COMMUNICATION

WITH

THE SPIRIT WORLD

OF

GOD

ITS LAWS and PURPOSE

Extraordinary Experiences of a Catholic Priest

JOHANNES GREBER

Stand up for the truth until death,
and God will defend you.
Ecclesiasticus (Sirach) 4:28

www.holyspiritanswers.com

INDEX

PART ONE

Personal Experiences in the Field of Spirit Manifestations

PART TWO

The Laws Governing Spirit-Communication with the Material Creation

PART THREE
Spirit-Communication in the Post Apostolic Age and in Modern Times

PART FOUR

Messages from the Good Spirit-World Concerning the Great Problems of Religion

Page

INTRODUCTION

"But these people scoff at anything they do not understand." *Jude 1 : 10.*

IS there for man a conscious existence after death? Is there a Beyond? Is there a world of spirits, into which the souls of our departed are received after leaving the body? And if these things are so, how shall we picture existence in that other world? What fate is in store for us there?

Or does everything come to an end within the cemetery-walls? When we bury the body there, do we inter the spirit also, and is nothing left of man, of all his hopes and fears, of all his struggles and cares, of all his joys and sorrows, of all his good deeds and bad, but a skull and a handful of ashes?

Again and again, these questions assail us. In the silent hours of deadly sickness they bear heavily upon the human heart. At every death-bed at which we stand, behind every coffin which we follow, they wring our innermost soul. They arise from the mound above each grave, and are cut deeply upon every tombstone.

Who will solve for us the great problem of the Beyond? To whom shall we carry our doubts, in order that we may learn the real truth? Shall we seek it of the various creeds and their ministers? True enough, they teach us to believe in a hereafter and in the survival of the soul of man, but they sadly weaken the force of their own teachings by denying, as regards the souls of animals, what they claim for the soul of man. For if there is no hereafter for the brute creation, what particular reason have we for believing in one for the human race? Is not the life-history of both the identical one? Both are conceived and born in the same way. To both are allotted pleasure and pain, to both a sense of right and wrong, and one dies as does the other. These very facts are confirmed by the Bible in the words: "For man's fate is a beast's fate, one fate befalls them both; as the one dies so the other dies; the same breath is in them all; man is no better than a beast, for both are vanity, both are bound for the same end; both sprang from the dust, and to the dust they both return. Who can tell if the spirit of man goes upward, while the spirit of a beast goes down into the earth?" *(Ecclesiastes 3 : 19-21.)*

Moreover, as regards the most important questions of religion our various Churches hold conflicting views. It is therefore, idle to look to them for a conclusive answer. Man, being fallible, is at the best a dubious guide in these matters.

To reach the truth concerning them there is but *one* way: if there is a Beyond, peopled by a world of spirits, conclusive proof is forthcoming only, if those spirits will visit and enlighten us, for they alone are able to tell us the truth about the great questions relating to an after-life. So long as this gap between the spirit-world and our own remains unbridged, so long shall we remain in the darkness of uncertainty and endure the pangs of gnawing doubt.

But today, people laugh at those who speak merely of the bare possibility of establishing communication between the world of men and that of spirits; laugh and ridicule, just as people have always ridiculed any views that conflicted with the popular beliefs of their time.

When Galilei taught that the earth revolves and the sun stands still, his contemporaries regarded him as mentally unsound. The Church looked upon him as a heretic and excommunicated him. He was thrown into prison, and could rid himself of his sufferings and persecution only by retracting what he had proclaimed.

When the first telephone was exhibited at the Academy of Sciences in Paris, one of the most eminent professors of that institution called the whole thing a hoax, carried out by means of ventriloquy.

The same thing has happened to the apostles of every other new truth. Their contemporaries have ridiculed, insulted, burned or crucified them.

So today the world laughs at those who seek to prove to mankind that there is a spirit-world, not barred to mankind, with which we can communicate if we go about it in the right way and if we observe the necessary requirements. For there are laws governing the spirit-world as immutable as any in force in the world of matter.

The art of communicating between men and the spirit-world has received the name of "*spiritism.*" Today this word is in poor repute with the masses, although very few persons really know what it means. Spiritism is regarded as an absurd vagary of ill-balanced minds. People speak of "those spiritistic fools" with a sneer. — "But these people scoff at anything they do not understand." *(Jude 1 : 10.)*

In this battle against spiritism, the churches are fighting in the front rank. Their attitude is indeed difficult to explain, for those self-same churches assure us that they have received the revelations of their religions through communication with the spirit-world. Judaism and Christianity are based upon the testimony of the Old and the New Testaments and hence rest entirely upon spiritism, for of all spiritist works the greatest is the Bible, the larger part of whose contents hinges upon messages sent hither from the Beyond. At every turn in the Scriptures we read of some communication between the world of spirits, and our own.

The churches are therefore in no position to deny the possibility of communicating with the spirit-world, unless they are prepared to saw off the limb upon which they themselves are seated. Yet they try to defend their war on spiritism by asserting that attempts to communicate with the spirit-world are forbidden by the Bible, citing the injunction: "Ye shall not question the dead."

Just what does the Bible mean by "questioning the dead"? When the Bible speaks of the "dead", it refers, not to those spirits which have become separated from the body by the death of the flesh, but to the *spiritually dead.* "Death", according to the Scriptures, is the separation of the spirit from God. The "dead" therefore are those who have been separated from God because of their unbelief and by defection. They are the spirits of darkness. The "kingdom of the dead" is the kingdom of Lucifer, the realm of the enemies of God, the realm of lies and woe.

According to the Scriptures there is a kingdom of the "dead" and a kingdom of the "living". It is within our power to communicate with spirits in either of these kingdoms, who have passed into the Beyond. We can seek counsel of the spiritually dead — in which case we would be consulting evil spirits, or, as the Bible terms it, *"questioning the dead."* Or else, we may turn to the living in the Beyond, which would be seeking counsel from the world of good spirits, or, to quote the Scriptures once more: *"Inquiring of God."*

To seek counsel from the "dead" or from the world of the apostate spirits would be the greatest possible affront to God. It would be idolatry, which consists of communicating with evil spirits.

The necromancers of old were generally recognized as being, knowingly and deliberately, in communication with the Powers of Darkness, — the Demons. Hence God's stringent command voiced in the old Testament, to root out the necromancers from among the people.

There is therefore only one, clearly defined, kind of Communication with spirits which the Scriptures forbid, namely: *intercourse with evil spirits.* On the other hand it is the duty of mankind to seek to establish communion with God and with the world of good spirits. "When they tell you to consult mediums and ghosts that cheep and gibber in low murmurs, ask them if people should not rather consult their God. Say, Why consult the dead on behalf of the living? Consult the message and the counsel of God!" *(Isaiah 8 : 19)* — "Ask me about things to come . . ." *(Isaiah 45 : 11.)*

The invitation to "inquire of God" was joyfully accepted by the faithful of all ages. Among the Israelites it was a matter of daily occurrence. "And it came to pass, that everyone which would inquire of the Lord went out into the tabernacle of the congregation. . ." *(Exodus 33 : 7.)*

God gave his answer in an endless variety of ways. His spirit-messengers stood in constant touch with the faithful. Throughout the New Testament we find references to them.

If, therefore, we, as faithful servants of God, or, at any rate, as honest seekers after the truth, try to get into touch with the world of good spirits we are committing no sin, but rather, obeying one of God's commandments; an important commandment, for only through contact with the world of good spirits can we arrive at the truth. *There is no other way.*

For this reason, nowhere in the entire Scriptures is the seeker after the truth told to go for guidance to his fellow-men, but always to God and His spirits. This holds good also for the New Testament. At the time of His departure from the earth, there were many things which Christ still wanted to tell his followers and which the latter had as yet not understood. These matters were to be more fully explained thereafter, not by any human agency, but through spirits whom the Father would send as messengers of the truth, whose participation would be visible to the human eye. "Truly, truly, I tell you all, you shall see heaven open wide and God's messengers ascending and descending upon the Son of man." *(John 1 : 51.)*

This ascent and descent of the angels was witnessed by the early Christians at their gatherings, whence the exhortation of the Apostle Paul to all Christians: "Therefore you in your endeavor to communicate with the spirits should seek to reach the greatest possible number of different spirits of God." *(1st Corinthians, 14 : 12.)*

It is fundamental for the religious life of mankind that the truth about the great questions of life and the hereafter be *sought not of men or in their interpretations, but by direct communication with God's spirit-realm, which is the source of all truth.* So God teaches us in the Old Testament, and Christ in the New. So, also, we are taught by the Apostles, and these precepts were obeyed by God's people before the birth of Christ and by the Christians of the early centuries of the present era.

As time went on, this fundamental doctrine was ignored. Erring men usurped God's place and that of His spirit-messengers, as prophets of the truth. To use the words of the Apostle Paul, the preaching of the gospel became a "trade". Religion was imparted by human teachers, just like any mundane knowledge. And so it has remained down to the present day.

The spiritual leaders of the people became absolute masters in all matters pertaining to religion, and in this way accumulated ever increasing temporal power. Constantly more numerous grew the man-made ordinances laid upon the shoulders of believers in the name of religion. *The one-time liberty of God's children was converted into religious serfdom.* Whoever rebelled, and tried to live according to his own convictions was punished with death. In the name of religion, the blood of millions has flowed.

The old first-hand texts of the New Testament disappeared, and were succeeded by copies that differed in many essentials from their originals. Wilful forgery was resorted to in order to lend the authority of the Bible to the man-made opinions and strictures that in the course of time crept into being. It was a repetition of that state of things of which God complained so bitterly in the Old Testament, through his prophets: "How do you say: We are wise, and the law of the Lord is with us? Lo, the pen of the falsifying copyists has converted it into lie. The wise men are ashamed, they are dismayed and taken: lo, they have rejected the word of the Lord, and what wisdom is in them?' *(Jeremiah 8 : 8 -9.)*

Modern research has disclosed the fact that these forgeries

extended like a devastating plague to all of the ancient documents. The Bible, the Church Fathers, the writings of Jewish and pagan authors, all of them were altered, to support the religious doctrines which happened to be current at the time.

Naturally, this was done out of sight of the common people, who accepted unquestioningly the so-called "religious revelations" and interpretations offered to them by their spiritual leaders, and bequeathed them to their children and their children's children. And so it goes to the present day. *Religion is a legacy* which each of us has inherited from his parents and his teachers, without stopping to use his own judgment as to its truth or lack of truth, which, it might be added, is rather beyond the mental capacity of the greater portion of mankind. For this reason, most of us who today are Christians would have been equally zealous followers of the Jewish or Mohammedan faith, if our parents had been Hebrews or Mussulmen.

This was not so in the days when men were in communication with the world of good spirits. Then they could ask: "What is the truth?", and received an answer. It was for this reason that Paul exhorted the early Christians *to seek counsel of God,* if their views on any point differed from his own. "And if in any matter your belief should differ, that also God will make clear to you." *(Philippians 3 : 15.)*

So plain an indication as to the only way by which to arrive at the truth, as that conveyed in the foregoing passage by the greatest of Christ's apostles could never have been given a few centuries later. Whoever disbelieved the doctrines taught by the Church, or whoever tried to arrive at the truth by a direct appeal to God, after the custom of the old Israelites or the early Christians, fell under the ban of the Church and not infrequently perished at the stake. It is true that the unorthodox are no longer consigned to the flames, because today the Church has lost the power to send them there, but the ban remains, and would fall upon the greatest of the early Church Fathers if they were alive today and taught those doctrines which in their time they preached to Christian folk.

The path that led to God's world of spirits has been blocked, and with it the road leading to the truth. Man-made doctrines and rules have been used to erect religious structures into which mankind is invited to enter. Hundreds of creeds claim to be the dispensers of truth, the first destroying what the second adores, and the third proclaiming as the simon-pure truth what the fourth condemns as abominable heresy.

From these fetters of error mankind can be freed only, if God will send us His spirits as heralds of the truth, as He did in the earlier millenniums.

It is not the "dead" nor the "Kingdom of Darkness" nor fallible men to whom we must turn, but to God. *He is the same God today that He was then. Before Him, we are all alike. He loves the people of today as dearly as He loved those of the ages which are gone.* And as then He revealed himself to mankind through His messengers, so will He today.

It is to be expected that the churches will do their utmost to obstruct this road to the truth. This they must, since they will be fighting for their very existence. They consider themselves as the only disseminators of truth. Every one of them has its Pope, whether or not he wears a tiara. Any doctrine which includes in its tenets instruction through God's messengers will be looked upon as destructive competition, endangering the integrity of the church, since it is to be feared that the revelations so made will not harmonize with the tenets held by the churches.

Obviously, there can be only *one single truth.* Either this is in the possession of one of the many creeds, in which case all other creeds are in error, or else, the truth is not to be found in any of them. When all is said, the words from Goethe's Faust: "In gaudy pictures there is little clearness, a wealth of error and a grain of truth," apply to *all religions without exception.*

For twenty-five years I was a Catholic priest. I believed that mine was the true religion; was it not, indeed, the faith of my parents, my teachers and my spiritual superiors? Even if the proofs of its verity did not completely convince me, I had no reason for refusing to accept that which was accepted by all of my co-religionists. Furthermore, any voluntary doubt as to the truth of the tenets of my church would have been mortal sin.

Of the possibility of communicating with the land of spirits I knew nothing. My acquaintance with spiritism was confined to casual readings about it in the daily papers. I regarded it as a swindle or as self-deception.

Then came a day on which I took, involuntarily, my first step in the direction of coming into contact with the spirit-world, and underwent experiences that stirred me to the bottom of my soul.

Once this step had been taken, I could not, durst not, stop.

I was compelled to go on in my search for enlightenment. Cautiously I advanced, keeping in mind the words of St. Paul: "Prove all things; hold fast to that which is good." *(1st Thessalonians 5 : 21.)*

It was only "that which is good," that I wanted. I was seeking the truth, ready to accept it, whatever the cost. I knew that God does not desert the upright, unselfish seeker, and that, as Christ says, He will not give a stone to those who humbly ask for bread.

I was not unaware of the serious consequences that I was incurring by my action. My position as an ordained minister, my entire material existence, my worldly future would be wrecked, were I to persist. I knew that insults, persecution and suffering without end would be my lot.

This price I was willing to pay.

On the new road which I had taken, I found the truth. It brought me inward freedom and happiness. The outward troubles that I suffered in consequence and that persist until today, fail to disturb the inward peace that I have won.

It is the purpose of this book to describe the path which brought me into communication with the world of spirits and laid the truth open to me. The book has been written in a spirit of love for my fellow-men, regardless of their creed or outlook on life.

It is intended for all seekers after the truth, as a guide for all those who desire to communicate with the *world of good spirits,* and thus, by the shortest path, to arrive at God and at the truth.

Guide-books for those who travel about the earth are written by persons who have visited the places which they describe in the texts of their works. Such books are not written for people who expect to stay at home, but for such as want to go to countries hitherto strange to them.

This book of mine is meant to be a guide-book of that sort. It is designed to direct the reader to that bridge on which the spirit messengers from the Beyond meet us. Whoever, in the light of what is herein set out, steps upon that spirit-bridge, will find every statement that appears in this book fully confirmed.

I do not, therefore, expect any of my readers to accept at their face value the statements contained in this book, without subjecting them to further proof. If he did, he would be basing his beliefs regarding the most important questions of life on the dictum of one who is no more infallible than other men. This he must not do, for my assertion that the truths I have set down in my book were derived, not from my own deductions but from communication with the world of good spirits in the Beyond, might well be based on error or self-deception, on my part.

I, who like all men am weak, fallible and sinning, can ask for myself no greater credence than is accorded to any of my fellow-men. I therefore do not ask to be believed blindly. But one thing I do demand: *That the truth which was revealed to me be sought by the same road by which I found it.* This road has been accurately described by me, in order that no one may fail to find it. Learned and ignorant, rich and poor alike, can travel it. No preparation, no special training, is required. No tolls are collected. Only one thing is indispensable: *The Will to the Truth.* Those who seek it must be ready to accept it at the moment at which they are convinced that it is being offered to them, and must be willing to model their lives accordingly. This book is not written for those who will not accept these terms. For them, no way leads to the truth, for God manifests His will to the well-disposed only.

They who have not the "Will to the Truth," who are not ready to explore the road which I am pointing out, thereby forfeit the right to pass judgment on my book. If, for instance, a chemist were to announce that he had found a method of making gold by combining certain substances, and were to describe his process minutely, only those would be capable of expressing an intelligent opinion as to his claims, who themselves had performed the experiments described by their author, and who had faithfully followed all of his directions.

I am certain that this book contains the truth, "For I know whom I have believed." *(2nd Timothy 1 : 12.)*

I feel no fear that those who follow the path indicated by me will find anything to conflict with what I found. Everyone who has heretofore followed my advice and has sought to get into communication with the world of good spirits has had experiences precisely like my own.

Nevertheless, my book is sure to encounter many bitter enemies. Not so much among the great mass of the people as in those circles for which the acceptance of the truth would mean heavy material sacrifices, as among all ministers of the various sects. The creed which they have been preaching to their congregations, heretofore, *has provided them with a means of living.* If now, in consequence of any change in their way of seeing the truth they are compelled to make alterations in those things which they have been professing, they will cease to be ministers of their respective creeds and lose their daily bread, for which they have been dependent on their position.

To give up a place supposedly bestowed for life and to go out into the uncertainties of the world poor and beset by enemies, is one of the greatest sacrifices that a man can make. Not many will make it: sooner, they will dispense with the truth.

It was for this reason that the Jewish priests waged so bitter a war on Christ and His doctrines. Their livelihood was in danger. They did not study Christ's teachings to enable them to say whether these were right or wrong, but unloosed their deadly hatred upon Him whose words threatened to alienate the people from them and thus to undermine their influence with the masses. For this, His death was decided upon and the curse of being the relentless opponent of the truth and of those who sought it and those who proclaimed it, rests to the present day on the *priesthood of all religions.* With fire and sword, priesthood has slain millions under color of war against heresy, just as the Jewish priests excused their slaughter of Christ by saying:

"He hath spoken blasphemy."

But the real reason then, as it was in later ages, was the fear of the total or partial loss of temporal influence, worldly honors, offices and revenues. Of course there have been and still are exceptions. Perhaps these are more numerous today than they were in the past. But these later-day Nicodemuses can do as little to prevent the spiritual leaders of today from passing the death-sentence upon the truth, as the first Nicodemus was able to accomplish.

The clergy of today will therefore not only repudiate my book, but will refuse to apply, in the manner therein prescribed, the tests of the veracity of the statements which it contains. And yet, there is nothing about these tests which can offend the conscience of anyone, unless, indeed, it is a reprehensible proceeding for a layman or a clergyman to sit down, alone or in company with others, to worship God in the privacy of his home, to turn to Him with song and prayer, and to beg of Him the fulfillment of Christ's promise: "If ye, then, being evil, know how to give good gifts unto your children, how much more shall your Heavenly Father give a holy spirit to them that ask Him?" *(Luke 11 : 13.)*

Is it by any possibility a sin to study the truths of the Holy

Scriptures at such a service, to discuss them with others and to pray for the true light? Is it a sin to join hands on such an occasion after the manner of the early Christians and to concentrate one's thoughts on higher things, repenting of evil, forgiving one another and beseeching God to help us and to grant us the *Spirit of Truth* which Christ promised to His followers? *Is there one of us who cannot do these things with a clear conscience?* More than this I do not ask, for this road, and no other, was the one which I travelled when I experienced what my book relates. No special privileges were extended to me; I received only that which any honest searcher will receive. Indeed, many who follow my trail may receive far more than I did.

The fact that the things which we learn in the manner to be described seem so incredible, is no reason for refusing to set out upon the path indicated, for God expressly promises to show us the unbelievable, in the words:

"Call unto me, and I will answer you, and show you great and mighty things which you did not know." *(Jeremiah 33 : 3.)*

The Author.

Easter, 1932.

PART ONE

Personal Experiences in the Field of Spirit Manifestations

My First Step Toward Communication with the Spirit World

"When I thought to know this, it was too hard for me; until I went into the sanctuary of God."
Psalms 73:16, 17.

IT was late in the summer of 1923. At that time I was the Catholic priest of a small rural community. In addition to my clerical duties, I was in charge of a charitable association, whose headquarters lay in a nearby city. I used to make two trips weekly to the office of this association in order to attend to the details of its activities.

It happened one day while I was at the office that a man came in and asked me: "What is your opinion of spiritism?"

Before I could answer, he went on to tell me of his own experiences, relating that he was in the habit of attending a sort of divine service held once a week by a small group, the members of which would pray, read the Scriptures and afterwards discuss the passages they had read. Among those who attended these gatherings was a young boy of unpretentious family and of very indifferent education, who was an apprentice in some private enterprise.

At the *seances* this boy would frequently fall over forward as though dead, but would be violently pushed back into an upright position apparently by an invisible force, after which he would sit with his eyes closed and impart wonderful tidings to his hearers. He would also answer questions addressed to him, ignoring, however, all queries of a purely materialistic nature. At the conclusion of his manifestations he would again droop forward and instantly regain full consciousness. Of what had happened and what he had said while under this spell he would have not the least recollection. The boy, said my informant, was healthy and bright and felt no discomfort, no headache nor any similar symptoms as a result of the ordeal.

My informant ended his story with the words: "Now, I am anxious to hear from you what you think of it all. But before you express an opinion, please attend one of our meetings, so that you may be in a position to convince yourself in person as to what goes on there. You will have the opportunity of addressing questions of your own to the boy."

I had been listening to him with the closest attention. What was I to say? I neither knew nor understood anything about "spiritism", as I had heard it called. True, I had occasionally read accounts in the daily papers describing the exposition of mediums and of similar spiritistic swindles, but now I, a seriously-minded individual and a clergyman into the bargain was being asked to enter upon this ground and to run the risk of making myself ridiculous. That was out of the question. I was, indeed, tempted to apply a purely scientific test to the phenomena that had been related to me, if this were possible when I was alone and in the privacy of my own study. But visit the homes of others and expose myself to gossip, I would not.

I therefore told my visitor frankly that I had had no personal experience with spiritism and that I was in no position to pass an opinion on the things he had witnessed. I said, furthermore, that I had grave doubts as to the propriety of my accepting his invitation to attend one of the meetings he had described; that I owed consideration to my cassock, and could not run the risk of being branded openly as a "spiritist", for my presence at his gatherings would undoubtedly become generally known speedily.

My acquaintance would not accept these reasons, but replied: "This is a most important matter, of which you, as a clergyman and a man holding a public position, should be informed. At any rate I consider it your duty to make an investigation, and after having done so, carefully, and impartially, you can pass judgment. You will probably be asked about these matters frequently in the course of your career, for to whom should we laymen look for information except to our spiritual guides, whom we trust to tell us the truth. The time has passed when this subject can be disposed of by being ignored. Right here in Germany the number of spiritists is growing daily. Every town of any size has its quota. I know that the churches would like to see this matter brushed aside as a fraud and as the invention of the Devil, but it will not be settled in that way.

"If it is unpleasant consequences that you fear, you need not worry on that score. Your presence at our meetings will not be made public, for the few who attend them are of the sort that knows how to be discreet and to avoid doing anything that might harm you. So the best thing you can do is to accept."

I could not deny the force of his arguments: he was right. If we clergymen who aspire to teach and guide the people refuse to make a personal investigation of the truth of such manifestations as he had described, who else is there to make it? Who could be more vitally interested in these matters than the clergy of all creeds? For if spiritism were to prove a source of the truth, it would be bound to have a most profound effect upon the belief of every sect.

Consequently, after a little hesitation, I agreed to go to the meeting that was to be held on the following Sunday.

For the next few days my mind was constantly busy with the subject. At times I regretted having accepted the invitation, as the unpleasant consequences which my action might bring upon me loomed ever larger in my imagination, the more I thought about them. Anxiously I awaited the coming Sunday.

After the conclusion of the afternoon service I drove to the city, intending to look after a few pressing matters at the office of the charitable organization before going to the place of meeting. In my coat pocket I carried a slip of paper on which I had jotted down the questions which I intended to ask the boy that evening; they were all such as to require rather lengthy answers, involving more than a casual acquaintance with religious lore. I myself was unable to answer them and merely wanted to find out what explanation the boy would have to offer.

On arriving at the office I found a letter for me from the man who had given me the invitation. In it he said that the meeting would be held, not as originally planned, at his home, but at that of another family whose address he gave. It had been so ordered.

This unexpected change caused me to hesitate and aroused my suspicions. Was I being trifled with? The family to whose residence the meeting had been transferred I did not know even by name. Was I to be subjected to the embarrassment of going among utter strangers? Perhaps after all the whole thing was a trap set for me. I made up my mind at once not to go.

In order not to keep the gathering waiting for me in vain, I sent my acquaintance a messenger with a note stating that I would not attend the meeting.

It was not long before he appeared at the office in person, asking me to reconsider my refusal. He said that the change in the place of meeting had been no doing of his, but had been ordered from a source which must be obeyed, and that perhaps the reason for making the change lay in the fact that the meeting, if held in the other house, would be less likely to attract attention than it would at his own. In the end, I went.

It was half past seven when we arrived. I was cordially greeted by the family and could see that my coming had given them pleasure. Since the meeting was not to open until eight, I had ample opportunity to talk with the boy, who had also arrived beforehand. I asked him a number of questions to enable me to judge of the extent of his learning, and found that in this respect he did not differ greatly from the average youth of his age.

The meeting opened at eight o'clock with very few present, and I was surprised to find that it was to be held not in the dark, as I had supposed was customary at all such meetings, but that the room was left brightly lighted.

The opening consisted of a short prayer offered by one of those in attendance with great reverence. In fact, everyone about me had the appearance of being deeply in earnest and thoroughly engrossed in the subject before him.

Scarcely was the prayer ended when the boy fell over forward with a slump and an exhalation of breath so sudden that I was startled. Had he not been supported by the arm of the chair in which he was seated, he would have dropped to the floor. After a few seconds he was pushed upright in a series of jerks as though by an invisible hand, and remained sitting with his eyes closed. I could feel my heart beating faster in the expectation of what was about to happen.

"*Gruess Gott* (God's greeting)", he began, and immediately turned to me with the question: "Why have you come here?", using the familiar form "du" (thou) which took me aback, as under ordinary circumstances he would never have dared to take this liberty.

"I came in search of the truth," I replied, "I heard of what takes place at these meetings and want to satisfy myself personally whether these things are true or false."

"Do you believe in God?" he went on and added, without waiting for my answer, "I know you do, but why do you believe in God?"

This question was so unexpected that I scarcely knew what to say. I had a feeling, too, of being confused, and consequently answered so inadequately that I myself was thoroughly dissatisfied with my own explanation.

"I had expected something better of you", returned the boy calmly, a remark which fell upon me like a slap in the face. I had come with the idea of exposing a piece of charlatanism, but after the first exchange of words it was I who was on the defensive.

"The question which you have answered so unsatisfactorily we will leave until later," he said soothingly, "and now it is your turn to ask me questions. I will answer them as far as I am permitted. You have with you a written list of the questions you want to put. Take out the slip on which you wrote them."

The others looked at me curiously for no one had known of my list. My first question read:

"Why is it that Christianity seems no longer to exert any influence upon the people of today?"

Without a moment's reflection or hesitation he began his reply. Incidental questions put to him or objections raised by others of his hearers he answered with amazing simplicity and clearness. According to my short-hand notes his statement ran as follows:

"The teachings of Christ are no longer to be found in their original purity and clearness in those documents which have come down to you. In what is called the New Testament, several paragraphs, indeed, entire chapters, have been omitted. What you have now are mutilated copies. Not knowing the originals, you are unable to determine what those mutilations are. Those who were guilty of these mutilations have been punished by God."

One of those present asked who it was that had thus made free with God's Holy Writ.

"That does not concern you," was the curt answer. "It is sufficient for you to know that it happened and that God has punished the culprits. What would it profit you to learn their names? You would use the information to pass judgment upon them, and you know that you shall not judge of your fellow-men. God judges, that is enough.

"Even the last letter of the Apostle Paul addressed to all Christian communities has been destroyed. In it he had carefully explained those passages in his earlier writings that had given rise to misunderstanding. But his explanations were not in accord with many erroneous doctrines that had subsequently crept into the Christian faith."

At this point I asked him when it was that the first views

which conflict with the true teachings had found their way into the Christian religion, to which he replied:

"To a small extent as early as the first century. As you know, even during the lifetime of the apostles there were not a few differences of opinion among the Christian communities. Later, many erroneous human opinions and dogmas, that do not agree with Christ's teachings, were introduced. If you had the complete and unamended text of Christ's doctrines, many a load imposed by man in the name of religion and Christianity would be taken from your shoulders. Many a precept which you are expected to believe, even though it seems out of all reason, would be discarded because it would be recognized as being wrong, and you, as God's children could again breathe freely. As it is, millions of people feel that much of what is being taught today as a part of the Christian faith, cannot be true. From force of habit, they may conform outwardly, but there is no true inner conviction.

"There are many today who do not profess even outward adherence to Christianity. Instead of rejecting only those parts of it which are untrue, they discard altogether their belief in religion and in God, because they think that these things are all of one piece.

"But the time will come when the teachings of Christ will be restored to man in their full purity and truth. In what way this will happen, you need not know for the present.

"Moreover, the originals of the documents relating to the New Testament, even when they have been preserved, have been altered in not a few places. The copyists substituted words and whole phrases, left out a word here or inserted one there, thus altering the sense of the text to suit their purposes. In most cases they were trying to create passages in the Bible which would lend support to the religious views of their times, and to that end they falsified its text. They were not always conscious of the enormity of their offense, but believed, rather, that they were serving the cause of religion. In this way the people were misled, and many of them feel in their hearts that they are not on the right path, even if they are in no position to be set right. The natural consequence is that a religion so deprived of its roots can no longer exert any fruitful influence."

"May I ask," I interposed with a feeling of oppression, "that you tell me of some place in the New Testament in which a word has been changed to the extent of altering the sense of the text?"

"While this is not the precise time," he replied, "which I should choose to go into the subject of these falsifications, as I shall later when I come to explain the Bible as a whole, I will grant your request and name two places, in one of which a word has been replaced by another, and in the second of which a word has been omitted entirely.

"You are familiar with the exclamation of the Apostle Thomas, as rendered by your modern Bible: 'My Lord and my God!' *(John 20 : 28.)* As a matter of fact, however, Thomas used the form of address always employed by the apostles toward Christ: 'My Lord and Master!' The word 'Master' was at a later date distorted to read 'God'. Why this was done, I shall explain on a later occasion.

"A phrase from which a word was omitted and thereby its whole meaning changed should be of great interest to you personally, since you are a Catholic priest and believe that you have the power, as such, to pardon sins. What passage in the New Testament can you cite to support the claim that such power was conferred upon priests?"

I recited the following passage: "Whose soever sins ye remit, they are remitted unto them. . ." *(John 20 : 23.)*

He corrected me, wording the passage thus: "If you forgive the sins of others, they are forgiven to them", and went on:

"The Greek word which you translate as 'them', has in that language also the meaning of 'selves'. Now, in the original text the word 'your' occurred before the word 'selves'. That which today is rendered as 'them', actually read in the original: 'yourselves'. In the original, therefore the passage reads: 'If you forgive the sins of others, they are forgiven to yourselves'. You can see how the sense of this passage has been distorted by the omission of the word 'your'. Christ here said nothing but what He had said repeatedly elsewhere, namely: 'Ye must forgive in your hearts your fellowmen the failings and sins which they have committed against you, so that ye may obtain forgiveness from God for your own sins.' 'Forgive us our trespasses, as we forgive those that trespass against us'! 'Forgiveness is the hardest task in your lives, and it is for this reason that God gives you His especial aid for the purpose. Christ, as you know, says in the same place: 'Receive ye a holy spirit! 'If you will forgive the sins of others, your sins shall be forgiven you; if, however, you retain them — that is, in your hearts — then your sins will be retained by God. Have you followed me?"

Greatly abashed and sobered I softly answered: "Yes", adding immediately:

"Is it then your opinion that it is of no value for me, as a priest, to receive the confessions of others, seeing that I cannot grant them absolution? Ought I not, therefore, discontinue the practice entirely?"

"That is not necessary," replied he. "Since the Christians of your Church believe that they must confess to a priest in order that their sins may be forgiven them, you may continue to take their confessions, with a good conscience, as your office requires. There is nothing evil or displeasing to God in revealing one's sins to a fellow man. But do not think that you can usurp God's office by forgiving the sins of your confessants. Your duty is confined to removing sinful thoughts from their hearts by advice, admonition and appeals to their better selves, so that they may return home as better men and women, and give proof of their change of heart by their future conduct. Perfunctory confession and absolution is not only purposeless, but a desecration of the idea of a reconciliation with God.

"These side issues which you have raised have led me away from my subject, to which I shall now return.

"Even though portions of Christ's teachings as contained in the copies which have come down to you of the old manuscripts have been purposely omitted or falsified to distort their meaning, enough of the true material still remains to enable men, by using as a guide, to draw nearer to their God. Unfortunately they cannot sift the true from the false.

"The foundation of Christ's teachings is: 'Love God before all things and love your neighbor as you love yourselves'. Whoever obeys this injunction, obeys every law of Christianity. All other precepts are merely supplementary to this fundamental one and are helpful as guides to its observance in the life of each individual.

"And now I shall speak of the last, but no less important reason why Christianity seems to have so little influence on the people of today.

"They do not find in their spiritual leaders any great observance, in practice, of the teachings of Christianity or of what these leaders themselves preach. That is true of the clergy of all creeds. There are exceptions, but these are comparatively rare. Where can you find clergymen who could stand before Christ without blushing? How many are there who share suffering, poverty and want with their brethren and sisters, for that is what the members of their congregations are? Do they serve these as Christ directs, or do they not, in fact, dominate and exploit them? Will they do anything for nothing? *Are there not clergymen who demand payment in money for the prayers they offer?*

"As to the lives they lead, of that I shall say nothing now. It is a matter of which some day I should like to speak to you in private."

At this point he turned to me and continued:

"You expect to visit your brother and sister to-morrow. There is no need of such haste. Stay over with us another day and come back here to-morrow evening at half past seven. Then we two can talk to each other in private. Therefore, when this boy, through whom I am speaking, comes to himself again, ask him to be here at that time."

In conclusion the boy offered a prayer in a language strange to me and raising his hands in an attitude of benediction uttered the words:

"Blessed be you in the name of the Lord! Gruess Gott!"

After this invocation the boy again drooped forward as he had at the beginning of the meeting, opened his eyes and gazed about in astonishment. He could not understand why the hour was so late; of what had occurred, he knew nothing. He said he had the sensation of having slept long and restfully and that he was feeling refreshed and perfectly well.

When I asked him to come back the next evening at the same hour he declared that that was impossible as there was some important work to be finished on that day at his shop, so that he could not come before nine o'clock. His employer had already notified him of this.

Nevertheless, I decided to be back the next evening at the same place and at the time which had been set for me.

As I walked back to my lodgings after the meeting I felt as though I had awakened from a heavy dream. The moon shed its silvery light over the housetops and the stars were shining peacefully in the clear sky, but within me the fires of my thoughts were blazing fiercely and I knew that their flames had already caught the beams on which the whole structure of my faith had heretofore rested.

Which was telling the truth: the creed of which I was a priest, or the Voice which had spoken through that boy? Or had he concocted it all out of his own head and staged a farce at our expense?

Out of his own head? That Boy? Rather would I accept any other explanation, however unlikely. I had, of course, read of "clairvoyance", "subconsciousness" and "telepathy", but none of these seemed to fit the case in hand. I decided therefore to carry my investigation further. The subject was of too great importance to allow me to pass it by. For me, there was no drawing back; I was bound to go through with it to the very end. Perhaps the next meeting would carry me forward another step on my journey.

The Decision

"I have chosen the way of the truth; thy judgments have I laid before me." *Psalms 119 : 30.*

AFTER a rather sleepless night I tried on the following day to relieve the torture of my mind by strenuous application to the work at the office of the charitable association.

Shortly before half past seven that evening I was back at the apartment at which the previous evening's meeting had been held. To my surprise, the boy was there before me. He told me that at four o'clock that afternoon his employer had come to him with the announcement that he had changed his mind about the work which he had intended to have finished by overtime, and that he would put it off until the next morning.

I was alone with the boy. As the clock struck half past seven he again fell forward as before into that state inexplicable to me, again greeted me with the salutation: *"Gruess Gott!"*, took my hand and said:

"I am glad that you have stayed, for I have much to tell you. First of all, however, I must finish with the last point of which I spoke yesterday.

"You remember that I told you we would speak of that when we were by ourselves."

He now drew a picture of the lives led by a great part of the clergy. I listened, shocked and pained. Then, however, he added in the most kindly way:

"Now talk to me openly and unreservedly, for I know that since yesterday your mind has been upset and that you feel lost."

In a voice trembling with inner emotion I answered:

"You are right, my thoughts are in a whirl. I do not know what to think of it all. Be kind enough to instruct me in everything, but first of all tell me who you are, and how you are able to speak to me through this boy?"

"You have a right to ask me who I am, for it is your first duty to test the spirits that speak to you and to assure yourself that they were sent by God, since otherwise you might become the victim of evil spirits which would ruin you, body and soul, and which would not reveal the truth, but by lies would guide you to the path which leads over the edge of the precipice. I swear to you before God that I am one of His good spirits, indeed one of His highest spirits, but my name keep to yourself."

He then made himself known to me.

"I am he who has brought you here at God's behest. I desire to teach you so that you, in turn, may teach your fellow-men."

All the while I hardly knew how I felt or what was happening to me.

"I shall now begin," he continued, "to instruct you in those things that take place here. You may think that what you see is something quite new and unheard of. It is as old as humanity. From the days of the first man down to the present, the spirit-world has communicated with mankind. That is true of both the good spirit-world and the bad. You, of course, have read often enough in the ancient texts which you men call the Old Testament, that God spoke to the people. God spoke to Adam, Cain, Isaac, Abraham and Jacob, to Moses and to many others. How do you think He did this? You know that God is a spirit and that spirits have no lips of flesh or vocal chords to allow them to speak after the manner of men. How then, did God speak to these people?"

"I cannot say," was all the answer I could make.

"And how do you explain the appearance of the three men before Abraham? He knew they were no human beings, but messengers sent by God. Still, he placed food before them and interceded with them regarding the destruction of Sodom and Gomorrha. How do you account for that?"

I had nothing to say in reply. All this I had read hundreds of times and even taught it to the children in school, but just how the communication of the spirits with man, as related in the Bible, was effected, I had never given a thought. Although he continued to examine me in these matters, there was not a single question which I succeeded in answering correctly.

"As you know, man has various means of communicating with his fellows at a distance from him. He writes letters, telephones or telegraphs, and lately has made use of even the ether-waves through the radio. Similarly, the world of spirits, which is separated from you materially, has various ways of communicating with you by means perceptible to your senses.

"But you men of today never think about these things. All you do is to read about them and let the matter rest there.

"Take the grand story of Moses! There you will find that

the angel of the Lord speaks to him from the burning bush; that God daily sends commands for Moses to follow; that the angel of the Lord moves before the people in a pillar of cloud from which he speaks; that Moses asks God for guidance as often as he wishes, and that God always makes answer.

"The people also could seek counsel of God. They went to the tent of meeting outside the camp in which Joshua, the servant of Moses, was always required to be present and from which he was not allowed to depart. Now stop and think: why was it that young Joshua was commanded to remain within the tent constantly? Was there any connection between this and the appeals to God for counsel?"

Like a flash of lightning the answer came to me and I quickly replied:

"I suppose that Joshua was like this boy here. Just as you are making use of his person in order to speak to me, so in those days the spirit world spoke through Joshua."

"You are right," he said, "But remember that when the Bible says: 'God spoke', it was not God himself who spoke, because as a rule, God speaks only through His spirit-messengers.

"And know, furthermore, that the spirit-world does not always speak through a human being when it wishes to speak to mankind. There are many ways in which the spirits can make themselves understood by you.

"Thus you find that God spoke through the 'pillar of cloud'. In very many cases communication with spirits has been made possible by the gift of clairvoyance, and clairaudience, vouchsafed to certain individuals. God's speech with Adam and Eve and with others later was effected by means of clairaudience.

"There was still another channel open to the Israelites for consulting God, namely the breastplate worn on the robe of the High Priest and hence also called the 'breast-plate of judgment'. On a later occasion I shall describe to you exactly the proceedings followed when God was consulted through this channel.

"It is not only in the Old Testament that you will find references to communication with the spirit-world, but to the same extent in the New. Each of the Gospels, and in particular the history of the Apostles, contains many accounts of revelations made by spirits. Christ himself solemnly promised all who would believe, that He would send them God's spirits. The phenomena witnessed during the divine service of the early Christians, for which you of today can find no explanation, were nothing else than the comings and goings of spirits which spoke through one of the worshippers in a foreign tongue and through a second in the mother-tongue of the congregation; which gave to a third the power of healing the sick and distributed other gifts, according to the fitness of those upon whom such gifts were bestowed. In those days these things were of daily occurrence and were looked upon as matters of course.

"Do not think that communication with the spirits ceased in the early days of the Christian era, as many of the 'churches' ask you to believe. On the contrary, it should and it will continue always, for it is the only way in which you can learn the truth.

"It is true that it rests with the people themselves whether or not they obtain communication with the spirits of God. Even in the days before Christ there were times when this communication ceased almost entirely. Those were the times of estrangement from God.

"Today, the people, in spite of the many temples which they build, have to a great extent fallen away from God and into the power of the Evil One. Whenever mankind again draws as close to God as it was in the days before Christ and in those of the early part of His era, all those things which to you seem so strange and which are recorded as having happened then will be repeated. For the God of today is also the God of Old. He loves His creatures as dearly now as He loved them then, and before Him we are all equal.

"These general teachings must suffice for today. As to the details concerning the communication between the spirits and mankind you will be taught later, if you are willing to receive instruction and to undertake the task which has been reserved for you. You are not compelled to do this. You are quite free to choose. You may accept what is being offered to you and testify to the truth, or you may decline it and continue on the road you have been travelling heretofore. If you are willing to accept, you will in all probability be called upon to make great worldly sacrifices. You will suffer persecution for the sake of the truth and of right. But you will find peace.

"If you reject this gift of God which I offer, the responsibility is yours. It is for you to decide."

"You are not asked to accept anything blindly. You are expected to determine for yourself whether it is true or merely a snare laid by the Evil One. Nor must you be satisfied with hearing of these things from me: you must, by your own observations, collect experience in this field, independently of what you learn here.

"So in conclusion I shall ask you to look about in your rural parish for persons who have had nothing to do with these matters. Hold weekly meetings with them, offering prayer and expounding the Scriptures, as did the early Christians. Then give close attention to whatever happens. In that way you will be in a position to compare what you see there with what you see and learn here.

"Also arrange things so that you can be at this place of gathering every Sunday evening at eight o'clock, in order that I may continue with your instruction."

"I am quite ready," I said "to come here every Sunday whenever it is at all possible, but I cannot quite make up my mind to ask any of the simple peasants among my parishioners to attend meetings of this sort. In the little village where I live that would attract an amount of attention, the consequences of which no man could foretell. Besides, I can think of no one whom I consider suitable for the purpose."

"If you will make up your mind to act, the rest will be taken care of,' he replied to my objection, "You are not being forced into this. The decision rests entirely with you. But I would advise you to accept. And now I must conclude."

Raising his hands in a gesture of benediction as he had on the day before, he pronounced the words:

"May God protect you. May He give you strength to carry out His will. Amen. *Gruess Gott!"*

Again the boy sank over forward and after a few moments came to himself, quite unaware of what had taken place.

All explanations on any natural grounds, that occurred to me, I was forced to reject as inadequate. They did not account for even a small fraction of what I had witnessed. What captivated me most of all and, I might say, irresistibly, was the clear-cut reasoning and the convincing logic of that to which I had listened for the first time in my life. Only the truth could exert so great an influence upon me, an influence from which I had not the power to withdraw, even had I been so inclined.

So much of the Bible which had heretofore been obscure to me, I now understood quite clearly.

What was more, I had merely made a beginning. I had been offered thorough instruction in everything connected with the subject, and had only to accept the offer. I was not required to be satisfied with what I had heard here, but was urged to draw upon another, independent source, so that there could be no mistake. I had been advised to sit down with unsophisticated, inexperienced country people who had not the remotest idea of "spiritism", to worship after the manner of the early Christians, far from all outside influence, in my own parsonage.

Ought I to take the risk? What would people say? I felt the fear of my fellowmen's opinion rising within me. Would not my own parishioners consider me mentally unsound if I were to undertake anything of that kind? And if my ecclesiastic superiors heard of it, would I not lose my place?

A desperate struggle raged within me. Which way was I to cast my decision? For I knew that decide I must, now or never. At no time in my life have I prayed more fervently to God than I did then. In the end, I resolved to follow the directions I had received, even though it meant the greatest personal sacrifice, the loss of my position and my means of support.

This, then, was my decision. No sooner had I taken it than I became inwardly quite calm and able to confront the future with the utmost confidence.

The Corroboration of the Truth

> "Now, you have been anointed by the holy One, and you all possess knowledge. I am not writing to you, because you do not know the truth . . . but the unction you received from him remains within you and you really need no teaching from anyone; simply remain in Him, for this unction teaches you about everything and is true and is no lie — remain in Him, as it has taught you to do."
>
> *1st John 2 : 20.*

I HAD decided, regardless of consequences, to select a few individuals in my own parish and to arrange for meetings with them, similar to those I had attended in the neighbouring town. As yet I had not made up my mind whom to select, for I had been told that everything would be taken care of whenever I was prepared to act. And so it turned out. I had no need of seeking the people; they were brought to me by a strange chain of circumstances, without any effort on my part.

There was in my parish an invalid woman who was partly lame, and on whom I used to call several times a week. A married sister of hers who had four children, three sons and a daughter from twenty to twenty-six years of age, lived in the village which was the seat of my parish.

One evening as I sat talking with the invalid, one of her sister's sons came in and asked whether his mother was at the house. He was told that she had been there but had left to attend to some errands, whereupon the boy sat down to wait for her. Very shortly afterwards his mother arrived, and a few moments later her other two sons who had called to fetch their brother. They had agreed with some of their companions that all were to meet that evening at the home of a certain family. After another short interval the daughter appeared; she was a nurse, and had come to ask me whether one of the sick people of the parish would have to be watched during the night. That made seven of us who were present.

Suddenly one of the sons began to speak of the sermon which I had delivered on the previous Sunday, in which I had cited a passage from the Bible with which they were entirely unfamiliar. I took the opportunity of explaining that particular part of the Holy Writ to my hearers, who listened to me with the greatest attention. When I had finished, one of the sons remarked that he wished he could often have a chance to have various parts of the Scriptures explained to him.

On this I told him that I should be glad to meet them all at the home of his invalid aunt and to answer any questions which they might lay before me, for in a like manner the early Christians had assembled at each others' homes to discuss matters of religion. All of those present eagerly welcomed my suggestion, and we immediately fixed upon the evenings on which we were to meet.

The first few of our meetings took place without any unusual incident. We always opened them with a prayer, after which, holding hands, we sat for a few minutes in silence, concentrating our thoughts. I would then read passages from the Scriptures, interpret and discuss their contents and answer any questions asked by my hearers. We would also deliberate how best to help the needy of our immediate neighbourhood and its surroundings.

I was much impressed with the earnestness with which the three brothers took the matter, and not only I, but their mother also, observed something peculiar: the faces of all of them were assuming a finer, nobler, expression. Even strangers remarked upon it. Furthermore, one of them confided to me that some inner change was taking place in him, for which he could not account; that when he was at work out in the field, an inner voice was constantly exhorting him to praise God and to give Him thanks. Such thoughts had never come to him formerly. And now, whenever, quick-tempered as he was, he gave way to a fit of rage, it would weigh so heavily upon his soul that he would feel compelled to leave his work until he had begged God to forgive his offense. Not until then could he resume his work with any peace of mind. In former times he had offended in this way dozens of times a day without experiencing any compunction.

It happened, at our fourth meeting, that I had been interpreting a certain passage in the Bible, my interpretation being the same as that given today by all Christian authorities on the Scriptures, for at that time I knew of no other. I had not yet completed what I was engaged in saying, when one of the boys became inexplicably excited, looking at me with a strange gleam in his eyes. I could see that he was struggling hard against some inward emotion. Suddenly turning to me he said in a trembling voice:

"I cannot help myself. I must tell you that your interpretation is not correct and that I am compelled to give the true one."

With that, he uttered the sentences which had been inspired in him for the elucidation of this passage of the Bible. What he said was so clear and convincing that neither I nor any of the others could have any doubts of its correctness.

We had not yet recovered from our amazement when the same boy exclaimed:

"I must write."

"Why, what are you going to write?" I asked him.

"That I do not know, but I am being compelled by an irresistible power. Give me a pencil and paper."

We gave him both, and immediately he began to write rapidly, continuing until he had covered a sheet of folio size. One letter was joined to the next, so that there were no spaces between words or sentences. At the bottom appeared the word "Celsior."

The document contained information of great value to us.

The boy asked me the meaning of the word "Celsior" and I told him it was a Latin one, signifying "The Higher One" or "A Higher One."

I now enquired of him what his sensations had been during his recent experience. He answered that he could not find the right words to describe them; that he had been under the influence of a power so great that he could not resist it, although he had done his utmost to strive against the impulse to tell me that my interpretation of the Bible was wrong, for he had, of course, believed at first that it was the correct one. But in the end he had been compelled, first to speak and then to write. He had felt as though his own thoughts had been crowded out of him and had been replaced by others. He had known that he was writing, and had been aware of the contents of each sentence, but only while uttering or writing that particular one. As soon as one sentence was completed, he had lost all recollection of it, his mind being fully taken up with the next, and he had been compelled to utter or to write it in the exact words in which he had received it. He had been unable to pay any attention to the letters, the spelling or the punctuation while writing. After concluding his interpretation of the Biblical passage mentioned and his writing, he had completely forgotten what he had said and written, so that he was quite unable to repeat a word of either.

We were still discussing the occurrence, when one of his brothers announced that he could no longer attend our meetings because he found that he could not keep his head still and that it was continually being turned from side to side against his will. He had done his best to control this tendency, but without success.

I, too, had noticed this motion of his head, and so had his mother who looked at me questioningly and in alarm. I reassured her and the young man by telling them that they need not fear, for that what we were doing could not possibly be wrong. It was true, I added, that we did not understand everything that was happening here, but that it would undoubtedly soon be made clear to us. Similar phenomena had been observed at the gatherings of the first Christians, a statement which I confirmed by reading aloud the 14th Chapter of the First Epistle to the Corinthians, which I expounded as best I could at that time.

To me, what had taken place on that evening was as new as it was to the rest. At the meetings in the city I had witnessed the manifestation of a spirit through a wholly *unconscious person*. The fact that spirits could use human beings in the full possession of their faculties as instruments, and especially, that they could cause these to speak and to write, was quite outside of my previous experience. Above all, I was completely at a loss to understand what was taking place in the boy whose head was being moved to and fro.

I was therefore very glad to have the opportunity of asking for an explanation of these matters on the occasion of my next attendance at the Sunday meeting in town, at which I was told as follows:

"Do not worry if you do not understand everything at the outset. The subject is still quite new to you and there are many points which you have not yet had time to grasp. But little by little you will come to understand them all.

"It is the same way with your human inventions and discoveries: at first a newly discovered fact is considered impossible and its discoverer as mentally abnormal. Years later the same discovery is universally admitted, and regarded as obvious. How many people a hundred years ago could have conceived of your modern airplanes, your telegraph, your telephone, let alone your radio? Had anyone then predicted that the time would come when man could fly through the air, speak with distant places and listen, in his own home, to a concert being given hundreds of miles away, he would not have been taken seriously. And it is precisely the scientists who would have scoffed the most at any such possibilities.

"You have been told and are seeing for yourself, that the spirit-world can communicate with mankind, as soon as the necessary conditions have been fulfilled. Most people will not believe this, just as formerly they did not believe in the possibility of what today are commonplaces.

"So too, your scientists now refuse to accept that the spirit-world is able to enter into your lives in a manner perceptible to your senses. And yet, even in your own day there are thousands of occurrences which those very scientists can verify as indisputable facts, and, what is more, as *facts which can be ascribed only to intervention by the spirit-world.* But your scientists seek other causes for these occurrences, and ask you to accept the most senseless and incredible explanations to account for 'human agencies' behind these occurrences, so that they themselves need not acknowledge the existence of a spirit-world and a Beyond. Some of them take this position because they deny a future life; others, because as scientists they lack the courage to admit the intervention of spirits, although inwardly convinced that it exists. They are afraid that their professional reputations will suffer in consequence.

"But the time is coming when your science will be forced to admit that both spirit-worlds, the good and the bad, intervene visibly and perceptibly in your lives and your fortunes, and do so in an infinite number of ways.

"You must not be surprised, therefore, if you are considered today as not quite normal, as soon as you announce that you have spoken with a spirit.

"It is indeed hard for me to understand why your various religious denominations should refuse to admit the possibility of the intervention of the spirit-world and of its intercourse with man today, or why, if they do admit it, they contend that it can be only the evil spirit-world which manifests itself now-a-days.

"Any such attitude is utterly untenable, for if it is impossible for spirits to reach you today, it was equally impossible in the past, and all Biblical accounts of communication with spirits must be relegated to the realm of myth. If, on the other hand, now-a-days it is only *evil* spirits which can make their presence known to you, then the same was true formerly. That means that all beliefs based on either the Old or the New Testament would fall to the ground, for they certainly claim to have received their religious truths and laws from spirits. If, then, *good spirits* were able to visit men in the past, there is no reason for doubting that they are able to do so today as well, for the same God who sent the spirits then, sends them today. Just as he tried then to guide mankind upon the right path, so does He today. Or do you think that you are no longer in need of any advice and guidance from God's spirits? Do you think you are better and wiser than the people of Old, and that you possess all the truth there is?

"That which you saw in your parish confirms what you are learning from me here. You will witness much more. Have no fear for the boy who cannot keep his head still; we are working on him and you will see how the different *'mediums'* are prepared for their duties.

"The word 'medium' means 'instrument'. Mediums are therefore human beings used by the spirit-world as instruments, to enable it to communicate with man. Animals also may be employed for the purpose, but of these we shall not speak for the moment.

"If human beings are to serve the spirit-world as instruments they require development, which is imparted by the spirit-world and requires more or less time, according to the individual but more particularly according to the purpose for which the medium is to be employed.

"When the time comes, I shall instruct you thoroughly as to the different kinds of mediums and the details of their development. Today, I shall tell you only enough about it to enable you to understand what will happen at the next meetings in your parish.

"You have there at present two kinds of mediums undergoing a course of preparation at the hands of the spirit-world. One is a so-called' inspirational medium' into whom certain thoughts, determined by the spirit, are instilled with such force, that the medium's own thoughts are completely expelled from him, leaving him wholly within the spirit's power. The medium not only receives all the thoughts from the spirit, but is compelled to write them down or to utter them, retaining the full use of his faculties meanwhile. Your 'inspirational medium' requires further training to perfect his receptiveness to messages from the spirit-world. It is still necessary to remove from him much that now obstructs this faculty. What that is, you cannot understand now, but you will, later.

"The other medium who has not yet entered into activity is

in the first stage of preparation. I mean the boy who could not keep his head still at your last meeting and who was frightened in consequence. He will become a 'speaking medium'; his own spirit will be expelled from his body and the latter will be occupied by another spirit which will speak through it. This state is called a 'trance'. There are various gradations of trances, according to whether the spirit of the medium is completely or only partly expelled from the body.

"The way in which this expulsion is accomplished is something that you will find difficult to understand, but it will be explained to you in detail on a later occasion.

"The development of a 'full trance' or a 'deep trance' medium is not a pleasant sight, but it is necessary and proceeds according to eternal laws.

"In order that the medium's mother may not be frightened unneccessarily by what takes place, it will be best for her to keep away from the meetings for the time being.

"The development of mediums is an important and a sacred matter and therefore you must, at your sittings, pray earnestly to God and ask Him to help them and to give them strength, so that everything may be done according to His will and that the mediums may become useful agents for the good, and may remain faithful to God.

"Whatever I have told you today is necessary, in order that you may have some knowledge of what happens during the development of mediums, and that you may not feel alarmed over the things which you may see happening to them."

Everything that I had been told about the training of the two mediums in my parish came true to the letter. The boy who had been described as an 'inspirational medium' progressed rapidly. Full instructions concerning the most important truths were instilled into him, and were committed by him to writing. Many of the things so revealed were entirely new to me and were, to a large extent, quite contrary to what the boy had hitherto believed and to what I myself had proclaimed in my sermons as the truth. In this instance there was no possibility of any subconsciousness or thought-transmission, by which so many people try to explain phenomena of this kind. Thought-transmission was utterly out of the question, if only for the reason that whatever, from this time on, the inspirational medium set down, was committed to writing not at our meetings but at his own home and without anyone else being present. The boy would not sit down to write of his own accord, but would on each occasion be obliged to do so by that same resistless power that had taken possession of him for the first time at the meeting that I have described. Even the precise time would be determined by that power. Once he was awakened very early in the morning, long before the usual time of rising, and was summoned to get up and write. He did not obey the summons, thinking the hour too early, when suddenly he felt himself pulled forcibly out of bed and laid upon the floor. Thoroughly frightened, he sprang to his feet and sat down to write. What he put down was a remarkable treatise on "Redemption," which did not agree in a single point with that which he, as a Catholic, had been taught on the subject, and which did not resemble, even remotely, anything that could have been gathered from any other known source. In a like manner he, an untutored country lad, wrote a paper on the "Holy Writ" which contains truths that are entirely new. Not only the contents but the phraseology of these writings are such, that the boy could never have created them out of his own head. He wrote treatises in prose on the following subjects: "The Spiritualization of the Soul"; "God's Mercy"; "What has your Redeemer done for you?"; "Spring, Summer, Fall and Winter"; "The Harvest"; "The Night"; "Beseech ye the Lord"; "The Holy Writ"; "A Child's Love"; "The Death of a Mortal."

Just as the sole subject of all of his prose writings was God's truths, so too in the case of his poems like: "The Heroes' Demand"; "The Language of Creation"; "Hail and Hosanna"; "In the Pathways of God"; "God's Shepherd and his Flock"; "The Stronger One"; "Thus wanders thy Creator."

The preparation of his brother as a 'speaking medium' required more time, while the aspect of his physical condition on these occasions was often alarm-inspiring. I was therefore glad that I had been warned of this beforehand, since otherwise I might not have had the courage to persist to the end. As for the boys' mother, I had asked her to stay away from the meetings for the time being.

After his course of preparation had been completed he used to fall into the same state of trance that I had observed in the case of the speaking medium in the city. The spirit-being that first spoke through him arrived with the greeting: *"Gott mit uns"*

(God be with us), swearing that it was one of God's good spirits and making known its name.

Through this spirit I received a wealth of knowledge and instruction, all of which was in harmony with what I had learned from the inspirational medium of my own parish and, especially, from the medium in the city.

In this connection there were two things that struck me: in the first place I could detect a difference in the rank of the spirit speaking through the medium at my parish, and that of the spirit employing the medium in the city, for several times when I asked some very important question of the former spirit, he would refuse to answer, with the remark: "I am not authorized to reply to that question. You must ask "Him" !

Whenever pronouncing the word "Him", the medium bowed low, the reference being to the spirit speaking through the lad in the city. On the first occasion on which I was referred to the latter spirit, I asked the spirit before me whether he knew the other one.

"I do," was the reply, uttered with a low bow.

At first I could not quite understand why the spirit speaking through the farmer-boy should not be permitted to answer questions as freely as that for which the boy in the city acted as a medium, and one day I asked the latter spirit for the reason. He informed me that the customs of the spirit-world were similar to those on earth insofar as when a messenger is sent on a definite errand, he is expected to deliver only the message entrusted to him and nothing else. Thus, being himself duly authorized by God, he had the right to answer any questions of mine if he considered such answers necessary or useful, but the spirit speaking through the boy in my parish, he added, was allowed no such latitude, and was in duty bound to refer me to his superior with respect to any questions which, in his subordinate capacity, he might not answer himself.

The other difference that I noticed was, that it was always *one and the same spirit* that spoke through the boy in the city, whereas there were several different spirits for which the speaking medium of my parish acted as spokesman, although it was the highest of these that made use of him the most frequently. It always came to us with the greeting: *"Gott mit uns!"*, and was recognizable by its gentle voice and its characteristic form of diction. It was also always the first one to speak at the meetings held in my parish.

One day I asked it how it happened that only one spirit would speak through the medium in the city, whereas the medium whom it employed served several other spirits as well. The answer was as follows:

"A definite task has been allotted to the other spirit, and for this purpose the medium in the city has been appointed to *its exclusive use*. For this reason no other spirit beings may enter that medium. On the other hand, the medium through whom I speak, although prepared for my use, may by God's will, be employed by other spirits, good and bad, high and low. In this way you are to be allowed to become familiar with the different kinds of spirits and to learn from their speech and actions about their state in the Beyond. Above all, you will learn something of the path which low spirits must follow in order to attain perfection. It is most important that you should gather such personal knowledge of the spirit-world by means of its manifestations through mediums, for thus you will learn far more of the subject than you could by any amount of oral instruction. However, any spirits which may manifest themselves through the medium here will not come and go as they please. They are subject to a controlling spirit appointed to determine which spirits may enter into the medium and how long they may remain there. Such a control exists in the case of all mediums who serve as instruments for the good, and the same is true of all meetings at which communication is held with spirits after the manner willed by God. In the absence of such control, nothing truly good or beautiful can be accomplished, because the good and high spirits do not appear. They come only to those places in which everything is done as directed by God, and in which one of His Spirits holds sway. At most of the spiritistic gatherings of today this control is lacking, and as a result they become the playgrounds of the lower spirit-world.

"During the early stages I shall tell you what spirits I shall admit and how you are to conduct yourself toward them. Later you will be able to distinguish between them for yourself, and will know what to do in each individual case."

That is precisely what happened.

A great number of spirits made use of the "speaking medium" of my parish.

Among them were *high spirits* which entered, lauding and praising the Lord, taught us matters of great importance and departed after bestowing God's blessing on us.

There were also *spirits undergoing great suffering,* which often implored our help in heart-rending words, beseeching us to pray with them. At times they spoke in some foreign language, and, finding that we could not understand them, turned away disconsolate.

Again, there were *spirits of a very low standing,* which cursed themselves and their fate, reviling us and scoffing at everything high and sacred in the most unmeasured terms. When urged by us to join us in prayer, they refused scornfully or spitefully. If we insisted on their uttering the name of God, they immediately departed out of the medium.

Very numerous indeed were the spirits which did not realize at all that they had been divorced from the flesh by death. They believed that they were still on earth and engaged in the occupations which they followed in life. These were the so-called "*earth-bound spirits.*"

Our most gruesome experiences were those with the spirits of criminals. They constantly saw themselves haunting the scene of their crime and again and again witnessed what had taken place during its perpetration, like a film which repeats itself over and over again. The spirit of the murderer was forever engaged in plotting and carrying out the assassination in all its details and described his thoughts and feelings during those terrible hours in words which made us shudder, telling us how the victim gazed steadily at it with a look that drove it to despair. A similar fate pursued the spirits of usurers and other evil doers who had brought want and misfortune upon their fellowmen. Wherever they might turn, they were confronted with the forms of their victims. The suicide's spirit ceaselessly re-experienced the sensations, the outbursts of despair and the events which had attended his self-destruction. No actor on earth could play his role so realistically as did these spirits, in depicting their emotions during the darkest hours of their lives through the person of this medium who was utterly inexperienced, uninstructed and innocent in such matters. Often what we saw and heard was enough to make us tremble at every limb.

Now and then we would be visited by so-called "bantering spirits" which tried to amuse us with their pranks and lies. As we showed no desire for their company, they would be obliged to depart as suddenly as they had come.

The appearance of these different types of spirits and the incidents connected therewith were of the utmost significance.

The high spirits brought us valuable instruction and at times earnest admonitions and, occasionally, reproved us so severely that not infrequently one or another of their hearers burst into tears. More than once the most secret thoughts of someone present were laid bare, although this was always done in such a manner as not to humiliate him in the eyes of the rest. It is, indeed, characteristic of the good spirit-world that it always administers its censure and reproof in such a way that it causes no offense, and it always accompanies its admonitions with expressions of consolation, cheer and love. The good spirits do not break the bruised reed nor extinguish the glowing spark, but with gentle hands bind up the wounds in the hearts of those committed to their care.

They do not, as a rule, repeat many times their warning or advice relating to the same subject. If no heed is paid to their words, they may, perhaps, remind their hearer of them once or twice, but not oftener, or if so, only in the rarest cases. But if he strives diligently to follow their advice or to obey the warning, they come back to the subject again and again and help him with their loving advice and encouragement, until he has reached his goal. Whenever genuine good will is shown by the mortal, their love and mercy knows no bounds, not even in those cases in which human frailty leads him astray. If, however the object of their endeavors makes no effort to do as one of these messengers from God bids him, and if later he asks for guidance in another matter, he will generally be told:

"Why do you consult me when you do not do as I say?"

The appearance of even the lowest spirits was most instructive. I shall never forget the evening on which the speaking medium was visited in quick succession by the spirits of three suicides which furnished us with the most gruesome sight that it is given to man to witness in this field. When the last of these spirits had departed from the medium and while we were still sitting there trembling, the guiding spirit entered and thus addressed us:

"There were weighty reasons why you have been shown what you saw this evening. In the first place you were to witness what sort of 'rest' there is in store for some people after death. You so often say, when standing by a grave: 'He is at rest at last.' Tonight you have seen something of that 'rest'. You cannot begin to realize what these unfortunate spirits have to suffer before they can be brought to understand their position and to turn to God. You were not allowed to enlighten them As yet they do not deserve it. They must go on suffering until they have been rendered fit to receive such enlightenment. Today it would have been to no purpose. But there was also another reason why their condition was shown to you."

With that, the spirit raised its voice and said solemnly:

"One of you has been harboring the thought of killing himself today, and was about to prepare for the deed."

On hearing these words, a member of our circle uttered a startled cry and exclaimed:

"It was I, oh God, it was I !"

"Yes, it was you," replied the spirit in a much gentler tone. "You had hoped to escape a burden that you have borne for years, by killing yourself and so finding rest. Today you have seen what kind of rest you would have found. Now, I am sure, you will be forever cured of such thoughts and this evening has been of the greatest benefit to you."

I was particularly anxious to determine whether the things that were told or predicted by the mediums were so or would come true, for if we could verify those statements which were susceptible of proof, we had no reason for doubting the truth of those which were not.

Of the many statements by spirits which I so verified, I shall cite a few which should convince any unprejudiced person.

1. *My Visit, in company with a Medium, to my Parish Church.* One day the medium from the city came to see me at my rectory. We were sitting together in my study, talking of casual matters, while my housekeeper who had been working in the kitchen, now and then entered the room. During one of her absences, the boy suddenly fell into a trance and the spirit addressed me with the words:

"Your houskeeper has just gone out to work in the garden. I want to make use of this opportunity to speak to you. Please show me your church."

The fact that my housekeeper had gone into the garden could have been known neither to me nor to the boy in his human capacity, for the garden lay behind the rectory and could be reached from the kitchen only by passing through the rear hallway, from which a door opened upon it. We were both seated in a room on the opposite side of the house and could neither hear nor see what was going on in the kitchen or the garden.

In response to the request to show the church, I rose, the boy, still in a trance and with his eyes closed, following me with unsteady steps. The church stood beside the rectory and was accessible from it without crossing the street. The church could be entered by a side door from my front yard. When we had done so the spirit said:

"The altar stands directly above a human skeleton that is buried in the ground, and there are other skeletons buried beneath the nave. Once upon a time there was a graveyard here."

I replied that I knew nothing of it; I did not think it possible, for the church stood on a little knoll and was not surrounded by any space available for burials.

"Ask the oldest residents," he replied," they may be able to tell you something about it."

Then he turned his tightly shut eyes toward the organ-loft and said:

"You know that I rarely give advice in purely material matters, but today I shall make an exception. You have bought an organ. Tell the organist that after he is through playing, he must always push the stops all the way back into place. Three of the stops are still halfway out, which allows dust and moisture to enter the pipes; in time, this will impair the purity of their notes. I speak of it because fine, pure music contributes to the beauty of divine service and thereby to the glory of God."

The keyboard of the organ was locked, so that neither the keys nor the stops could have been seen, even by a person standing directly at the instrument and certainly not by anyone near the altar. From that distance we could have seen nothing even if the organ had been open. Its key was hanging in a closet in the vestry.

We next went to one of the side altars. The altar-piece represented the death of St. Joseph, with Jesus and Mary standing by his bedside.

"This picture is not true to fact," said the boy, "Jesus was not present when Joseph died."

We now passed several pictures showing the Stations of the Cross. When we reached the one depicting Veronica receiving back her kerchief on which the image of the blood-stained features of Jesus had appeared, I asked whether this had really happened or whether it was merely a legend.

"It is the truth, and no legend," was the reply.

Before the picture of the Crucifixion, the spirit suddenly asked me:

"What do you think caused Christ the greatest agony?"

"The nailing to the Cross," I answered.

"Not that," rejoined the spirit," but thirst. The nails were driven suddenly by the brutal executioner's assistants through His hands and feet with a few quick blows, and caused a numbness which for some time was not excessively painful, just as in the late War many wounded men did not feel at the moment bullet or shell wounds, even severe ones. The worst is the thirst that follows loss of blood, as your wounded found. No physical suffering can equal that of dying of thirst."

As we walked on we came to a side-chapel in which there was an ancient wood-carving of Mary, which centuries ago had stood in a nearby convent whose ruins could still be traced.

"This carving," said the spirit, "has long been sought by the suffering spirits bound to remain near the ruined convent in the valley below."

Lost in amazement I asked:

"Why is it that those spirits have not been able, in all that time, to find this carving which is so close at hand? And besides, what good could it do them?"

"Since you do not understand, I will tell you. Spirits which are punished for their misdeeds by being banned to a certain spot, may not pass beyond the limits set for them. For this reason the spirits banned to that valley may not wander as far as this church and may seek the statue of Mary only within their prescribed limits. As to the good it would do them to find it, it is true that the statue itself cannot help them, but there was something connected with the statue that formerly brought them some relief.

"While the statue was still in the convent, many people went before it to pray. On these occasions, prayers were said for the 'poor souls' as you call spirits in torment. Such prayers cannot, indeed, lessen the guilt of the spirits or reduce their penalty, but they *hear* the prayers, and their thoughts are thereby turned toward God. This alleviates their agony, but since the time when the statue was taken away from the convent, nobody goes there to pray and the spirits miss the consolation which the prayers brought them. They know that these were associated with the statue, and are eager to recover it."

By this time we had reached the stairway leading to the organ-loft. I was curious to know the facts as to the stops which had not been pushed back into place, but at the moment my mind was occupied with another thought. I was wondering whether the spirit beside me could play the organ; that the boy could not, I knew for a fact. There seemed to be only one difficulty, namely, the question whether he could move his hands and feet as rapidly as playing an organ requires. It was with some hesitation, therefore, that I asked him to play.

"Gladly," replied the spirit, — "if it will give you pleasure."

I returned to the vestry for the key and we ascended the stairs leading to the organ-loft. Unlocking the keyboard, I immediately looked at the stops; sure enough, three of them were part-way out. The spirit repeated its injunction to warn the organist of this matter.

The boy then sat down at the organ to play, at first softly and in sweet, harmonious chords, the notes gradually gathering in volume as he went on. When he reached the climax, the voice of the organ pealed and crashed with the sound of the hurricane that levels trees in its sweep, then slowly ebbed until it died away in gentle murmurs. There could be no doubt: the touch was that of a master hand.

When he had finished playing he pushed all the stops into place and rose from his seat; then stepping in front of me, he asked:

"Do you know what it was that I have just played?"

"No," I answered.

"That was your life," said the spirit quietly.

I must have shown my astonishment, for I could not have believed that a man's life could be portrayed by the notes of an organ. As though reading my thoughts, the spirit went on:

"The life of man is like a painting, which can be done in colors and also in notes. Every color presents a note, and every note a color. There are clairvoyants who read all tones in their colors, and who cannot distinguish harmony from discord by ear, but only by sight and from the way in which the colors are blended. It is therefore possible, in any event for spirits, to reproduce every painting in music."

I was unable to comprehend this: the thought was too new to me.

Silently we descended the stairway to the nave of the church and went to the door by which we had entered. Here my companion stopped and said:

"Now I must leave you. I cannot go with you to the rectory because your housekeeper is on the point of leaving the garden and going into the house, and I do not want her to see this boy in his state of trance. I shall now stand close to the wall; do you support the boy's body, so that he may not fall down when I depart from him."

I did as I was bidden and found that it required my full strength to keep the boy from sinking over forward while the spirit was leaving him. He at once regained his faculties and was much surprised to find himself in the church with me, as he remembered only that he had sat with me in the rectory. Of what had happened in the meantime he knew nothing. When I told him that he had played the organ beautifully, he shook his head incredulously.

At the moment at which we opened the rectory door my housekeeper stepped from the garden into the rear of the hallway. Had the spirit not left the medium when it did, she could not have failed to see the boy in his trance.

Later, when I spoke to the boy about the several events, he disclaimed all knowledge of skeletons, organ stops, the death of St. Joseph, Veronica's kerchief, the agony of the Crucifixion, the statue of Mary and its history, the spirits banned to the neighbourhood of the convent-ruins, the effect of prayer upon them, and the organ recital and what I had been told in connection therewith.

On that very evening I learned by inquiry that the site now occupied by the church had at one time been a graveyard.

2. *The Member of a Monastic Order who Attended Spiritist Meetings.* One message, delivered one evening through the farmer boy of my parish as a speaking medium, seemed to me very improbable. It was to the effect that a monk from the neighbouring

Benedictine monastery was attending spiritist meetings held in a city not far removed. We could scarcely believe that a father, wearing the habits of his order, would take his seat at a spiritist gathering, in view of the intense hostility of the Catholic church toward spiritism. There was no way for us to verify this communication but its correctness was soon to be demonstrated through an unforseen channel.

I had been reported to by ecclesiastic authorities as a frequenter of spiritist meetings, and a commission was sent to investigate the charges against me. The hearing was to be held at the very Benedictine monastery in question and I was ordered to appear there.

At the hearing I frankly admitted having attended spiritist meetings and instituted them in my parish. I was reminded that all Catholics had received an order, emanating from Rome, not to attend any such meetings. I protested that I had heard nothing of this but that, if the facts were as alleged, I could not understand why a father from that selfsame monastery should also be attending meetings of that sort. I said this, not to protect myself, but merely to learn in this way whether what had been reported by the medium was true.

The head of the investigating committee indignantly denied the truth of my assertion and heatedly maintained that such a thing was impossible and that he must reject my statement as calumny.

I answered calmly that I had not brought the matter up to cause the father or his monastery any trouble, but that I had heard of it through a certain source and was taking this way of verifying the truth of the story. Should my statement prove false, I would see to it that my informant was set right. The head of the commission suspended the proceedings and went, presumably, to see the abbot of the convent. After a short absence he returned rather crestfallen, and admitted that I was right, but added as an excuse that the monk in question had received permission from the abbot to visit spiritist meetings.

The truth of what the medium had told me was thus established.

3. In the course of the proceedings brought against me I received confirmation after confirmation of the reports and predictions made, by the mediums *about my affairs*.

One day I was summoned before the bishop. Scarcely had

his letter reached me, when the farmer boy of my parish, the speaking medium, came to my rectory and said:

"I have been obliged to come to see you. You have received a letter from your episcopal superior, ordering you to repair to ——————, to appear before him."

I asked the boy how many lines there were in the letter; even that he knew exactly. Thereupon he passed into a state of trance and the spirit which spoke through him cheered me with the words:

"Have no fear! Trust God and be not afraid! What can man do to you?"

I replied that I intended to confess to the bishop the convictions I had acquired as a result of my communications with the spirit-world, and that I fully expected to lose my place as a minister of the Catholic church in consequence.

"The bishop will ask no questions on spiritism, or about any convictions you may have derived from it;" said the spirit, "at some time in the future you will be granted leave. Your separation from your parish will come about in peace between you and your church, and not by way of expulsion."

I could hardly believe that the bishop would fail to ask me about the spiritist meetings and the truths revealed there, but it turned out just as the medium had predicted. The bishop read to me the edict issued by the Congregation of Rome in 1917, which provided that Catholics might not attend spiritist meetings, caused me to sign a paper acknowledging that he had brought the edict to my notice and imposed a penance on me for my past transgressions of the same. But of spiritism itself he said not a word.

Somewhat later I had the painful experience of seeing a certain prediction communicated through the medium in the city come true. I had been told at a meeting that one of our number was going to betray me. We did not believe that there was anyone among us capable of such baseness, and yet, the seemingly impossible happened: a woman of our circle denounced me to the episcopal authorities for my continued attendance at spiritist meetings.

This seemed to make my expulsion a foregone conclusion. I had, as it happened, applied for a leave of absence to allow me to devote myself to charitable work, but the episcopal vicariate had rejected my application in terms so unamiable, that humanly speaking there seemed to be no hope of its being granted. The case against me in the ecclesiastical courts pursued its course, and a day was set for the final proceedings at which I was ordered to be present. It lacked but a very few days of the date on which the verdict, which was sure to result in my expulsion, would be rendered. Nevertheless, I still had faith in the prediction that had been made to me that I should be allowed to depart from my parish, in peace with my church. Then, at the eleventh hour, I had a telegram from the ecclesiastic council notifying me that proceedings against me had been dropped at the instance of the bishop. Soon afterwards he wrote me, granting me leave of absence and asking me when I would like to surrender my parish. I replied giving him the date, December 31st, 1925, the day which had long before been predicted as that on which my connection with my parish would terminate.

4. In the Whitsuntide week of 1924 I was travelling to Graz in Styria. On the stretch between Passau and Vienna I was alone with a young man in a railroad compartment, seated opposite him and reading, when I saw his head suddenly bow forward as though he had fallen asleep. Almost instantly he straightened himself again, sat with his eyes closed, took a notebook out of his pocket and covered a page of it with writing. Then he tore out the page and handed it to me saying:

"Take this and keep it. What its meaning is, you will be told elsewhere."

I looked at the writing but could not decipher the characters. At that moment the young man recovered consciousness. He did not know that he had written anything or that he had given me the paper, nor did he remember a word of what he had said to me. He too was unable to read the characters set down on the paper.

After my return from Graz to my parish I carried the paper about in my pocket for a couple of weeks, when one Saturday evening I happened to be at the home of my speaking medium's family. The boy was alone in the room. After a few moments he fell into a trance and said:

"Show me the paper you have with you, that was given you on your journey to Graz."

When I had given it to him he read it and observed:

"Tomorrow afternoon you will have a visit from a Jew. People think he is sick, but as a matter of fact he is being tormented by a malignant spirit which has such power over him that he can scarcely utter a word. As soon as he comes, call the boy through whom I am speaking. Leave all the rest to me. You will see mighty things.

"The writing on this sheet is that of the Jew's guardian spirit done through the medium whom you met on your trip to Graz. It is the spirit of a deceased uncle of the Jew's, who lived in Cologne. The malignant spirit tormenting the Jew is also that of a deceased relative."

At four o'clock on the next afternoon someone rang my doorbell. I opened the door and was startled at seeing a man whose limbs were contorted and whose head was jerking back and forth nervously. He tried to speak but could not utter a word. I took his hand and led him to my room, and at once sent for the boy who, upon his arrival, fell into a trance before the Jew. Then he arose, stretched out his hand as though conjuring the visitor, and addressed him in a foreign language which I could not understand. Back and forth the Jew was tossed as if by an invisible force; then he was freed from the evil influence; he wept for joy and began to speak without any difficulty, telling me that he knew quite well what had just taken place. He himself, he said, had the power of clairvoyance and could distinguish the spirits about him, good and evil ones. His good spirit was that of an uncle of his of Cologne; his evil one, that of a relative whom he had not known in life. The evil spirit had tried to prevent him from coming to see me and on his way to my house shouted the vilest epithets and curses in the Hebrew tongue at him, some of which he repeated to me. Now he hoped that he was forever rid of that spirit. He knew also whose spirit it was that had set him free. Then taking out his prayer book he showed me a Hebrew prayer to one of the high celestial powers. The Jew had not been mistaken: it was the very spirit who was then present.

While I was still talking to the Jew the boy once more went into a trance and turned to me saying:

"What I am telling you now cannot be heard by that man; his senses are being dulled so that he cannot understand me. The things that have just happened were shown as an object lesson to you and to him also. He will be freed from his evil spirit, but for a short time only, for the spirit will come back and torment him until he dies. He has merited this punishment; but he will not come to see you again, for he will never again be able to muster up the strength to do so."

I asked the Jew whether he had understood what had just been said and he replied that he had heard nothing. Deeply moved, I bade him farewell and have never seen him since.

5. I had often had my attention called by the various mediums to the fact that many falsifications had been introduced into the documents that dated back to the early days of the Christian era and had asked myself repeatedly whether there were not some work of scientific merit in which the attempt had been made to uncover these falsifications. I knew of no such work and could find no one else who did. At our meetings I had purposely refrained from asking about the matter, as I had been told that everything that could be of use to me would be brought into my hands.

Unexpectedly on one day portions of a work of this were sent to me by two separate deliveries. *The pages had not been cut.* At the same time there came a letter from a lady whom I had met only once in my life. It read:

"The books I am sending were given to me day before yesterday by Mrs. H. of F., for you. She *had* to send them to you at once, without even reading them herself.

"Mighty things are happening to her. Be sure to look her up before long.

N. N."

The Mrs. H. who had been compelled to send those works to me was a total stranger to me, even by name.

In these books, of whose contents she knew absolutely nothing, proof was adduced to show that a document by the Jewish author Flavius Josephus had been most brazenly falsified in favor of the Christian religion by interested copyists, who had represented Flavius Josephus, a *despiser* of Christ, as one of His *votaries.*

There were also many references to the systematic falsifications of the writings of the first few centuries, thus confirming everything that I had been told by mediums entirely unfamiliar with such matters. This discovery pleased me greatly.

6. Confirmation of the general truth of communication with spirits and of many individual facts relating to the same field was vouchsafed me in America. In that country, spiritism is widely

disseminated under the appellation of "spiritualism", there being great numbers of so-called "spiritualistic churches."

At the outset I made use of the opportunity of becoming acquainted with the way in which spiritism was practiced in these churches by attending the services in many of them.

Unfortunately my visits confirmed what I had heard from mediums in Germany, who had again and again assured me that God's good spirits will not go near places frequented by people more concerned with temporal matters than with progress on the paths leading to God. Only spirits of the lower orders, I had been informed, appeared at meetings at which materialistic views predominated. I was told also that there is no control over the spirits at such gatherings which become the stamping ground for spirits of the class mentioned, although not necessarily evil ones. Generally they are those of relatives, friends or acquaintances of members of the congregation, spirits which have progressed but little in the Beyond and which are therefore more interested in the temporal affairs than in the spiritual advancement of those whom they have left behind. Such meetings are thus no longer a divine service, but information bureaus for worldly questions and come dangerously close to offering the same sort of things that took place at the idolatrous ceremonies of pagans and that owed their attraction to the fact that the mediums functioning thereat were expected to impart information relating to the worldly success and careers of their hearers.

Much as I had hoped to find something lofty and edifying in at least some of these churches, I was completely disappointed. On the contrary, what I generally found was of a nature to hurt rather than to advance the cause of spiritism. I had also the impression that these meetings were attended merely for the sake of messages relating to *worldly matters,* and that the question of money seems to play no minor part with the leaders of these churches. A fixed admission fee is charged, which means that the really poor are debarred from attending.

All this substantiated what I had been told in Germany about modern spiritism, even when conducted with an outward show of respect for religious forms, and I became convinced that spiritism of this kind will not bring humanity much closer to God; it is not the spiritism of the early Christians.

Nevertheless it was my good fortune to meet with the finer

aspects of spiritism in America also, and through it to corroborate my previous experiences.

During my stay in New York I lived with a German family named Niemann at 148 East 18th Street. I am giving the name and address because this family played a leading role in the events to be related, and has authorized me to make public its identity. Elsewhere in this book I have refrained on principle from mentioning names, to preclude the possibility of any unpleasant consequences to anyone, at the hands of ill-disposed persons, as a result of anything that may appear herein.

I had never spoken to Mr. Niemann about spiritism and had gone no further than to tell him of some of my experiences in the spiritist churches of New York. He himself belonged to no denomination and seemed to have suffered his belief in God to lapse. As for what I told him of the occurrences at the spiritist meetings, he considered the whole thing a fraud and a money-making scheme.

Nevertheless, out of curiosity he decided one evening to accompany me to a meeting at one of these churches. What was told to him there was correct in all particulars, in spite of the fact that the medium had never seen him before, and naturally did not know who he was. He was informed among other things that he possessed great mediumistic powers and was urged to cultivate them.

After we had returned home he asked me what the medium had meant by urging him to cultivate his mediumistic powers, upon which I explained the situation and offered to hold services with him and Mrs. Niemann once a week. Incidentally, this would give me a further opportunity to verify what I had learned in Germany, even though I no longer had any doubts on that score.

I held the services as they had been conducted in the small circle in my parish, in the manner already described, and here, on the opposite side of the ocean, in a family which had abandoned its belief in God but which was ready and eager to accept the truth, I watched the schooling of mediums progress exactly as it had progressed in the case of the mediums with whom I had been in touch in the past. Thus, both there and here, the laws governing the development of mediums were the same.

On the very first evening Mr. Niemann began to write down spirit messages, conscious of the fact *that* he was doing so, but unaware of *what* he was writing. The various paragraphs of what he wrote were done in different handwritings and were signed with the several names of relatives and friends whom Mr. Niemann remembered only when he saw their signatures affixed to what he had just written. They all assured him that in acting as he did, he was choosing the right path and that he should hold to it, for they themselves would have been but too grateful if someone had shown them the way to God while they were alive. The messages stated that there was a Beyond and a God, in Whom the new convert should trust.

When Mr. Niemann came out of his trance and read what he himself had set down in different handwritings, he was speechless with amazement.

Subsequently he and his wife held the service in my absence and again he wrote as on the first occasion, much to his wife's surprise, for she still believed that I had hypnotized her husband and had transmitted to him by telepathy the thoughts which he had committed to writing. Now, however, she had proof to the contrary, because he had done his mediumistic writing in the same manner as he had when I was present. Incidentally, she might have reflected on the first occasion that I had no way of knowing the names of the deceased which appeared in the writing, and could not, therefore, have transmitted them to the writer.

At that same session she had an even more convincing proof, for she herself was compelled by an invisible power to take the pencil and write, while tears rolled down her cheeks. Unlike her husband, she knew what she was writing, her sensations being the same as those of the boy in my home parish. As in his case too, the thoughts to be written down were forcibly instilled into her. She was, therefore, an "inspirational medium", like that boy, and like him, was unable to repeat, at the conclusion of her writing, the ideas with which she had been inspired.

The schooling of these two mediums progressed from week to week. For a short time Mr. Niemann continued to write, but soon entered upon his development as a speaking medium, with all of those outward manifestations which I had observed in the case of the speaking medium in my former home. The spirit which spoke through him always came with the greeting: *"Der Friede Gottes sei mit Euch!"* (God's peace be with you) or, *whenever the message was especially important,* with the words: *"Gottes Wort sei mit Euch!"* (God's word be with you.)

We were soon to receive confirmation in a way which affected us all deeply, of the truth of the messages brought us by this spirit.

I had a very dear friend in Germany, a plain man of the people, who lived in a small rural community, and of whom I had taken leave personally before I sailed for America.

On July 20th, 1930 at one of our services, the spirit speaking through Mr. Niemann announced that my friend in Germany was dangerously ill and would soon die. The actual text of the message was:

"Your friend H. S. is dangerously ill. He is suffering from a lingering sickness. You will never again see him on earth."

Seeing that the shock of this news brought tears to my eyes the spirit went on consolingly:

"Your friend is a noble man. He is in good hands with us. If you want to write him, do so at once, so that your letter may reach him before he dies."

Then, seemingly to make sure that my letter would still arrive in time, the medium turned his head to one side as though questioning someone; then, facing me again he assured me:

"Yes, the letter will reach him in time, but do not put off writing it."

I wrote on the following day and as a sort of farewell message enclosed my picture. Naturally I said nothing of the prediction of his impending death; on the contrary, I expressed my pleasure at the prospect of seeing him again shortly and begged him to meet me in Bremen on my return.

On August 20th, 1930 I had a letter from my sister in Germany who lived near my friend's home. This letter was dated August 11th and began as follows: "It pains me to tell you that your best friend, H. S., of O., is dead. I heard that only last Monday he had a letter from you together with your picture. So after all, he saw you once more and could bid you goodbye. They say he wept bitterly, as you had written asking him to meet you in Bremen on your return home. He is now in eternity."

On the day on which my sister's letter came, our little circle held a service. Since the evening on which my friend's approaching end had been foretold, the spirit which had manifested itself through Mr. Niemann had not spoken, but now it entered the medium and pronounced the following words which were taken down in shorthand by Mrs. Niemann:

"God's word be with you! Amen! It is by way of an exception that I am speaking through him today, so that your prayer may be granted." (During the day I had been praying to God for words of comfort.)

"You have suffered a loss which weighs heavily on you as a mortal. But do not mourn. He (meaning my friend) is now much, much happier. And as a reward to you, he is standing by your right side, his face turned toward you. He is smiling at you and stroking your head with his right hand. He sends you his love and bids you not to take it so hard. On a later day you may hear from him, (meaning that my friend would perhaps speak to me himself through the medium) but not yet. His last struggle was not painful. He wanted to see you and to speak to you once more. Now he can do the first, but not the second. (The spirit here referred to seeing and speaking.) He died in the midst of a prayer to God. Oh, you poor mortals! Life is so hard for you, but keep your faith! Do not weaken, do not falter, and your rewards will not be lacking. Many whose lot on earth was not of the happiest stand far higher in the Beyond than those who were rulers on earth. 'Matter' does not bring happiness." (By matter, spirits mean money, a word which they seldom pronounce, using 'matter' instead.)

"Therefore do not take things so hard! Oh, if you could only see him! You may know by the fact of his being here that he stands very high. He still has to undergo a slight purification before reaching the eleventh sphere; he will not be required to pass through the tenth. In life he was one of those who truly are and were children of God."

Then speaking through the medium who stood with his hands raised aloft, the spirit pronounced the prayer:

"Heavenly Father, be merciful to us! Turn Thy countenance upon us! Give comfort to him who sits here mourning for the loss of his friend. Send him peace and cheerfulness, so that he may conquer his sorrow. Let the departed, who was an example among men, come to Thee in Thy mercy. Receive him into Thy circle that he may grow quickly in grace and confer mercies and blessings upon mankind. Father, he whom Thou hast chosen is coming to Thee; let him then fulfill the task which Thou hast allotted to him. Be gracious, Father, and give them both Thy blessing. Amen!"

At the service which followed, Mrs. Niemann, acting under

the influence of my departed friend, wrote things of which humanly speaking, she could have no knowledge, among others, a reference to a walk which I had taken, years previously, with my friend through a little valley in the Hunsrueck Range. On that occasion we had spoken of God and of the great questions of a future existence. I myself recalled the incident only when I saw it set down in Mrs. Niemann's mediumistic writing, in which the valley in question was called by its proper name, known only to people of the locality.

Even years before my friend died I received from him proofs, sufficient in themselves, of the truth of what I had learned in my communication with the spirit-world, to have carried conviction, for when in consequence of my spiritistic experiences I was obliged to alter my religious beliefs radically, I feared that this dear friend of mine, who was a good Catholic, would become estranged from me like so many others. When I expressed this apprehension at one of the meetings in Germany to the spirit which manifested itself there, I was assured:

"Your fear of losing your friend is groundless. We ourselves will instruct him and you will not find it necessary to make any explanations."

It was not long before my friend looked me up and related to me some remarkable visions which he had had. In them he had been shown a number of fundamental truths at variance with his creed as a Catholic, primarily the truth revealed in a vision which had come to him in a churchyard of the final pardon of the souls of the condemned and of a universal reconciliation with God. He had also had many visions showing the fate of the spirits of the departed, and at the same time had received instruction bearing on that subject. He was even informed of the life task that had been assigned to me personally. These experiences had convinced him so thoroughly that I felt it unnecessary to go beyond confirming the correctness of his visions.

7. *Egyptian Tombs.* There was one message the full significance of which I cannot grasp even today, and which, although it has not yet been fulfilled, I do not want to leave unmentioned.

It relates to the discovery of two royal Egyptian tombs of about 5000 B.C. I have not the least doubt that what I was told about them is true; that these tombs will ultimately be located and will be found to contain everything reported to me by four different mediums.

Let me relate first of all the strange way in which my attention was called to these tombs.

On February 1st, 1924 I was sitting in my private office at the headquarters of the charitable organization after business hours, when there arrived two young men some twenty to twenty-three years of age and announced that they had been sent to do me a service. Scarcely had they said so when both fell into a deep trance, and the spirits speaking through them called for paper and pencils. I brought these materials and my visitors sat down at a table and began to draw. When they stopped after a while I saw that they were making sketches of royal Egyptian tombs bearing inscriptions in an ancient script illegible to me.

I asked them who they were; only one of them could understand German, and answered in that language. The other spoke a tongue unknown to me, his remarks being translated by his companion. His story ran as follows:

"Both of us who are speaking and writing through these instruments were Egyptian princes. Our names are Arras and Isaris. I, Arras, was the ruler of the upper Nile country while my friend Isaris ruled over the Lower Nile. We were both indulgent to our subjects. We did not flog our slaves and allowed our people to have their own way. They were rich: there were no real paupers among them. The land produced three crops a year, so that there was a surplus of food-stuffs and abundance of all things. Our people had everything they needed, held the most magnificent festivals, indulged in every extravagance and took no thought of tomorrow, forgetful of the Almighty God. They consumed the fruits and grains of the soil which God caused to grow. The water they drank was of the purest, their wine of the very choicest, but yet they never paused to think of Him to Whom they owed these blessings. Their ways of living and their festivals grew ever more riotous.

"Nor were the people content with the customs that had come down to them from ancient days, but created new gods of gold and precious stones. They prayed to these manmade idols and worshipped them. Indeed there were those among them who allowed themselves to be immolated for the sake of these images.

"We watched all this unconcernedly and allowed the people to follow their practices, instead of putting a stop to them as we should have done. On the contrary we encouraged these idolatrous doings in order to gain favor with the people. I myself sent to the idol Amojo ten cartloads of objects of gold for the completion of the image, merely to raise myself in my people's esteem; Isaris did the like for the idol Lachitju, and for the same reason. At the head of our subjects we marched to the dedication of the images and stationed soldiers to protect them, when we should have ordered their destruction. Before each image stood a golden basin holding the blood of a newly born infant. This blood was never allowed to dry, care being taken to keep the supply always replenished. If by chance this was neglected, the priest guilty of the omission was executed with the sword by the High Priest, in front of the idol.

"Our madness grew apace, but God's vengeance came at last. First he sent a drought which killed all growing things; yet the people would not pray to Him. Had it then recognized His omnipotence, He would not have judged it too harshly, but there was no one who would bow down to Him in prayer, until at last God as a punishment decreed the utter destruction of the apostate nation which would not own Him as its Creator. It could have learned to know the true God, for there were not lacking astrologers and wise men to proclaim the truth in order to prepare the people for the day of reckoning and who did not fail to do so, but they were scorned and flouted by the masses. Their warnings went unheeded and those who uttered these warnings were slain.

"One day the heavens darkened. Gray clouds gathered, and the sky turned black. A storm arose, lightning flashed, shattering the idols until not a vestige of them could be found. Then followed calamities which destroyed the people: fire and brimstone rained from the heavens, fouling the air with vapors that smothered man, woman and child; stone palaces collapsed burying all within them beneath their ruins. At last, God sent a furious tempest that covered the face of the land with a mantle of gray and yellow sand. Such was His vengeance for the offense done to Him; it was an act of justice.

"Both of us were dead before the day of destruction came. I, Arras, died by the dagger of a priest who coveted my wife. My bosom friend Isaris died fighting against his own general Zyclov who lived under the same roof with him and lusted for power, impure of heart and seeking to undermine the throne of his master, against whom he rebelled and whom he slew.

"Our city and our tombs are buried and have not yet been unearthed. We lived five thousand years before the birth of Christ, when the whole country of Egypt was governed by a number of princes all under one ruler who today would be called emperor. They were princes of federated states and both of us were among them, but Isaris was also counsellor for the entire State, or as you would say today, imperial chancellor. The capital of the Federation was Memph. The sovereign was always the member of a certain family and was chosen by the leading families, the priests and the military chiefs."

When I asked him what other nations existed at the time, the reply was:

"The peninsula of Arabia was inhabited by tribes of nomad Arabs. There was a great nation near the mouth of the Euphrates extending as far as the Ganges, and another country inhabited by the Moors, which may still be traced on ancient charts."

When the mediums recovered consciousness they were surprised at seeing the drawings they had made, and disclaimed all knowledge of their significance. All told, these young men came seven times within three months; I never knew when to expect them.

One morning as I was on the point of leaving my parish for the city to go to the office of the charitable association, the farmer boy who was the speaking medium came into the rectory and said he had received instructions to accompany me to town on this occasion; why, he did not know. I therefore took him with me, knowing from experience that the boy never received such instructions unless something important was at stake.

On this particular day the two mediums who had been making the Egyptian sketches appeared again and, simultaneously with the farmer boy, went into a trance. For some time the latter sat in silence while both of the others were busy with their drawings. Suddenly the boy stood up, and walking over to one of the other mediums, spoke to him in a foreign tongue, seemingly to explain something connected with the drawing. Then he approached me and asked for an eraser. When I had given him one, he again went to the medium to whom he had been talking; on this, I also went nearer and could see that the drawing represented the course of the Nile. The medium now took the eraser from the boy, rubbed out a short section representing the river, and made an alteration. I asked the medium from my parish who was still in a trance whether he was free to tell me what these proceedings signified. The spirit speaking through him answered that for this day he was charged with supervising the work of the two mediums making the sketches, for these related to the most important item of the information which would lead to the discovery of the tombs, namely, the course of the Nile. The spirit of one of the former Egyptian princes had caused his medium to draw the bed of the Nile as it was in his day, but since then its burden of sand had caused the river to shift its bed in places, and it was from precisely one of these spots that the measurements for locating the tombs would have to be taken. It was for this reason that he had influenced the boy to accompany me to the city on this day.

Upon the completion of the last drawing I received a message to trace whatever had been drawn and to deposit a full set of tracings at a specified place. Thereupon one of the Egyptian princes dictated to me a statement which I was required to sign and which ran:

"In the year 1924 I received a communication of the existence of the spirits of two former princes named Arras and Isaris. From the same source I received various drawings and depositions covering an account of the lives of the said princes and of their fate. I was commissioned to travel to their country and to open their tombs, as well as to uncover the surrounding portions of the buried sites. This material was collected by me between February 1st and May 1st 1924.

"Isaris deposes on behalf of Arras and in his own name: 'Acting under instructions, we two have made known to you what is herein related, in order that you may find our resting-places. The execution of the task lies in your hands. You have worked faithfully for us both psychically and spiritually. We thank you for this. We ask you to continue to do so, and today we take our leave of you. We shall return only once more. That will be on the day on which that which we have communicated to you is fulfilled and on which it is not only believed by you but acknowledged as history.

"Pray for us and *Gott zum Gruss!*

" 'When you are standing by our graves and have found our remains, we shall be there. Our task here has been fulfilled. *Gott zum Gruss* — until we can speak to you again.' "

I signed this declaration and added it to the rest of the Egyptian papers.

On this occasion I had asked several other questions relating to the subject in hand and had been answered as follows:

"I can assure you that everything bearing on the locality itself where the graves are situated has been put into the drawings; the precise details we can give you only on the spot. It is merely a question of *executing this commission*. You have only to seek the tombs to find them. You will find in them different objects of cultural interest much resembling others that have been found elsewhere and hence of no special importance in themselves. The important things are the *'Appeal to the People'* and the *'Scroll'* containing the laws of *'White Magic'* which relates to communication with spirits, and also various directions for healing diseases. There are also directions for the manufacture of products from plants, salts and the like, for the preservation of objects, and formulas for the making of durable fabrics from plants. Finally, you will find gold, coined and uncoined, enough and to spare to cover the expenses of your search.

"Your fate will not be that of so many others who opened such tombs and died soon afterwards, for although there is on each tomb an inscription reading: 'Whosoever violates this grave or inspires its violation, shall come to grief,' you are going in the name of God and undertaking your excavations in our name with God's help. Hence, no harm can befall you.

"You ask me regarding the characters on the drawings. They vary in type, for the same characters were then not employed in every locality. The writing is that of our times; you cannot read nor write it. I could indeed dictate each letter to you, but that would not help you because a letter may stand for a whole word, or for a character only. The same script appears on our tombs, our palaces, on the stones, pillars and walls. Your learned men may break their heads against these stones, but they will not succeed in deciphering the script. Perhaps an occasional one may tell you that the writing on the drawings is probably Egyptian, because he can recognize a character here and there, but most of them will inform you that you have lost your wits, and will throw all manner of obstacles in your way.

"The name of the Great King under whom we governed as princes of the federation was: 'AM-EL'. He died after us, and his burial place has not been discovered.

"There are in Egypt about ten thousand graves of kings, princes, and nobles, without counting those of others. Hence you may be sure that there are many undiscovered graves remaining."

Later, at various *seances* with the mediums of my parish, I inquired about this Egyptian disclosure, in order to find out when the tombs would be found, and was informed:

"That will come in due time. Events affecting the whole world will take place, which will bring this matter to a head. Today the search is not feasible and would cost the lives of a great many people for reasons which you cannot understand. *The great ends which God proposes to accomplish in this way are far beyond human comprehension.*"

I have devoted so much space to the Egyptian matter because, with a full documentary record in my possession I shall, when the time comes, be in a position to establish that which was revealed to me as being correct in every particular.

Personally, I feel that the discovery of the tombs under consideration will furnish science of today with the most powerful proof of the truth of the claims advanced in this book, for then, not even those who disbelieve in a future existence will be able to dismiss the evidence, but will be forced to acknowledge its genuine value. That, however, is merely my personal opinion. As to the significance of finding the tombs, no further information was vouchsafed to me, but I received further confirmation with regard to the revelations on Egypt, through the medium in the city, who gave the additional information that the prince called Arras had borne the name of "Hario" also.

If the examples recorded above, constituting only a small part of my experiences, are duly weighed, it will be clear to anyone that they cannot in any way be explained by ascribing them, as is customary in such cases, to "natural" processes. They cannot be traced to "suggestion", "thought-transmission", nor "subconsciousness", for the things related by the mediums were unknown to them in their human capacity, as well as to any other human being.

Those things of which a person was never conscious cannot become part of his subconsciousness, any more than I can transmit to another, thoughts which I do not possess myself.

The words "suggestion", "subconsciousness", and "thought-transmission", are generally, in this connection, *mere words,* used with the intention of conveying a deep meaning and, as a rule, making a great impression on people not accustomed to think for themselves. In reality, however, they are words which convey no applicable ideas. "When thoughts are lacking, their place is often taken by a happy word."

As for thought-transmission, I have often done my level best, both before a medium had entered a trance and while he was in that state, to transmit my thoughts to him, but in not one instance did his disclosures contain a single word of the message I had tried to convey in this manner.

Similarly, I have also induced others to try to influence a medium's utterances through suggestion, by joining me in concentrating their thoughts upon a subject agreed upon among us, but none of these attempts was even in the least successful.

What was told me by mediums, untaught and inexperienced in all branches of learning, surpasses any human knowledge of the subjects in question.

But *one* satisfactory explanation remains, namely: *There are such things as ultra-mundane spirit-beings which make use of these mediums as their instruments, to convince us of the existence of a God and of a spirit-world and to guide us to the path leading to Him.*

The matter reproduced in the succeeding chapters, relative to the "Laws Governing Communication with Spirits" and "The Great Questions of the Here and the Hereafter" will furnish additional evidence in support of what I have attempted to demonstrate.

PART TWO

The Laws Governing Communication by Spirits with the Material Creation

General Remarks

WHEN first I came into contact with the spirit-world, I was promised that I should be taught concerning the laws governing the way in which communication by spirits with the material world and especially with mankind, is effected.

The fulfillment of this promise meant for me a new and incontrovertible proof of the truth of what I had previously learned from the same source. I myself knew nothing of those laws; still less did the mediums, who were utterly unversed in all branches of science and hence unable to impart any information on the subject from their own knowledge.

The promise given to me was kept in a far greater measure than I had dared to expect. The instruction which I received in the laws relating to communicating with the spirit-world, possessed a clearness and a power of conviction inherent to truth only. All my questions were answered exhaustively, to their least details. Never did I detect the slightest discrepancies in what was taught me. Everything interlocked, as in the movement of a well-made watch. My teacher was the same spirit-being which on the second occasion of our meeting had promised to initiate me into every truth, and which used as its instrument the same boy who had served as such on the occasion mentioned. As this boy had enjoyed a very mediocre education only, he exemplified in this respect the words of the Apostle Paul: "God has chosen such as the world calls foolish, to confound the wise, and the things which the world calls lowly and of no esteem have been chosen by God to bring to naught the things which loom large in its eyes, for no mortal shall boast of his deeds before God." *(1st Corinthians, 1 : 27, 28.)*

"You mortals," so the spirit opened its discourse, "seem to assume that only the world of matter is subject to laws. You are mistaken, for God is a God of system and of law in all creation, terrestrial or spiritual. In His doings he observes the laws which He Himself made, and disregards none of them.

"Thus we spirits too must observe the God-given laws of Nature whenever we wish to communicate with the world of matter. This is true of the good spirit-world as well as of the evil.

"You are in the habit of calling everything a 'miracle', unless you can bring it to conform with Nature's laws as you know them. For those familiar with the forces acting in the world of matter and in the spirit-world, there is no such thing as a 'miracle', for everything happens according to the same immutable laws, not one of which supersedes or conflicts with another.

"If you raise a stone with your hand, the law of what you call gravitation acting on the stone is not thereby set aside, but is overcome by a greater force. If however, a stone were raised *by a hand invisible to you, you would consider that a miracle because you do not see the force,* and hence would think the stone was rising *of its own volition. And yet a force that causes the stone to be lifted must be present in either case.* Whether or not you you can see the force does not affect the operation itself. *In either case the force of gravitation acting on the stone is overcome by a superior force.*

"In consequence of the laws enacted by *His Own omnipotence, God Himself cannot make a stone raise itself by its own efforts.* He might indeed have made the laws governing matter differently from what He did, but having made them as they are, He must, even when only the lifting of a stone is involved, permit the action of a force upon that stone greater than that of gravitation.

"The same thing is true in all fields, nor is there anything 'miraculous' in the fact that the spirit-world should communicate and speak with mankind. Whenever I speak to you through this boy I do so according to fixed laws which I am bound to observe and which would have to be observed equally by any evil spirit which might desire to speak through him.

"Consider the mechanism of your telephones! How many of Nature's laws must be complied with before you can use these for speaking! You must have a current. Wires and other parts required to transmit speech and adapted to the laws of acoustics and electricity must be installed, and these laws apply, whether the instrument is used by a good citizen or by a criminal.

"In order that you may understand the things which you will witness in connection with spirit-communication, it is essential that you learn the more important laws involved in the intercourse between the spirit-world and material creation. When you have grasped these, you will be able to understand most of what you will encounter in this field, things for which you mortals have not yet succeeded in finding an explanation."

The Law of Vital, or Odic Force

> I find, whatever God may do shall stand unchanged; nothing can be added to it, nothing can be taken from it. So God orders things, that man may stand in awe of him. *Ecclesiastes 3:14.*

"BECAUSE of their different natures, spirit and substance cannot react upon each other directly. Not even your own spirit is capable by itself of imparting activity to a limb or organ of your body. No more am I, who have taken possession of the person of this boy, able to lift his body erect or to raise his hands or to produce a sound from his organs of speech by my own efforts. For the purposes I have mentioned, your spirit, as well as I, require a *power-current.*

"Thus an engineer requires a constant supply of power furnished by steam or electricity if his engine is to operate. If that supply is lacking or is inadequate, his engine will stand still.

"In our case it is the spirit which is the engineer and its engine the body or the substance. If the substance is to be set in motion by the spirit, a supply of power is necessary.

"The learned men of old called this power-current the "soul" as distinguished from man's 'spirit' and from his 'body'. Thus they taught, quite correctly, that man is made up of spirit, soul and body.

"The Bible calls the power-current of the vital energy the 'breath of life'. . . "and God breathed into man's nostrils the breath of life; so man became a living being." *(Genesis 2:7.)*

"You people of today speak of the power-current in man as the 'odic force'.

"This 'odic' or vital force exists in and about all things created by God. It is found in every human being, in every animal, in every plant, in every stone, in every mineral, in all water, in every star, in every spirit and in all other existing things. It is nothing material, but is spiritual and is always associated with a spirit. It is the vital force of the spirit, which is therefore always its conveyor. Hence, wherever there is life, there is od, and wherever there is od, there also is spirit. Since, therefore, this od exists in and about all things created by God and is always associated with spirit, it follows that every created thing harbors a spirit.

"That may seem incredible to you, but it is true.

"Any spirit associated with a material body possesses, first of all, the odic force required *for its own existence as a spirit,* and next, sufficient *additional odic force* to induce life, growth and activity in the terrestrial body. Thus, to make use of an inadequate simile, a locomotive requires a certain amount of steam-power to enable it to travel alone, and a certain amount in addition to the first to enable it to draw the train which is coupled to it. The train coupled to your spirit is your body, for which your spirit requires additional odic power.

"However, the od allotted to the body differs from that allotted to the spirit, since anything intended to react upon substance must be assimilated and adapted to it to some extent. Hence the od of the bodies of your earth is less spiritual than that of the spirits inhabiting them.

"The physical od resembles your terrestrial power-currents, which are neither purely material nor purely spiritual. Their true nature is unknown to you although their effect comes within range of your daily experience.

"For your terrestrial power-currents you employ material conductors, designed to carry a current of the strength best suited to your needs. You have machines and plants of all kinds whose operation requires current of a certain strength. If the current is too powerful, it will destroy your installation. If it is too feeble, your plant will stop running.

"In a like manner the odic current of all physical beings is carried by a conductor through the body and all of its wonderful parts which you call organs, in a strength necessary for the purpose intended. If that current exerts too powerful an effect on a given organ, it will derange the same. If it is too feeble, the functions of the organ cease.

"In the case of odic energy the conductor is the blood. If the conductor is destroyed by loss or decomposition of blood, the odic current ceases, just as your power-currents cease to flow when your conducting wires are damaged by outside agencies or by disintegration.

"As blood acts as conductor for the od, and, hence since without blood physical life is impossible the Bible calls blood "the life". ' . . . for the blood is the life.' *(Deuteronomy 12 : 23.)*

"The physical od is not created by the spirit of the respective body, but is derived from the food taken into that body.

"In order that you may understand what I shall have to say further about odic energy, I must give you an explanation of the *nature of substance.*

"Have you ever thought of how the bodies of living organisms are formed? Consider your own body and its growth! Was it built up, by any chance, by additions of finished substance, as a house is built by placing one stone upon another? You know for yourself that it was not. The body is nothing but od *condensed into substance,* and this is true of all bodies, not only those of human beings, but of those of animals, plants and minerals. Their growth and their taking material shape are subject to those selfsame *laws of odic condensation.*

"The od of individual material organisms represents a mixture of ods of the most varied strength and kinds, produced by wonderful laws unknown to you mortals. In man, this mixture is different from that found in animals; in animals, different from that found in plants; and in plants, different from that found in minerals.

"This difference obtains not only between the primary groups of Nature, but between individual organisms within the same group. Thus the odic composition of the various human races differs: that of the Negro is not the same as that of the white man or of the Indian, and again, not all members of the white race have the same odic composition. This statement holds good for all the other races of man. Every individual has his own odic composition, which is not the same in any two human beings, and the same thing applies to beasts, plants and minerals.

"Since therefore the physical structure of a living organism consists of the condensation of the odic compound peculiar to that organism, each body has its own individual properties. Flesh, bones, nails, hair, and all other parts of the body have their distinctive characteristics which are governed by the odic composition of the individual in question.

"In your eyes it is one of Nature's deep secrets how it is possible for od, which exists in an ethereal form and is invisible to you, to be condensed into tangible matter. The fact that such things *are* possible you know from your own experience, for you can see that your body does not grow by the direct application to it of finished substances. You know that the acorn does not grow into the oak by continued increments of wood attached to its surface, but that its growth represents a process taking place within the organism, although to you this process is inexplicable.

You know that the food which you eat does not attach itself to the inner surfaces of your body and promote growth in that way, but that *something flows into all parts,* great and small, of your entire frame, consolidating into flesh, bone, nails, hair and other tissue, and by thus consolidating becomes substance. *That 'something', which is unknown to you, is "od".*

"Whence comes this od, which is so necessary for the formation and support of all living beings? You yourself know, if you stop to think, what the needs of your physical existence are: you require air, water and food. But not everything present in air, water or food can be utilized by the body. Above all, not every ingredient of these substances can be assimilated by the various parts of your body in the shape in which it occurs in the air, the water or the food, that is to say, not in the same material shape. Even air is matter. Everything must first be converted into an etherialized shape, and conducted in the form of od to the parts and particles of the body.

"The conversion of the material forms of nourishment into od follows by way of the solution which takes place in your bodies during the *process of digestion.*

"The air which you breathe represents a material mixture of od from which your lungs extract only those portions of the od which your bodies require, exhaling those which they cannot use, in the process of breathing.

"Water also has an odic composition of its own. The od of water is that which is needed most of all by the bodies of men, animals and plants, for these are chiefly the condensed product of the od taken from water. Hence, water-od predominates in the foods derived from the plant and animal kingdoms, so that when this food is taken into the system, the necessary quantity of water-od is generally present also. Owing to the fact that the od of water plays so important a role in all bodies, they cannot go without it for any great length of time. Your professional fasters may be able to do without solid food for weeks on end, but if they were deprived of water they would quickly die. For the same reason animals and plants perish when denied the od of water for a prolonged period.

"Now you understand why the tortures of thirst are the greatest that any living being can experience; they represent death in its most painful form.

"The od of the air does not enter into the structure of the body to the same extent, but is used in the main to build up the various currents which effect the disintegration of food and its conversion into od; to mix the various kinds of od, and to bring about their ultimate condensation into matter. All disintegration is caused by *hot* odic currents and all condensation by *cold* ones. For this reason you cannot live more than a few moments if deprived of the aerial od, for where this is absent, all other odic activity ceases automatically.

"There still remains to be answered the question: whence comes the od found in air, water and food?

"It comes from the earth, which as a heavenly body possesses a supply of odic mixture and has the power to radiate this mixture that contains every kind of od required for the support of all life on earth. The terrestrial od consists of the od peculiar to the earth as a heavenly body, and in addition to this, the earth receives by radiation into its own odic mixture, that of all other heavenly bodies within range. Each of these heavenly bodies has a specific od peculiar to itself, of a nature and composition not found in that of any other heavenly body.

"According to the position of these heavenly bodies with respect to the earth, their odic radiations will be of a smaller or a greater effect upon it, and since this position to each other changes every second, the odic radiations sent by these bodies to the earth, will vary accordingly.

"The mingling of the od of your earth with that of the bodies around it is of the greatest importance to life and growth upon earth.

"You must remember that every kind of od possesses powers peculiar to itself. To the extent then that an infant at the moment of its birth is subjected to the influence of the od of one or more heavenly bodies, to that extent will the infant's own odic composition be affected. At the time of birth, this composition is still fairly neutral, but at that instant it is given a fixed permanent trend by the odic radiations and mixtures acting upon it.

"If now a certain kind of od represents the main component of the whole, it will determine the infant's growth and development for all time. And since the different kinds of od produce each a *characteristic type of vitality,* the characteristic of the predominant odic component will give to the infant a definite individual physique and an individual behavior.

"It is therefore neither superstition nor idle fancy to assume that a person's physical, mental and moral attributes can be foretold if the moment of his birth is known. The influence of the odic mixture of the heavenly bodies on your life upon earth, upon your vital energy, your character and your temperament, is much greater than you realize. You yourselves have a saying: 'He was born under a lucky or an unlucky star', which means that you are referring to the effect exerted by the odic radiations of a heavenly body on living beings at the moment of their birth.

"All this is so closely related to the great questions of the fate of men, that I could not refrain entirely from speaking of it.

"All bodies of terrestrial beings are therefore condensed od, derived from the odic radiation of the earth and that of its surrounding heavenly bodies.

"An example taken from Nature will illustrate to you this process of disintegration and condensation.

"You know that under the influence of heat the moisture from the land and waters evaporates by stages generally imperceptible to your eyes. At a certain height above the earth, the vapor, which was invisible at lower levels, is condensed into a thin, barely perceptible veil. As condensation progresses, this veil becomes distinctly visible as a cloud, which grows denser and denser under the influence of cold, until, after being condensed beyond a certain point, it falls to the ground as rain or snow. If the water is chilled still further, it is condensed into ice and becomes a solid. Here you have the condensation, step by step, of an ethereal substance invisible to your eyes into solid matter, which you cannot only see and touch, but which possesses also considerable resistance. Thus the ice which covers your ponds, lakes and rivers is solidified water, of the same composition and distinctive properties as the water from which it is formed and which in turn is condensed vapor.

"Thus, just as vapor rises from the earth and step by step turns into solid matter as ice, only to dissolve again into water and back into vapor, so is the case of all terrestrial bodies. They are derived from the od of the earth, invisible to you, which is condensed into substance by the process of growth and which returns to the od of the earth after the death of the living organism. The words: 'Of earth thou art, to earth shalt thou return', therefore apply to all terrestrial things. That is the continual cycle which will endure until all substance is finally dissolved into od, never again to be condensed into material organisms. Of this I shall tell you more on a future occasion.

"From what I have said you can deduce that in every terrestrial being there are three forms of od: the od of the spirit; the somewhat more condensed, but to the human eye invisible od represented by the vital force; and the od which has become solid matter and which you call the body.

"The od representing the vital force of the body always remains associated with the od of the spirit and hence with the spirit itself. It is the motive power for the body at the disposal of the spirit, just as your terrestrial motive powers are at the engineer's command. If then the supply of motive power for the body is diminished below the point required to maintain life in the body, the spirit departs from the same and corporeal death ensues, just as the engineer abandons his engine when he cannot keep it running for lack of power.

"At the death of terrestrial bodies, the odic force remains vested in the spirit, for those bodies possess no independent odic force of their own; it is only the spirits which have taken possession of the bodies which have that power.

"Nevertheless, thanks to the odic power at its command, the spirit can strengthen the od of its body, which may have become weakened by sickness, through the exercise of its *will-power;* it can stimulate the activity of sluggish bodily organs and thereby eliminate injurious matter from the system. In these circumstances it is of course essential that the weakened body avoid the use of improper food, and that it promote the efforts of the spirit-od by means of a wholesome diet. To use another concrete metaphor, the spirit in this instance works by its own odic energy like a powerful pressure-pump upon the physical od and on the conductor of the current of the same, namely, the blood.

"The extent to which the spirit of a person can infuse strength into his physical od through the spirit's own odic power and by the exercise of its will-power, is shown by numerous illustrations. The physical odic force of paralyzed persons threatened with great danger often receives a sufficient access of strength through the will-power of the spirit, to banish their disability and to restore to them the use of their limbs, temporarily at least.

"The same effect is produced by a patient's firm expectation of getting well. This is also an act of will, and, through the strength which it imparts to the odic force of the body, leads to many sudden recoveries which you regard as miracles.

"Will-power expressed in courage, hope, faith and cheerfulness is therefore the best remedy, and is, incidentally, the best safeguard against contagious diseases. The od of the body, reinforced by will-power, forms as it were a protecting wall which bars the entry of noxious germs. The greater the will-power, the stronger this invisible armor.

"Lack of will-power and of courage, fear and timidity have the opposite effect. They act like an exhaust pump which draws the physical od, together with the blood, out of the body and the organs *inward,* thus weakening the system and paving the way for contagion.

"Just as the od of the spirit of a body is able to lend strength to the latter's physical od when this has become weakened by sickness, so the odic force of healthy persons may be *transmitted* to, and invigorate, the sick. Odic transmissions of this sort are what you call 'magnetization'.

"Od can be transmitted by any living being to another, not only by man to man, but by man to animals, plants and minerals. By transmitting your own personal od to plants you can promote their growth. You can magnetize water, oil and similar substances, infusing them, so to speak, with your od, and thereby hasten the recovery of the sick who drink of that water or who are anointed with that oil.

"Man can use also the od of plants, beasts and minerals as remedies for his own ailments. *It is upon this reciprocal transfer of od that the laws of healing within God's creation are based.* Thus many living animals radiate a definite od which has healing powers. Those of many plants are widely known, although unfortunately the people of today are not as familiar with the curative properties of certain plants in the case of various diseases as were the ancients. The same is true of the minerals. Most people think it superstition to believe that every precious stone has an odic power of its own, and yet it is precisely the od of precious stones which possesses unusual purity and strength, and invigorates the persons wearing them. It is, of course, essential for the wearer to select the stone best suited to his personal od and possessed of no odic forces which would conflict with the odic radiations of the individual. You have books which will instruct you further as to the right precious stones, the kind of which is determined by the date of their wearer's birth.

"A very important factor in all healing is the *transmission of od by one person to another.* A sick child feels better immediately when its mother snuggles it against her body, for by so doing she transmits her own healthy od to the sick child and strengthens the latter's od which has become enfeebled by sickness. A healthy person who sleeps with sick or old people imparts a share of his odic force to them. His sick or old bed-fellows are invigorated thereby while the healthy person grows steadily weaker by the continued expenditure of his od. That is the reason why healthy persons who sleep with old or sick people for any great length of time take on a sickly appearance, which is a consequence of the loss of their odic force, and for the same reason children should not be allowed to sleep in the same bed with old folks.

"Od *flows through all* parts of terrestrial bodies and *radiates beyond them to a certain distance.* This radiation which surrounds terrestrial bodies has been called '*aura*' by your scientists. Everything in creation has such an odic aura, even the great heavenly bodies. What you call the force of attraction of the earth is the power of odic radiation, whose range bears a certain relation to the size of the globe. This is true of all other cosmic bodies. There is not a point anywhere in the universe which is unaffected by the odic radiation of one heavenly body or another.

"The odic aura surrounds the material body like a halo and extends to an equal distance from it at every point, *having in consequence the same shape as the body to which it belongs* and which it encompasses. For this reason use is made of the expressions the '*odic body*', '*astral body*', or '*fluid body*', of concrete beings, as distinguished from their material bodies. It is what the Bible calls the '*spiritual body*'. It is not visible to your corporeal eyes, but these odic radiations or 'odic bodies' can be seen by the so-called clairvoyants endowed with the gift of seeing spirits.

"*The spirit is the source of life* but the shaping and the scope of your lives are determined by the odic force associated with the spirit, and hence called the vital force. This force manifests itself by *vibrations of the od.* Every manifestation of the intellectual life, every manifestation of all life about you in nature, all natural forces are odic *vibrations.* All thought and all volition are expressed in the corresponding odic vibrations, set in motion by the spirit, as the bearer of the od. Every physical sensation, every psychic state of feeling is caused by odic vibrations. All impressions conveyed by tones, colors, odors, tastes and responses to the touch are produced by definite odic vibrations. In the spiritual world these are vibrations of the pure ethereal od; in material creation, they are vibrations of od in its more or less condensed form.

"All phenomena witnessed on earth, all growth, blossoming and ripening, all power and radiation; electricity, radio, ether-waves, light, darkness, and the whole gamut of sensations produced by tone, color, odor, taste and touch; all currents of power in the Universe, the attraction exercised by the heavenly bodies and their motion in space, everything rests upon these odic vibrations. A sage of ancient times observed: 'Everything is in a state of flux'. He should have said: 'Everything is in a state of vibration'. The *divine secret of numbers* rests on the vibrations of the odic force flowing through the entire universe and permeating its tiniest particle. You human pygmies will never fathom this secret. You are seeking the *unit* in what goes on about you, but you will not find it. It is true that you have discovered many facts connected with this secret of numbers. You know the number of vibrations which produce the notes familiar to you, and you are trying to find out the number of odic vibrations on which color is based, but what does all that represent in the vast ocean of truth inaccessible to you? You cannot break the seven seals of God's Creation; you can only bow your heads in wonder and reverence before the Almighty's wisdom and omnipotence.

"From what little I have told you of odic vibrations, let us now deduce a few of the conclusions that are most important for our purposes.

"You will see at once that *harmony* in odic vibrations stands for beauty, health, happiness, peace and good fortune, whereas *discord* in such vibrations must be the cause of ugliness, sickness, suffering and unhappiness. Just as discordant tones and colors affront your esthetic sense and are, as it were, actually painful, so a discordant attitude on the part of a created spirit toward its Creator acts in spiritual matters, producing spiritual ugliness, sickness and discontent, in short, spiritual suffering which grows in the same measure as the spirit's attitude toward God grows more inharmonious. The extreme limit of such an attitude, namely, open hostility on the part of the spirit toward its Maker means also the greatest measure of spiritual anguish and misery, or the state of what you call 'Hell'. And since extreme discord in odic vibrations represents the opposite extreme to beauty and light, which presuppose the most perfect harmony, so Hell must be a state of the utmost repulsiveness of the odic body and of the most profound darkness. These conclusions are based on eternal laws. It is not God who pushes you down to Hell, but your want of harmony with everything good and beautiful, with everything that is spiritually wholesome and pure, with light and with life. That is why Hell is a spiritual death, into which he plunges, whose spiritual nature is in extreme discord with the Divine nature. Discordant odic vibrations of the spirit are the diving-rudder of spirit-flight; harmony, the elevating-rudder. *To banish this inharmonious attitude out of its spiritual life is the most important task of every living being.*

"However, the odic vibrations of no living thing are influenced by the thoughts and moods of its own spirit only, but also by those of *other* beings whose odic vibrations it receives. If, therefore, clairsentient people come into close enough contact with the odic vibrations of others, they will receive the sensations of the latter also. This law is the basis for the ability to 'fit ones self' in with the moods, character, way of thinking and fortunes of another.

"All odic vibrations leave in their own odic bodies certain impressions similar to those made by the vibrations of the notes of a song on a phonographic record, allowing that song to be rendered audible again and again afterwards, and not alone so far as the mere notes are concerned, but with the same expression of feeling which the singer gave to the air while singing it. This also is the basis of the power of memory: the deeper the impressions made on this odic plate, the more easily can they be reproduced.

"The same process that takes place in material form in the case of a phonographic record, goes on spiritually in the case of the sensations impressed on the consciousness of clairsentients as soon as they come into close enough contact with the spiritual odic record of other persons. This contact produces in their own od the same vibrations, and consequently the same sensations, as those present on the records of the others.

"From what you have learned you know that given vibrations of odic forces produce not only a given tone, but also a definite color, smell, taste and response to the touch. The sensations of cold and heat are likewise based on such odic vibrations. There are clairsentients to whom a tone represents a color and who can even tell colors by the sense of touch, being able to detect the differences by the radiations of heat or cold given off by the various hues. Others can discern the psychic sensations of love or hatred, of good or of ill-will, of courage or cowardice, of faithfulness or of unfaithfulness in their fellow-men not only through their own sensations, but in the corresponding color-schemes, and are hence able to portray the conceptions of love, faithfulness, sorrow, joy, hatred or envy in colors. All this rests on the odic vibrations by which their sensations are accompanied.

"*Od is therefore also the conveyor of our physical sensations.* Hence, if the od is forced out of a limb of your body, that limb loses all feeling also. The od may be forced out of the entire system or out of a part thereof in a great many ways. It may be expelled by paralysis or by internal ruptures which interfere with the duties of the blood as the od-carrier. Physicians habitually expel the od by means of narcotics. Alcohol taken in excess will cause the expulsion of od and thereby bring on partial or complete insensibility. The sense of feeling returns as soon as the system has been rid of those foreign substances.

"Contrariwise, feeling may persist even after a corporeal limb has been separated from its body, for the odic body of a terrestrial being remains intact, even after a limb of the corporeal body has been removed. In the case of a person who has lost a leg the odic leg remains, and since od is the conveyor of feeling, the person often feels as though he had not lost the limb at all, even after it is gone. He feels pains in the knee, the heel or the toes of a leg that is no longer part of his body. Anyone who has undergone amputation will bear out this statement.

"Because the od remains with the spirit when the latter leaves the body at corporeal death, it is possible for the spirit to experience the same sensations as those it felt while still inhabiting the body. For this reason the spirits of the departed feel pain as acutely as they could during their life on earth.

"Spirits of those of the deceased who because of the lives they led have been condemned to a lower (inferior) sphere, believe that they still inhabit the earth as human beings, and base this belief on the following grounds: firstly, they still have the same sensations which they had as living human beings; secondly, they look upon their odic bodies as bodies of flesh and blood, because the odic body has exactly the same shape and appearance as the material one; and lastly, they have lost all recollection of their corporeal death.

"*The od of all individual beings has a distinctive odor.* Since od is spiritual in its nature, its odor is perceived through spirtual powers of perception and not through the physical sense of smell. The smell of the od of each living being differs from that of any other. Just as there are no two individuals of the same figure and features, so no two have the same odic odor, and as every spirit, even a disembodied one, possesses an odic body, so, likewise, disembodied spirits have their own characteristic odor which is the more unpleasant, the lower the category of the spirit. That is why the old books when referring to appearances of the Devil, speak of the vile stench which attended his presence.

"Due to the fact that the od extends beyond the body in the shape of an aura, it can be perceived by others from its smell. Something of the odic scent of a living being adheres to every object which its odic radiations touch.

"It is by the odic scent that a dog can tell its master's belongings and tracks, and by which police dogs can trail criminals. Only when the original trail has been obscured by later ones whose odic scent is fresh, does it become difficult or impossible to follow the old trail.

"Not alone does the odic radiation of a living organism and its characteristic scent adhere to matter of a coarser grain with which it comes into contact, but also to such tenuous substances as the ether through which the organism has passed.

"Thus every created thing leaves behind it an odic trace of its existence uniting the day of its coming into being with the last day of its life.

"I can best explain this by an example: if a wagon is driven along a road, dropping a constant stream of some substance that runs through a crack in the bottom of the wagon-box, the course travelled by the wagon can be told by following up the trail of the substance dropped, which forms, as it were, a band connecting the point of departure of the wagon with that of its destination.

"Such a band is formed by the od of every creature on its way through life. It is by a trail like this that migratory birds return to their old haunts and that the swallow comes back to the same eaves under which it built last year's nest. The odic sensitiveness of these creatures is extremely delicate, but is active *only so long as they are in good health,* for because of the weakening of their odic powers, sick animals lose the odic sensitiveness necessary to enable them to follow their own or another creature's trail. For this reason, too, migratory birds which are in poor health cannot find their way home, nor can a sick dog follow its master's trail or its own.

"There are human beings also whose odic sensitiveness is so acute that they can perceive the odic scent of others at some distance and feel such persons to be attractive (sympathetic) or repulsive (antipathetic) even if they have never met or otherwise come to know the individual in question. Mutual attraction or repulsion 'at first sight' is merely the reaction of odic sensitiveness. Hence the popular expression: 'They cannot bear the smell of each other'.

"Od is among the most wonderful things in God's Creation. The odic band not alone connects you with everything with which you come into contact in life, but it also reflects your entire existence; every act, every utterance, *every thought of yours is reproduced by it as in a film.* It is a *"Book of Life"*, into which everything is entered. It is a *phonographic record* which retains and reproduces everything. It is a film which does not lie, and whose revelations cannot be denied. And it is the evidence by which in the end you will be judged by your Creator.

"For every terrestrial being its *predestined fate is impressed upon its od from the outset* and can be seen both in the entire odic body as well as in every particle of the od. Its fate can therefore also be read in the odic particles adhering as radiations to everything with which that being has come into touch.

"Not all that you do or suffer in life is predestined. Most of it results from the acts of your own free will. Only the general path of your lives, together with certain turning points along that part, is predestined. What you do while travelling that path and how you act at those turning points, is for you to decide. For that much, you are responsible. *Your life has one purpose only: to raise your spirit to a higher level on the road that has been mapped for you, and to bring it nearer to God.* Your path through life is one of tests. Its nature and length are fixed in advance, beyond your control, and these you cannot change, do what you will. The turning points on that path are stations at which you have to pass those tests, and at the end, corporeal death awaits you. Whether or not you do your duty as you go, depends on yourselves. Whoever passes the tests, his spirit will continue to progress in the Beyond until it reaches its final goal: union with God. Whoever fails to pass must take the tests over again until he can meet them successfully. Passing or failure are not predestined, but depend on your own merit or shortcomings.

"The Christian creeds do not recognize this truth. They do not know that the Creator works like an architect who first draws his plans for the erection of a building. These plans do not give all the details of the *interior construction* of the building or of the materials to be used for that purpose, but only the *outer trace*.

"In a like way, God has laid out the ground lines for the life-structure of every man, according to which his life is fixed in outline, *leaving man free to decide upon the interior details*, according to his own liking.

"There are many references in the Bible to the fact that man's fate is predestined. 'For no man knows his hour.' *(Ecclesiastes 9 : 12.)* 'All the days of my life were foreseen by thee, set down within thy book; ere ever they took shape, they were assigned me, ere ever one of them was mine'. *(Psalms 139 : 16.)* And you read furthermore in the Book of Ecclesiastes: 'Whatever happens has been determined long ago'. *Ecclesiastes 6 : 10.)* 'My fate lies in thy hands'. *(Psalms 31 : 15.)* The prophet Jeremiah utters the words: 'Oh Lord, thou knowest that man's course lies not in his own hands; it is not in a man to keep control over his actions'. *(Jeremiah 10 : 23.)*

"Birth and death and the span that lies between are predestined and beyond man's control. No one, not even a physician, can therefore save a person's life. Every man dies at the appointed moment. 'No man can control the day of death'. *(Ecclesiastes 8 : 8.)* Christ confirms this axiom with the words: 'Who is there among you, who by worrying can prolong his allotted time of life by a single span?' *(Matthew 6 : 27.)*

"Just as a human architect can make *ulterior* alterations in his plans, so it is within the realm of possibility for God, by way of exception, to permit changes in the destiny of certain individuals. The power of lengthening or shortening the time of a man's life rests with Him alone. As the Bible teaches you, God sometimes prolongs the life of one of His servants who has proved faithful and has shown himself to be a trustworthy helper in God's plan of salvation for winning back the erring. Thus to Hezekiah he sends the message: 'and I will add fifteen years to your life.' *(2nd Kings 20 : 6.)* The foreordained span of the life of others is shortened by the Lord because they have failed to perform the life-work allotted to them or because they have tried to disuade their fellow-men from fulfilling their duty to God. 'Bloody and deceitful men shall not live out half their days.' *(Psalms 55 : 23.)* By bloody men' the Bible means not those guilty of actual bloodshed on earth, but of killing the souls of fellow-men by enticing them away from God. 'The fear of the Lord prolongs days: but the days of the wicked shall be shortened.' *(Proverbs 10 : 27.)* God inspires the prophet Jeremiah to announce to Hananiah: 'I will send you off the face of the earth! This very year you are to die, for having taught disloyalty to the Eternal.' *(Jeremiah 28 : 16.)*

"So, too, the destiny of the various nations is foreordained.

"You do not understand these matters because you have no true conception of the causes and ends of the great events of the world. Above all, you are ignorant of the purpose underlying the material creation and do not know the relations that exist between the incarnated spirit and God's handiwork.

"Of these things I shall tell you more hereafter.

"I have inserted my remarks relating to predestination because they were necessary in connection with my explanation of the odic force, since otherwise you would be unable to understand what I am about to say of clairvoyance in its relation to od.

" 'Clairvoyants' are living beings, men or animals, whose spirit is able to detach itself from the body to such an extent that it attains a power of vision equal to that of the spirits of the Beyond which have left their terrestrial bodies altogether.

"A well-trained clairvoyant is able in certain circumstances to read the destiny of another person, impressed upon that person's od. He can read the whole past of a person whose od he sees, and not only that part of it which was predestined, but also those events which resulted from the unrestricted exercise of the individual's will. Of the future, however, he can read only what is foreordained, but not that which lies within man's control.

"The manner of a person's death can be foreseen by a clairvoyant only when this also is predestined, for it is not a part of a person's destiny in every instance; in fact, generally speaking, what is foreordained in some cases, is left for the individual to determine in others. It is only the *hour of his death* which is appointed for every man.

"In order that clairvoyance in this field may be possible, the clairvoyant must in some way establish contact with the od of the person whose destiny is under consideration. He must either have that person before him in the flesh, or else he must get into touch with some object that has been in that person's possession and to which, consequently, something of his odic radiation clings.

"The ability of a clairvoyant to read sealed letters or to recognize objects which he cannot see with his corporeal eyes is also something that rests on this odic reaction. *The more powerful* the odic action emanating from the object, *the more distinct* the clairvoyant's vision.

"If a clairvoyant's spirit is able to detach itself *completely* from his body and actually to leave the same, it is in a position to follow the odic trail of another person and to ascertain his whereabouts at the moment.

"Not all clairvoyance however results through the odic radiation. Many events that happen at a great distance from the clairvoyant are seen by him at the instant of their occurrence due to the fact that his spirit, having left the body, is present at the scene of the event, or else, even though the spirit remains with the body, because the news is imparted to him by the spirit-world through clairaudience, or is shown to him as in a picture through clairvoyance.

"The future of individuals with whose odic radiations the clairvoyant has not come into touch, as well as the future of peoples, countries, cities and other communities can be seen by a clairvoyant only when it is shown to him by the spirit-world by means of pictures. To produce such pictures which may either depict the coming events with faithful accuracy, or else by means of symbols, is well within the power of the spirits charged with that task. Od is the material employed by them for pictures of this kind.

"The future of nations and other coming events were generally revealed to the prophets of the days before Christ by means of symbolical pictures.

"*Od also possesses color,* which varies for each creature, running from the deepest black through billions of shades to the most resplendent white. You mortals cannot even conceive of the variety of these colors. On some autumn day, study the yellow of the withered leaves. You will not find two among them having exactly the same shade. A similar variation you will find in the color of all things.

"I have repeatedly intimated to you where to seek for the reason for the great differences in the odor and color of od, namely in the spirits of living creatures. The lower the spirit's trend of thought, and attitude toward God, the more repulsive it becomes as a spirit. *Spirits too have shape.* Your human spirits have that of the human body, or, to put it more correctly, your human bodies have the shape of your spirits. So also the bodies of beasts are shaped like their spirits, for the physical body has the same form as the odic one, and the odic body is shaped to conform with the spirit. Remember that the spirit builds up the physical body with the aid of od, to correspond with its own form and lineaments.

"Your so-called scientists will of course ridicule you if you tell them that the incarnated spirits have the shape of the bodies which they inhabit. Scientists cannot conceive of a spirit which has a shape. They believe that only what is material, and limited by time and space, can have shape. They are badly mistaken. Spirits are not shapeless, as indeed there is nothing in all creation but what has shape. Spirits have form and shape, and yet they are not bound by either time or space, as are material bodies. How, unless each of us had its shape, could we spirits recognize one another? The Angel Michael is different from Gabriel, and Gabriel from Raphael and other spirits, to mention only these Biblical characters. The fact of the matter is, then, that all spirits have shape, beginning with God and passing from Him down through His higher spirits, to the most hideous figures of the depths, and to the incarnated spirits on earth.

"Beauty is harmony, ugliness, absence of harmony. That is a law which applies to all creation. The most beautiful face in a portrait can be made utterly hideous by an inharmonious stroke of the brush, and in the same way the spirit becomes the more repulsive in form, and especially in the features of its face, the more it lacks in harmony in its attitude toward the Creator, in whose image and likeness it was originally created.

"Just as the od surrounding the spirit takes on the latter's shape, *so too it shares in the beauty or ugliness of the spirit's color and odor.* For this reason you witness in the materialization of spirits as it takes place nowadays, that the odic radiations of a good spirit give off a beautiful light and, as the condensation of the od progresses, emit a sweet odor, whereas the od of base spirits is shrouded in darkness and always causes an offensive smell. It is true that mortals cannot always perceive this odor, as it can be detected by your physical sense of smell only in rare instances.

"These are facts which your scientists have had ample opportunity to confirm.

"The harmony or the discord of the spirit is also transmitted through the odic to the physical body. For this reason man's character is expressed in the lines of his body, particularly in the features of his face, and even in the shape of his limbs. Those who are familiar with this law can therefore read the character of the spirit from the lines and shape of the various parts of the body, and for this reason also a man's nature can be judged from his handwriting. That is why the messages sent by the spirit of one who has died, will, when written down by a human medium, be in the handwriting peculiar to the sender while he was alive on earth, and such handwriting changes only when the character of the deceased has undergone a marked improvement in the Beyond.

"Since a man's destiny appears pictured in his od like the plan of a building and is transmitted by the od to his physical body, it can be read also in the lines and marks of his body. Hence, whoever is familiar with these marks will be able to see at least a part of that which a clairvoyant can determine in full by examining the od.

"I could dictate to you a very interesting book on all of these interrelated facts, but it is not my task to enrich human knowledge; I am charged only with telling you enough of these matters to enable you to understand the facts of communication by spirits with the material world, and the laws on which that communication is based.

"Inasmuch as od is spiritual in its nature, it also has the property, in common with spirits, *of being unaffected by the resistance offered by matter of any kind.* In the same way as it permeates the body pertaining to it, it can pass through any other substance, once it has left that body. There is nothing that can obstruct it.

"You have something similar in the case of the so-called Roentgen rays, so that it will not be difficult for you to understand what I am saying.

"Furthermore, just as in Nature powerful forces are developed under the influence of heat, accompanied by the formation of clouds, and become visible in the shape of lightning, so the spirit-world can, with the assistance of od, create *very powerful currents,* either hot or cold. In the case of lightning you speak of hot flashes, which fuse whatever they strike, and of cold flashes, which do not set fire to things but act only through the enormous pressure which they exert.

"Heat expands and dissolves, while cold contracts and condenses. This is a law that applies not only to the world of matter, but to that of spirit as well.

"As you are able to convert matter into steam with the aid of high temperatures and even to cause this steam to become invisible to the human eye, so also is the spirit-world able to dissolve matter completely. It too makes use of hot power-currents, by means of which it converts matter into an od-like, etherealized form. *For, as I have explained to you, all matter is nothing but corporealized od which can be dissolved into spiritual od.* Matter which has been converted into od penetrates all substances without meeting resistance, as does all other od, and can be transported to any place whatever, there to be condensed anew into matter.

"You speak of this dissolution of matter as 'dematerialization' and of the condensation of od into matter as 'materialization'.

"Whereas the spirit-world causes matter to dissolve by means of hot, high-power odic currents, it uses cold currents for condensing od, in keeping with the general laws of Nature. And just as you, when employing powerful terrestrial currents observe great care to prevent any accident, so the spirit-world takes equal precautions when using the power-currents employed by it.

"When you handle high-tension wires, you make use of so-called 'insulating devices'. You speak of 'short-circuits' and similar contingencies. So too when using odic currents for purposes of dematerialization or of materialization in the presence of living terrestrial creatures, the spirits must use the same degree of care in order to keep harm from coming to those creatures and to accomplish the desired dissolution or condensation of the matter involved.

"For this reason any unforeseen interference on the part of the spectators at a spiritistic *seance* with the efforts of the spirit-world may be dangerous for the medium who serves as the drive-shaft, or for the spectators, and may make the production of the desired phenomena difficult or even impossible. For in this field also, such a thing as a short-circuit is possible, unless provision has been made betimes for the necessary insulation.

"All this may sound entirely too human to you, but I cannot repeat too often that everything which you have on earth in a state of matter, exists also in the spirit-world in the state of spirit, *without any exception whatever.* It is not easy for you to understand this, seeing that all your ideas are derived from the world of matter, whence you find it hard to convert them into terms of the spiritual.

"The od with which your own spirit works in your physical body requires a given degree of condensation, as I have already pointed out to you, for a certain compromise must be struck between spirit and matter. For the same reason, the spirit-world, when working through corporeal beings, must condense the necessary od to a degree suited to the purpose in hand. *Light* and *heat* act in a highly obstructive sense in the case of condensations of this kind. That this should be true of heat you will readily see, since heat expands and dissolves. The fact that light also may exert a disturbing influence on the condensation of od will be fairly clear to you by analogy, when I remind you of the dark-room which is necessary for the development of your photographic plates.

"The condensation of od in the presence of heat and in bright daylight is not entirely impossible, but requires a quantity of od far greater than that available, except in the rarest instances, to the spirit-world for communicating with man. Otherwise, for Creation as a whole and for the performance of special tasks, the good spirit-world has at its disposal odic energy in unlimited amount and strength.

"It is therefore childish and a sign of your profound ignorance in such matters, to ridicule the fact that many spiritistic phenomena can be produced successfully only in the dark. Some of your scientists even assert that darkness is insisted upon only because it facilitates the concealment of 'spiritistic humbug'. It would be as reasonable to demand of the photographer that he develop his plates in broad daylight instead of in a dark-room and to call him a fraud because he can do his developing in the dark only. Unfortunately almost everybody is ignorant of the fact that the work of the spirit-world proceeds according to the same laws as those governing your actions on earth.

"What might be called 'odic feeding', a method of administering nourishment by means invisible to the human eye and seemingly utterly incomprehensible to the human mind, is also accomplished by the dissolution and recondensation of od.

"It happens that at all times there have been people who took no food whatever and still remained alive. In their case nourishment was administered by spirit methods, the spirit-world dissolving the food into od and introducing it into the digestive tract in that state. There the odic sustenance is condensed into material food and is digested. For this reason those people who to you seem to have eaten nothing, evacuate quite normally, just as though they had eaten and digested tangible food. This method of nourishment is always associated with other displays of activity on the part of the spirit-world in connection with the individuals in question. It is not an end in itself, but a link in the chain of events designed to serve a higher purpose.

"From what I have told you so far you are able to deduce for yourself that sufficient odic power is a pre-requisite for every task performed by the spirit-world on terrestrial beings, in a manner perceptible to your senses. *Odic force is the motive power throughout all of God's Creation as well as in the spirits' workshop on earth.*

"The question now comes up of its own accord: *Where do spirit-beings get the odic energy which they need for their communication with terrestrial creatures?*

"You might conclude offhand that spirits possess *sufficient odic power of their own* to enable them to work with matter. This however, is not the case, for spirit-beings require their odic energy to sustain their own existence and perform their work in the spirit-world. Above all things, however, the od of the superior spirit-world is far too fine and pure to combine with the very differently constituted od of terrestrial beings. Thus you too have fine substances which you cannot mix homogeneously with coarser ones.

"It follows that for its work on earth the spirit-world must use od of a type suited to the terrestrial od, and, as a rule, finds the type it needs in those terrestrial beings within whose sphere that work is to be performed.

"Men, beasts, plants and minerals are therefore the sources of od from which the spirits take the necessary motive power, and these sources of od are called 'mediums'. Terrestrial beings able to spare sufficient odic energy are said to be 'mediumistic'.

"All tangible created things are mediumistic, for all possess odic energy and are able to spare part of it, but in most cases their ability to do so is so slight, that they cannot be considered as sources of od by the spirit-world.

"Again, the odic power of mediums, although it may be sufficient in quantity, is not always fit for immediate use. It must first, in all cases in which it is to be employed by the 'superior spirit-world' as a motive force, be purified, or, so to speak, 'filtered'. Many of the substances you have on earth must be similarly 'filtered' before you can use them.

"To be sure, the *inferior spirit-world* need not undertake any purification of the od of the mediums, for the more impure this is, the better it is adapted to the od of such spirits. Hence it is also much easier for them to use mediums for their purposes, and they arrive at this end much more quickly than do the *superior spirits*.

"What more I may have to say as to the employment of odic force you could, as a matter of fact, discover for yourself by logical reasoning. It concerns finding an answer to the question: *In what way does the spirit-world employ terrestrial od for work to be performed with concrete beings?*

"The best and most concise answer would be: *Exactly as your own spirit must make use of the flesh and blood members of your body in order to perform acts which can be perceived by the senses, so, in most cases, a disembodied spirit must provide itself with members composed of matter.* This end it can achieve only by clothing its spiritual members with the od taken from mediums, and subsequently condensed to a suitable degree.

"Whenever *your own* spirit wants to grasp a concrete object it can do so only by means of *your* hand. But your physical hand is really nothing but the shell of the materialized hand of your spirit, formed by the condensation of terrestrial od. If therefore a disembodied spirit wants to grasp the same concrete substances it must first materialize its own spirit-hand by condensing the terrestrial od at its disposal. It has no other feasible means. The materialization need not, of course, be as thorough as that of your physical hand and perhaps not even thorough enough to render the spirit-hand visible to you, but still thorough enough to allow it to grasp the object. If the available od is insufficient to effect such condensation, the strange spirit will be as little able to grasp the object as you would be if your arms had been cut off.

"It is true that a spirit can grasp and move concrete objects without materializing its spirit-hands, *provided that object has been previously dissolved into od,* for any matter which has been converted into od, and hence, etherealized, is directly accessible to a disembodied spirit. But unless such dissolution has taken place, a concrete object can be grasped by a disembodied spirit only when the latter's spirit-hand has undergone materialization, for only like can grasp like.

"There are many degrees of odic condensation or materialization, from that visible only to a clairvoyant's eye to the complete materialization of spirits, in which case they differ in no respect from a material body. *The degree of condensation is therefore dependent upon the amount of od available to the spirit-world for the given purpose.*

"Let me cite a few more examples. *Your own spirit* wants to speak so that your fellow men may hear with their corporeal ears. *What must it do?* It must seek the aid of the flesh and blood organs of speech of your body; without them it is helpless. And whenever a spirit which has no body, and consequently no organs of speech, desires to say something, what must it do to produce sounds intelligible to human ears? It has the choice of two ways: it may either materialize its own spirit-organs of speech by condensing them with the aid of terrestrial od, or it may condense the *spirit-sounds* by means of the od of the medium at its disposal, to such an extent that they become audible to human ears. In the latter case therefore, the spirit does not need materialized organs of speech, but merely the condensed od of the sounds. You describe this method of speech by spirits as 'direct voices' which can be heard with more or less distinctness, according to the greater or lesser amount of odic energy supplied to the spirits by the mediums for the purpose of condensing the odic sound.

"You are visible to your fellow creatures from the fact that you have a material body. *Your material body, however, is only the material shell of your spirit with all of its organs, for every organ found in your body has its counterpart in a spiritual state in your spirit.* If therefore a disembodied spirit wants to appear to terrestrial eyes in such a guise that it will be taken for a terrestrial being, it must clothe its spirit-form and all of the members thereof with a shell of matter, which it produces by means of the condensation of terrestrial od. In the case of a spirit so materialized, the human eye can discover nothing to distinguish it from an everyday person. The spirit has skin, bones, all external organs, fingernails, hair and teeth, as well as inner organs like a heart which beats, blood which circulates, and whatever else is present in any normal, flesh and blood human being. A complete materialization of this kind requires so much od that no one medium is capable of supplying it; in such cases, therefore, *part of the substance of the medium's corporeal body* must be dissolved and used for materializing the spirit. For this reason, in materializations of this nature, a medium surrenders a great part of his physical weight, which is restored to him in full when the materialization has come to an end.

"I am constantly surprised that your scientists who investigate this field so closely do not discover these facts for themselves, for surely they witness phenomena enough to indicate the right path. They see *materialized hands* grasping and moving objects. They hear *direct voices,* and simultaneously they often see the *cloudlet of od* out which these voices proceed. When they photograph some of these phenomena, they may find upon the plate something that looks like an *Adam's apple,* formed by the spirit by means of the materialization of od, in order to provide it with a voice. When investigating *complete materializations* they find everything that is present in a normal human being, and yet they cannot hit upon the track of the truth.

"The greatest obstacle in the way of seeing the truth is *the erroneous conception of the terms 'spirit' and 'matter'.* Once the fact is recognized *that the nature of the spirit-creation is the same as that of material creation,* and *that they differ only in the manner in which they manifest their existence,* most of the difficulties that now prevent a proper understanding in the field of spirit-communication will disappear of their own accord. It will then be recognized that created spirits possess the *same organism* in spirit form, as terrestrial beings possess in material form; that the body has been cast over the shape of the spirit, and hence, that nothing can be contained in the material casting which is not present in the spirit-shape also. And it will further be recognized *that the Beyond resembles the Here in every way, with the sole difference that Here all things are matter, and that There all things are spirit.*

"But all life, in both the material world and in the world of spirit, *is bound up with the odic force.* This is the most powerful force in Creation, and it is the force by means of which God, who is the source of this force, can overthrow all things, the means by which He and His spirit-world perform the greatest 'miracles' as you call them. It is the force which renders the Magician capable of superhuman performances, inasmuch as his own powers are increased by the spirit-world, either the good or the evil, depending upon with which of the two he is in communication.

"In the case of the evil spirits, those which have severed their relations with God, this power is however circumscribed within very definite limits, whereas it can be put to use by God's spirits to an unrestricted extent.

"It was with this force that Christ healed the sick and raised the dead. With this force also He cast out the demons from those possessed of them, and it is the same force which the world of good spirits used at His behest to effect the miraculous increase of the loaves, by means of the materialization of the bread which had been brought to the spot as od.

"Christ promised this same power to all who would believe in Him. 'And for those who believe, these miracles will follow: they will cast out demons in my name; they will talk in foreign tongues; they will handle serpents; and if they drink any deadly poison, it will not hurt them; they will lay hands on the sick, and make them well; and they went out, and preached everywhere, the Lord working with them, and confirming the word by the miracles that endorsed it.' *(Mark 16 : 17 et seq.)* For a belief in God, meaning not only a belief in His existence, but unshakable faith in Him and faithful obedience to His will, *brings man into the closest union with God, Who is the exhaustless source of power.* Such belief will also place God's spirit-world at the service of man whose faith will render him capable of all things. 'Anything can be done by one who believes.' *(Mark 9 : 23.)*

"Every true believer in God will therefore experience those things that were fulfilled in Christ:

"If we do as God will, God on His part will grant us what we desire."

Biblical References to the Utilization of Odic Force in Spirit-Communication

And the Lord came down in the cloud of od, and spoke to him . . . *Numbers 11:25.*

"NATURE'S laws apply universally. They admit of no exception. If therefore the law relating to the odic force of which I have told you is the fundamental one which covers all spirit-communication, it must apply wherever spirits communicate with man.

"In order to prove to you that an odic current was necessary in every case of communication by spirits with man related in the Bible, I shall go over some of the accounts in the Old and New Testaments with you, and explain them to you.

"Naturally, as regards most of the spirit-manifestations of which the Bible speaks, mention is made only of the *fact* of such communication, nothing being said of the accompanying phenomena. Nevertheless, there are instances in plenty in which the utilization of od is expressly indicated.

"The first indication of this kind occurs in the story of Abraham. 'When the sun went down, and it turned dark, there was a smoking furnace, and a blazing torch that passed between the pieces'. *(Genesis 15 : 17.)* This happened while the Lord was speaking with Abraham. The odic current, when only slightly condensed, looks like a *cloud of smoke* and has a reddish-yellow gleam in the dark, like the *flame of fire.*

"The story of Moses is full of instances bearing on this subject. 'And the angel of the Lord appeared to him in a flame of fire rising out of a thorn-bush: when he looked, there was the thorn-bush ablaze with fire, yet not consumed'. *(Exodus 3 : 2.)* In this case also it was od that the spirit employed in order to speak to Moses. Hence it must have been at night that Moses saw this apparition, for in the daytime, the od would have looked, not like a flame, but like a cloudlet enfolding the thorny bush. This conclusion is confirmed by the following Biblical account: 'And the Lord went in front of them in a column of cloud, to lead them by day, and in a column of fire, to light them through the night; so that they might travel both by day and by night'. *(Exodus 13 : 21.)* The column of cloud was nothing else than the cloud of od, which, both in the case of the thorny bush and in guiding the Israelites, formed the *odic shell* which surrounded the angel of the Lord and was needed by him to make himself perceptible to men. I have already told you that od is always associated with a spirit. *There is no such thing as perfectly free, uncombined od.* This statement is borne out by all manifestations witnessed by the people of Israel.

"Hence, as often as mention is made in the Old Testament of the 'column of cloud', this is always done in connection with some act on the part of God's spirits. 'When the *"angel of God"*, in front of the army of Israel moved to their rear — the column of cloud moved from before them to behind them'. *(Exodus 14 : 19.)* 'When Moses entered the Tent, the *column of cloud* used to come down and stand at the entrance of the tent, when the Eternal was speaking to Moses'. *(Exodus 33 : 9.) And the Lord came down in the cloud, and spoke to him. . . (Numbers 11 : 25.)*

"On Mount Sinai, when the Lord wanted to speak with Moses in tones loud enough for all the people to hear, He said to Moses: 'I am coming to you in a *thick cloud,* so that the people may hear me speaking to you'. *(Exodus 19 : 9.)* This indicates expressly that the cloud of od was necessary to enable the Lord to speak to man. It also indicates plainly that the denser the od the louder the sounds produced by means of od. Much the same is true of your radio. The stronger the current, the stronger the sound transmitted.

"When therefore, the Lord appeared upon Mount Sinai amid a mighty blare of trumpets, it was essential that there should be an amount of odic power to correspond. Hence we are told: '*And the mount of Sinai was all wrapped in smoke,* as the Eternal descended in fire upon it; the smoke rose like steam from a kiln, till the people all trembled terribly'. *(Exodus 19 : 18.)*

"While explaining the law of odic force, I pointed out that the condensation of od is produced with the aid of powerful currents. The same is true of the dissolution of condensed od. Even the great masses of od about Mount Sinai were condensed by such high-tension currents. It was therefore dangerous to life to venture within the field of these high-tension currents. Hence the Lord forbade the people to approach the mount. Every man or beast that went up to the mount or touched its border, was surely to be put to death. *(Exodus 19 : 12.)* This was not an empty threat to inspire the people with the fear of the Lord as you mortals believe. It was rather a justifiable warning of the danger to life attending any contact with those currents. Just as you dwellers on earth call attention to danger from high-voltage currents by erecting warning signs, so the warning issued to the people of Israel was given for a similar purpose. Only after these currents had been turned off were the people to be allowed to ascend the mount. In the words of the Lord, this moment was to be proclaimed: 'When the ram's horn is sounded, then they may come up to the mount'. *(Exodus 19 : 13.)* Only those whom the Lord had previously authorized to enter the odic currents, namely Moses and Aaron, could do so without danger to their lives. In their cases, 'insulation' not unlike the kind you use for persons exposed to high voltages, had been provided.

"And if the Lord commanded further that every man or beast should be killed for even touching the border of the smoking mount, this was not meant as a punishment for disobedience, since obviously in the case of beasts the question of sinning could scarcely arise. It was rather a measure for preventing any interruption of the currents at all costs. Such interruption would have followed, had any incarnate beings exposed themselves to the currents without warrant, that is to say without being provided with proper means of insulation.

"The explanation of the events recorded in the Scriptures may surprise you and may strike you as too mundane and matter-of-fact. But it is the truth, and furnishes you with a fresh proof of the universal sway of the God-given laws, to which even the Creator Himself submits in His dealings with matter. He suspends not a single law, or, as the Holy Writ expresses it: 'Also, I find, whatever God may do shall stand unchanged. . .' *(Ecclesiastes 3 : 14.)*

"After this explanation you will probably understand also, why Christ, immediately after His resurrection, forbade Mary Magdalene to touch Him, for the materialization of His spirit was then only beginning, and Magdalene, by touching Him, would not only have prevented any further progress of the process of materialization, but would have destroyed what had already taken effect. A later-day, ignorant copyist sought to explain Christ's refusal to allow the woman to touch Him, by inserting the words: '. . . I have not ascended yet to the Father'. *(John 20 : 17.)* That this could not have been the true reason is evident from the circumstance that somewhat later, Christ expressly invited His apostles to touch Him, although at the time He was not yet ascended. But the materialization of His body was then complete, and therefore any contact with Him could cause no bodily harm to His disciples or interfere with the materialization.

"Let us consider a few more examples taken from the New Testament. In the transfiguration on Mount Tabor, 'a bright cloud overshadowed them: and from the cloud a voice said. . .' *(Matthew 17 :5.)* Here too a cloud of od was necessary, in order that there might be a voice that could be heard by human ears. That cloud was used by Moses and Elijah to render themselves visible as a mass of condensed od, to the three apostles present.

"It was in a form fashioned of materialized od that Christ appeared after His resurrection, and in a similar form that He stood before His disciples on the Day of the Ascension. They saw His odic body dissolve into a cloud of od before their eyes, and when the cloud itself had become invisible by further attention, Christ had disappeared from sight. The general belief that it was an ordinary cloud which hid Christ from His disciples, is utterly wrong.

"On the day of Pentecost there appeared above the heads of the Apostles and of those who were with them, *'tongues like flames'*. These were *flashes of blazing od,* like the flame seen in the burning bush, 'one resting on the head of each'. And they were all filled with a spirit of God, enclosed in these shells of od. These spirits, with the aid of odic power, began to speak through their human instruments in as many strange tongues as there were men of different nations among their hearers. From the circumstance that the tongues of od looked like streaks of flame, we see that it was at night that God's spirits descended. The actual time by your method of reckoning was half past one o'clock in the morning.

"A passage from the Revelation will prove to you that the *evil* spirit-world is equally bound by the laws governing odic phenomena. 'And I saw a star dropped from heaven to earth: he was given the key of the pit of the abyss. And he opened the pit of the abyss; and *smoke poured out of the pit,* like the smoke of a huge furnace, till the sun and the air were darkened by the smoke from the pit. And out of the smoke came locusts on the earth'. *(Revelation 9 : 1, 3.)* Further, in the same place, you are told how at God's behest and as a punishment to men, the evil spirits materialized themselves with the aid of the odic force into locusts having men's faces. I cite the foregoing passage only because it expressly mentions the 'clouds of od' which were indispensable for the materialization of the evil spirits.

"Naturally all of the many materializations and manifestations of spirits recorded in the Bible presupposed the employment of a corresponding amount of odic power, even if this fact is not expressly stated in each individual case.

"*The sacrifices prescribed in the Old Testament were the sources from which God drew the od required to enable Him to speak.* Among those portions of the Old Testament which are incomprehensible to you, are first and foremost the laws of sacrifice of the Israelites. You ask yourselves, rightly enough: How can an infinitely perfect God, Who is the source of all life and happiness, of everything that is good and beautiful, find pleasure in the offering of beasts, plants and herbs? Does he derive comfort from the blood of slaughtered animals, from the reeking fat of bulls, goats and lambs? Why should He delight in the fragrance spread by myhrr, cinnamon, calamus, cassia and olive oil? Why should spices be especially grateful to Him? And it may strike you as childish, that the great God, Whom Heaven itself cannot contain, should command a small, manmade tent to be erected for Himself, and should determine upon each trivial detail of its construction, on every beam and bolt, on every rug and curtain, on every garment to be worn by the priests, from headdress to underclothing. As a matter of fact, does it not savor of human vanity that God should insist upon the use of the most precious materials: gold, silver and the rarest of precious stones, so that the tabernacle and its fittings must have cost a huge sum in your money?

"If you look at these things from a purely human standpoint they may seem to you unworthy of a God. But once you recognize the purpose which God had in mind and understand that this purpose could be achieved only through means that seem so uncomprehensible to you, you will not cease to marvel at His infinite wisdom and love, as manifested herein also.

"Unhappily a knowledge of this purpose is concealed from you, although the purpose itself is expressly stated and pointed out to you in the Holy Writ. You have lost the art of reading the Scriptures with a view of understanding them. Your eye glances over their contents as it would over those of any worldly book. That which you read, you judge in a purely human light. Your worldly inclined minds fail to discern therein the mighty doings of God. Thus they are likewise incapable of grasping the significance of what is laid before you concerning the physical conformation of the tabernacle and the offerings described in the Old Testament.

"Open your Bible, and I will make clear to you the things therein contained concerning the tent of the testimony and its furnishings, and concerning sacrifice and priesthood.

The sole purpose for which all of those directions were issued is indicated in the words: 'This is to be a regular burnt-offering made age after age at the entrance of the Trysting tent before the Lord *where I meet you and speak to you'. (2nd Moses 29 : 42.)*

"Thus *communication by God with the Israelites* was the *sole purpose* in the mind of the Lord in commanding the erection of the tabernacle and in giving directions regarding sacrifices.

"You know that every spirit requires terrestrial odic force whenever it desires to communicate with the material creatures of the earth in a manner perceptible to the terrestrial senses. That is a God-given law which applies to all spirit-beings, from God, the highest of spirits, to the lowest spirits of the abyss.

"Whenever, therefore, God Himself, or God's spirits, either at His behest or with His sanction, desired to meet with the Israelites and speak to them, it was necessary that od of a suitable kind should be available.

"*All of the measures taken by Moses at God's command* in the erection of the tabernacle and in the presentation of the offerings, *were designed to procure the purest of all terrestrial od.*

"Inasmuch as terrestrial beings are carriers of terrestrial od, and since the od of human beings is a wonderful mixture of varieties of od taken from all over the earth, the od required to enable God to speak with men was drawn from a great variety of earthly sources, including minerals, plants, herbs, trees and animals. Above all things, however, it was necessary to take care that the od collected for that purpose should not be contaminated with the impure od radiated by terrestrial matter, which might find its way into the pure od that was being prepared. Hence all materials used in the construction of the tabernacle and for making its fittings, had to be such as contained the purest of od only.

"Among the *minerals,* gold, silver and copper possess the purest mineral odic mixture, as shown by the fact that they do not rust, for rust collects by the absorption of impure od, which has a destructive effect on any other od into which it penetrates.

"The same thing is true of the fabrics which were used, partly for the garments of the priests, partly for curtains and veils, and partly for covering the tent. Stuffs of blue, purple and scarlet, fine twined linen and byssus, have the purest odic mixture found in fabrics. Therefore the ephod of the High Priest, who approached the closest to the spirit of God that spoke through the cloud of od, had to be of these colors and materials, embroidered with gold.

"In the same way the '*breastplate of judgment*' worn over the ephod, was made. It consisted, besides, of twelve precious stones, for these contain large quantities of the most valuable od of all.

"The *robe of the ephod* was all of blue and upon its skirts were pomegranates of blue, purple and scarlet and bells of gold round about. All these details were of the greatest significance.

"The *undergarments* were of byssus, the breeches of pure linen. It is known to you also that clean linen worn next to the body or used for bed clothes is especially conducive to health. That is because this stuff contains a particularly pure od which is imparted to your body and exerts a stimulating effect.

"Of all *woods,* acacia is the purest, and was therefore the only lumber that could be used in the construction of the tabernacle.

"All other directions, which you can find for yourself in detail by consulting the Bible, concerning the composition of the utensils, screens, carpets and tent-coverings, were likewise issued solely to ensure the greatest purity of the od.

"Everything I have spoken of so far served as a *precaution* against the contamination of the od which was prepared in the shape of an *od-cloud* hanging above the ark of the covenant, and which was intended to serve to convey God's utterances. It was to prevent such contamination also, that the priests were required to wash their hands and feet in the water contained in the laver that stood at the entrance to the Holy of Holies, before they went near the ark of the covenant.

"The most important thing, however, was the preparation of the od itself which, floating as a cloud above the ark, was required for the production of the sounds by which God spoke to Moses. In this case the speech was not through a medium, but by 'direct voice'. The spirit-sounds were condensed by the terrestrial od of the cloud to the extent necessary to make them audible to human ears. As the Bible says: 'And when Moses entered the Trysting tent to speak to him, *he heard the Voice speaking to him* from above the cover on the ark of the presence, between the two cherubs: and the Eternal said to him'. *(Numbers 7 : 89.)*

"*The offerings which were prescribed were designed to assist in the preparation of the od-cloud.* You are sufficiently familiar with the fact that blood is the conductor of od in physical bodies. Hence the greatest amount of, and the most soluble, od is found in blood, and hence also blood is the best source of od for communicating with the spirit-world. And it was only for the sake of obtaining od that animals were slaughtered, both by the heathens to their idols and by the Jews in their divine service. The blood was sprinkled over the altar, and certain of the solid parts particularly the fat, the kidneys and the caul from the liver were disintegrated into od by being burned, for, next to the blood, the parts named are richest in od.

"The heathens prepared od for communicating with evil spirits by means of their idolatrous offerings. In the tent of testimony of God, the preparation of od was undertaken to make it possible for God and His higher spirits to communicate with the people of Israel, as witness the words spoken by the Lord to Moses: 'The priest must splash the blood on the altar of the Lord the entrance of the Trysting tent, burning the fat as a soothing odour for the Lord. They shall no longer offer their sacrifices to the evil spirits to whom they have deserted'. *(Leviticus 17 : 6, 7.)*

"Since the od-cloud above the ark of the covenant represented a mixture of the purest terrestrial od, only those beasts whose od was of the purest were allowed to be slaughtered. The beasts called 'unclean' in the Bible are those having the lowest and most impure od of any creatures whose flesh could conceivably serve for human food. That also is the reason why the people were forbidden to eat the flesh of unclean animals. Your physicians know well enough that swine's flesh is not to be recommended as an article of diet, particularly for growing children. What you call scrofula would scarcely be found among children if they were denied the flesh of swine, which is not wholesome even for adults if it forms a substantial part of the daily diet.

"There was, however, another reason for forbidding the Jews to eat the flesh of unclean beasts. You know that any impure od which may be present in a man, offers a dangerous opening to the evil spirit-world to work upon the worst side of his nature, for impure od is the breath of life to evil spirits, and whenever they find someone whose od is like their own, they can very readily not only influence his thoughts and imagination, but also arouse his physical passions to a dangerous pitch. On the other hand, a man whose od is pure is not easily accessible to evil, which is kept from coming into direct contact with him by the radiation of his pure od. For evil can bear such radiations as little as a person whose eyes are affected can bear strong light. The purity of a man's od depends upon the purity of his spirit, and since most men, because of their impure minds, have already quite sufficient impure od to offer an opening to evil, it is most undesirable to allow additional terrestrial odic impurities to reach them through the consumption of unclean food.

"God therefore had very important reasons for forbidding the eating of the flesh of unclean beasts. At that very time the influence of the Powers of Evil was particularly strong, owing to the universal prevalence of idolatry, and it was God's wish that a people chosen by Him as the bearer of His faith should be shielded as far as possible against this pernicious influence.

"For the same reason He issued the numerous rules to govern those cases in which the Israelites came into contact with impure od, and were considered unclean in consequence.

"However, the od of clean, unblemished beasts was not sufficient by itself alone for the preparation of the odic mixture needed for the tent of the testimony, but required in addition the purest od that could be procured from plants and minerals. The od of flowing myhrr, cinnamon, calamus, cassia, rye-bread, meal, wine and olive-oil was mixed with that of herbs like stacte, onycha and galbanum, and pure frankincense seasoned with salt. So it became a 'sweet savor unto the Lord'. You know from what I have taught you, what is meant by the 'sweet savor unto the Lord', and you know too that the purest od likewise diffuses the sweetest odor.

"The odic mixture for the tent of meeting was prepared by God's spirits in a state of purity corresponding to that of the spirit which manifested itself. The 'chemists of the Beyond' were those beings that you call 'cherubs'. That is why their image of beaten gold was placed above the mercy-seat over the ark, and was also embroidered on the curtains and hangings.

"Inasmuch as the od was collected above the mercy-seat and was employed by God's spirits for their speech, the preparation of the od had to be conducted in the immediate vicinity of the ark, for the source of od must always be in close proximity to the spirit which needs this force. Hence the altars and the tables on which the various offerings were made ready were close to the screen behind which stood the ark.

"The collection, retention and condensation of the od was facilitated by the fact that the ark was enclosed by curtains and a screen. You dwellers on earth, when you desire to collect od in quantity and to give it a high degree of condensation, require a so-called cabinet, within which or at whose entrance the medium who is the source of the od takes his place. The laws governing spirit-communication with mankind are the same everywhere.

"The fact that the wings of the two cherubim were extended like a roof, to cover the mercy-seat, further contributed to retain the od.

"The great strictness of the injunctions for keeping any impure od well away from the tent of meeting was due to another cause also, namely that if the pure and very powerful odic currents produced in the tent by the spirits of God were allowed to come into contact with impure currents, the bearer of the impure od would be killed by the high-tension currents, just as surely as a man who comes into contact with a high-voltage electric current will die, unless the proper insulation has been provided.

"For this reason Aaron was not allowed to enter the sanctuary whenever he pleased, but only after the condensation of the od above the ark was completed and when the high-tension currents employed for the purpose had been cut off. The exact time was prescribed to him; had he not heeded the directions, he would have been killed as were his sons when they violated the instructions for keeping the process of preparing the od undefiled during the burning of incense.

"After what you have just learned, the laws concerning offerings, and everything relating to the tent of meeting will appear to you in a far different light than has been the case heretofore.

Mediums

'Many were the forms and fashions in which God spoke of old to our fathers by the prophets.'
Hebrews 1 : 1.

"IN the days when men sought after God from their inmost hearts, their communication with His spirit-world was a *direct* one. Each individual possessed by nature most of the qualifications needed for such communication. His own spirit, attuned to lofty and divine thoughts, was capable of receiving messages from the spirit-world through *a spiritual sense of sight, hearing and feeling.* This was what you call nowadays 'clairvoyance', 'clairaudience', and 'clairsentience'. No intermediaries were needed for the messages sent from the Beyond.

"This gift disappeared as mankind fell away from God and began to devote all its thought and care to worldly things. In their reckless race after money and other worldly goods, men forgot God. This not only weakened the communication with the good spirit-world, but brought about the disappearance of those gifts which had made it possible theretofore. To-day the majority of mankind goes so far as to disbelieve altogether in the possibility of such communication. There are relatively few people today who possess the gifts in question and who are in touch with the world of good spirits after the manner of the God-fearing folks of old.

"But the time is coming when things will again be as they were in this respect, that is to say, when each individual can communicate by spirit-sight and hearing with the Beyond.

"Until that time, however, those who still believe in God may converse with spirits through another channel, and many who do not believe may witness the workings of the spirit-world with their corporeal senses, and thereby be aroused to return to a belief in the Almighty and in survival after the death of the body.

"For this purpose God has given mankind of today the so-called *mediums.* The meaning of this term has already been made clear to you, but since a correct understanding of the nature of mediums is among the most important points connected with spirit communication, I must not fail to instruct you minutely in this particular. In so doing I shall confine myself to discussing *human* mediums, omitting those cases in which *animals* may serve as such.

"Mediums are intermediaries or human instruments employed by the spirit-world to make itself manifest to man. Inasmuch as the spirit-beings require odic power for the purpose, mediums are persons who serve the spirit-world as *sources of odic power.*

"It is chiefly *their own od* which mediums surrender to the spirits manifesting themselves. *The mediums are, however, at the same time points for collecting the od liberated by the non-mediums in attendance at the so-called spiritistic seances.* Exactly as sometimes happens in building an aqueduct, when the water from the main spring is supplemented by that of many smaller springs, so the medium's capacity to supply od is increased by his collecting within himself the feebler odic power of the other persons present.

"While all people possess odic power, in most cases this is too closely bound to the body to be surrendered readily. Hence it is not available to the spirit-world in adequate strength.

"People qualified to function as mediums are highly sensitive. This means that because of the ease with which they can part with their od, the impressions made upon them are deeper than in the case of other people. This is not a morbid condition as your scientists think, and has no relation with nervousness, hysteria or lack of will-power; on the contrary, good spirits cannot use nervous, irresolute or sick persons as mediums. A good medium must have more will-power, stronger nerves and better physical health than the average person.

"Mediums are divided into different groups according to the purpose for which their odic power is employed by the spirit-world.

"1. If this power is used to raise or lower a table or to cause the same to emit raps, the medium employed in this connection is called a '*medium for table-communication*'. The rising and falling, or the rapping of the table are used as a sign-language for obtaining messages from the spirit-world. *This is the lowest form of spirit-communication,* for the spirits which appear at table-tipping *seances* are almost without exception those of a low order. *Spirits of the superior kind do not select this way in which to manifest themselves.* Thus it happens that at such gatherings the low spirits which appear often carry on much mischief, occasionally assisted by the tricks of the spectators. Unfortunately, table-tipping with its manifestations which are either ridiculous or mendacious, does much to discredit the higher forms of spirit-communication.

"Seekers after God and lovers of the truth will therefore shun communication of this kind and choose only those methods which are worthy of the high ends in view.

"2. Whenever messages from the spirit-world *through writing* are set down by a person, you speak of him as a *'writing medium'*.

"The manner in which the writing is accomplished differs widely in the case of the various writing mediums. In one instance the thoughts may be inspired into the medium and written down by him; he is therefore sometimes known as an *'inspirational medium'*. Another's hand may be guided at the same time that the words he writes are inspired into his mind. All the while he is fully conscious of his actions. Contemporaneous inspiration is necessary in those cases in which the medium offers strong resistance to the guidance of his hand. Others again know only *that* they are writing, *but are quite ignorant of what they set down.* Still others write in a state of utter unconsciousness; they know neither that they are writing nor *what* they are writing.

"Moreover it not infrequently happens that one and the same medium will write in several of the ways I have described.

"*'Direct writing'* as it is called is entirely different from the writing done by mediums, being produced by the spirit itself which makes use of the odic force only of the medium and not of the latter's hand. By means of the od which it takes from the medium the spirit materializes its own hand, and with it writes upon a surface like a sheet of paper, a slate or something similar with which the medium does not come into contact. The amount of od required for this method is much greater than when the medium's hand is used in writing.

"There are two references in the Bible to 'direct writing', with both of which you are of course familiar. The tablets bearing the Commandments were written on Mount Sinai by the hand of God as related in the books of Moses: 'The tablets were the work of God, the writing inscribed on the tablets being God's own writing'. *(Exodus 32 : 16.)*

"When King Belshazzer made a great feast to his lords and drank from the sacred vessels which his father had taken from the temple which was in Jerusalem and praised the gods of gold, and of silver and of brass, 'that very hour the fingers of a man's hand appeared writing on the plaster of His royal palace opposite the lampstand. The king saw the palm of the hand as it wrote'. *(Daniel 5 : 5.)*

"The medium's hand may also be used for drawing or for painting, rather than for writing. In such cases the mediums are designated accordingly, the general process being the same as in writing.

"3. There is another class of what might be called writing mediums, namely the 'planchette mediums'. A 'planchette' is a slab of wood, metal or other material upon which are marked the letters of the alphabet, figures and other symbols. The surface of the planchette is smooth, so that an object may readily be slid about upon it. The medium, who retains his full consciousness, lays his hand on some object provided with a hand or pointer, which rests upon the slab. He now waits until the object moves so that the pointer will touch a letter. It indicates, one after another, a series of letters which when put together will spell out words and sentences.

"The planchette-medium sits with his eyes closed or, better still, blindfolded, so that he cannot see the letters himself, since otherwise he would be prone to assist the motion of his hand and thus to record his own thoughts.

"The most famous of all planchettes was the *breastplate* on the robe of the High Priest, who himself was a medium.

"In your modern version of the Bible this breastplate is referred to as the 'breastplate of judgment', because it was used by the Israelites when they desired that God's judgment be revealed to them. It was in the shape of a square and consisted of four rows of precious stones, the first row being composed of a sardius, a topaz and a carbuncle; the second of an emerald, a sapphire and a diamond; the third of a jacinth, an agate and amethyst; and the fourth of a beryl, an onyx and a jasper. *(Exodus 39 : 8 et seq.)*

"On each stone was engraved a character, standing for one of the names of the twelve tribes of Israel, a kind of alphabet being thus formed. The reason why precious stones were used was, because they possess odic power to a high degree and thus strengthened the High Priest's hand. Between the stones was a wide, smooth, groove of gold having no sharp corners or edges. A part of the equipment was the plate of pure gold worn upon the mitre and engraved with the words: HOLY TO THE LORD. This was fastened to the mitre with a lace of blue, and was the most important of the objects used in consulting the Lord. Hence it bore its inscription with good reason. *(Exodus 39 : 30, 31.)*

"Whenever invoking God for counsel, the High Priest untied

the lower edge of the breastplate from the ephod and brought the breastplate into a horizontal position. He then removed the engraved plate of gold, or the diadem, from the mitre and laid it into a groove between the precious stones. Thereupon he extended his hand over the breastplate, without touching either it or the diadem which rested upon it. His great odic power was used by God's spirit-world to set the golden diadem in motion. It glided along the grooves, touching, with a small eyelet by means of which it was fastened to the mitre, those stones whose characters were to be joined into a *word* in the order in which the stones were touched. When a *word* had thus been spelled out, the diadem glided to the right edge of the breastplate where it struck a small bell, to indicate that the word was completed. At the end of a *sentence,* the diadem slid first to the right and then to the left side of the breastplate, striking the bells there in succession. This double signal indicated the conclusion of a *sentence.* In this way all possibility of error was eliminated, since no character belonging to one word could be transposed to an adjoining word, nor could an entire word be transposed from one sentence to another.

"Inasmuch as this method excluded any possibility of mistakes in recording God's answer, the diadem and the bells were known collectively as the 'sacred lots', to indicate the truthfulness of their revelations. In the Hebrew text they are called 'the Urim and the Thummim', words which signify also truth and clearness.

"In the days of the kings of Israel the breastplate of judgment was often used when God's counsel was sought, the priests acting as mediums. David in particular thus appealed to God in almost all important matters through the priest Abiathar, making use of the breastplate, and by means of it receiving God's answer.

"4. The most important of the mediums for communicating truth are the *'speaking mediums'* as soon as they have been trained to act as *'deep-trance mediums'.* A medium is said to be in a *deep trance* when his spirit has left his body entirely. In this state he resembles a corpse, the only difference being that the spirit, which has gone forth from him, is still connected with its body by a band of od, whereas in the case of a corpse there is no such connection. Through this band of od the medium's body receives enough vitality from the spirit to keep its organs functioning. It is along this band of od also that the spirit finds its way back into the body of the medium.

"In the place of its own spirit, another spirit-being enters the body and delivers its message by means of the medium's organs of speech. In so doing it makes use of the odic energy remaining in the medium's body after his spirit has left it.

"A deep-trance medium naturally knows nothing of what the strange spirit has said. When consciousness returns he feels as though he had been asleep. Hence you speak of the 'mediumistic sleep of deep-trance mediums.

"It is of the greatest importance to those to whom a strange spirit is speaking through a medium, to know *the nature of the spirit* that has taken possession of the medium's body and whether it is a high or an inferior, a good or an evil spirit. For this reason I advise everyone to test the spirits in order to learn whether they were truly sent by God, or whether they are evil. This can be done *by making them swear in the name of God, to their identity and to that of the place from which they came.* A good spirit will take this oath, an evil one will not. If you are dealing with a good spirit, it will inform, admonish, instruct and advise you for your good. If, however, the spirit is an evil one, send it away at once, but first admonish it to pray to the Lord.

"If spirits of a humble, suffering type, but well-disposed, enter a speaking medium, it is your duty to teach them the cause of their condition, to direct them toward God and to pray with them. In this way you will be doing a great kindness to many of these 'poor souls' as you call them, and they will be grateful to you for it ever after.

"The duty of applying such tests to spirits was emphasized by the Apostles when preaching to the early Christians. Every Christian community was carefully instructed in the matter; not less well-instructed in this field were the people of pre-Christian times.

"5. *'Apport-mediums'* are generally deep-trance mediums whose odic force is used by the spirit-world to transfer tangible objects into enclosed spaces from without, or from within such spaces to the outside. The deep-trance state is here necessary in most cases, since the spirits require all of the medium's physical od in order to make these 'apports', as the objects apported must be disintegrated into od in one place, and re-materialized into substance in the other.

"There are, it is true, mediums who, without going into a deep trance are able to release enough od to effect apports, especially if *several* powerful mediums are used simultaneously as sources of od. Although you may not have any physical perception of the extremely high heat which is developed by the odic currents for the purpose of disintegrating matter, you can feel some of the heat that remains after the objects have been re-materialized. An example may make this clear to you: there are so-called 'spooks' which occasionally 'apport' stones, sand and the like from the street into locked rooms of houses. They can do this only when they have at their disposal enough odic force to produce hot, high-tension currents. With these they disintegrate the substance of the objects and carry it in the shape of od into the rooms, where it is reconverted into solid matter, which now feels hot to the touch, for although it has been recondensed by cold currents, it retains part of the heat used in its disintegration, just as glowing steel, after being quenched in water, will remain hot for a considerable time to come.

"At times the medium's body itself is transported from one place to another, occasionally over great distances. This is also done by de-materializing it at one spot and re-converting it into substance at the other.

"When, as related in the Old Testament, the prophet Habakuk, together with the food he carried to Daniel in the lions' den, was to be transported by an angel of the Lord, the angel did not carry Habakuk through the air as people seem to believe, but disintegrated him and his belongings and re-materialized him at the den. The same happened in the case of Philip, as related in the Acts: when he had enlightened and baptized the treasurer of Queen Candace of Ethiopia, 'the Spirit of the Lord caught away Philip and carried him to Azotus'. That is to say, the spirit disintegrated Philip's body, causing it to disappear before the eunuch's eyes in an instant, and re-materialized it in the city of Azotus. *(Acts 8 : 26 et seq.)*

"Such happenings are beyond the comprehension of man because he cannot see the forces at work in the matter. The fact that substance, and even bodies of living people can be disintegrated at one place and re-materialized elsewhere can no longer be denied, since well-authenticated instances of this phenomenon are too numerous to admit of such denial. The natural laws according to which the process takes place should be abundantly clear to you after the explanation I have given.

"6. In the case of *'materialization mediums'* the medium's whole physical odic force is used to enable one or more spirits to make themselves visible to human eyes. Since this requires all of the od possessed by the medium, his own spirit must be removed from his body. According to the amount of the od available, the strange spirit uses the same to clothe either its entire figure, that is to say, its body and all of its members, or only certain parts as for instance, the eyes, the face or the hands. If the materialization is to be complete enough to allow the spirit in question to look like a terrestrial being, the od alone of the medium is not sufficient, and matter must be taken from his body, and used *in the state of od* for the materialization of the spirit. On such occasions a medium loses physical weight equivalent to the substance surrendered to the strange spirit. Your scientists have determined this loss of weight by means of automatic scales, on which they had caused the medium to take his place at the beginning of the investigation. Cases are known in which a materializational medium lost as much as eighty pounds of his weight within a few minutes. However, the od as well as the substance surrendered remain connected with the medium by means of band of od of which I have spoken, and flow back into the medium when the spirit is again de-materialized. That is why materialization always takes place in proximity to the medium. You may often notice, also, that the motions of a materialized spirit are attended by similar motions on the part of the medium, for the connection between the two is a very close one. If your hands and arms were bound together with those of someone else by means of tightly drawn cords, and if you were to gesticulate with your own members, you would cause the other person to make similar gestures with his. The materialized spirit and the medium are bound together in an analogous manner by odic bands.

"This intimate connection between the medium and the materialized spirit explains another phenomenon for which, also, your scientists can give no reason, namely, the different odors often diffused by mediums during materialization. At times these odors are pleasant, at others they are offensive; they may indeed resemble that given off by a decomposing corpse. The nature of these odors depends on that of the spirit incorporated by means of the medium's od. When I spoke to you about od, I explained that it assumes an odor in keeping with the qualities of the spirit which it clothes. The od taken from a medium and used by a spirit for its materialization therefore assumes an odor corresponding to the nature of the spirit in question, and since the materialized od of the spirit remains closely connected with the medium, the spirit's odic scent is transmitted to the medium as well. This gives the impression that the medium himself is the cause of the pleasant or unpleasant smell, whereas one or the other proceeds from the spirit which has materialized itself with the medium's od.

"7. There is yet another type of medium which is of no benefit to mankind, the so-called *'physical mediums'* who are used chiefly by *evil* spirits. These utilize the odic power of such mediums for the *moving about of objects* in proximity to the medium. Tables, chairs, utensils of all kinds, rise and float from one spot to another; instruments begin to play; a bugle rises into the air and blows; a drum near at hand gives off beats; bells fly across the room and ring, and numberless similar things happen.

"It goes without saying that *good* spirits do not stoop to these tricks, for it is not their place to produce phenomena intended only to gratify man's taste for the extraordinary. To be sure, similar phenomena are witnessed in the case of other mediums also, but with them not nearly so regularly as with the 'physical mediums'.

"You ask to what purpose the low spirits hold such 'a carnival at modern spiritistic seances', or why indeed they are allowed to do so. To this I can only reply that low spirits have the same latitude of conduct as low and wicked people. Precisely as the latter are left free to act as they please, so no restrictions are placed upon the liberties of the former, at least not up to a certain point. True enough, their liberty is not altogether unlimited, for if it were, they would do mankind even more harm than they can do as it is. For man's goal is to arrive at God, and with this in consideration, He has set bounds to the activities of evil-doers. But even the 'high carnival of evil' as you call it, which goes on at modern spiritistic meetings, has not infrequently a good effect in spite of everything. For nowadays when there are so many people who believe in no God, no Beyond, no spirit-world and no survival after death, it does some good that they should witness the kind of things of which you speak, if only because it compels them to think of these matters, to relinquish their skeptical attitude and to make a beginning of trying to discover the truth. This statement applies to everything that happens at your spiritistic meetings of today, from levitation and table-rapping to the physical phenomena and to materialization. Even if the only interest in these things springs from a craving for new sensations, it often happens that many people do retain the impression that ultra-mundane forces must exist, and if this result is not all that could be desired, it is at least better than if those individuals had not had their attention called at all to the Beyond.

"What mankind does need, and need badly, is a thorough-going explanation of the nature of spirit-communication and of the manner in which such communication can be established with the *good* spirit-world. This is to be your life-work, and for this reason you are receiving all of these teachings. They are not meant for you alone, but for your fellow men as well. It is your duty to teach them these facts, as you would teach them to your own brothers and sisters. When people have been taught how to seek communication with the good spirit-world, every spiritistic gathering will become an inspiring divine service.

"8. Your scientists include among mediums those individuals who have the gift of *clairvoyance and clairaudience*. This is not correct. It is true that clairvoyants, clairaudients and clairsentients have *mediumistic powers,* but they are not true mediums. With them, it is *their own* spirit which is active, which sees and hears, whereas in mediums properly so called it is a strange spirit which acts while the medium's spirit is temporarily dispossessed. The gifts of clairvoyance and clairaudience do indeed enable the spirit of a man to see and hear the spirits about him, but a clairvoyant is not an instrument of these spirits and should therefore not be classed as a medium. The spirit of a person endowed with clairvoyance, clairaudience and with supernatural powers of feeling, smelling and tasting, owes these faculties exclusively to the fact that it can detach itself from the body to a greater or less degree. A spirit so detached and partly withdrawn from the body thereby becomes independent of the latter's physical senses of perception and assumes the faculties and properties of a discarnate spirit, seeing, hearing and feeling after the manner of ultra-mundane spirits, according to the extent to which it is detached and according to the purity of the od surrounding it. This purity is of particular significance to clairvoyants, for, as in the case of glass, impurities affect its transparency. By the same token, the sensory powers of ultra-mundane spirits vary greatly with the composition of their od. Some of these spirits can see, feel, and hear things that others are unable to detect. The same thing is true of human beings gifted with clairvoyance, clairaudience and clairsentience. In their case there are countless degrees of the keenness of these faculties, from the most rudimentary to the highest. Some merely *sense* the proximity of the spirits about them and vaguely feel the impression which the latter create upon them, but to see and hear the spirits is beyond their power. Others are able to *see* the spirits, but not to *hear* them. Still others see them plainly, hear their words and can tell the different spirits apart by their appearance. The many mistakes made by your clairvoyants in their statements are explained by the fact that with most of them the faculty is present in a very imperfect state only.

"You will find many references to clairvoyance in both the Old and the New Testament. Of the patriarch Jacob we are told: 'Jacob went his way, and encountered the *angels of God*. On seeing them Jacob said: This is God's camp. . .' *(Genesis 32 : 1, 2.)*

"During the reign of King David when the angel of the Lord smote the people of Israel with the pestilence as a punishment, *David actually saw the angel.* 'David saw the angel who was striking down the people'. *(2nd Samuel 24 : 16.)*

"The prophet Elisha had the gift of clairvoyance. It is related of him in the Book of Kings that he perceived by this power how his servant Gehazi followed after the captain Naaman who had been cured of leprosy, and by false pretexts extorted presents from him for Elisha. When Gehazi had hidden these presents in his house for his own use, and had gone in and was standing before his master, Elisha asked him: 'Where have you been, Gehazi? And he answered: Your servant has not been anywhere. But Elisha said to him: Was I not with you in spirit, when someone came back from his chariot to meet you? You have taken the money and you mean to get garments, olive-yards, vineyards, sheep, oxen, and slaves, male and female'. *(2nd King 5 : 25 et seq.)*

"Elisha also foresaw the destiny of Hazael by clairvoyance as recorded in the same book of the Bible: 'As he spoke, the man of God's face became rigid with horror. Then he burst into tears. And Hazael said: Why does my lord weep? And he answered: Because I know the cruelties you will practise on the Israelites, setting fortresses ablaze, murdering young men, dashing children to pieces and ripping up pregnant women! God the Lord has let me see your reigning over Aram'. *(2nd Kings 8 : 11 et seq.)*

"It was by clairvoyance also that the great prophets saw the spirits sent to them, as well as the fate in store for humanity, for nations and for individuals. This fate was generally revealed to them by the spirit-world symbolically. In addition to the gift of clairvoyance, the prophets were also endowed with clairaudience. You will find an example of this if you will read over again the Book of Daniel, especially those of its passages relating to the apparition of the archangel Gabriel: 'While I was uttering my prayer, the ANGEL Gabriel whom I had seen in the former vision, sped swiftly to me about the hour of the evening sacrifice. He came and talked to me saying: O Daniel, I now come to give you insight. When you began your supplications this divine oracle was granted, which I now come to impart to you, for you are a man greatly loved by God; so ponder the oracle and understand the vision'. *(Daniel 9 : 21 et seq.)*

'Then in the twenty-fourth day of the first month, when I was on the banks of the great river, which is Tigris, I raised my eyes, and as I looked there I saw a spirit standing robed in linen, with a girdel of fine gold from Ophir round his waist, his body gleaming like a topaz, his face like lightning, his eyes like lamps of fire, his arms and legs like the colour of burnished bronze, and the sound of his words like the noise of a multitude. I, Daniel, alone saw the vision; for the men beside me did not see it; shuddering had seized them, and they ran to hide themselves. So I was left alone to see the great vision. No strength was left in me; paleness ruined my fresh colour; I heard the sound of what he was saying, but when I heard his voice I fell down into a dead faint, my face upon the ground. Then a hand touched me, and set me on my knees and hands all shaking . *(Daniel 10 : 4-10.)*

"I have quoted these two passages from the Book of Daniel at length, because they are especially instructive for your purposes and because they confirm much of what I have told you so far. In the first place you have here a most pronounced instance of the actual occurrence of clairvoyance and clairaudience. Daniel sees the spirit-shape, whereas his companions do not. But since they also were mediumistic, they *felt* the proximity of the spirit and its mighty odic power, and fled in terror. This supports my statement that some people, while they may not be able to see or to hear spirits, can *feel* their presence. Furthermore, these passages of the Bible, like so many others, prove that spirits have a figure and limbs similar to those of mortals. Finally, Daniel felt a hand which touched him and raised him upon his knees and upon the palms of his hands; it was the hand of Gabriel who had materialized it with the aid of the odic force borrowed from Daniel. The audible speech of the spirit and the materialization of its hand required so much odic force that Daniel, who had sunk powerlessly to the ground, had to be strengthened by Gabriel with his own odic energy.

"Coming to the New Testament, I shall mention only the clairvoyance of the Apostle Paul. When Saint Paul had come to Troas, there appeared suddenly in the night a man of Macedonia, who besought Paul: 'Come over into Macedonia, and help us'. *(Acts 16 : 9.)*

"On another night, the Lord stood beside Paul and said: 'Courage! As you have testified to me at Jerusalem, so you must testify at Rome'. *(Acts 23 : 11.)*

"On the voyage to Italy, Paul said to the crew of the ship that carried him: 'Men, I see this voyage is going to be attended with hardship and serious loss not only to the cargo and the ship, but also to our own lives'. *(Acts 27 : 10, 11.)*

"I have already told you that the great events of the future can be foreseen only if revealed to the clairvoyant by the spirit-world as in a picture. That statement also is confirmed in this instance, for when the crew failed to heed Paul's warning and ventured upon the voyage in disregard thereof, they encountered a storm which obliged them to throw overboard part of their cargo and the tackling of the ship, and had already abandoned all hope of being saved, when 'Paul stood up among them and said: Men, you should have listened to me and spared yourselves this hardship and loss by refusing to set sail from Crete. I now bid you cheer up! There will be no loss of life, only of the ship. For last night an angel of the God I belong to and serve stood before me saying: Have no fear Paul; you must stand before Caesar. God has granted to you the lives of all your fellow-voyagers. Cheer up, men! I believe God, I believe it will turn out just as I have been told. However, we are to be stranded on an island'. *(Acts 27 : 21 et seq.)*

"To the Corinthians Paul writes: 'For my part, present with you in spirit, though absent in body, I have already as in your presence, passed sentence on such an offender as this'. *1st Corinthians 5 : 3.)*

"Similarly he writes to the Colossians: 'For though I am absent in body, I am with you in spirit, and it is a joy to note your steadiness and the solid front of your faith in Christ'. *(Collosians 2 : 5.)*

"From these last two passages we see that Paul's spirit could leave his body and be present at events that occurred in distant places."

The Development of Mediums

For I will pour water on the thirsty land and streams on the dry ground; I pour my spirit on your children, and my blessing on your offspring. *Isaiah 44 : 3.*

"WHATEVER is intended to serve a particular purpose must first be suitably produced, prepared and adapted, as your machinery and utensils are constructed to meet the ends for which they were designed.

"Mediums are the instruments of the spirit-world and are intended to make possible communication between the spirits and material beings. Hence these mediums must be rendered capable of doing whatever may be necessary for attaining that object. This is accomplished *by the development of their mediumistic powers.*

"Mediums are primarily *sources of energy* from which the spirit-beings draw the motive power for their work. *It is they who furnish the odic force.*

"To make the steps in the training of mediums as intelligible to you as possible, I shall again make use of a comparison. To run your motor cars, you require a substance derived from petroleum. When opening up the sources of the latter, the first step is to obtain enough petroleum by drilling, to make its production profitable. But the crude oil as it flows from the wells cannot be used as such. It must first be refined and undergo a number of forms of treatment to make it suitable for the various uses to which it is to be put.

"In the same way the spirit-world must provide for obtaining *as great an amount of od as possible* from the mediums. This od, however, is firmly united with the medium's body, and it is essential that it be so treated that it can be liberated freely and lent to the spirit in the quantity required.

"When dealing with artificial fertilizers, you speak of the *solubility* of their components. You differentiate between *total phosphorous, potassium, nitrogen and calcium contents* and the *soluble* percentage of these elements. Only the latter portion is of value to you, and it alone commands a price.

"Similarly, only that od is of value to the spirits which can be released by reason of its ability to detach itself from a terrestrial body. The more readily detachable a medium's od, the greater the amount which can be liberated, and the more striking and comprehensive the phenomena which the spirit-beings can produce.

"While speaking of the od which is made available by the training of the mediums and which is used by the spirits concerned, I must not omit a very important observation. If the activity of a spirit relates to the execution of a *special command of the Lord,* the spirit will have at its disposal more od than is possessed by all creatures on earth put together. In this case the spirit stands in a particular connection with the sources of all odic force, God Himself, and can draw upon this source to the extent required for carrying out the divine mission assigned to it.

"If, for instance, God commands a spirit to impart instruction to mankind, the requisite amount of od is supplied to that spirit. The spirit will, however, make use of your od also, for the spirit-world employs this precious force as sparingly as you mortals do your worldly valuables. In this case you reinforce the od at the spirit's disposal with your own, and enable the spirit to prolong its disclosures beyond the time originally planned. To make use of an illustration taken from your daily experience, it is like adding fresh water to the water of a cooling-jacket that has been cooled off already, in order to increase the efficiency of the cooling-jacket and the duration of the operation.

"If, however, the good spirits are acting, not at God's command but upon their own responsibility, albeit with His sanction, the work they can accomplish depends on the quantity of od available from terrestrial sources, that is to say, from the mediums.

"The amount of od which can be liberated differs with each medium. With one, it barely suffices for the simplest tasks of the spirit-world; with a second, it permits of a much greater scope, while with a third it may be plentiful enough for the most difficult undertakings in this field. Among these is the corporealization of a spirit by means of a condensation of od so pronounced, that the spirit stands before you as a complete body, differing in no respect from an ordinary human being. It was in a thus embodied state that three of God's messengers appeared to Abraham, that the Archangel Raphael accompanied young Tobias, and that Christ stood before His disciples after His resurrection.

"It rests primarily with the medium to render his physical od as readily detachable as possible. This he can accomplish by steadfast fixity of purpose, or by what you call 'concentration'. Only persons who are able to fix their minds on a given subject and to divert their thoughts from all worldly matters can therefore become good mediums. Hence your most powerful mediums are found among races in whose religious training concentration is an important feature. Of all races, the Hindoos produce the most mediums because their religion exacts of them daily practice in concentrating their minds, from childhood on. They call it 'submersion of the spirit' and many of them attain great perfection in this direction. Since the human spirit employs only its *own specific od* during such periods of concentration, the *physical* od is allowed to rest in the meantime. No strain is put upon it, and it may hence be liberated all the more readily for the use of the spirit-world.

"The oftener a person devotes himself to such spiritual concentration, the easier it is for him to release his quiescent odic energy and to surrender it by means of radiation. The proceeding is like the behavior of a magnet. The first time this is used, its power is very slight, not enough to attract even the smallest particle of iron, but the more the magnet is used, the stronger it grows, and in the end becomes capable of sustaining relatively heavy iron objects.

"It is the same with the odic force: in the early stages of a medium's development it is feeble, but the oftener he practices concentration, the more powerful does the odic radiation suitable for spirit-communication become.

"The primary object of the training of mediums is therefore to develop their ability to release as much od as possible by mental concentration. The amount or the strength of this terrestrial od is of equal importance, alike to all spirits good or evil.

"A second problem in the training of the mediums is the adaptation of the medium's od to that of the spirit which works through him. To solve this problem is the task of the spirit-world. The adaptation of the od varies greatly, according to whether it is to be used by superior or by inferior spirits. A superior spirit must purify and refine all mediumistic od, or filter it, so to speak, whereas an inferior spirit does not find this necessary, as its own od is impure, and readily accommodates itself to the unpurified terrestrial od.

"With some mediums there is still a third purpose to be achieved by training. If, namely, a medium's *entire physical od* is to be used by the spirits in their work, this is possible only provided the medium's spirit leaves his body; hence, provision must be made for the liberation of his spirit. To accomplish this is not easy, and requires much painful, time-consuming labor on the part of the spirit-world. During the process the medium's sensations are not unlike those of a dying person. In the case of the latter, death ensues from the separation of the spirit from the body, as you know. As to the difference between the body of a medium whose spirit has projected itself from it, and a dead body, I have already explained this to you. You will remember that when the spirit of a 'deep-trance medium' leaves his body, it still maintains connection with the same by means of a *band or cord of od,* whereas in the case of the bodies of the dead, death has been caused by the breaking of this cord.

"From what I have said you must have gathered a clear idea of the object pursued in the training given to mediums. This object includes the liberation of the greatest possible amount of od, the purification of the same for the tasks undertaken by the superior spirit-world, and finally, the release of the spirits of 'deep-trance mediums' from their bodies.

"The development of the faculties of clairvoyance and clairaudience likewise requires training. Here too, the spirit is released in part from the clairvoyant's body, and the od which surrounds his spirit must undergo an appropriate degree of purification, but such partial separation in the case of clairvoyants differs radically from that in the case of the spirit of a 'deep-trance medium'. It is true that the clairvoyant's spirit is projected; nevertheless it remains bound to the entire physical od and to all parts of the body. The od merely expands, to use an everyday term, and by its expansion allows the partial projection of the spirit. With a clairvoyant, a separation of the physical od from the spirit does not take place.

"With a 'deep-trance medium' the entire od, except an odic cord, is separated from the spirit, which is thereby set free, being enabled to leave the body and to travel for great distances from it, thanks to the high elasticity of that cord. When the medium's spirit has left his body its place is taken by a strange spirit, which proceeds to deliver its messages. With a clairvoyant this is not possible, for in his case no strange spirit can enter, seeing that his own is still united with the whole physical od of his body and that, in consequence, no space is left available for occupation by a strange spirit.

"In the case of the clairvoyant therefore, we have a close union which is maintained between his own spirit and the od of his body, and in that of a 'deep-trance medium' an almost complete liberation of the spirit from the physical od. With the clairvoyant, it is *his own spirit* which tries to see and hear; with the deep-trance medium, the medium's spirit surrenders its place to *another spirit,* allowing the same to manifest itself through the medium's body by means of the utilization of the physical od remaining therein. There are, however, clairvoyants who are also 'trance mediums', be it of the 'part-trance' or the 'deep-trance' type.

"You will readily understand that the spirit-world has varied and difficult work to perform in educating and perfecting the mediums. You can, of course, form no conception of what it costs the spirit-world — to use a worldly term —, to train mediums. How much power, how many precious remedies are consumed in the process! Spirit-operations, often much more difficult and serious than those undertaken by your surgeons upon terrestrial human bodies, are necessary. Many mediums have inner defects which must first be cured before their training for the part can be begun.

"We have our instruments and medicines, just as your surgeons have theirs for the operations which they undertake, for with us there is a spirit-counterpart for everything that you possess in material shape. It goes without saying that we spirits are never ill and never require operations or treatment. We use our ample knowledge and resources only on behalf of the incarnate creation, to cure men and beasts and to educate mediums to serve as vehicles for communication with the spirit-world. We, too, have specialists in all departments. We have our chief and assistant physicians, and help trained in the most varied duties. We have a great store of spirit-instruments, anesthetics, stimulants and medicines, all of which find employment in the education of the mediums.

"Consequently, the number of spirits which take part in the training of a medium to serve the good cause, is very great. Just as a definite duty is assigned to each assistant at an operation conducted by human beings, so, while a medium is being trained, each spirit connected with the process has its special work to do. Everything is beautifully systematized. Your mediums while undergoing their course of preparation are therefore in good hands, provided that they place themselves at the disposal of the *good* spirits, that they shun all evil and walk in the way of the Lord.

"No one need therefore be alarmed at witnessing what goes on during the training of a medium, particularly during that of a deep-trance medium. Everything follows fixed laws. The good spirits are the best friends you have, and you have nothing whatever to fear from them.

"The training of mediums is accomplished most speedily at the so-called 'spiritistic seances'.

"On this account and in view of the great importance of such training I shall go into great detail as to the way in which these *seances* should be held. At the same time I shall give you the reasons for the particulars which must be observed on such occasions. I shall also explain to you the things that happen at these *seances* in the course of a medium's training.

"When a group of seekers after God and the Truth has decided to unite in an effort to get into communication with the good spirit-world, the first thing to be determined upon is the place at which its meetings are to be held *regularly*. This place should be chosen so as to ensure the greatest possible privacy. You too, when conducting the more important of your worldly affairs, are careful to provide against intrusion, and this is the more essential when the question at issue is the establishment of a purely spiritual bond, which would be much more susceptible to disturbing influences than would any worldly undertaking.

"The best time for such meetings is in the evening after eight o'clock, when the day's work with its worldly cares and worries is over, and people can devote themselves to calm reflection.

"Generally speaking, *seances* should not be held oftener than twice a week.

"Before the meeting, the premises should be thoroughly aired to rid them of all vapor, tobacco-smoke and stale air, for the odic power of the participants is greatly lowered by vitiated atmosphere, and in consequence, the odic radiation, which is so important to the spirit-world, is obstructed.

"To keep the air pure a large bowl of fresh water is placed in the room; this absorbs a part of the air which becomes contaminated in the course of the *seance*.

"Upon the table at which the participants are to be seated are placed for each a few sheets of paper and a soft pencil.

"Immediately before the opening of the *seance* those present must not converse on material subjects, but must concentrate their thoughts and dismiss all purely worldly matters from their minds. Remember, it is for the purpose of serving God that they have met!

"The place chosen by each member at the first meeting should be regularly occupied by him thereafter, because the odic radiation, which varies with each individual, must gradually be brought into a certain equilibrium. For this reason those present should seat themselves alternately according to sex, for the od of the male is preeminently positive, while that of the female is negative, and to offset one with the other is the best way of establishing a balance. However, this alternate seating arrangement is not imperative; it merely facilitates the balancing of the od for producing an effective current. A change in the order of seating after this has been adopted should be made only in response to an order to that effect from the spirit-world, transmitted by a trained medium or by a medium undergoing training.

"If there is a musical instrument like a piano or a harmonium in the assembly-room, it is best that the meeting be opened with a religious anthem, sung to instrumental accompaniment. For want of anything better, the phonographic record of a hymn or other solemn air may be played. The singing and playing of a beautiful song inspire the hearts of the hearers with harmony and solemnity and turn their thoughts to higher things. Such music is also a good safeguard against the influence of the world of evil spirits which will try to force their way into the meeting for the purpose of obstructing and disturbing its efforts, since evil is discord and does not feel at home in surroundings in which the harmony of lofty thought and sentiment finds expression in song and words. That was why, as the Bible relates, the evil spirit departed from Saul whenever David played the harp before him and sang psalms to the Lord.

"After the singing is over someone present must pronounce a simple prayer of his own composing. Should he be too bashful to deliver this without the aid of notes, he may write it down beforehand and read it aloud with due reverence. Everyone who attends these meetings should take his turn at offering prayer.

"Following the prayer, someone must read a passage from the Old or the New Testament, which must be discussed by those present. The aggregate time given to the singing, the prayer, the reading and the discussion should be about half an hour.

"At the termination of the discussion, the participants join hands, the light being dimmed as much as possible, each person laying his right hand over the left hand of his neighbor. This is called 'forming a chain', and is necessary in order that the odic force of each individual may be united into a single current, just as separate lengths of wire must be connected whenever it is desired to pass an electric current over a line. It must always be borne in mind that the ability of the spirit-world to perform its work at a *seance* depends on the strength of the odic current, and that the efficiency of the od is greatly enhanced by dimming the lights.

"The formation of the chain has also a highly symbolic significance, for, just as those present join hands and thereby become linked outwardly into one unit, so they are held to be of one heart and *one* soul among each other. They must love one another, help one another forgive each others' faults and banish from their hearts everything that might disturb the internal harmony of the group.

"It was for the reasons I have cited that the early Christians used to join hands when they gathered together for worship. They thus sought to typify unity of mind, but primarily they strove to create a powerful odic current in order to enable the good spirit-world to deliver its messages.

"The 'chain' should be maintained for twelve or fifteen minutes. During this time everyone must strive to keep his mind concentrated, to exclude therefrom all worldly subjects and to harbor nothing but good thoughts. To this end he may engage in introspection, review his own past life, his shortcomings, his bearing toward God and his fellow men, his sins of omission, and the like. He should give thanks to God for all blessings received, praise and exalt Him and reverently beseech Him to be allowed to converse with the good spirit-world. He may include in his prayer anything conducive to his spiritual welfare.

"When the time allotted to the 'chain' has elapsed, the leader of the assembly causes the same to be broken. Each person now takes up the pencil before him and lays his hand lightly on the sheet of paper at his place. When doing this he must have the strength of mind not to write of his own volition, all the while keeping his hand relaxed so that it will yield to any motion which may be imparted by the spirit-world.

"At the first few *seances* the available odic force is usually very small in amount and the obstacles encountered by the participants are very serious. Everything is still too new to them. They find it difficult to keep their thoughts collected and fall into a state of *tense* expectation. It is precisely this *tensity* which militates most of all against the liberation of their od, as I shall have occasion to speak of presently. As for the rest, the participants are like a new, unused magnet, which develops strength only through repeated use.

"However, it often happens that the mediumistic development of a participant is much further advanced than he himself realizes. In such instances it may be that the workings of the spirit-world are manifested at the very first *seance*.. He may feel a pulling at or a stiffening of the hand which holds the pencil and which then begins to move. He must not pose the slightest resistance to this impulse, but must allow the hand to yield. At the first few *seances* nothing more convincing may be executed with the pencil by the spirit-world than some straight lines, curves, circles or other elementary attempts at writing, before a letter, a word, or a sentence is formed. This is because the odic force released by those present is not yet powerful enough, but primarily, because the odic power of the medium in the making is still in its initial stage. Practice in writing will progressively strengthen this power. If the workings of the spirit-world are manifested in this or in some other way, the great obstacle, originating in the tense attitude of those present will now make itself felt. They usually watch with the greatest intentness what is happening to the other person. Tense expectancy, however, always represses the odic radiation of a person, just as someone who is listening intently involuntarily holds his breath. This diminishes the odic current and adds to the difficulties of the spirit-world, for even the best engineer cannot make his engine run properly if deprived of all or of a large part of his power.

"Fear, fright, distrust, doubt and all other forms of inward opposition exert upon the odic current an effect as unfavorable as that produced by mental tension. Whoever, harboring such feelings, takes part in a spiritistic meeting, not only fails to release any odic force himself, but interrupts the current liberated by the others. Hence mediums can tell at once when there is someone present who acts like an extraneous, obstructive body, and are justified in demanding the exclusion of such a person until he has adopted a different mental attitude.

"Whenever, therefore, at spiritistic gatherings, there is a lack of harmony of thought and feeling, there can be no homogeneous odic current, and the successful outcome of the meeting becomes problematical, if not indeed impossible.

This explains why scientific committees which experiment with mediums often meet with little or no success. The mediums, who, as we know, are the sources of power for the manifestations of the spirit-beings, feel discouraged and nervous when surrounded by an atmosphere of distrust. They realize all the while that their investigators consider them capable of committing fraud and that they have no faith in the thing itself. Sensations of this kind are bound to check the release of energy on the part of the mediums, if not to prevent it altogether.

"That is a law of Nature, and, incidentally, it is the same law as that which causes the blood to forsake the cheeks of a person seized with fear, and to rush to his inner organs, making him turn pale. What happens is, that the person's od as it retreats inward, draws the blood to his heart.

"How unjustly do your scientists therefore so often judge of a medium's failure to meet their tests! They would do better to consider the obstacles placed in the way of mediums as sources of power for the spirit-world, more particularly by the scientists themselves, who need only remove these obstacles in order to obtain a satisfactory demonstration of the ability of spirits to make themselves manifest.

"It is true that the *good* spirit-world very rarely engages in communications which do not deal exclusively with the purposes of good, but which serve merely to satisfy scientific inquiry, if not, indeed, sheer curiosity. The latter is the province in which the *low* spirit-world is especially active and in which, unfortunately it only too often causes a great deal of harm.

"Those who attend good spiritistic conferences should constantly be reminded that it is their duty to banish all doubt and distrust from their hearts and to await what may happen with the utmost patience and composure.

"Whenever, during the course of a *seance* a person feels an inner impulse to write down a thought which arises within him, he must do so. In time he will learn to distinguish between his own thoughts and those which are inspired, for the thoughts instilled by the spirit-world will force themselves upon you insistently as you try to dismiss your own, and will keep on recurring, try as you will to disregard them.

"If anyone present should feel a certain giddiness in his brain or a heaviness in his limbs, if his head is turned from side to side or if his body should perform motions inexplicable to him, it is a sign that the spirit-world has taken him in hand, These sympathetic motions of the body are the most marked in persons who become 'deep-trance mediums'. The back and forth, up and down contortions of the body are connected with the release of the spirit of the medium in the making, from his body and from his physical od. The physical symptoms exhibited on these occasions are often alarming to those who witness them, for they are a sort of death-struggle, though unattended by any pain to the medium. But all alarm on their account is groundless, for everything happens according to established laws.

"The most difficult period of a deep-trance mediums training is the stage of what is known as the 'semi-trance' or 'part-trance'. His own spirit has not yet been completely liberated and has not left his body, while a strange spirit is already making use of the same for its manifestations. The medium's spirit, being still present, hears the words spoken through the medium by the strange spirit, and thereby the medium is easily led to believe that the words and thoughts uttered are his own. He thus incurs the danger of misunderstanding the entire proceeding and of regarding the manifestations as so much self-deception. It may easily happen, also, *that the medium's own spirit breaks into the communications being delivered by the strange spirit,* a proceeding which naturally awakens doubt among the others present.

"It might seem at first glance that the strange spirit would do better not to attempt to deliver its messages until the medium's training was complete, thereby avoiding unpleasant consequences like those described, but the reasons which impel the strange spirit to communicate through a medium who has reached only the 'part-trance' stage are so weighty, that it will sooner accept all the disagreeable features enumerated than postpone its communications until the medium has completed his training. For it is precisely during the early stages, when no fully trained medium is available at the meetings, that the participants thereat require instruction and elucidation on too many points to permit of postponement until a later date. So much that is of the utmost importance to them depends on what they are taught at the very beginning, that the imperfect manner in which the messages are transmitted is regarded as a much smaller evil than would be a total neglect of instruction.

"The transition from the 'part-trance' to the 'deep-trance' stage is generally of relatively short duration *provided that the medium will take pains to progress within himself and to combat his human failings.* As soon as he has reached the 'full-trance' phase, a medium is entirely unaware of what the strange spirit is saying or doing.

"The most serious obstacles of all are the ones put by the evil spirit-world in the way of those who are seeking in good faith to communicate with the Beyond, for in this case as in all others, Evil does its best to prevent the accomplishment of Good. It neglects no means of trying to divert the seekers from their purpose, beginning by instilling into them the idea that the whole question is one of self-deception, auto-suggestion or hypnosis, and doing its best to dissuade them from engaging in matters which will expose them to ridicule.

"The evil ones will have accomplished much if they succeed in arousing serious doubts in one person or another as to the truth, genuineness and worth of the cause. For this purpose they also often exploit the most trivial superficial pretexts, especially minor errors and shortcomings, which are bound to happen as long as men are human.

"The evil spirit-world likewise tries to terrify persons being educated as clairvoyants, by showing them the most abhorrent monstrosities, grimacing likenesses of the Devil and other sights of that sort, in order to induce them thereby to discontinue their training and to abandon the cause.

"Naturally, people who devote themselves to a *low form* of spiritism are spared these demonstrations, for spiritism of this type is a connecting link with Evil, which consequently has no inducement to divert men from its pursuit.

"It is when the evil spirits are active that all participants, and more especially the mediums, are put to the test. A personal test is applied to everybody, and always at his weakest point. Only those who can meet this test are granted the gifts of mediumship. Whoever fails, will either abandon his search altogether, or fall wholly under the sway of the evil spirits. On this account all should pray for help and strength, in order that they may resist the temptations presented by the evil spirits.

"As to the *duration of the seances,* these should not be unduly prolonged. Generally speaking, one hour should be enough. As soon as the spirits manifest themselves through the medium, they usually decide when the meeting ought to be adjourned. For the Lord is a God who loves order, and His spirits are spirits that love order. This is made evident in a wondrous manner at all meetings held under God's protection, by the invariable attendance of a *controlling spirit* which conducts everything. It decides what the participants must do to facilitate the training of the medium and tells them how to go about to promote their own progress, what faults to correct and what virtues to cultivate. The controlling spirit often decides upon the passages from the Holy Writ which are to be read at the beginning of the *seance* and occasionally alters the order of seating of the participants as may be required for obtaining an increase of odic energy. It furthermore determines what spirits are to be admitted into the mediums, the nature of the messages they may deliver and how long they may stay in the medium. It may also admit evil spirits into him, so that the other persons present shall come to know such spirits by their dispositions and actions, and thereby acquire practical experience in how to comport themselves in their presence. Nothing, however, pleases the controlling spirit more than to admit spirits which are in deep distress but whose disposition remains fairly good, into the mediums, in order to give these spirits an opportunity of being advised, and directed to turn to God, by those present. This is a great kindness which those in attendance at such meetings can thus do to their suffering brethren in the Other World. Sometimes the controlling spirit will later on explain its reasons for the admission of the various spirits.

"At every meeting the controlling spirit is the first of the spirits to arrive, *and always with a greeting that makes a reference to God.* It is the spiritual guide of those gathered together, whom it admonishes, warns, criticises and instructs. In particular, both during the course of the medium's training and afterwards, it emphasizes the need of an ever greater belief and trust in God.

"The closer man's soul approaches to God, the greater his share in the power that emanates from Him, and the greater and more wonderful the gifts which the Lord bestows upon him for the benefit of his fellow men. Thus the aim of every *seance* in which God's spirits are active is: "Nearer my God to Thee!"

"In the early stages of the medium's education, when the first written messages from the Beyond are received, it is usually only your departed kin and friends who are allowed to communicate with you, provided that they are on the road to God in the

Beyond and do not belong to the evil spirits. They too will earnestly exhort you to believe in God, and will not weary of telling you that in communicating with the good spirits, you have chosen the right path. They will also express their regret that this path was not pointed out to them while they were among the dwellers on earth.

"As the training makes further progress, the messages from departed relatives and friends cease *entirely,* and the higher spirit-beings make themselves manifest. *This, however, presupposes that the participants strive for spiritual perfection and that their intentions are pure.* If anyone who attends such gatherings should be lacking in good intention or should lose interest, and if he should fail to heed repeated admonitions addressed to him by the good spirits, he will be excluded from future gatherings by order of the controlling spirit. This is necessary, not only because he himself is making no progress, but because he is a detriment to the rest, forming, as he does, a rallying-point for the evil spirits which follow him to the meeting and exert their baneful influence upon the others present. Furthermore, the odic force is adversely affected by the discord which he introduces into the assembly, as a result of his inward obstructive attitude.

"Gatherings held for the purpose of communicating with the spirit-world without the supervision of one of God's spirits, do not enjoy His sanction. They may have all the external features of a divine service; nevertheless, the entire trend which spirit-communication takes under these conditions will not be toward God. They contribute nothing toward the purification and uplift of the soul. Wherever the divinely appointed control is lacking is not the place for the spirits assigned to the service of those who seek salvation. *To save the souls of the communicants is the only lawful purpose of spiritistic meetings.*

"Therefore, although many of the so-called 'spiritist churches' of today go through the outward form of offering prayer and singing hymns at their gatherings, the real object of what takes place at these is far removed from serving any divine ends.

"The persons acting as leaders or collaborators of these churches are generally gifted with clairvoyance, clairaudience and clairsentience, and through these gifts are able to communicate with the spirits which accompany the members of their congregations. The odic radiation of these spirits establishes contact with that of the mediumistic servitors, male and female, of these churches, who thereby not only obtain a personal impression of the spirits present and of their relations to the persons whom they attend, but are enabled to receive the messages brought by the spirits for the good of their friends among the living.

"The chief feature of these ecclesiastical assemblies is the delivery of messages relating almost exclusively to worldly fortune and trouble and to *material success,* and this is the principal inducement for the attendance of the majority of the participants. They look upon such churches as so many information bureaus, where, on payment of a given admission-fee, they can learn something about their own worldly future from the spirits of departed friends or relatives, through the clairvoyants connected with the church. Because of this, the leaders of churches of this type are careful to see to it that no one shall leave the service without having received a message of the kind mentioned.

"Inasmuch as God's spirits keep away from meetings of this character and hence exercise no control over them, the low spirit-world is left free to do as it pleases. Even if the spirits which do attend them are not necessarily evil ones, the communications delivered are of a nature which can be of small benefit to the soul.

"If it should happen further that the clairvoyants who officiate at these churches are also 'part-trance mediums', they act like open windows through which the low spirit-world can enter at will, since there is no controlling spirit on hand to keep them out or to maintain order. Hence the spirit-messages are jumbled together in a fashion which cannot fail to be repugnant and which is bound to reflect most unfavorably on good, divinely-sanctioned spirit-communication, for because of the religious cast given to the service at these churches, the impression is created that spiritism as it is practiced there is of *the kind that is pleasing to God.*

"The leaders of these churches therefore have a heavy responsibility toward God for anything that may happen at their meetings. It is their duty to devote their gifts entirely to the service of God, unselfishly and regardless of worldly considerations. They must pray for 'spirit-control', which will gladly be granted them, and having received it, *they must obey it implicitly.* If they will do this, their meetings will become divine service in fact and will inure to the edification and the spiritual welfare of their congregations. Then the higher spirit-world will become active and the low spirits will be denied access.

"If the meetings are held according to my directions, they will bring you untold blessings, much joy and true peace of soul.

"Every meeting must be closed with a brief prayer of thanksgiving spoken by the presiding member, and, if possible, with a song.

"The training of a medium and the other particulars relating to communication with the good spirits may however be carried out in other ways than at '*communal seances*'. Any individual may, *by himself alone,* devote a definite time, such as half an hour or even less daily, or perhaps several times a week, to mental concentration. When so engaged he must proceed in the same manner as that prescribed for *seances* held in common. He must begin with a brief prayer, read a passage from the Scriptures and reflect upon it. Thereupon he must take a pencil and lay his hand on a sheet of paper lying before him, and wait patiently, in a state of perfect relaxation. If he is impelled to write down thoughts which are very insistently urged upon him, he should commit them to paper. If his hand is set in motion by an external force, he should yield to its impulse.

"At the end of the time which he has allowed himself for his devotions in private, he should conclude these with a prayer. He may rest assured that from the first moment at which he seeks contact with the good spirit-world, it will begin its work on him and create all the conditions pre-requisite to such contact. In fact, this work will often be begun as soon as a person turns his thoughts seriously to this subject. It often happens that mediumistically gifted persons experience what to them is an inexplicable sensation during the first serious conversation about the spirit-world and its contact with mankind in which they take part. This sensation arises from the fact that the spirits of the Beyond, of whom some are always hovering about you, immediately begin to exert their influence on such persons who, on account of their mediumistic tendencies, are highly susceptible to any odic action on the part of the spirit-world. But until a person knows at least something of the possibility of communicating with the spirit-world it would serve no purpose for the spirits about him to begin to work on him, and not only that, but it might have very unpleasant practical consequences, for neither he nor any of those about him would be capable of understanding the mediumistic symptoms which he would develop. He would be thought to be suffering from some nervous disorder and would be put under the care of a physician or sent to a sanatorium. Hence the good spirit-world begins its work only when there is some prospect of success, but not otherwise.

"In connection with these teachings I shall answer a question which many persons ask, reasonably enough: *'Does spiritism have an injurious effect on the health of mediums or of persons who frequent spiritistic seances?'* My answer to this is: *'No'*, and *'Yes'*.

"If a meeting at which spirits appear is held *under God's auspices;* if everything done at that meeting is done in His name; if you will *put yourselves under His protection,* and if you will *love Him* and *seek only what is good,* contact with the spirit-world *can never harm you. On the contrary,* you will be strengthened *physically* and *spiritually,* and above all, the mediums who fall into a deep trance will be benefitted, because sleep, which you require to refresh you, is not needed by them while they are in that state. All this, of course, holds true only provided you are serving the good cause and keep the evil spirits at a distance. So long as mediums are in a state of trance, their bodies are resting and are thereby invigorated. Even though we, the good spirits, may be at work on them or through them, they are in no way harmed. On the contrary, they enjoy physical repose, and feel better at the end of a *seance* than they felt before it. The odic energy taken from the mediums and other participants at a *seance* is replaced by the good spirit-world with fresh od. Furthermore, during a medium's training, any internal defects of his which might interfere with or prevent a deep-trance state are removed through the good offices of the spirit-world, so that the medium in question is in a better state of health after he has been trained as a deep-trance medium than he was previously thereto.

"On the other hand, *spiritism is certainly injurious* if, in its pursuit, *God is disregarded; if everything is done under evil influences;* if, indeed, *amusement is sought from such contact with evil* and *if prayer is neglected.* In this way, step by step, *you fall into evil ways,* all the worse because not only are you led by the evil spirits to stray from the path of truth and righteousness, but because you suffer serious bodily harm, since the odic force taken from you by those spirits is never again replaced by them. In consequence the health of all participants and particularly that of the mediums is greatly impaired and in time, utterly ruined. There is, therefore, a grain of truth in the popular belief that he who makes a league with the Devil must pledge his own life as a forfeit, for his odic force is gradually sapped by evil and his body loses its power to retain life. Many mediums who engage in the lower forms of spiritism suffer mental and physical breakdown.

"Hence spiritism is injurious and dangerous only, if followed not for the sake of learning the divine truth and of growing in inward grace, but merely to satisfy curiosity and a craving for the marvellous, or to obtain information relating to material affairs or of purely scientific interest.

"Therefore, warn your fellow-men against participating in spirit-communication *which serves no higher ends.* Instruct them in spirit-communication of a good, divinely sanctioned nature, for this should be practiced by everyone. It is man's only path to the truth, and is the shortest road that leads to God.

"But even those who have not fought their way through to a belief in God should practice spiritism in its good form, if they have honestly resolved to accept the truth as soon as it is convincingly presented to them. Truth-seekers who follow this path in such a frame of mind will find the truth, and that freedom that is the heritage of the children of God. They will come to know the true meaning of religion. It was of such that Christ said, '*Seek and you will find.*'

"Those who have not yet learned to believe in God should nevertheless pray to Him, if only conditionally. They may adapt their prayer to the immediate exigencies of the occasion. The following supplication may be uttered by an unbeliever, if his intention is good and if he is ready to accept the truth:

'Oh God! If it is true that Thou dost exist, I pray to Thee with all my heart to guide me to the right path. Amen.'

"His prayer will surely be granted, for God is merciful to all who mean well. As to the particular religious denomination to which a man may belong, this has no bearing whatever upon his attendance at spiritistic meetings of the right kind.

Biblical Accounts of Mediums and of Schools for Mediums

'I raised up sons of yours as prophets and young men to be Nazarites.' *Amos 2:11.*

"THE people of today seem to find something strange and new in the idea of the possibility of communication between spirits and mankind. This is because you read the Bible superficially and do no reflect upon its teachings as you should. If you did, you would inevitably ask yourselves as you read: 'How did all these things happen? In what way could they have been brought about? What am I to think of them? How am I to explain them'?

"Seeing that the very opening chapters of the Bible relate that God conversed with mortals, that He spoke with Adam and Eve, with Cain and Abel, with Abraham, Isaac, Jacob and Moses, you, as rational beings, should at least make the attempt to form a clear conception of the manner in which this was done. They to whom God's spirits spoke in those days, were human beings like yourselves. They had their sins and shortcomings as you have yours. The laws of Nature which governed their life on earth were no different from those of today. God and God's spirits are the same today as they were then. And as you read further and find that there was daily intercourse between the people of Israel and the spirit-realm of the Beyond; that every man could ask counsel of God and would be answered; that the leaders of the people undertook nothing without the advice of the good spirit-world, your own common sense should tell you that communication with the spirit-world *is possible*. And if it *is possible*, and was maintained for thousands of years by mankind in the past, why should it be denied to the men of today?

"It is true that you seem to believe that it rests entirely with the spirit-world to communicate with you or not, and that the same is able, of its own accord and at its own will, to bring about such contact, without any help from you. You may think that the spirits are free to visit men at any time and at all times, and that all that is required of man is to admit the spirits and to listen to what messages they may bring. And since you see no evidence today of the spirit-communication of old, which plays so important a part in the Bible, you have come to the conclusion that the Beyond has definitely abandoned all communication with the world of the living. This is a lamentable error. On the contrary, the good spirit-world is only too anxious today to come to you and is ready to cross the bridge leading from the Beyond to the Here. *But you must lend a hand in the building of that bridge.* It was true in the past also, that mankind on its part had to fulfill all the conditions required to enable the spirit-world to communicate with it. The peoples of old were familiar with these conditions, and observed them accordingly.

"Nowadays when you read in the Bible the description of the phenomena that accompanied the manifestations of spirits, you think that these phenomena were mere external trappings, having no connection with the spirit-communications themselves. Do you honestly believe that there was nothing more than foolery and idle outward show in the fact that the angel of the Lord spoke to Moses from the 'bush which burned with fire' and to the Israelites from the pillar of cloud, or that he could have made himself understood without the aid of that flame and that pillar of od? Do you by any chance imagine that God was diverting Himself when He said to Moses: 'Lo, I come to thee in a thick cloud, that the people may hear when I speak with thee'? and that He could have increased the carrying-power of His voice without increasing the cloud of od? Or do you believe that the great cloud that settled upon Mount Sinai amidst thunder and the sound of trumpets, was also merely outward show, and that these sounds could have been produced without the cloud? And when David besought Abiathar, the priest, to bring him the ephod with the breastplate of judgment, so that he might consult God and receive His answer, was that too only foolery? Or were the flames of the thorny bush, the pillar of cloud, the breastplate of judgment, and the other things with which you meet in the Bible as you read of the intercourse of the spirit-world with mankind, not rather the conductors imperatively required for telephonic conversation from the Beyond to the Here.

"As a matter of fact, they constituted the bridge over which God's spirits travelled to reach the people of those times. Without that bridge, they could not have come. The material contributed by terrestrial beings was odic force, which became visible to all in the shape of a flame during the burning of the thorny bush, and in the case of the pillar of cloud as odic vapor; by the same token, odic energy was required for the many materializations of spirits into incarnate form, recorded in the chronicles of those days. An adequate amount of the same force had to be available to those spirits which indicated the letters on the breastplate of judgment forming the words which constituted the answer sent from the Beyond.

"The sources of odic force for the spirit-communications recorded in the Bible were, then as now, the 'mediums'.

"In the Old Testament you will find a great deal written of 'prophets' and 'schools of prophets'. What meaning does this convey to you? Do you imagine that the gift of prophecy can be learned at school, as a scientific education is acquired? In your modern parlance you use the word 'prophet' to designate a person who can foretell the future, and according to that connotation it would be natural to assume that it was possible to acquire at the ancient schools of prophets, the faculty of predicting events to come.

"That is a misconception of the meaning of the terms 'prophet' and 'schools for prophets' as used in the Bible.

"A 'prophet' is a person from whom not his own, but a strange spirit, speaks. It was in this sense that the Apostle Paul wrote of 'the spirits of the prophets'. *(1st Corinthians 14 : 32.)*

"If the spirits which speak through a prophet are truthful ones, he is called a 'true' or 'real' prophet. If, however, they are lying, or, in other words, evil spirits, he is branded in the Bible as a 'false' prophet.

"What were called 'prophets' in Biblical times are today known as 'mediums'. The choice of words is immaterial; it is the substance that counts. All prominent characters of the Old and the New Testament were great 'mediums', and although the mediumistic conditions under which they surrendered their odic force to the spirit-world are not minutely described in the Holy Writ, they are plainly indicated in not a few of the accounts recorded therein.

"*Abraham was a medium.* The state of trance into which he passed to enable him to release his od during his intercourse with the Beyond can be clearly recognized in one passage: 'When the sun was going down, a deep sleep fell upon Abraham; a great horror of a darkness came over him. . . When the sun went down, and it turned dark, there was a smoking furnace, and a blazing torch that passed between the pieces'. *(Genesis 15 : 12, 17.)*

"The 'deep sleep' was not a normal sleep, but what you call

today a 'mediumistic sleep', in which the medium's od is set free to be used by the spirit-world for its manifestations. The 'horror' and the 'great darkness' mentioned here, which not seldom overcome a medium serving the good cause, are produced by the evil spirit-world in its attempts to frustrate the messages brought by the good spirits, seeing that the sensation of fear will interfere with the surrender of any medium's od, and make the delivery of spirit-tidings impossible. But previous to this the forces of evil had already tried to exert their pernicious influence upon Abraham. When, at the Lord's command, he had slaughtered beasts and divided them, 'birds of prey' descended upon the carcasses, 'and Abraham drove them away'. The sacrifice had been offered with the object of opening up a source of od supplementary to that of Abraham, namely the od of the slain beasts. What the Bible here speaks of as 'birds of prey' were not actually birds, but evil spirits materialized as such. Only in that shape were they able to carry off the pieces of flesh. Now you can understand what they had in mind. They first tried to choke the source of od that had been opened by the slaughter of the beasts, and next, to check the flow of Abraham's own od by inspiring him with terror. The time chosen for Abraham's mediumistic activities was after dark, because, according to the familiar laws, light and heat have an adverse effect on the required condensation of od. As you already know, the *'smoking furnace'* and the *'flaming torch'* mentioned in the passage I have quoted, were odic manifestations.

"*Moses too was a medium.* It was the od liberated by him that shone in the bush like a flame, his own od being supplemented by that of the herd which he was tending. This incident also occurred at night. The odic condensation took place in a bush whose branches acted somewhat like a screen to hold the odic mass together, much as this was effected by the screen of the 'tent of testimony' or is accomplished by the 'cabinets' used in the spiritistic *seances* of today. The bush also possessed od of its own, which united with the other od.

"In very ancient times 'mediums' were called *'seers'* because they generally possessed the gift of clairvoyance in addition to their other mediumistic qualifications. The word 'prophet' is of a later coinage.

"Such 'seers' or 'prophets' were found everywhere.

"When Saul, in the company of his servant, sought his father's asses which had strayed, the servant said: 'There is a man of

God in this city, a man who is highly respected. Whatever he says is sure to come true; perhaps he can tell us something about the errand we are on'. And at this point the Biblical account adds by way of explanation: 'Formerly in Israel, when a man went to consult God, he said: Come, and let us go to the 'seer'; for he that is now called a prophet was formerly called a 'seer'. *(1st Samuel 9 : 5-9.)* In this way Saul and his servant happened to go to the house of Samuel.

"Samuel was not only a medium himself, but was the head of the 'school of mediums' in Ramah. In those days such institutions were called 'schools of prophets'.

"When Saul was returning homeward and had come to Gibeah, he was met by a band of 'mediums' who were in a state of trance, and out of whom spirits were sounding the praises of the Lord. Saul straightway fell into the same state, 'and a spirit of the Lord came mightily upon him'.

"Your translators of the Bible who do not grasp the significance of this state, render the phrase 'and the Spirit of the Lord came mightily upon him and he prophesied', an expression from which the reader will find it hard to get much meaning. It was not Saul's spirit nor those of the mediums he had met that were inspired; the manifestations were those of good spirits from the Beyond who had taken possession of Saul and of the others. For this purpose it was not necessary for the mediums to have been in a 'deep-trance', for what you would now call a 'part-trance' or a 'semi-trance' would have been quite sufficient.

"The Bible further relates that David fled to Samuel at Ramah, where both of them lived at the 'house of the prophets' or, in other words, at the 'school of mediums'. When the messengers sent thither by Saul to take David arrived, Samuel was engaged in a *seance* with the mediums who at that moment were in a state of trance. Your version of the Bible reads: 'When they saw the company of the prophets prophesying, with Samuel at their head, a spirit of God came over the messengers of Saul, till they too prophesied'. 'And when it was told Saul, he sent other messengers, and they also prophesied. And Saul sent messengers again the third time, and they also prophesied. Then he went also to Ramah, and a spirit of God came upon him also, and he went on and prophesied, until he came to Naioth in Ramah. And he also stripped off his clothes, and he also prophesied before Samuel, and lay down naked all that day and all that night. Wherefore they say, Is Saul also among the prophets?' *(1st Samuel 19 : 18-24.)*

"There is much in this account that requires explanation. The circumstance that all of Saul's messengers fell into a 'trance' so quickly can be accounted for by the fact that they were highly mediumistic. And in a great and powerful odic current, such as is present at any gathering of mediums, developed or in the process of development, like the meeting at Samuel's school for mediums at Ramah, it was not difficult for the spirit-world to bring about a state of 'semi-trance' in persons mediumistically inclined.

"Saul himself was a medium, and hence in his case no outside odic force was required to enable him to go into a semi-trance. For this reason he had entered this state while still on his way to Ramah.

"You need not be shocked at the idea of the mediums at the school in Ramah sitting about, or, according to the custom of the times, lying about scantily clad. Even today, mediums dress as lightly as possible when engaged in *seances,* as everything must be done to prevent them from developing a great amount of heat, since heat, as you know, has a disturbing and retarding effect on odic condensation. For this reason Saul lay down naked. When it is stated that he lay there all that day and all that night, this does not mean that he was in a 'trance' during the entire period. He was kept lying down for that length of time, because it was the good spirit-world's last effort to bring him back unto God from Whom he had become estranged by his disobedience. He was no longer in touch with the good spirit-world but had fallen under the spell of an evil spirit. He had in fact come to Ramah on that very day for the purpose of capturing and killing David. All this was now held up before his eyes as a last appeal in the various messages brought by the spirits of God, speaking through the mediums present. Samuel himself, by earnest expostulation, did his utmost to save the king whom he had anointed, from the destruction which threatened. This was the purpose also of the various acts of worship which Samuel performed in the presence of Saul and to which the Bible makes no reference: he sought to touch the king's heart and to induce him to retrace his steps.

"*Divine service* was indeed the most important part of the curriculum at the 'schools of mediums'. It was the aim to bring the mediums being educated there or 'student prophets' as they were called in those days, heart and soul into the closest communion with God. Unshakable belief and abiding trust in the Lord formed the foundation upon which the mediumistic acquirements of the students were built. In this way they were designed to become qualified to serve their fellow men as worthy instruments of God and His world of spirits, for the dangers to which mediums are exposed were the same in those times as the ones which exist today.

"The greatest of these dangers, then as in all ages, was the craving for honors and money. Mediums were highly regarded. Not only were the reigning princes eager to have numerous mediums in their retinues, but many well-to-do families kept a medium whom they called 'priest', in their employ for consulting the spirits. These mediums received valuable presents and their living was provided for them. Most of them were what would be called today 'planchette-mediums', who consulted the spirit-world by means of a 'breastplate of judgment' made in imitation of the breastplate of judgment used in the tabernacle.

"You will find this statement of mine confirmed in the Book of Judges. There it is related that a man named Micah restored to his mother the silver which he had taken from her, and that she caused a part of the metal to be made into a 'graven image' and a 'molten image' which were installed in the house of Micah, who consecrated one of his sons to serve him as a 'priest'.

"He furthermore induced a Levite from Bethlehem to serve him in the same capacity, saying unto him: 'Stay with me, be my father and priest; I will give you a pound of silver every year, a suit of clothes and your food. So the Levite agreed to live with the man . . .' *(Judges 17 : 10, 11.)* What appears in your versions as a 'graven image' and a 'molten image' were the two parts of a 'planchette'.

"The mediums, being human, exerted themselves to remain in the good graces of those from whom they made their living, and therein lay the real source of danger. In their anxiety to transmit no tidings except such as would be agreeable to their employers, they sometimes did not hesitate to conceal unpleasant truths from them and to utter falsehood instead. By so doing they became 'lying prophets', thus severing their connection with the good spirit-world and becoming instruments of evil, even though they sought to maintain appearances by invoking the name of the Lord when engaged in their mediumistic work.

"More especially, mediums in the service of powerful temporal rulers were prone to yield to this temptation, as shown by the story of King Ahab. *(1st Kings, 22.)* There you read of four hundred mediums who conspire to tell the king nothing but agreeable news, a conspiracy which grew out of their own evil leanings. They thus cut themselves adrift from the good spirit-world, realizing as they did that they were making themselves the instruments of lying spirits. Naturally they feared that their faleshood would be exposed, should the king consult a truthful medium, and therefore, when Ahab summoned into his presence Micaiah, a medium in the service of the good spirit-world, the other mediums sent a messenger to intercept Micaiah with instructions to persuade him to enter into the plot, Micaiah however, refused to connive at the proceeding and warned Ahab of impending disaster, whereupon one of the lying prophets present 'stepped forward and struck Micaiah on the cheek saying: 'Which way went a spirit of the Lord from me to speak through you?' Here you have an instance of an utterly corrupt prophethood, which did not scruple to resort to falsehood and deceit for the sake of riches and worldly honors, and which, nevertheless, gave the impression of being an instrument of the Lord. Its mediumistic utterances are inspired by lying spirits, a fact of which those prophets were well aware and which they did their utmost to conceal.

"Mediumship of this character, especially if under the patronage of a king estranged from God, was bound to be disastrous to the whole nation *as soon as it ranged itself openly upon the side of undisguised idolatry'*. 'Prophets of Baal' was the name by which they were known, and they became exceedingly numerous. At times there was scarcely one good medium left among them. Thus it is said of the age of Eli, the High Priest: 'And the word of the Lord was rare in those days; visions were not common'. *(1st Samuel 3 : 1.)*

"On Mount Carmel Elijah said to the people: 'I, even I only, am left a prophet of the Lord but Baal's prophets are four hundred and fifty men'. *(1st Kings 18 : 22.)*

"The fact that the mediums of old allowed themselves to be swayed by worldly considerations to misuse their gifts can be gathered from the words uttered by God through the prophet Micah: 'And as for the prophets' — the Eternal says — 'who lead that make my flock astray; who cry 'All's well'! if they get food to eat, — and open war on any who refuse them. *(Micah 3 :5.)* ' . . . and the prophets are divining for money, and all the while relying on the Eternal'. *(Micah 3 : 11.)*

"You must not think that the people of those days accepted out of hand and as genuine all phenomena evoked by mediums. They too realized that they might be imposed upon and were just as suspicious of mediums as you are nowadays. In order to guard against being tricked by sleight of hand performances, they were in the habit of binding the mediums. Hence those of the mediums who lived by their calling kept on hand suitable fastenings for the head, feet and hands, with which they submitted to being fettered by their visitors. If after they had been fettered, demonstrations occurred which could be ascribed to, and as a matter of fact were produced by, the work of spirits, the visitors would be duly impressed and would be converted to a belief in the type of spirit-communication witnessed by them. But since it was not the good spirits which used such mediums as their instruments, persons who frequented these demonstrations eventually fell into evil ways. The teachings which they received from the evil spirits through the mediums turned them from the true God, and led them into vices of the vilest kind. It was the female mediums in particular who were the most patronized, and against whom was directed the threat pronounced by the Lord through the prophet Ezekiel: 'Son of man, face the women of your country who only prophesy from what they feel; and prophesy against them, and say: Thus saith God the Lord: Woe to the women that sew pillows upon all joints of the hand, and make kerchiefs for the head of persons of every stature to hunt souls! . . . And you have profaned me among my people for handfuls of barley and for pieces of bread'. *(Ezekiel 13 : 18.)*

"The method followed in the development of mediums in the 'schools of mediums' of Biblical times is not given in detail in the original documents of the Scriptures. First of all, however, the applicants for mediumship were tested as to their general aptitude for the calling and those who possessed the necessary qualifications were very soon picked out; those who did not, were dismissed.

"But even applicants highly gifted by nature as mediums were retained as students only if their character warranted the belief that they would employ their talents in the service of what was good and sacred. It was on this factor that the heads of the good schools of mediums laid special stress, whereas in the schools conducted by priests who worshipped idols only the applicant's mediumistic qualifications were taken into consideration. The same difference existed in those days with respect to the development of mediums, that you may find today. You yourself have witnessed with your own eyes the development of more than one medium. You have arranged for and conducted meetings at which this development was taken in hand. You invested such meetings with the character of a *divine service* and you did your utmost to bring yourself and the other participants nearer unto God. All of you put yourselves under His protection. You opened and closed the gathering with prayer and with praise to the Lord. Your readings were chosen from the word of God as recorded in the Scriptures. You sought only that which is good, and were ready, if it pleased God, to become useful instruments of the good cause.

"In that same way the development of mediums was conducted by the God-fearing among the Israelites.

"As compared with this, however, you should observe what goes on at most 'spiritistic *seances*' nowadays. Of God and of His praise there is generally not even a suggestion. People attend them for the sake of seeing something out of the ordinary and for excitement. By whom these demonstrations are brought about, whether by good spirits or evil ones, is of no consequence, and many of those who go to such meetings do not even believe that the phenomena witnessed there are the work of the spirit-world, but persist in ascribing them to human agencies. This nullifies at the outset the sole purpose entertained by the good spirit-world through its communication with mankind, namely, to bring man nearer to his God.

"It was at meetings of this sort that 'Baal's mediums' were developed. True enough, the people of those times knew that what they saw involved communication with spirits, but everyone engaged in this low form of spiritism was interested only in witnessing and learning things through this channel which would promote his worldly undertakings and ambitions. His fate in the next world was as far from his thoughts as it is from those of most people of the present age. Hence it was quite natural that the people of that time should not be at all interested in seeing to it that the mediums were developed with a view to fitting them for lofty and sacred purposes.

"No space is devoted in the Bible to a minute description of the schools of mediums conducted by the idolatrous priests because the development of 'Baal's mediums' took place at the general gatherings held to pay homage to the idols. No special form of development is required to fit people to serve evil ends: this comes about by itself, for: 'Man is inclined to evil from the days of his youth'. But to attain what is good and pleasing to the Lord requires great effort and a hard struggle, and for these, special preparation is imperative. Hence such preparation was necessary for those mediums who had resolved to become instruments of the Divine will. They were educated at the 'schools of prophets' as related in the Bible, under the guidance of men of God, like Samuel, Eli and Elijah.

"In the days when great and God-gifted men like these stood at the head of such 'schools for mediums' there were vast numbers of applicants seeking admission, for the God-fearing families considered it a mark of Divine favor if among their children there were any gifted with mediumistic powers which could be developed under a leadership of this high type.

"In the times of Eli and Elijah there was a school for mediums in every city of importance, such as Ramah, Gilgal, Bethel, Jericho and others. The student prophets under Elijah were so numerous that their places of assembly could not hold them, and so it came to pass that one day they said to him: 'This dwelling of ours as you see for yourself is too small for us. Pray, let us go, to the Jordan, and get each of us a log, to build a dwelling-house for ourselves there'. And he answered: 'Go'! *(2nd Kings 6 : 1, 2.)*

"In the days to which the New Testament refers there were no special schools for mediums among the Christians. They were not needed, because the assemblies of worshippers were held in such a manner that they took the place in every respect of the functions of the earlier schools for mediums. The worshippers joined hands when they offered prayer, to signify that they were 'all of *one* heart and of *one* soul'; that they were *united* by love into one community, and that they were addressing their prayer to God as a single unit, all of them as members of *one* spiritual body, inspired by *one* spirit, cherishing *one* hope, bound together by *one* common faith, supplicating *one* God.

"For the mediumistically gifted members of the community this custom of joining hands was of great importance, since in this way the odic power of all was collected into a single odic current. This could be utilized by the spirits of God, both for the purpose of manifesting themselves through the mediums already developed, as well as for developing those in process of preparation for the calling. The steps in the development of mediums were perfectly familiar to the early Christians from their days of heathenism, so that they were well aware of what they were about. As heathens they had been in the habit of communicating with evil spirits, and the natural laws governing such communication were well known to them. They also knew that heathen idol-worship was nothing but an intercourse with demons, carried out under the same natural laws that apply to communion with good spirits.

"Hence Saint Paul did not find it necessary to instruct the Corinthians regarding the laws by which spirit-communication can be brought about at all, but confined himself to telling them of the influence exerted upon them by the good spirits, as contrasted with that exerted by the evil ones.

"Chapters 12 and 14 of the First Epistle to the Corinthians contain everything relating to communication with the good spirits that any devout, God-seeking person need know of the subject. Unfortunately your present generation no longer comprehends the teachings imparted to the Corinthians by the Apostle in those chapters. This is due first of all to the fact that you are generally ignorant in matters relating to spirit-communication. Again, blame must be placed upon your incorrect translations of the Bible and upon the erroneous explanations offered to Christians on the strength of those incorrect translations.

"Because of the importance of the subject, I shall go through Chapters 12 and 14 of the First Epistle to the Corinthians with you, and interpret them to you correctly.

"According to your versions, Chapter 12 begins with the words: 'But I want you to understand about spiritual gifts, brothers. You know when you were pagans, how your impulses led you to dumb idols'.

"The very first words: '. . . about spiritual gifts . . .' contain a misleading error in translation. The reader can construe them only as meaning that the gifts in question are the gifts bestowed by the Lord on man's spirit, whereas the Greek text at your disposal reads quite differently, its literal translation being as follows: 'About matters relating to spirit-communication". Today we should put it more briefly and say: 'About spiritism'. Again, the original text does not say 'dumb idols' but 'dead gods', the latter term being universally understood to mean the 'demons' or spirits severed from God, which are always referred to in the Bible as the 'dead'.

"In what follows, there are two sentences that are lacking in the Greek text now available to you. They ran: 'Thus you became companions of the evil spirits, who would not recognize Jesus as their Lord. But now, that you belong to Christ and are subject to His rule, you may communicate with holy spirits'. Immediately after these sentences which have been omitted in the Bible, came Verse 3, which reads according to your translation: 'So I tell you, that no one is speaking in the Spirit of God' when he says: 'Cursed be Jesus' — and that no one can say, 'Jesus is Lord', except in the Holy Spirit.

"But also in the translation of this verse there is an error that obscures the sense, namely in that the Greek text does not read: 'in *the* Spirit of God' and: 'in *the* Holy Spirit' but: 'in *a* spirit of God' and: 'in *a holy spirit*'.

"The true meaning is, that the several results are brought about, not directly by God Himself, but by the spirits serving Him, who accomplish His will among His creatures on earth with the aid of His power.

"Due to the fact that your translators of the Scriptures have, in countless passages, used the expression: '*the* Holy Spirit', whereas the Greek text reads: '*a* holy spirit', they have not only occasioned erroneous interpretations of the passages in question, but above all, they have caused such confusion regarding the meaning of the term 'holy spirit', as to give rise to the false doctrine that the Holy Spirit is a Divinity.

"For the sake of giving you a clear insight into what is meant by spirit and spirits, so that you may be able to understand the two chapters under consideration, of the First Epistle to the Corinthians, I shall illustrate my meaning by an example taken from worldly conditions.

"In the days when your kings were absolute rulers, *only the king's will* had any weight in matters that might happen within his dominions. Within his jurisdiction only *one* will, only *one* spirit, existed, namely, the will and the spirit of the king. His servants and officials performed their acts of office subject to his authority entirely, and only according to his will and his spirit. From this it did not follow that they were obliged to obtain the king's consent for every individual official act; they had his laws and his general instructions by which to go, and from these they could decide for themselves what should be done in each separate instance.

"There were, therefore, many people engaged in governing the kingdom, but only one real ruler: the king.

"This is true also of the Kingdom of God. Within this, there is only *one* absolute ruler, whose will is law in all things. That ruler is God, or, as sometimes expressed in the Bible, the Spirit of God, or *the* Holy Spirit. The other spirits, likewise known as God's spirits or holy spirits, are merely God's executive agents, His servants and officials. Their functions also are defined by laws and directions, subject to which they act. Hence they, too, do not require special instructions from God on every occasion. They all co-operate in the same spirit and the same sense, in the furtherance of God's will and intention. They represent, so to speak, a great governing body composed of many parts which, although individually distinct and independent of each other, are ruled as the parts of a whole by the spirit which appointed the spirit-world as a governing body, and which has conferred thereon its own might and authority. This was in the mind of Saint Paul when he wrote: 'Now there are diversities of gifts, but *the same* Spirit. And there are diversities of ministrations, and *the same Lord*. And there are diversities of workings, but *the same* God, who works all things in all'. *(1st Corinthians 12 : 4.)*

'"Thus if it happened at the meetings of the Christians in Corinth that one spirit spoke through a medium in a strange tongue, a second through another medium in the language of the country, a third endowed its medium with healing-power, and still other spirits worked in other ways, these spirits were not acting at their own pleasure nor under their own authority, but at the will and under the authority of the *one* God, the highest, almighty spirit.

"The Corinthians were naturally greatly impressed and astonished whenever a spirit spoke through one of their mediums in a strange language. They therefore eagerly desired, and included this wish in their prayers, that as many spirits as possible might manifest themselves in this way. Since this wish arose only from human curiosity and love of the sensational, they were reprimanded because of it by Saint Paul, who told them that the workings of the spirits which visited them were for the sole purpose of serving the edification and the internal growth of the church, and were not undertaken for the sake of gratifying purely personal desires. What would it profit them, he asked, if the spirits which came to them spoke 'in tongues'? Neither the medium's spirit would thereby be benefitted, since it could not understand the words that were uttered, nor would the medium's hearers profit, as the strange speech would be equally unintelligible to them. Let them rather pray to be visited by spirits which would impart teachings to them in their mother tongue, and if spirits spoke to them in strange tongues, let them pray that their speech might be interpreted, which could be done either by those spirits themselves or by others.

"It may seem extraordinary that spirits should speak at all in a language unknown to their hearers, but there was a good reason for this, since it served to prove the reality of spirit-communication, or, as Paul aptly says, as a sign to the unbelieving.

"Here I must pause to explain that your versions of the Bible refer to speaking in foreign languages as 'speaking in tongues', and to communications imparted in the language of the country as 'prophesying'.

"That Paul heartily approved of the efforts of the Corinthians to communicate with the spirit-world is shown by his words: 'So also you, since you are zealous of spiritual gifts, seek that you may abound to the edifying of the church'. *(1st Corinthians 14 : 12.)* Your translators have rendered this sentence also unintelligible by substituting the term 'spiritual gifts' for the word 'spirits', in spite of the fact that the original text expressly says 'spirits' and not 'spiritual gifts'.

"At the conclusion of his teaching, Paul exhorts the Corinthians to 'let all things be done decently and in order', for 'God is not a God of confusion, but of order and peace'. By this rule the mediums also are directed to abide. Not more than two, or at the utmost three of them may put themselves at the disposal of spirits speaking in a strange tongue, and then only, if spirits able to interpret are present, but if there be no interpreter, let him keep silent in the church'. As to the revelations made in the mother-tongue of the participants, these also are to be restricted to two or three, in order that the hearers may have time to discuss what they have heard and to express their views as to its meaning, or, in Paul's own words: 'Let the others exercise their judgment upon what is said'! The admonition which Paul gives to the Corinthians in this passage is the same as that which I, as you know, have uttered so often at your gatherings. I, as well as the other spirits that have spoken with you, have been in the habit of urging you, at the conclusion of our visits, to discuss among yourselves what you had just heard, and to exchange your opinions concerning it, for the question at issue is not one of how much you may hear at any single meeting, but of how well you understand what you have heard. If, then you will talk over among yourselves the things that we spirits have told you, we shall be able to say who there is among you that has understood us correctly, and who has not, for we remain present during your discussion and listen to what you are saying. If we gather from your remarks that your interpretation is incorrect or that there are differences of opinion among you, we again enter into the mediums and clear up any points which remain doubtful.

"Anyone not familiar through personal experience with the interrelated factors in spirit-communication and with the relation in which the spirits stand to the mediums will be unable to understand the rules of procedure laid down by Saint Paul. Therefore I shall add a brief explanation.

"You cannot possibly overestimate the human character of the relations of the good spirits with respect to you. They are the best friends you have, and are always present in large numbers at your religious gatherings. In the most cases they are spirits which were mortals like yourselves, and which in the Beyond have progressed toward God. They have been assigned as your guides, counsellors and guardians. They have the most fervent desire to lead you along the path toward God while you are still on earth, in order that, when you depart thence, you may enter as high as possible a sphere in the spirit-world. It not infrequently happens that your friends among the spirits, while they were on earth, belonged to other countries than your own and spoke the languages of those countries. Many of them cannot speak your native tongue, for spirits, like everyone else, must learn those languages of the human race with which they were unfamiliar during their stay on earth. All of them, however, are eager to speak a good word, and crowd about the mediums for the purpose of using them to deliver a spoken or a written message. For the sake of preserving order on such occasions, a 'controlling spirit' is present at each gathering devoted to communicating with good spirits, it being that 'controlling-spirit's' duty to decide, which of the spirits may speak and how long they may speak. In making its decisions regarding the admission of the individual spirits, the 'controlling spirit' is guided somewhat by the rules and resolutions adopted by the assembly itself; if, for instance, the participants agree not to allow communications in a language unknown to them, the controlling spirit will admit no spirit unable to express itself in the mother-tongue of those present. The mediums too have the power to deny the admission of a spirit-being into their bodies, for a state of 'trance' occurs only when no resistance is offered on the medium's part. Hence, as Paul says: 'the spirits of the prophets are subject to the prophets', or, in other words, to the 'mediums'.

"There is one passage of Paul's teaching which is obscure, partly in itself and partly because of its incorrect rendering. This passage reads: 'When ye come together, each one has a psalm, has a teaching, has a revelation, has a tongue, has an interpretation. Let all things be done to edifying'.

"First and foremost, the translation is wrong, as I have said, for it should read: 'When you have come together, each one *receiveth* a psalm', and so forth. Each one *receives* whatever it may be, through a medium present. He does not bring it with him, already prepared, but during the course of the meeting the spirits offer these various things through the mediums. One spirit may offer a hymn; another, an instructive discourse; a third, a revelation; still others, a message in a foreign language and a translation of that message into the native tongue. Out of the great variety of spiritual fare offered, everyone present may choose what will best satisfy the immediate needs of his soul, for the object in view is the edification of the whole congregation, rather than that of only one or another of its members. The offerings are made as diversified as possible because of the wide variation of the spiritual requirements of the participants. One, who personally, or whose family, has experienced particularly good fortune, will be able to express his feelings best by words of praise to the Lord, which will be pronounced by a spirit through a medium; another feeling downcast, will be cheered by a message of consolation. A third may be assailed by doubts as to whether the things he is witnessing are indeed the workings of the spirit-world, and will be relieved of these doubts when he hears a medium speak in a strange tongue.

"Paul's teachings to the Corinthians regarding the manner of holding communication with the spirit-world were not evolved in his own mind, but were uttered at the Lord's behest, for he ends them with the words: 'If any man thinks himself to be a prophet, or spiritual, let him take knowledge of the things which I write to you, that they are the commandment of the Lord'. *(1st Corinthians 14 : 37.)* And he adds: 'So do I teach in all churches of the saints'.

Inquiring of God as Recorded in the Holy Writ

"Thus says the Lord, the Holy One of Israel, and his Maker: Ask me of things that are to come!'

Isaiah 45:11.

"GOD is the fountain of truth. Whosoever shall draw from it will receive the truth and will be preserved from error. A knowledge of this led the faithful of olden times to enter into communion with God when seeking the truth. They did not expect this communion to come about and to bring conviction by way of *inner illumination, but by way of revelations of the truth received from without, and sent by the Lord in a manner perceptible to the human senses.* They inquired of God by means of human *expedients,* and were answered by Him through the same channel.

"They were well aware that the good spirit-world in the service of God is the agent of His will, *and that to consult the spirit-beings of God's kingdom is equivalent to inquiring of God Himself.*

"They were equally well aware that there is such a thing as an evil spirit-world, and daily experience had taught them the possibility of communicating with this also.

"At all times before the birth of Christ and in the early days of His era, the godly made liberal use of the privilege of inquiring of God. The writings of the Old and the New Testament abound in instances in which it is related that the faithful, when desirous of learning the truth, 'inquired of God' and received their answers, transmitted to them through God's spirits.

"If you will open your Bible and carefully read through its Books one by one, you will find my statement confirmed.

"You will find mention made of 'inquiring of God' in one of its very early chapters, it being related of Rebekah, the wife of Isaac, who feared that she was barren: 'Twins were struggling in her womb and she said: 'Why has this befallen me'? So she went to consult the Lord'. *(Genesis 25:22.)* The manner in which she 'consulted the Lord' is not recorded, nor yet the way in which she received the answer which was vouchsafed to her, but the casual way in which the story is told shows that inquiring of God was not an unusual practice.

"After the exodus of the Israelites from Egypt, the people

daily appealed to Moses to 'inquire of God' on their behalf. 'And when Moses' father-in-law saw all that he did to the people, he said, What is this thing that thou doest to the people? Why sittest thou thyself alone, and all the people stand about thee from morning unto even? And Moses said unto his father-in-law, *Because the people come to me to inquire of God:* when they have a matter, they come to me; and I judge between a man and his neighbor, *and I make them know the statutes of God, and his laws. (Exodus 18 : 14-16.)* Here also nothing is said to show the method by which the inquiries were addressed to God. Not until later, when Moses at God's command had built the tabernacle, do you find a more detailed account of the means by which 'inquiries of God' and the answers thereto were made possible: 'It came to pass, when Moses entered into the Tent, *the pillar of cloud descended,* and stood at the door of the Tent:*and the Lord spoke with Moses.* . . . And the Lord spoke unto Moses face to face, as a man speaks to his friend. And he turned again into the camp: but his minister Joshua, the son of Nun, a young man, departed not out of the Tent'. *(Exodus 33 : 9-11.)*

"The essential parts of this account are already familiar to you from my former teachings, but now you will probably notice also that there is a difference between the manner in which *Moses* inquired of God, and that in which it was done by the *people.* To the *solemn* inquiries addressed to God as here related, Moses, *as the representative of all the people,* is answered by the Lord through the *pillar of cloud,* whereas when individuals of the people inquired of God, their answer came, not through the pillar of cloud but through another channel, which, although not clearly defined in this passage, is sufficiently well indicated to leave no doubts on that score in the mind of anyone familiar with the subject. You learn that Joshua, the servant of Moses, was not allowed to leave the Tent; evidently therefore, there must have been a reason for his constant presence there. This reason was directly connected with the practice of inquiring of God, *Joshua having been especially appointed to act as a medium for those of the people,* who desired to inquire of God concerning their *private affairs.* It is expressly stated that 'every one that sought the Lord went out unto the tent of meeting'. No fixed hours for 'inquiring of God' having been set, Joshua was obliged to be present in the Tent at all times, so that he might be available to all as a medium for transmitting the Lord's answers. *He was employed as an instrument by God's spirits, in the same manner in which they employ the mediums of today.*

"After the death of Joshua, the Israelites inquired of God: 'Who shall go up for us first against the Canaanites, to fight against them? And the Lord said, Judah shall go up: I have delivered the land into his hand'. *(Judges 1 : 1, 2.)*

"When the Danites sought an inheritance to dwell in, they sent five men to spy out the land. These came to the house of Micah where they met a Levite who lived there as a medium. 'And they said to him, Ask counsel, we pray thee, of God, that we may know whether our way which we go shall be prosperous. And the priest said to them, Go in peace: Before the Lord is your way wherein you go'. *(Judges 18 : 5, 6.)* In this chapter there is also a detailed account of the manner in which the Levite inquired of God. It is related that Micah had caused a founder to make him a 'graven image' and a 'molten image', as your translators express it, not knowing the true meaning of the term and even assuming that these images were 'idols'. As a matter of fact they were made *in imitation of the breastplate of judgment worn on the garments of the High Priest* and so called, as you know, because it was used for inquiring of God.

"Imitations of the High Priest's breastplate of judgment were used whenever the people of Israel consulted the Lord in matters of private interest. These imitations corresponded perfectly to what is now called a 'planchette' and consisted of two parts: a lower, stationary part, generally cast as a plate and engraved with the letters of the alphabet or other symbols, and an upper part, light and handsomely carved and provided with a pointer. The cast plate was either set upon a table or fastened to a base or a pillar, and was highly polished to allow the upper part to slide over it with ease. Whenever counsel was sought of God, the movable upper part was sent upon the plate, and the medium, laying his hand on it, waited for it to be moved by the spirit-beings to the letters on the plate with the aid of his own odic power. If this happened, the pointer indicated in the proper order the characters which, when combined into words and sentences, spelled out the answer returned by God. It was, therefore, substantially the same thing as the High Priest's breastplate of judgment.

"The imitation of that breastplate was even carried to the extent of having precious stones engraved with characters, set into the cast plate by expert jewelers, large sums of money being spent for the purpose. And precisely as the High Priest wore costly robes when seeking counsel of God, similar garments were provided for the *private mediums* who attended the breastplate of judgment. Thus we read of Micah: 'And he made an ephod and a breastplate of divination, and consecrated one of his sons, who became his priest'. *(Judges 17 : 5.)*

"Gideon also made the spoils taken from the Midianites into an 'oracle' of the kind described, and 'put it in his city, even in Ophrah', where it could be consulted by all. But before long it was used by the people to consult evil spirits. *(Judges 8 : 27.)*

"Gideon had caused it to be made for the use of inquiring of God only, but it was misused by the people, who employed it to inquire of the 'dead' or, in other words, to communicate with the evil spirit-world, and who thereby fell into idolatry.

"However, those among the Israelites who observed God's commandments made use of private channels for communicating with Him only in emergencies. In matters of great importance they still preferred, when inquiring of God, to repair to the spot which He Himself had appointed for the purpose in the days of Moses. They used to go to the 'tent of meeting' where the High Priest inquired of God for them by means of his breastplate of judgment. Thus when the Israelites went up to Beth-el they 'asked counsel of God: Who shall go up for us first to battle against the children of Benjamin? And the Lord said, Judah shall go up first'. *(Judges 20 : 18.)*

"When Saul wanted to pursue the defeated Philistines by night and to destroy them utterly, and his people were willing to follow him, the priest said: 'Let us consult God here. So Saul asked God: Shall I go down after the Philistines? Wilt thou deliver them into the hand of Israel? But God did not answer him that day'. *(1st Samuel 14 : 36, 37.)* God did not answer Saul on that day because Saul's son had violated a command of the Lord, Who intimated by His silence that He would answer only those who obey Him.

"David almost invariably inquired of God through the breastplate of judgment. His medium was Abiathar, the priest. '. . . but David strengthened himself in the Lord, his God, and David said to Abiathar, I pray you, bring me the 'ephod' (breastplate of judgment). And Abiathar brought the ephod to David. And David inquired of the Lord saying, If I pursue after this troop, shall I overtake them? And he answered him, Pursue; for you will surely overtake them, and will without fail recover all'. *(1st Samuel 30 : 7, 8.)*

"Only those will God allow to inquire of Him who put their whole faith in Him and who look to Him for help. But all those who hold communion with the Evil One and who look for help to the spirits of the Abyss, God will reject. 'These men have taken the idols into their heart, and put the stumbling-block of their iniquity before their face: should I be inquired of at all by them'? *(Ezekiel 14 : 2.)*

"It is not the half-hearted, not those who today turn to God and tomorrow to Baal, not those who today attend church and devote tomorrow to wickedness, whose appeals for counsel God will answer. This was true in olden times and it is true today. Of such, God has drawn a true picture through the mouth of Isaiah the Prophet: 'Yet they ask me daily, and delight in knowing my ways: as a nation that did righteousness, and forsook not the ordinance of their God, they ask of me righteous judgments; they delight to draw near God. . . Is not this the fact that I have chosen: to loose the bonds of wickedness, to undo the bands of the yoke, and to let the oppressed go free, and that you break every yoke? Is it not to deal thy bread to the hungry, and that thou bring the poor that are cast out to thy house? when thou seest the naked, that thou cover him; and that thou hide not thyself from thine own flesh? Then shall thy light break forth as the morning, and thy healing shall spring forth speedily . . . *Then thou shalt ask, and the Lord will answer'. (Isaiah 58:2-9.)*

"There were many different ways in which God manifested Himself to the faithful who sought His counsel in their troubles. The story of Saul relates the manner in which this prince, the first of the Kings of Israel, was answered by the Lord while he was still an obedient servant of the Lord. On the day before the battle of Gilboa, Saul, who because of his disobedience had been deserted by God's spirit, 'inquired of the Lord' but 'the Lord' answered him not, neither by 'dreams' nor by the 'Urim', nor by the 'prophets'. *(1st Samuel 28 : 6.)* This indicates that on previous occasions Saul had been answered in one or another of these ways. What your Bible translators express by the word 'dreams' is spirit-sight, or a vision, in which a person sees the truth in an unmistakable picture. Such visions are vouchsafed only to those who have mediumistic powers of clairvoyance. The spirit-world therefore finds it necessary, in selecting the way of delivering its messages, to take into account the receptivity of those to whom these messages are directed.

"When use was made of the 'Urim' or 'breastplate of judgment' God's answers were given in collaboration with a medium, as I have already explained to you.

"As for the 'prophets' who figure so frequently in the Bible as bearers of messages from God, they were 'speaking mediums' who in not a few instances were capable of receiving God's words either by clairvoyance or by clairaudience, and who then transmitted them.

"Wherever in the Scriptures you find a reference to 'inquiring of God', you will also find confirmation of the truth that God will send His answer in some way that men can understand, to all those who turn to Him confidingly and who appeal to Him for counsel.

What is meant in the Bible by "Inquiring of the Dead"

"Why consult the dead on behalf of the living? Consult the message and the counsel of God!"
Isaiah 8 : 19.

"WHEN you of the present generation speak or write of the 'dead' you are referring to those who have departed from the earth and whose bodies are at rest in the churchyard. You put no other meaning upon the word 'dead'. 'Death' therefore signifies to you the severance of the spirit from its earthly body."

"The Scriptures constantly refer to 'death' and to 'the dead', but rarely to designate thereby corporeal death. 'The dead' of whom the Bible speaks are not those whose days on earth are over. When the Bible mentions 'death' it does not mean the separation of the spirit from the body, *but the separation of the spirit from God.* To be united with God and to belong to Him, is 'life'. To be severed from God is 'death'."

"This teaching recurs throughout the Old and the New Testament."

"The *'dead'* are those who are *severed from God,* the *'spiritually dead',* be they spirits in the Beyond or passing through life on earth as men who have forsaken God."

"The very first reference to 'death' in the Bible signifies *separation from God,* for when God forbade the first people, dwelling in Paradise, to eat of a certain fruit, He added the warning: 'For on the day you eat from that tree you shall die'. *(Genesis 2 : 17.)* It was not the death of the body that was meant by these words, but separation from God, for, as you know, the first people suffered not bodily, but *spiritual* death when they had violated His Command. By their disobedience, they went over to the side of Evil, and thereby severed themselves from God."

"When Moses, as his life on earth drew to an end, bade farewell to the people, he gave them this admonition: ' . . . I have put life and death before you, the blessing and the curse: Choose life, than, that you and your children may live, by loving the Eternal, your God, obeying his voice and holding fast to him. . .' *(Deuteronomy 30 : 19, 20.)*"

"It was not *terrestrial life* nor *bodily death* that he had set before the people, but *spiritual life*, which should endure while they held fast to God, and *spiritual death*, which would ensue at the instant of their forsaking God and severing themselves from Him. 'He that keepeth the commandment keepeth his soul; but he that is careless of his ways shall die'. *(Proverbs 19 : 16.)* 'Verily, verily, I say unto you, if a man keep my word, he shall never see death'. *(John 8 : 51.)*"

"*The sin of apostasy from God therefore carries with it spiritual death.* 'Do you not know that you are the servants of him whom you obey, either the servants of the sin which brings to you the spiritual death, or servants who obey the call of righteousness'? *(Romans 6 : 16.)* 'What fruit had you to show in those days? Was it not of which you are now ashamed? Is not the end of it all spiritual death? But now, being rid of sin and having become God's children, you have fruit which makes for your sanctity, and which in the end leads to the life hereafter. For the wages of sin is the spiritual death but God's gift of grace is a life to come. . .' *(Romans, 6 : 21, 23.)*"

"*Not all sin leads to separation from God,* but '*only the sin when it is fullgrown brings forth death*'. *(James 1 : 15.)* It is not the stumbling and falling of those who believe in God and seek unto Him that bring forth spiritual death, for the stumbling is through human weakness, and the falls are suffered on the road Godward. *But to abandon God, to turn your back upon Him, and to live as though there were no God, that is the sin which bringeth forth spiritual death.*"

"*The 'dead' are God's enemies.* They have placed themselves under the rule of the spirits of Evil. 'They have transgressed the covenant: there have they dealt treacherously against me'. *(Hosea 6 : 7.)* They have deserted their colors and serve the Prince of Darkness. They have chosen him as their god. That is the meaning of the word 'whoredom' which occurs so often in the Holy Writ. 'Their doings will not suffer them to turn unto their God; for the spirit of whoredom is within them, and they know not the Lord! *(Hosea 5 : 4.)* And because of this spirit they are not ripe for a return to their God. 'Will I ransom them from the power of Sheol; *will I redeem them from death?* O death, where are they plagues? O Sheol, where is thy destruction'? *(Hosea 13 : 14)*. Plagues and destruction are the punishments which God visits upon apostates through the spirit-powers of evil."

"It is natural that God, who wants only what is good in spiritual life, should have strictly forbidden all intercourse with the 'dead' as being His enemies. There is nothing good, there is no truth and no virtue, that can be learned of them."

"Appalling indeed were the consequences of the dealings held by the nations of old with the evil apostate spirits through the agency of low spiritism, to which the Bible refers as harlotry or idolatry. There were no abominations in which the 'dead' did not lead the misguided people through their human mediums. Not only did the people eat the flesh of the offerings that had been dedicated to the demons, intoken of fellowship with the latter; but they did not shrink from sacrificing their sons and daughters to the evil spirits and from committing the most shameful excesses at the sacrificial rites. All of these practices were instigated by the Powers of Evil, once the people had entered into communion with them. 'They joined themselves also unto Baal-Peor, and ate the sacrifices of the 'dead'. *(Psalms 106 : 28.)* 'Yea, they sacrificed their sons and daughters to demons'. *(Psalms 106 : 37.)*"

"The consequences of idolatry are thus pictured in the Wisdom of Solomon: 'For whilst they slew their children in sacrifice, or used secret ceremonies, or made revellings of strange rites; they kept neither lives nor marriage any longer undefiled: but either one slew another traitorously, or grieved him by adultery. So that there reigned in all men without exception blood, manslaughter, theft, and dissimulation, corruption, unfaithfulness, tumults, perjury, disquieting of good men, forgetfulness of good turns, defiling of souls, changing of kind, disorder in marriages, and shameless uncleanness. For the worshipping of idols not to be named is the beginning, the cause, and the end of all evil. For either they are mad when they be merry, or *prophesy lies,* or live unjustly, or else lightly forswear themselves'. *(Wisdom 14 : 23-28.)*"

"When you read of these things you may be led to conclude that those people acted thus because they were no longer in their right minds. They were, nevertheless, as normal as you are today. But such is the power of evil, and so subtle are its ways of misleading men, that those who have once fallen into its snares find it almost impossible to extricate themselves from them. Of all the weapons of the Powers of Darkness, the mightiest is a *mixture of truth and falsehood.*"

"They convinced those who communicated with them by "inquiring of the dead' that animals, the sun, the moon and the stars were the embodiment of mighty spirits which had great power over men, and could shape their fortunes for good or ill, and that, in consequence, these beasts and heavenly bodies must be worshipped in order to ensure worldly well-being and to avert calamity. They taught, furthermore, that communication with them could be had by means of sacrifices, particularly by the sacrifice of children."

"This doctrine was true to the extent that it taught that spirits are incorporated in all material things, and also, that communication can be had with these spirits through sacrificial offerings. The fatal underlying falsehood was, that the spirits of the Lower World were powerful benevolent spirits, having the good of their worshippers at heart. Once the evil spirits had impressed their adherents with this belief, the step to human sacrifice was a short one. The parents of a child marked for sacrifice were told that after its death, its spirit would constantly hover about them and bring them good fortune, but that both they and their child were doomed to the direst misfortune should they refuse to allow it to be offered to the idols. Obsessed as they were, they always gave way in the end."

"You need not wonder at this, for during the rites performed before the idols and at idolatrous gatherings generally, the evil spirits announced these doctrines through their trance-mediums and supported them by the exhibition of miracles which accompanied their discourse. Not infrequently, the idols themselves spoke. Such speech was a 'direct voice' produced by the low spirit-world with the aid of the od of the offerings and that of the mediums in attendance."

"The cause of apostasy from God was then, as it is now, the craving for worldly success and prosperity, but in those days all of the prerequisites for communicating with the spirit-world were well known, while today they have fallen into oblivion. Consequently, apostasy manifested itself in those times not only in *inward defection from God,* but in deliberately fostered, palpable, communication with the evil spirit-world, held through spiritistic idol-worship. 'Seeking unto the dead' was as much a part of the daily lives of the worldly minded, as was *seeking unto God* an integral part of the worship of the faithful."

"The messages sent by the 'dead' through their mediums were such as to flatter the human foibles of the recipients, who heard nothing but what was agreeable to them and who had no desire to listen to God's instruments, the good mediums. 'For it is a rebellious people, lying children, children that will not hear the law of the Lord that say to the seers, See not; and to the prophets, Prophesy not unto us right things, speak unto us smooth things, prophesy deceits, get you out of the way, turn aside out of the path, cause the Holy One of Israel to cease from before us'. *(Isaiah 30 : 9-11.)*"

"It was only what would please them that they wanted to hear, especially such things as would further their worldly interests, as Saul when consulting the witch of Endor summoned the spirit of Samuel. Good spirits will not allow themselves to be summoned at the whim and pleasure of men. They come of their own accord with God's sanction, or, in certain cases, at His express command. But they come only to those who seek unto God, in order that they may point out the way to Him. Which particular one of the good spirits is to manifest itself is not for man to determine, but rests with the good spirit-world. It is also true that of the evil spirits, not always those whose visit people desire are allowed to appear, for they too may communicate only by permission. They will, however, invariably claim to be the ones that were summoned, whether or not this is true, for they are spirits of falsehood whose only concern is to tell their adherents what these would like to hear."

"It is, therefore, an act of great folly for people to agree among themselves that whoever dies first will let the survivors know whether or not there is a future life. Whoever enters into such an agreement and makes his belief in a future existence contingent upon the fulfillment thereof, will invariably fail to receive the evidence he desires, for agreements of that kind are proof in themselves of an absence of belief in God, and the fate in store in the Beyond for those who die unbelieving is such that they are in no position to communicate with the living. The spirits of the lowest spheres remember nothing of life on earth or of any agreements which they may have made there; even if they did remember, they could not leave the place to which they are confined because of their transgressions. But whosoever believes in God will be able, without any such agreement and without any conscious effort on his part, to communicate during life with the spirits of his dear departed, if these too have been believers. In this case also the words of Christ hold true: 'Yet seek ye his kingdom, and these things shall be added unto you'." *(Matthew 6 : 33,)*

"But there was no seeking of the Kingdom of God by those who associated with the low spirit-world. It was not in them to seek unto God; they considered their worldly well-being only, and for this reason they desired no connection with the good spirit-world. As has been the case in all ages, the truths which they heard from the good spirit-world were too harsh and unpalatable for people who had given themselves up to the indulgence of their passions. The utterances of God they regarded as an oppressive burden, even going so far as to describe the reprimands, warnings and threats pronounced by the prophets at God's command by the blasphemous phrase of '*the burden of the Lord*' 'What is the burden of the Lord'?, was the usual question, whenever men desired to know what the Lord had caused to be proclaimed. It was for this that God sent them the message: 'When a layman or a prophet or a priest asks you: 'What is the burden of the Eternal's oracle'? tell them this from the Eternal: 'Burden'! you are the burden, and I mean to throw you off. Any prophet or priest or layman who talks of the 'Eternal oracle' or of 'what the Eternal says', I will punish that man and his household. No, this is what every man of you must say to his fellow, to his brother: 'What is the Eternal's answer'? 'What is the Eternal's message'? You must never again mention the Eternal's 'burden'. *(Jeremiah 23 : 33, 38.)*"

"Whoever, therefore, aspired to belong to God's people, might not have relations with that spirit-world which had forsaken Him. *Nor might they 'inquire of the dead',* for to do so was to commit high treason to God and to desert the truth. For truth was not to be found among the 'dead'. 'The dead know nothing'. What they speak is falsehood and imposture, calculated only to lead the faithful astray.

"Hence God thus admonishes His people: 'Ask me of the things that are to come; concerning my sons, and concerning the work of my hands, command me ye'. *(Isaiah 45 : 11.)* 'I am the Eternal, your God, training you for your good, leading you by the right way.' *(Isaiah 48 : 17.)* 'When they tell you to consult mediums and ghosts that cheep and gibber in low murmurs, ask them, if people should not rather consult their God. Say, 'Why consult the dead on behalf of the living? Consult the message and the counsel of God'! *(Isaiah 8 : 19.)* 'You befoul yourselves like your fathers, you break your troth with me for their detestable impieties, and you befoul yourselves with all your sacrifices to idols — burning your sons alive — down to this very day! And I am to be consulted by you, O Israel? By my life! Says the Lord, the Eternal. No, I will not be consulted by you'. *(Ezekiel 20 : 30, 31.)*"

"The Israelites had acquired the practice of seeking unto the '*spiritually dead*' while dwelling in Egypt and had to a great extent adopted idolatrous customs there. Hence among the first injunctions laid upon them by the Lord after their exodus from that country was the one forbidding them to inquire of the dead. 'You shall not practice augury nor practice witchcraft'. *(Leviticus 19 : 26.)* 'Never go to a medium or a wizard, never defile yourselves by consulting them. I am the Eternal'. *(Leviticus 19 : 31.)* 'Any person who consults a medium or a wizard, deserting me for them, I will set my face against that person and outlaw him from his kinsfolk'. *(Leviticus 20 : 6.)* These passages show that the men and women who had familiar spirits or who were wizards, were mediums through whom the evil spirits spoke. These mediums were themselves responsible for their evil associations from which they could have kept aloof had they turned confidingly to God and sought communion with the good spirit-world. Their punishment was therefore amply deserved."

"Besides the mediums, there were persons engaged in communicating with the evil spirit-world through 'clairvoyance'."

"References to the 'blood-guilt' of the wizards do not mean that these had committed actual bloodshed or physical murder, but relate to the *slaying of souls,* or the estrangement of spirits from God. They had indeed incurred blood-guilt in the sense that they had brought those who went to them into communication with the spirits of evil, in that way leading them away from God and becoming the cause of their spiritual death."

"The contamination to which those who associate with wizards expose themselves is not of a physical nature, but proceeds from the vicious od which they absorb from the contact and which defiles their own od, making it a hotbed for the activities of evil spirit-beings."

"There occurs in the Bible at least one detailed account of a case of necromancy, namely that of Saul's visit to the witch of Endor."

"When Samuel had died, all Israel had mourned for him and buried him in his own town of Ramah. Now Saul had cleared the mediums and wizards out of the country. But when the Philistines mustered and went into camp at Shunem, and when Saul mustered all Israel to encamp at Gilboa, Saul was afraid, and, his heart trembling with terror at the sight of the Philistine army, he consulted the Eternal, but the Eternal would not answer him either by dreams or by the sacred lot or by prophets. Then Saul said to his courtiers, 'Find me a witch, that I may go and consult her'. His courtiers said, 'There is a witch at Endor'. So Saul, disguising himself and changing his clothes, went with two men to the woman by night; he said to her, 'Inquire for me as a medium; bring me up the ghost of some one whom I name to you'. The woman said to him, 'You know what Saul has done, cutting mediums and wizards out of the country! Why, then, are you laying a trap for my life, to have me put to death'? Then Saul swore to her by the Eternal, 'By the life of the Eternal, this will not involve you in any guilt'! So the woman said, 'Whom shall I bring up for you'? 'Bring up Samuel', he said. The woman looked at Saul and screamed; the woman said to Saul, 'Why have you deceived me? You are Saul'! The king said to her, 'Have no fear! What do you see'? The woman said to Saul: 'I see a god coming up out of the earth'. He said to her, 'What is he like'? She said, 'It is an old man coming up; he is covered with a mantle'. So Saul knew it was Samuel; he bowed with his face to the ground and did obeisance. Then Samuel said to Saul, 'Why have you disturbed me by bringing me up'? Saul answered, 'I am so distressed the Philistines make war against me and God has abandoned me; he answers me no more, either by prophet or by dreams; so I have called you to tell me what to do' But Samuel said, 'Why ask me when the Eternal has abandoned you, to side with your rival? The Eternal has treated you as he declared by me that he would; the Eternal has torn the kingdom out of your hand and given it to David, your neighbour. It is because you did not obey the voice of the Eternal, because you did not carry out his fierce anger against Amalek, that the Eternal has done this to you to-day. And the Eternal will put Israel along with yourself into the power of the Philistines, and to-morrow shall you and your sons be with me'. *(1st Samuel 28 : 3-19.)"*

"There is much in this account which you will find hard to understand and which ought therefore to be explained to you."

"Does it not strike you as singular that Saul should have trembled at the sight of the Philistine host? That was not at all like Saul, who was a brave man and had been in countless battles, always facing death fearlessly. Why then this sudden attack of faint-heartedness? Here you find one of those strange occurrences with which you so often meet in life. It is what you call a 'premonition of death'. The expression is not well chosen; it would be more correct to speak of an 'assurance of death'. At the very first sight of the army of the Philistines, something within him told Saul that the hour of his death was at hand. That hour is indeed appointed for all, by fate. But what was the nature of the inner voice that caused Saul to feel sure that he would meet death in the coming battle? It was the same kind of a voice as that which called to so many of your soldiers in the Great War: 'You will not live through the next attack', or 'You will not live through the day', or, 'This is your last leave of absence; you will never again see your family and friends'. Why did so many soldiers who had often been home on leave before, find it so hard to return to the front on the occasion which proved to be their last? In the case of Saul as in that of all others who know to a certainty that their death is at hand, it was the guardian spirits that announced this hour, the most momentous one in a man's life. During your lifetime their voice has often warned you of impending danger. Again and again they have intervened to save you from peril, but when the inevitable moment approaches, these friendly spirits shake your inmost being so violently that the striking of the hour of your death sounds in your ears too loudly to pass unheard. Then you *know* that your time has come. Not in every case are the spirits allowed to sound this warning; when they are, it is a special mark of Divine favor, granted to give the person to whom this warning is issued, time to make his peace with God and implore His help at the moment when the fateful step must be taken."

"With Saul also it was the last appeal by the Lord's spirit-messengers urging him to return to that God to Whom he had become faithless. But Saul, although he knew he was about to die, so far from turning inwardly to God and renewing his oath of fealty to Him, contented himself with the outward formality of calling upon God through mediums and of asking for help in his *worldly troubles*. He sought no inner communion with the Lord in repentance of his past behavior. Because of this, God did not answer the questions inspired by worldly interest, and Saul, fearing for his earthly existence, sought out the necromancers. When he used the words: 'I am sore distressed', he was speaking of the foreboding of death that weighed upon him."

"At this point I wish to speak briefly of the many other ways in which the approach of someone's death is foretold. As you know, it is a popular belief that the howling of dogs, the appearance of certain birds, the turning white of plants, and other occurrences are signs of an impending death. This is not superstition, as your scientifically enlightened age pronounces it to be: it is true, and even if such signs fail to point out the person for whom they are meant, everyone familiar with them should take them to heart and pause to reflect upon his own state. These signs are the calling of your spirit-friends, to remind you of the reckoning which you will have to render after you leave this life upon earth. They are the manifestations of the spirit-world given through those animals, causing them to do things that you regard as omens. As I have told you repeatedly, animals also may be used as mediums by either the good or the evil spirit-world. The same is true of plants and flowers, but the spirit-world employs such signs only for the benefit of persons able to read them, for it does nothing without a purpose. That is all I need tell you regarding this point."

"Coming back to the necromancer of Endor, it may appear strange that Samuel should have answered her summons at all. He was not one of the 'dead', not one of those who had departed from God. He was not one of the spirits of the Abyss with which that woman was in the habit of communicating. He was one of God's good spirits. This fact the woman herself recognized from the godlike appearance of Samuel's ghost. It came as a judgment of God, to punish Saul for his offense of consulting the Powers of Evil. If in Samuel's place an evil spirit had come, it would not have predicted truthfully the terrible fate awaiting Saul, but would have beguiled him with some acceptable falsehood. Hence it was God's will that the good spirit of Samuel should appear before the clairvoyant, who was likewise clairaudient, and through her announce to Saul what the coming day held in store for him. To learn this so long in advance was the hardest part of what Saul had to bear. 'Tomorrow shall you and your sons be with me; the Lord will deliver the host of Israel also into the hand of the Philistines'. This prediction was the beginning of Saul's death-agony, which tortured his inmost soul unto the hour of its fulfillment. Hence, on receiving the fatal message, 'he fell his full length upon the earth, and was sore afraid'. What he had hoped to hear from the necromancer, namely, advice as to how he could best overcome his enemies, was not given him; in its stead, the terrible fate, which he had not come to learn, was revealed to him as a punishment. In Saul was fulfilled the prophecy pronounced by the Lord through Ezekiel: 'For every one of the house of Israel, or of the strangers that sojourn in Israel, that separate himself from me, and takes his idols into his heart, and puts the stumbling block of his iniquity before his face, and comes to a prophet to inquire for himself of me; I the Lord will answer him by myself: and I will set my face against that man, and will make him an astonishment, for a sign and a proverb, and I will cut him off from the midst of my people; and you shall know that I am the Lord. *Ezekiel 14 : 7, 8.)"*

"The necromancer's recognition of Saul when Samuel appeared was due to her power of clairaudience, which enabled her to hear Saul's name when it was uttered by the spirit of Samuel."

"When Samuel further told Saul: 'Tomorrow shalt thou and thy sons be with me', this is not to be construed as meaning that Saul and his sons were to share Samuel's lot in the Beyond. All that Samuel intended to convey to Saul was, that he and his sons were doomed to die on the following day, and that Samuel would be present to await them as they passed over into the other life. For the spirits of the dying are received and greeted at the deathbed by those of their beloved ones who have gone before, and are instructed and advised by them until they reach the place to which their lot has assigned them. That, for the spirit-world, is an invariable a rule as it is for you to meet your friends on their arrival at some foreign port to which you have preceded them, regardless of any difference, however great, between their ultimate destination and yours."

"The necromancer of Endor held communication with the 'dead' both by clairvoyance and by clairaudience. She could tell those who consulted her only what she herself saw and heard. Other necromancers were true mediums who passed into a trance while the strange spirit was speaking through them."

"Finally, when you read that the spirit of Samuel 'came up out of the earth', you must make allowances for an optical delusion. To render itself visible, a spirit requires a cloud of od, and it procures this od from the odic radiation of the persons in its immediate proximity. The cloud of od does not evolve suddenly, but develops little by little, generally increasing in size from below upward and thus giving the impression of a body which is rising. Samuel's appearance in the form of an old man, wrapped in the robe which he used to wear while on earth, was so designed for the purpose of making him recognizable. Spirits habitually show themselves in an odic form bearing all of those distinguishing marks by which they were known during their terrestrial existence.

Precisely as you are able to choose your material manner of dressing at will, so spirits can give to their garments of od the character which they consider the best adapted to their purposes."

"Inasmuch as the laws governing communication with the evil spirit-world are the same as those which apply to intercourse with good spirits, you find, according to the Scriptures, that the same means were employed in consulting the dead that were used when inquiring of God. In both cases you read of mediums acting as bearers of the odic force, whether they were prophets of Baal or prophets of God. In both cases beasts are sacrificed and incense is burned to increase the odic power. In both cases spots are selected, immune from any disturbing element, at which the unfavorable influences of light and heat upon the condensation of the od have been eliminated as far as possible. On this account the Bible pronounces anathema alike upon idolatry and upon the places at which communication with evil spirits was held. 'My people ask a piece of wood to guide them, a pole gives them their oracles! For a harlot-spirit has led them astray, they have left their God for a faithless way; they sacrifice on mountain heights and offer incense on the hills, below the oak, the terebinth, the poplar — so pleasant is their shade'. *(Hosea 4 : 12, 13.)*"

"Everything that you learn of the 'dead' from the Bible points to the fact that the 'dead' are the Powers of Evil. Whoever joins these powers, departs from God and suffers spiritual death. 'When Ephraim spoke, there was trembling; he exalted himself in Israel; but when he offended in Baal, he died'. *(Hosea 13 : 1.)*"

"It must not be supposed, however, that the worship of Baal consists only of the making of tangible idols by man and deliberately sought association with the evil spirit-world, as was the general custom in ancient times and as occurs today among pagan peoples. Rather, idolatry is any state of mind that excludes God from our daily lives; that turns wholly to temporal affairs, and that, under the influence of Evil, ignores God for worldly considerations."

"Mankind of today is not less idolatrous than were the people of whom the Bible speaks, even though in what you call enlightened communities, idols of wood or of stone are no longer erected. But there are other idols, set up within the hearts of people; money, fame and success. And to these idols as many victims are sacrificed today as were offered to the tangible idols of milleniums ago. It is to these modern idols that millions of adults, millions of children, are sacrificed each year. The evil spirit-forces of the 'kingdom of the dead' hold sway even today over by far the greater part of mankind, and what the prophet Micah said of the generation of his time is equally true at present: 'The devout have vanished from the land, not an honest soul remains; everyone lurks for bloodshed, each man preys upon his fellow; they have quick fingers for foul play; the judge must handle a bribe; the high official acts as he pleases, and between them they baffle justice. The best of them are no better than briars, the straightest are like thorns twisted in a hedge. Their hour of punishment is coming; it will be wrack and ruin. Never trust your fellow, never confide in a friend; keep your secret close from the wife of your own bosom. For sons insult their fathers, girls defy their mothers; daughters-in-law defy their mothers-in-law, and a man's household are his enemies. As for me, I will look out for the Eternal, I will await my saviour God: my God will aid me.' *(Micah 7 : 2-7.)*"

"But even to mankind of today the Lord will be merciful. He will so order it that men shall enter into communication with the good spirit-world and thereby be *raised from the dead.* "And it shall come to pass afterward, that I will pour out my spirit upon all flesh; and your sons and your daughters shall prophesy, your old men shall dream dreams, your young men shall see visions: and also upon the servants and upon the handmaids in those days will I pour out my Spirit'. *(Joel 2.: 28 -29.)* "

PART THREE

Spirit-Communication in the Post-Apostolic Age and in Modern Times

Introductory Remarks

AFTER I had received the teachings set down in the second part of this book, relating to the laws of spirit-communication and to the manifestations recorded in the Bible, it was left to me to study spirit-communication in other ages of the history of mankind and to compare the result with those things that I had learned from the spirit-world.

I was particularly enjoined to investigate everything that happens at the spiritistic *seances* of today, as well as whatever modern science has to say on 'mediums' and the messages delivered by them.

I would gladly have applied the test to the writings of the past by ancient authors, pagan as well as Christian, insofar as they dealt with communication with the spirit-world. For this I should have had to study the works of the ancient Greek and Roman philosophers. I should have had to go through all the writings of the Fathers of the Church and of ecclesiastical authors, from the post-apostolic age down into the Middle Ages not to speak of the works of the Mystics. Neither could I have ignored the innumerable accounts of the lives and acts of the saints of the Catholic Church if I hoped to lay claim to an exhaustive study of the subject. Furthermore, I should have had to look through the endless material supplied by books and periodicals on modern 'occultism'.

At the very first glance I was forced to admit to myself that such an undertaking would require the labor of a whole lifetime.

I therefore decided to add only three more chapters to this book. In these, it was my intention to prove *from my own investigation* that spirit-communication was not only a generally known and accepted fact in the post-apostolic age, but that it exists today, even though this may not yet be recognized by the people of the present, and that, furthermore, it is effected according to the same laws as those set out in this book, which were those which applied throughout the past and which will apply for all time to come.

The chapters which were the result of my decision are entitled as follows: "Spirit-Communication in the Post-Apostolic Age." "The Part Played by the Spirits in the Lives of a Protestant and a Catholic Clergyman of the 19th Century." "Spiritism in the Light of Modern Science."

Spirit-Communication in the Post-Apostolic Age [1]

"Is there a thing of which it may be said, See, this is new! it has been long ago, in the ages which were before us."
Ecclesiastes 1 : 10.

THE conflict that followed the advent of Christianity, between the pagan world and the adherents of Christ, was a desperate one. In this life and death struggle, the Christians of the post-apostolic age held the general belief that the Powers of Evil were the true rulers of all paganism, and that the temporal potentates and their subjects were nothing more than the instruments of those malignant powers. Hell saw its former dominion over mankind threatened by the good spirit-world, which found its expression in Christianity. "It now faced battle with a prince greater than the Roman emperor, and with forces stronger than his lieutenants and officials. The influence of these forces had been at work even before the birth of the Roman Empire, and extended to Rome's furthermost provinces, where Roman authority existed in name only. It had extended also into the hearts and minds of men, which acknowledge no alien rule.

"The Life of the State as well as the lives of individuals was inseparably bound up with this ultra-mundane world of spirits, known to the heathens as gods, heroes, or demons. The functions of the State were exercised largely under their auspices. A great part of the public communal ceremonies involving offerings and festivals was devoted to the worship of these deities." (Weinel, pp. 2 and 3.) Although their idols might to all outward appearances be dead things, people were convinced that behind these statues of stone and wood there existed living spirit-beings which could make themselves manifest. Referring to them the Christian martyr Justin says: "Those images bear the names and shapes of evil spirits which have appeared." It was these demons that were worshipped by the heathens. "In ancient times demons (in human mediums), appeared, committing adultery with women, subjecting boys to nameless abuse, and exhibiting scenes of horror that struck fear into the hearts of those who did not understand these doings.

[1] The citations in this chapter are taken from *Weinel's* book entitled: Die Wirkungen des Geistes und der Geister im nach-apostolischen Zeitalter bis auf Irenaeus, published by J. C. B. Mohr, Freiburg im Breisgau. Wherever Weinel is quoted, it is from the book mentioned.

People called these demons gods, and designated each god by the name which the corresponding demon assumed. Fear impelled them to do this, since they did not know that the demons were evil ones." (Justin I : 5, 2.)

Not only had the evil spirits been active in the past, but their doings were witnessed personally by the Christians of the early centuries.

Among the most obvious of these doings was the prevalence of various diseases in which a spirit, other than the patient's, spoke and acted through him. The maniac was possessed of a demon. The hysterical and epileptic were obsessed. Such was the universal popular belief among Jews, pagans and Christians.

These invisible spirit-creatures spoke at times through human mediums. The Christian writer Tatian thus describes a female medium of Apollo "After drinking water, she falls in a state of frenzy; incense drives her out of her senses and makes it appear that she is prophesying." (Tatian 19, p. 86.) A state of frenzy invariably indicates that a low spirit has taken possession of a medium, the presence of good spirits being always marked by the medium's quiet and peaceful demeanor.

The ravings of the priests of Baal as described in the Bible, the frenzied motions of the Bacchantes at the pagan feasts of the Greeks and the Romans, contortions of the dancing dervishes of our times, as well as the numerous similar exhibitions given by modern mediums, must be ascribed to the influence of evil spirits.

These spirit-beings could also be seen by the clairvoyants of that age. Persons endowed with clairvoyance or other mediumistic powers through which they could enter into communication with the spirit-world were known in that day as "Pneumaticians", a term derived from the Greek word "pneuma", meaning "a spirit." In the present age which knows nothing of the laws of spirit-communication, the word "pneumatician" is interpreted as "gifted in spirit", thus creating the impression that it was the spirits of those persons themselves which were the cause of the extraordinary phenomena. As a matter of fact, however, the "pneumaticians" were either full-fledged "mediums", or persons having mediumistic tendencies, or else individuals gifted with the power of clairvoyance or clairaudience. Thus "pneumaticians" were not only those who were in touch with the good spirit-world, but also persons who had dealings with the spirits of evil, the laws according to which such communication was held being the same in both cases.

"Demons are also visible to men, to whom they show themselves in order to create the belief that they are beings of great power." "Their aerial, fiery bodies are easily and often seen, although, to be sure, only by 'pneumaticians', but the fact that they are seen, and frequently seen, admits of no dispute," says Tatian. (Or. 15, p. 70.)

The aerial and fiery demoniac bodies mentioned above are odic bodies. All spirits have these, but the appearance of the forms of the various spirits differs according to the sphere which each spirit inhabits.

It is true also that the idols spoke, and performed miracles. Not even the Christians could deny this fact, since it was a matter of general knowledge. It was on this very fact that the heathens based the belief, that the idols which they adored were living spirit-creatures, endowed with great powers. They asked: "How does it come that certain images can work marvels, unless the beings to which we erect our statues are deities? Is it not highly improbable that lifeless, motionless, images should develop power through their own efforts, without some impelling force?" To this the Christian, Athenagoras, replies: *"Not even we Christians deny* that in certain places, cities and countries, miracles have occurred in the name of the idols, but we do not regard these as gods." (Athenagoras, leg. 23, p. 116.) Of a statue set up to a certain Neryllius in Troas he relates: "It is believed that this statue prophesies, and heals the sick. The inhabitants of Troas therefore offer sacrifices to it, and bedeck it with gold and wreathes. It is likewise believed that of the statues erected in Parion to Alexander and to Proteus, one can prophesy, while to the other, that of Alexander, offerings and festivals are dedicated at the expense of the state, as to a god who will hear the prayers addressed to him."

Athenagoras does not deny the doings of these images, but maintains that those who execute them are evil spirits.

"Thus people witnessed and experienced the phenomena, and through them received proof of the existence of a mysterious world of spirit-beings, lying beyond these occurrences — of spirit-beings mightier, wiser and also more ruthless than man. Beyond and above the Roman Empire lay the realm of one who was the true ruler of the world; Zeus, or the Devil. And it was precisely the Roman Empire whose governing classes so stubbornly resisted Christianity, which that spirit-kingdom seemed to be using as a bulwark." (Weinel, p. 12.)

Of the workings of the invisible prince of the world and of those of his tools, the Christians had terrifying proofs in their own persons.

What then was the end which the Devil and his demons tried to achieve by all their attacks on the Christians? It was: to decoy them from God, into the error of polytheism; to tear them out of their spiritual lives and to hurl them to spiritual death. "For the demons as they are called desire only to lead men astray from their God and Creator, and from Christ, His First-born. And those who proved unable to rise above worldly matters, they have fettered to manmade objects (statues), and they do so to this day." (Justin 1, 58.) "The demons have accomplished this end by inventing myths and mysteries, thus aping God's plan for the salvation of humanity. To those who sought communion with God they have, by means of their imagery, offered a pleasant but soul-destroying substitute for the true Revelation." (Justin 1, 56.)

The evil spirits which spoke through the idols at the pagan ceremonies produced speech audible to human ears by employing the od at their disposal to create so-called "direct voices." It was, in fact, an imitation of the speech of God through the cloud of od above the Ark in the Tent of Testimony, for that speech came also as a "direct voice", as has been clearly demonstrated in a previous chapter. And just as during God's speech the cloud of od required was produced by the blood of the offerings and by the smoke of the sacrificial fires, so the blood of the pagan offerings and the smoke of their fires were the sources of the od required for the "direct voices" of the evil spirits.

In view of the great danger that threatened Christians from the side of the Devil and his hosts, there was a very widespread fear of these Powers of Darkness. The question was not one of shadows and pictures drawn by fancy, as is believed by most people in modern times, nor was it one of tenaciously-held, undemonstrated dogmas, such as are held by Christians of all denominations even today; on the contrary, the evil spirits were powers that made themselves felt and put themselves in evidence daily, intervening in the lives of men at every turn, mysteriously, but potently. (Weinel, p. 24.)

"Let us picture to ourselves the sensations of a Christian, stared at in the house in which he lived by the *lares* and *penates* (images of the idols), ranged against the walls; exposed to what seemed to him the threatening gaze of the statues standing in the streets and public squares; passing by temples, in whose gloomy recesses that lay behind the rows of gleaming pillars the mysterious powers carried on their work, attracting crowds of adherents. Among these images were many, whose fearful shapes, with their grotesque combination of human and animal bodies, at once repelled, and inspired awe into those who knew of the personal spirit-power that lay back of them, alive and active. Far more dangerous still were the demons, when they breathed life into softly shimmering marble, when the joyously lovely bodies of the Greek gods and goddesses became the sense-seducing magic through which the Devil enslaved mankind. Christians realized with horror that all this life-breathing beauty had been stolen from God, to be used for sinful purposes; that the majesty which clothed these deities represented a theft of God's grandeur and of His sovereignty over the hearts of men.

"And when, at private entertainments or municipal or provincial festivals the awestruck Christian was made aware of the unspeakable lengths to which defection from God had gone; when at such festivals he saw the foulest crimes of demons and heroes enacted on the stage in all their setting of the passions which beset men and gods, like greed, hatred, vindictiveness, sensual love and their consequences, such as war, murder, adultery, displayed with magical seductiveness before the eyes of young and old, of the mature and the immature, his heart was stirred with a feeling of loathing and contempt for those who had led the souls of men astray from the true God and His eternal goodness and purity, by their jugglers' tricks and phantasmagoria.

"Fortunate indeed was the Christian in whom no other feelings were aroused. For if the beauty of the statues and that of their worshippers, or the sensual appeal of the drama stole into his heart; if at the gladiatorial combats the craving for blood that lies latent in man was awakened in him, he could hear, with terror and dismay, how these same Powers of Darkness called to him, now in the soft tones of flattery, now in wildly challenging tones, to arouse his lower instincts. He not only imagined that he heard these voices: the more he listened to them, the deeper he became engrossed in his experiences with the spirit-world, *the more of a "pneumatician" he grew to be, and the more frequently and clearly he would hear the spirits calling; indeed, he would actually see the forms of the evil spirits and experience the physical torments of their presence.*

"If in spite of all, he remained true to his God, the very worst might yet be in store for him. In that age of persecution, Satan and his minions developed their greatest strength. With abhorrence and dread the Christian came to know the cruelty of these mighty and ruthless forces, either through the torture of his friends or in the sufferings that racked his own tormented body." (Weinel, pp. 24 and 25.)

What then was the power which enabled the Christians to overcome the forces of the evil spirits? They themselves have given us the answer: *"It is a holy spirit, a spirit of God, which gives us that power."* The spirits of God came to them as they had come to the earlier Christian communities. Thus Justin, speaking of the Christians of his own day, says:

"They receive gifts, each according to his merit, and are enlightened in the name of this Christ. One may receive a spirit of insight, another, that of counsel; a third, a spirit of strength; still others, a spirit of foreknowledge, of doctrine or of piety." (Justin, Dialogue, 39, p. 132.)

"There are among us men and women, upon whom a spirit of God has bestowed gifts of grace." (Justin, Dialogue 88, p. 318.)

In his dialogues with Tryphon the Jew, Justin says: "There still exist among us the gifts of prophecy, whereby you may see what the things formerly given to your race have now descended on us. And just as there were false diviners in the days of the holy prophets, so there are false teachers among us today." (Justin, Dialogue 82, p. 296.)

Those who were in favor of rejecting spirit-communication as a religious dogma are taken to task by Irenaeus, who speaks from the standpoint of the entire Christian church of his time when he says of the sect of the Alogians: "They would destroy the gift of the spirit, which in the latter days was poured out to mankind according to God's will. They would reject the Gospel of Saint John, in which we are promised that the Lord *will send us* the spirit. And they reject not only the Gospel, but the doctrine of the spirit of prophecy."

The term "latter days" used by Irenaeus was understood by the Christians to mean the time from the appearance of Christ until the end of the world. By "spirit of prophecy" they understood a spirit which announced God's truth to mankind through a human medium, as was the rule in the first Christian communities. According to the early Christian doctrine, the truth was to be learned only where God's spirits appeared. This doctrine was expressed in the formula: "The truth must be learned where God's gifts of grace are to be found."

Inasmuch as intercourse with the good spirit-world was, and still is, effected according to the same laws as those governing intercourse with evil spirits, communication with both spirit-worlds bears an external resemblance, and only from the *contents* of the messages and from the *behavior* of the spirits that have entered the human mediums can we judge whether these messages come from good spirits or evil, from the superior or the low ones. As for the messages themselves, they were regarded in those times by Jews, pagans, and Christians, Catholic and non-Catholic, as being brought by invisible spirits.

"Whenever a Christian sees the apparition of an angel or a demon, of Christ or of the Devil, or whenever a pagan or a Gnostic has a vision, it is not true, contrary to what many modern theologians assert, that what in the case of the Christian is a real experience, is merely hallucination in that of the Jew, since in each of the instances considered above, invisible, superhuman spirit-creatures actually revealed themselves for the time being. And these visions may recur at any time and in the same manner." (Weinel, p. 64.)

"The activities of the holy spirits and those of the demons are, however, phenomena which not only bear a general resemblance to each other, but one and the same phenomenon may be construed as the work of either a good or a bad spirit, according to the religious viewpoint of him who records it. What might be considered as the work of good and holy spirits by a member of the Christian sect of the Gnostics, might appear to a Catholic as a hallucination produced by demons, and vice versa." (Weinel, p. 64.)

"Wherever pneumatic manifestations appear within a given psycho-physical field, their resemblance to each other *throughout the centuries is most striking*. The monastic Mystic of the Middle Ages, the Quaker of Protestant England, the Hugenotic inspirationist, the faith healer of the 19th Century, all act precisely as did the pneumaticians of the church in its formative stage." (Weinel, p. 65.)

"According to the Christian doctrine, there is no *neutral* ground in the field of pneumatic (mediumistic) phenomena. Either the spirit at work is good, or it is evil." (Weinel, p. 67.)

The methods by which spirits communicated in post-apostolic times were the same as those described in the earlier chapters of this book.

The spirits did their speaking through mediums. Among these there were "part-trance mediums" whose own spirits hear whatever the strange spirits say through the mediums. There were also "deep-trance mediums", in whom a strange spirit spoke, while the medium himself was quite unconscious. A medium who used to speak in a part-trance thus describes his sensations: "On these occasions I always felt myself being uplifted to God, in Whose name I therefore solemnly declare that I have never been bribed nor enticed by anyone, nor influenced by any worldly consideration whatever, to speak any words other than those *which God's spirit or angel itself utters through my organs of speech.* To such a spirit I therefore yield the guidance of my tongue during my state of ecstasy, meanwhile bending all my efforts to direct my spirit toward God and to remember the words pronounced by my lips. *My own words thus seem to me to have been spoken by someone else,* but leave a deep impression on my spirit." (Weinel. p. 77-78.)

Often, also, a spirit *prays* through a medium, while the latter is in a part-trance. An example of such a prayer offered "while filled with a spirit" is strikingly presented by the martyrdom of Saint Polycarp, in which, also, the sensation of being under the influence of a powerful emotion is well illustrated.

Polycarp had descended from the upper story of the house where he had been hidden and had surrendered himself to the soldiers waiting below, of whom he requested an hour's undisturbed respite for prayer. "When these things were granted he stood before them and prayed, *filled with the grace of God* (with a spirit), so fervently, *that for two hours he could not cease,* and that all of his hearers were seized with fear, while many of them repented having come to capture an old man so highly favored of God. *He could not cease from prayer,* for it was not he himself that was speaking, but something else within him which did not allow him to fall silent. Meanwhile he knows nothing of what is going on about him. He is utterly insensible to exhaustion, which ordinarily would not have allowed a man of his advanced age to remain standing. Everyone present realized that it was not Polycarp himself who spoke, but that someone else was speaking through him. Any such sight as this is unnerving to those who witness it, especially to those who witness it for the first time, and this is true in general whenever the ultra-mundane spirit-world comes into touch with a person in a manner patent to the human senses.

Undoubtedly the Swabian clergyman Blumhardt, at whose prayer the sick felt the *spirits of disease* leave them, was another such supplicant as Polycarp. (Weinel, p. 83.)

The state of "deep-trance" or "ecstasy" properly so called was very prevalent among the mediums of the Montanists. Eusebius, the enemy of Montanus, relates of him: "The recently baptized Montanus, inspired by boundless ambition, has allowed the Evil One to enter his soul. He has become filled with a spirit, and, having suddenly fallen into obsession and ecstasy, falls into a state of great emotion and utters words that sound like a strange language. Similarly, two women incited by him spoke while unconscious, quite suddenly and in a strange language like that spoken by Montanus, filled with the same evil spirit."

The spirit which speaks through Montanus explains his mediumistic state in the following words: "Behold, man is like a lyre, and I fly to him like a plectrum." This describes accurately the relation in which a spirit stands to the medium through whom it speaks. The medium is merely the instrument in the hands of the spirit; he is the piano and the strange spirit is the musician. This is so of all true mediums, without exception.

The condemnation expressed in the foregoing sentences by Eusebius, of the spirit-influences at work in the sect of the Montanists, who, after all, were Christians like himself, is the opinion of a religious opponent, and it must be remembered that of all enmities, the bitterest are those aroused by religious differences of opinion, in which the freest use is made of the weapons of slander and distortion of the truth. That the spirit-manifestations among the Montanists could not have been of the nature imputed to them by their Catholic opponents is obvious from the fact that Tertullian, the most learned and earnest Church Father of the time, went over from the Catholic to the Montanist Church. Whoever is familiar with the writings of this Father of the Church will understand at once that unless the manifestations of the spirits witnessed among the Montanists had been of a sacred and serious character, a man of his type would never have joined that sect.

Inasmuch as the spirit-workings among the Montanists attracted great attention and made serious inroads on the theretofore recognized Christian Church known as the Catholic, the leaders of the Catholic Church of the day promptly proclaimed the dogma that no true instrument of God speaks while in ecstasy, that is to say, a deep-trance condition, and this in spite of the fact that it was generally recognized that there had been many people in all ages who had spoken as instruments of God while in a state of ecstasy. Thus Athenagoras, Catholic though he was, who lived during those times, says:

"The prophets, while in a state of ecstatic insensibility and actuated by a Divine spirit, have uttered things instilled into them, a holy spirit breathing through them as a flutist breathes through his flute." (Athenagoras, Legatio pro Christianis 9, p. 42.) Elsewhere Athenagoras repeats that "the spirits have caused the prophets' organs of speech to function as though they were instruments." In the Justinian Oratio ad Graecos we read: "The Heaven-sent plectrum touched the just as it would a musical instrument, a zither or a lyre." Justin and Theophilus make use of the same simile, their language being the same as that of the spirit which spoke out of Montanus. Among the Montanists the methods of spirit-communication were the same as those practiced by the earliest Christian communities.

The book entitled "The Shepherd of Hermas", a spiritistic work through and through, was so highly regarded in post-apostolic days as to be classed among the Scriptures. This book likewise relates minutely the manner in which the speaking mediums of good spirits can be told from those of the evil ones. From what is laid down therein the fact is established *that as regards the form of speech there is nothing by which a celestial spirit can be distinguished from a terrestrial one.* Hermas records the following features which characterize the speech of good spirits through a medium: "No Divinely sent spirit will submit to being examined." *This means that such a spirit will not allow itself to be used for purposes of divination, to satisfy human curiosity.* Naturally, people may ask questions of a spirit, if they have failed to understand its message or if they remain in doubt as to some point or other contained therein. The good spirit-world even demands this of its hearers, for it imparts its messages, teachings, and admonitions for their benefit and earnestly desires that its words be thoroughly understood and correctly construed, and hence welcomes any necessary questions. Indeed, the spirits often invite their hearers to ask questions, even such as may have no bearing on the immediate subject of the communication. This happens in those cases in which a spirit knows that there is someone present desirous of information, which, however, must never relate to subjects of purely material interest.

A second mark which distinguishes the presence of a good spirit in a medium is: "It is not for men to determine whether or not and when a spirit shall speak. A spirit speaks only when God pleases that it shall do so." In all intercourse with good spirits it is therefore impossible to put a medium into a trance for the sake of obtaining a spirit-message. This comes when it ought to come. Man cannot control its coming. Man can, indeed, create the conditions required for spirit-communication by making the necessary odic power available, but whether or not communication will follow, does not depend on his will.

The proceeding is described by Hermas in the words: "The angel of the attending prophetic spirit fills man, and man, filled with a holy spirit, speaks to the congregation as the Lord wills."

The accounts of the initial stages of the deep-trance state among the Montanist mediums agree with the symptoms exhibited by all deep-trance mediums: "They bow their faces to the ground."

This appears to refer to the beginning of the deep-trance, for, as the medium's own spirit leaves him, his body sinks over forward and is returned to an erect posture only when the strange spirit enters it. The egress or departure of the medium's spirit is accurately expressed by the word "ecstasy" the meaning of which is "exit". After the strange spirit enters, the communication follows amid perfect decorum, if that spirit is a good one. If, on the other hand an evil spirit takes possession of the medium, a condition frequently arises which produces the impression of demoniacal obsession, even upon witnesses inexperienced in such matters. As the Christian Tatian says: "Ravings are the work of demons."

Clairvoyance, clairaudience and clairsentience as well as supernatural powers of the sense of smell and taste were of frequent occurrence among the Christians of the first few centuries.

Much space in the book of Hermas is devoted to clairvoyance and clairaudience, for most of the communications received by him came through these channels. A female figure which he saw and heard, explained to him the truths of the Other World. She was a guide to him, as was Beatrice to the clairvoyant Dante. For

Dante also derived the main theme of his Divina Comedia from what he learned through clairvoyance.

Saint Polycarp Martyr also foresaw his aproaching end by clairvoyance. At the country-seat to which he had fled, he spent his time with a handful of companions, "doing nothing day and night but pray for all the churches in the world, as he had previously been in the habit of doing. Three days before his capture, while he was at prayer, he had a vision in which he saw his pillow in flames. At this, he turned to those about him and said: "God has willed that I am to be burned alive."

The most frequent visions vouchsafed to the clairvoyant devout are those of ultra-mundane figures and landscapes, and, in general, revelations of the spirit-realm which resembles our world on earth, from which however it differs in that it is ethereal instead of being composed of matter.

Needless to add, pagan clairvoyants had similar visions, for clairvoyance is a gift of the human race resulting from the configuration of the od surrounding the human spirit, enabling it to see in the same manner as does a discarnate spirit. The things seen by a clairvoyant are as faithful an image as are the images of the material world caught by our physical eyes. The spirit-world can show these images to a clairvoyant whenever it pleases. Od is the substance of which they are composed. It depends entirely on the mental attitude of the clairvoyant whether his visions of the ultra-mundane are actuated by the good or by the evil spirit-world. Clairvoyance relating to things on earth and dependent on odic radiations of terrestrial being, is not affected by the clairvoyant's mental attitude and for this reason the pagan clairvoyants were able to see events on earth quite as well as were Christian clairvoyants, although the Christians charged them with employing demons for the purpose.

The records of the early centuries of the Christian era are filled with accounts of such instances of clairvoyance and clairaudience. When Saint Polycarp died a martyr's death in Smyrna, Irenaeus, who happened to be in Rome at the time heard a trumpet-like voice proclaiming: "Polycarp has sealed his testimony with his blood."

As regards mediumistic writing, many leading Christians of the time assert that while writing, they were inspired by the spirit-world.

The development of mediums in the post-apostolic age followed along the same lines as those pursued among the first Christian communities, taking place at the religious gatherings. According to Hermas, a prophet would enter the pneumatic state while the congregation united in prayer, all of its members at such times joining hands in token of unity. The odic current thus formed furnished the spirit-world with the material it needed for developing mediums and for delivering its messages through mediums already developed. Anyone who has watched the development of mediums will readily follow the description of the mediumistic proceedings of those times, since they were the same as those witnessed today.

When Eusebius states that the Church did not permit its adherents to allow themselves to be developed as prophets by others, or to undertake to do so by their own efforts, these proceedings also are perfectly clear to anyone familiar with the subject, for just as a person could become a medium at meetings held for worship, the same end could be accomplished with a mediumistically inclined individual if he foregathered with a few co-religionists for worship in private, or if he merely sat down by himself to engage in spiritual concentration, the only difference being that the development of a medium progressed much more rapidly at larger gatherings at which harmony prevailed, than in the presence of but few associates or if he were alone, since the combined odic power of a large congregation is far more effective in promoting the labors of the spirit-world than the much less powerful odic force of a handful of people or that of a single individual. Nevertheless, the odic power of an individual who knows how to concentrate his mind will, little by little, become so great that he may develop into a medium, although in this case much more time is required.

The action of the later Christian, or, to speak more accurately, of the Catholic Church, in forbidding the self-development of a medium and the acceptance of the help of others toward the same end, originated in an age in which dealings with spirits had ceased, even at religious meetings, due to the forcible suppression of such dealings by the leaders of the Church.

Their reasons for so doing were the same as those obtaining in the Christian churches of today in their opposition to spiritism. The leaders of an institution which has become a *close temporal corporation* are not willing to tolerate the competition of a spirit-world.

Even in the days of Irenaeus the old Church had become a

well-knit temporal body, in which clerical officialdom ruled the faithful. The bishops were no longer named by the manifesting spirit-world, but were appointed or elected by human agencies. Nor were they any longer content to perform the services assigned to the "episkopos" of the first Christians, but regarded themselves as the bearers of the revealed doctrinal truths and as the legitimate interpreters of the same. But whenever mortals, not chosen for the task by the spirits of God, touch things that are holy, instant desecration results. This same statement applies to the "elders" of later days contrasted with the "elders" of apostolic times.

If then, we should be called upon to define in a few words the difference, from the standpoint of the history of religion, between original Christianity and the later "Catholic Church", we might say: "In Christianity, in its original form, the word of God's spirits was everything and the word of men was nothing. In the Catholic Church of later days, the word of men was everything, and the word of God's spirits was nothing."

The Part Played by the Spirits in the Lives of a Protestant and a Catholic Clergyman in the Nineteenth Century

THE noteworthy events in the life of *Johann Christoph Blumhardt,* one of the most prominent clergymen of the German Protestant Church of the 19th Century, who lived from 1805 to 1880, are described in a book written by Friedrich Zuendel.[1] A great part of this book is devoted to accounts of the manifestations of the spirit-world that played an important part in Blumhardt's life and in his pastoral activities. The facts related are of particular importance in the understanding of modern spirit-communication, since not the slightest doubt can attach to the accuracy of the account and because the occurrences recorded are identical with those observed in all ages of the history of mankind.

Blumhardt has set down his experiences with the spirit-world in a memorandum addressed to his ecclesiastical superiors, and has done so with strict regard for the truth, adding nothing and suppressing nothing. In support of this statement I shall quote the foreword with which he introduced his memorandum:

"In submitting the following paper to my ecclesiastical authorities I feel it incumbent on me to state that heretofore I have not expressed myself concerning my experiences to anyone with equal boldness and freedom from restraint. Therefore, since most of what I have set down has so far been a secret which I could have carried to the grave with me, I was entirely free to select whatever I felt inclined to include in my statement, and it would have been easy for me to give an account which anyone could read without taking the least offense. This, however, I could not force myself to do, and although at almost every paragraph I was assailed by the fear that I might be acting hastily and recklessly in laying bare everything, a voice within me was continually urging me: Speak out!

"May the risk be taken, then, and so it shall be in the name of Jesus, the Victorious. For to act openly and honestly in this

[1] Friedrich Zuendel: Johann Christoph Blumhardt. Ein Lebensbild. Brunnen-Gliessen Publishing Co. The facts presented in the present chapter have been taken from the work in question, to which all suoplementary references also refer. The Author.

very matter, I regarded not only as my duty toward my reverend ecclesiastic authorities who have every right to expect frankness on my part, but as my duty to the Lord Jesus, Whose cause alone it was for which I had to do battle. However, since this is the first time that I am speaking without any reserve whatever, it is my earnest wish that my statements be regarded as private and as though an intimate friend were confiding his secrets to those whom he can trust implicitly.

"My second request, which I hope will also be pardoned, is: that my honored readers may read everything I have set down several times, before passing judgment. In the meantime I put my trust in Him Who has our heart in His keeping, and whatever the verdict may be, I shall have the consolation of knowing that I have spoken the truth without reservation, and of the unshakable conviction that Jesus is victorious!"

Further light is thrown on his memorandum by Blumhardt in his reply to an attack by a Dr. Valenti, in which Blumhardt says:

"I might, indeed, as may be contended, have been more discreet and might have omitted those parts of my report which could be construed as the most boundless conceit, since we have long been accustomed to stories of no particular point, dealing with demonistic phenomena, especially those relating to somnambulism. All this I felt very clearly, and I hope therefore that my exceeding frankness will not be attributed to stupidity. Assuming that I had to make a report, which I had been called upon to do, I did not want to distort the truth to the extent of creating the impression that my experiences had been nothing more than another case of demonistic charlatanism or an unusual occurrence, such as have been heard and witnessed so often within the past few decades. I would have been ashamed to take my place in the ranks of those eccentric adventurers who only too often use the apparitions and manifestations from the other world for frivolous ends; I approached the subject with the fear of God in my heart, and if the matter assumed a much more serious aspect than usually happens in similar cases, that was the very fact which I was bound to impress upon my authorities for my own justification, if for no other reason. If I was to write down *anything at all,* I was bound to write down *everything,* hence I related openly and unreservedly how I acted and thought. By so doing, I put myself into a position to await any outcome with perfect confidence, and if I had made a mistake, or erred on the side of presumption, it was right that my superiors should know this and be in a position to express their opinion. For I am not willing to take a dumbly secretive stand, such as is adopted today by many erroneous schools of thought and clerical bodies in regard to demonology, for people who know they have been misled brood over many things in private, and allow no one a look at their secrets who is not wholly committed to their side. My case was to be brought out into the open light and judged in the open light, but, be it added, only as something on the order of a secret of the confessional and insofar as my superiors were concerned. In them I would confide, and for the present, in nobody else. And I have kept my word."

In Blumhardt's parish there lived a poor family named Dittus, consisting of three sisters and two brothers. One of the sisters, Theophila, was twenty-five years of age. In the spring of 1840 this family had moved into the ground floor of a miserable house in Moettlingen which was included in the parish.

It was not long before Theophila Dittus thought that she was experiencing inexplicable happenings. She had the sensation of hearing and seeing uncanny things about the house; indeed, on the very first day on which they had moved into it, she had, while saying grace, been seized with an attack that caused her to fall to the floor senseless. Often, also, there were constantly recurring sounds of banging and shuffling in the bedroom, the living room and the kitchen. This naturally terrified the Dittus family as well as the tenants who occupied the upper story, but no one had the courage to speak of the matter. Theophila felt that her hands were laid forcibly across each other during the night, and saw figures and lights.

Only occasional rumors of these matters reached the clergyman, Blumhardt, who paid no further attention to them.

These spectral doings had been going on for more than two years, when relatives of the girl called Blumhardt's attention to her pitiful condition and asked for his help. In the meantime the uproar in the house had become so terrible, that it could be heard for some distance through the neighborhood, the sounds being like those produced by a gang of laborers at work. Theophila had particularly frequent visions of a Moettlingen woman who had died two years previously and who appeared carrying a dead child in her arms. This woman, whose name at first Theophila would not mention, always stood in the same place by her bed, occasionally moved toward her and kept repeating the words: "I want rest", or: "Give me paper, and I will not come any more!"

Blumhardt made arrangement to have a woman friend sleep with Theophila, in order to divert her mind from these matters, but the friend also heard the nightly uproar. Both of them saw a light flare up; following the direction from which its rays came they found, under a board, a sooty sheet of paper bearing illegible writing. Beside it lay three crown-pieces and several other papers, also covered with soot on the folded side.

From that time on there was a cessation of the noises, and Blumhardt had begun to hope that the spectral manifestations were at an end.

However, after two weeks the uproar began again, and increased from day to day. Dr. Spaeth, a physician to whom Theophila had confided everything, spent two nights in her room in the company of several other persons, witnessing things that exceeded all his expectations. The interest created by the affair extended in an ever-growing circle, drawing the curious from far and near as is always the case when people are looking for a sensational experience, especially in matters of this nature.

Resolved to end the nuisance by drastic measures, Blumhardt chose six of the most serious-minded and responsible men of his parish to assist him in investigating the occurrences reported. Accompanied by them he went one evening to the house, he himself remaining in the bedroom in order to observe Theophila, while the rest scattered about the building by twos. On this evening all seven men were witnesses to the fact that within three hours, twenty-five blows were struck at a certain point in the bedroom, so violently as to cause an empty chair which stood there to leap clear of the floor, the windows to rattle and the plaster to fall from the ceiling. These terrific blows, which resounded in the street with the distinctness of the discharge of fire-arms at a New Year's celebration, were heard by all the inhabitants of the village.

When Theophila, to whom the vision of the woman carrying the dead child had appeared again, asked Blumhardt whether he wished her to mention the woman's name, he emphatically declined the offer. On the following day Blumhardt was informed that Theophila was in a state of utter insensibility, and apparently on the point of death. He hastened to her and found her stretched out rigidly on the bed, the epidermis of her head and arms aglow and twitching. From her other symptoms she seemed to be on the verge of asphyxiation. The room was packed with people, among them a physician from a neighboring village who had happened to be present and tried to restore her to life, but who went away shaking his head, obviously helpless. Half an hour later she awoke, and told Blumhardt that she had again seen the figure of the woman with the dead child, but that she had fallen down unconscious the instant the vision had appeared.

Blumhardt now removed the girl out of the house and had quarters provided for her in the home of a responsible family, where no one, not even her own brothers and sisters, were allowed to visit her.

Blumhardt relates his own sensations in the following words: "I had a particular dread of somnambulistic visions, which so often give rise to most unpleasant notoriety and which heretofore have been of so little benefit to anyone. But since in any event the prospect that had been revealed to me was a mysterious and a dangerous one, I could not refrain from laying the matter before the Lord in solitary prayer, begging Him to preserve me and others from any folly and error into which we might be led. It distressed us deeply to feel that the Devil should still be so powerful and should be able to spread such hitherto unsuspected diabolical nets before mankind. Our heartfelt sympathy extended not only to the poor woman, whose pitiful state we could see, but to the millions who have departed from God and who have become enmeshed in the secret toils of magic. We prayed that in this instance at least, God might grant us victory, and trample Satan underfoot."

Presently, however, the uproar recommenced at the new quarters into which Theophila had moved. As soon as these sounds were heard, she would fall into violent convulsions, which kept increasing in severity and duration.

One day, when these spasms were so violent that the bedstead fell apart, Dr. Spaeth, who was in attendance, remarked as the tears rose to his eyes: "It would almost seem from the way this girl is allowed to suffer, that there were no clergyman hereabouts. *What we see here is nothing natural.*"

Blumhardt took the physician's words to heart and visited Theophila oftener. One day when both he and Dr. Spaeth were at her bedside, her whole body began to tremble while every muscle in her head and arms twitched feverishly, although otherwise her entire frame was stiff and rigid. Meanwhile there were frequent emissions of foam from her mouth. The physician, who had never before seen anything of the kind, seemed at his wits' end. Suddenly she awoke and was able to sit up and drink some water; almost in an instant she seemed to have become a different person altogether.

Day by day Blumhardt grew more convinced that demoniacal influences were at work in this matter. As though by inspiration, therefore, on the occasion of one of her attacks, he stepped up to the patient, forcibly folded her rigidly cramped hands in the attitude of prayer, and calling her loudly by name, although he knew she was unconscious, said: "Fold your hands and pray: 'Lord Jesus, help me! We have long enough witnessed the doings of the Devil; now we want to see what Jesus can do!" After a few moments the girl woke up, and repeated the words of the prayer; to the great astonishment of all present, her cramps ceased almost immediately.

This, according to Blumhardt's own admission, was the turning point of his life. For the next few hours the patient rested peacefully, when the cramps returned more violently than ever. Again Blumhardt caused her to repeat the petition: "Lord Jesus, help me." Again the cramps left her at once.

Somewhat later, when Blumhardt visited her again, she exhibited new symptoms, for she flew into a rage at his appearance and struck at him, without, however, actually touching him. Finally she beat upon the bed with her hands, which looked as though they were radiating some ethereal force from their finger-tips. This lasted for some time, whereupon she became calm again.

Her relief, however, was of short duration. Presently sounds like finger-tappings were heard all about her and she received a sudden blow on the chest which caused her to sink down backwards. The female shape which she had seen at her former lodging re-appeared to her, and this time Theophila revealed the apparition's name to the clergyman. It was that of a widow who had died a few years previously and whom Blumhardt remembered well in connection with his pastoral activities. Her manner, while she was alive, had been one of great dejection, as of one who seeks peace without finding it.

Thereupon Blumhardt began to pray aloud and pronounced the name of Jesus. Immediately Theophila rolled her eyes and drew her hands apart, while a voice became audible which was at once recognizable as a strange one, not so much because of its sound as because of the expressions used and the tenor of the remarks. It cried: "I cannot bear to hear that name." Everyone present shuddered. Blumhardt relates: "I had never before heard anything of the kind and silently appealed to God for wisdom and caution. Finally I put the question: 'Can you find no peace in the grave'. The voice answered: 'No'. — 'Why not?' — Answer: 'As a punishment for my sins. I murdered two children and buried them in the fields'. — 'Do you know of no way in which you can be helped? Can you not pray'? — Answer: 'I cannot pray'. — 'Do you know Jesus, who pardons all sins'? — Answer: 'I cannot bear to hear that name'. — 'Are you alone'? — Answer: 'No'. — 'Who is with you'? — There was a short pause; then, in a sudden burst the voice said: 'The worst of them all'. The speaker now accused herself of sorcery, because of which she had put herself in the power of the Devil. She said that she had already departed out of Theophila seven times, but would do so no more. I asked whether I might pray for her, to which she consented after some hesitation. I told her that she could not remain in Theophila, upon which she at first began to supplicate, but quickly assumed a defiant attitude. I now commanded her to depart, whereupon Theophila beat the bed violently with her hands, and was at once relieved of her visitor."

Some days later the obsession returned. At times it seemed as though hundreds of demons were issuing from her in regular relays, whereat on each occasion the patient's countenance would change and assume a new threatening mien toward Blumhardt. It also happened that the men who accompanied the clergyman were pushed about and struck as though with fists, without being able to see the source of these attacks. Blumhardt himself was immune, for, as the demons said, they were not allowed to touch him. At such times Theophila would tear her hair, beat her breast, strike her head against the wall, and do what she could to injure herself. It seemed as though these scenes were becoming more and more terrifying and as though Blumhardt's intervention had only made matters worse. "What I suffered at that time in mind and soul," he says, "cannot be told in words."

"My anxiety to put an end to the matter grew from day to day. Although on each occasion I had the satisfaction of feeling when I left her that the power of the demons must yield to my efforts, and of knowing that the patient seemed quite normal, nevertheless the sinister power always appeared to gather fresh strength, as though it hoped in the end to enmesh me in its toils and thus to ruin both me and my usefulness as a clergyman. All of my friends urged me to desist. But I could not bear to think of what would happen to the patient if I withdrew my help from her, or of how I would be regarded by all as being responsible, should the worst happen. I felt as though I were in a net, from which I could not escape by merely *giving up the struggle,* without danger to myself and others. Besides, I frankly admit that I would have felt disgraced in my own eyes and in the eyes of my Savior, to Whom I prayed so often, to Whom I confided so many things, and Who had given me so many proofs of His help, had I meekly given in to the Devil. Who is the Master Here? I was often forced to ask myself. And trusting in Him Who is the Master, I again and again heard the call within me: Forward! we must reach a worthy goal, though we descend to the deepest paths, unless it be indeed untrue that Jesus has crushed the serpent with his heel."

The symptoms that seemed to indicate the departure of demons from the patient grew worse. At the same time other uncanny phenomena appeared and even became perceptible physically. Thus one night while Theophila was asleep she felt as though her throat had been clutched by a burning hand, which left great blisters in evidence of its contact. Before her aunt, who was sleeping in the same room could strike a light, these blisters which encircled her whole neck had already filled. The physician, who called on the following morning, was dumbfounded at this occurrence. Furthermore, by day and night she felt as though someone were pushing her sides and her head, or her feet were seized, causing her to fall down in the street, on the stairs or wherever else she happened to be, with the result that she suffered bruises and other hurts.

On June 25th, 1842 when Blumhardt had been called away to attend a children's festival, he heard on his return that Theophila was on the verge of madness. He hastened to her, and before long she seemed to have recovered thoroughly, but on the same afternoon matters took an extraordinary turn. The patient suffered so violent an attack that she lay there as though dead; again it seemed as though demons were departing from her, but this time to an extent far exceeding any previous experience, arousing in Blumhardt the conviction that he had won an unexpectedly sweeping victory. As a matter of fact there was no further trouble for several weeks, during which Theophila was free to go where she pleased.

One day, however, she suddenly appeared at his house for the purpose of making a confession which she had hitherto withheld out of bashfulness. She confided to Blumhardt that on every Wednesday and Friday she was attacked by a disorder attended by painful and copious hemorrhages, and that unless this disorder were checked, it would soon lead to her death. Her accounts of certain other experiences associated with this trouble cannot be repeated here, and were of such a nature that Blumhardt was forced to see in them a confirmation of the most grewsome figments of the imagination conjured up by popular superstition. "At first," writes Blumhardt, "it took me some time to force myself to accept the melancholy conviction that Darkness should have acquired such power over mankind. My next thought was: 'It is all over now! You are getting into witchcraft and sorcery, and what do you hope to accomplish against these forces?' And when I looked at that piteous figure I shuddered to think that such sinister forces could exist against which there seemed to be no possible help. It occurred to me that there were people reputed to possess mysterious arts which insured protection against demoniacal evils of all kinds, and sympathetic magical expedients, implicitly believed in by high and low. Ought I to seek recourse in things like these? That, I had long since made up my mind, would be fighting the Devil with his own weapons.

"Would not sincere prayer accomplish something against the powers of Satan as they stood revealed, regardless of their strength? What hope indeed is there for us poor, puny mortals, if we cannot obtain direct help from Above? If there is such a thing as sorcery and witchcraft, is it not a sin to allow these forces to have their way unchecked, when we have the opportunity of combatting them in earnest?"

Blumhardt therefore called out to the patient: "We must pray! Come what will of it, we must give prayer a trial. At least in this way we risk nothing. On every page of the Scriptures we are assured that our prayers are heard, and the Lord will do as He has promised."

On the following day which proved to be a memorable one for him and for those who were with him, Blumhardt again visited the sick girl. Outside, a heavy thunderstorm was gathering, promising to break a dry spell that had lasted several months. Theophila, suffering from an attack of veritable madness, seemed determined to put an end to her own life. Tearing about through both rooms she called wildly for a knife; next, she rushed up into the attic, sprang up on the window-sill and had already climbed out into the open, retaining her hold on the window frame with one hand only, when the first flash of lightning of the approaching storm met her eyes, startling and awakening her. Coming to her senses she cried out: "For God's sake! No, I will not do such a thing." But the lucid interval quickly vanished, and as her delirium returned she seized a rope which she skillfully tied to a beam and at the end of which she fashioned a noose which could readily be tightened. She had almost thrust her head into this noose when a second stroke of lightning, flashing through the window, caught her eye, and like the first one, brought her back to consciousness. On the following morning she burst into tears on seeing the rope that dangled from the beam, with its complicated knots which, in a normal state of mind, she could never have tied so skillfully.

At eight o'clock of the evening of the same day Blumhardt was summoned again and found her literally weltering in blood. Nothing need be said about certain other terrible experiences which she had undergone. Fervently Blumhardt addressed himself to prayer, after having tried with little success to hearten the girl with a few words of cheer, while the storm raged outside. Within fifteen minutes, all of her alarming symptoms had disappeared; she became quite normal again and Blumhardt left the room for a few minutes to allow her to change her clothes.

Quite unexpectedly the patient suffered a renewed attack, just like certain previous ones resulting from demoniacal influences. Suddenly, however, the full rage and disappointment of the demons burst forth in a chorus of exclamations uttered for the most part in howling and whining tones: "Now everything is lost; we have been betrayed at every turn; you are upsetting everything; our whole league is broken up; it is all over; everything is in a snarl; you are to blame with your everlasting prayers; alas, you will end by driving us away altogether. There are 1067 of us, and many more who are still alive. They should be warned. Alas, they are lost, they have forsworn God and are lost forever." "The roars of the demons, the flashing lightning, the rolling peals of thunder, the splashing of the down-pouring rain, the prayers on my part, answered by the demons in the manner related above, all combined to produce a scene, the like of which the most vivid imagination could scarcely conjure up."

Although the particular disorder in question completely disappeared from this time on, it was not long before demoniacal phenomena of a different kind made themselves noticeable. However, the demons which appeared from now on showed marked differences in their behavior. Some of them were defiant and filled with hatred for Blumhardt, often uttering words worthy of being recorded. They felt a dread of the abyss which they now felt yawned close before them, and said among other things: " You are our worst enemy and we are yours. If we only could do as we liked! If only there were no God in Heaven!" At the same time they admitted that only they themselves were to blame for their perdition. Grewsome indeed was the behavior of one of the demons who had appeared at former times to Theophilia in her home and who now confessed himself to have been a perjurer. He distorted his face, stiffly uplifted three fingers, shuddered violently and burst into groans. Similar scenes, of which Blumhardt would gladly have had more witnesses, occurred in plenty. But most of the demons which appeared from August 1842 until February 1843 and even later, were among those which fervently longed for release from the bonds of Satan. Numerous different languages were spoken by them, for the most part non-European ones. In some cases the attempts of such demons to speak the German language were peculiar and at times truly ludicrous, particularly when they tried by circumlocution to express ideas, the German terms for which were unfamiliar to them. Their speech also included words which Blumhardt was unable to ascribe to any of the demons of the class in question, sounding, as they did, like the language of a higher region. They were words of instruction and of reference to God, addressed in part to the people present, and in part to the demons themselves, to arouse them to the impious nature of their doings.

For a long while Blumhardt did not know what attitude to take toward the different kinds of spirits, particularly toward those which entreated his help. "It was some time before I paid any attention to what they said," he writes, "and I was often sorely depressed on seeing their woeful expression of countenance, their hands raised in entreaty, and the tears that streamed from their eyes, while listening to their words of terror and despair, and to their appeals, which would have moved a heart of stone. But reluctant as I was to undertake anything for their release, having at heart the integrity of my creed as a Protestant, I could not refrain in the end from making the attempt, the less so as neither threats nor exhortations were of the slightest use in making the demons desist. The first demon with which I ventured the experiment was the spirit of that woman who seemed to have been the origin of the whole matter. She again appeared to Theophila, and announced in a firm and determined manner that she wanted to belong to the Savior, and not to the Devil. She then related the great changes that had taken place in the spirit-world as a result of the recent battles, adding that it had been most fortunate for me that I had resorted only to the word of God and to prayer. Had I taken recourse to any of the mystic expedients so currently in use among people, as the demons had expected me to do, I should have been irretriveably lost. As she said this she raised her finger significantly and closed her remarks with the words: 'That was a terrible fight that you undertook.' She then entreated me urgently to pray that she might be granted complete freedom from the power of the Devil."

Day by day Blumhardt saw more clearly that the communications of the well-disposed among the suffering spirits were made under Divine guidance. Incidentally, they were effected without disturbances of any kind; nevertheless, he does not seem to have grasped the true correlation of the entire sequence of events.

I shall cite here only one more case, a particularly interesting one, taken from Blumhardt's report. One of the spirits begged that he might be permitted to enter the church for a while. Blumhardt replied: "You can see that it is the Lord Who points out the way to you. Go, wherever He directs." The spirit continued: "Might I visit your home?" This request surprised Blumhardt who, thinking of his wife and children, was not inclined to grant it, but on second thought he said: "Very well, if you will annoy no one and if Jesus is willing, you may come." Upon this a voice called from the patient's lips: "Not within walls! God is the advocate of widows and orphans!" The spirit bursting into tears, now entreated to be allowed at least to enter Blumhardt's garden, a petition which the Divine control appeared to grant. From all indications, this was the spirit of a man who during life had robbed widows and orphans of house and home.

Certain other experiences related by Blumhardt in his report have been purposely omitted by Zuendel in his biography of the clergyman. Zuendel's reason for so doing was, that in his opinion the weird and agonizing tricks of the Powers of Darkness witnessed by Blumhardt would dwarf the impression of the powerful Divine aid extended, and, in the minds of his readers, would tend to belittle the same. It would, however, undoubtedly have been better had Zuendel related the facts in full, for the truth need never shun the light of day.

The things omitted by him unquestionably refer to manifestations of the Powers of Evil through the materialization of spirits or similar phenomena of materialization, through the apport of objects or their removal, or in one of the many other ways described elsewhere in this book. Assuredly also there were physical phenomena and "direct voices", so often produced by spirits of a low order.

"Finally," relates Blumhardt, "when there appeared to be no end in sight to these phenomena, I summoned up all my resolution and implored of God, that He, since His is the power which had created everything from nothing, might now convert these realities into nothingness, in order that the arts of the Devil might be utterly annihilated. In this way I battled for several days, and the Lord, Who has promised us: 'Whatsoever ye shall ask in my name, shall be given unto you', kept His word. The fight was won."

Again, however, when everything seemed over, Theophila suffered a sudden and terrible recurrence of symptoms of illness, apparently aimed deliberately at her life. On one occasion when she had inflicted incredibly horrible wounds on herself, these were miraculously healed. Suddenly, however, they broke open again and a friend of the girl ran in haste to Blumhardt to tell him that her death might be expected at any moment. "On hearing this," writes Blumhardt, "I fell on my knees in my study and spoke out boldly. So strong had I come to feel, that on this occasion I would not even give the Devil the satisfaction of going to see the patient in person, but instead of doing so, sent word throug her friend that Theophila should get up and come to me, as she could, if she had faith. It was not long before she was walking up my stairway. What my sensations were, no one else can ever realize."

The end of the story is given by Blumhardt in the following words: "Every single thing that had happened heretofore, now seemed to come on at once. The most unfortunate part of it was that in these days the sinister effects extended to the patient's half-blind brother and to her sister Catherine, with the result that I was forced to fight for all three of them at the same time, it being quite evident to me meanwhile that their cases were closely interrelated. From this point on I cannot go into each individual occurrence in detail, as the things that happened were too many and too varied to be remembered by me. But these were days, the like of which I hope I shall never see again, for matters had reached a point at which I had to risk everything, so to speak, it being a case of "conquer or die." In the measure, however, as my exertions increased, I became more and more conscious of a Divine protection. The brother was the first to be liberated, and so completely, that he was able to render effective aid in what followed. My main concern on this occasion was not Theophila, who in the end, after a few further battles, also appeared to be quite free of the demons, but her sister Catherine who had never had the slightest trouble in the past, but who now became so raving that she could be kept in restraint only with the greatest difficulty. She threatened to tear me into a thousand pieces and I could not venture to approach her. She constantly attempted to rip herself open, as she expressed it, with her own hands, or lurked about as though waiting for a chance to commit some terrible deed upon the persons holding her. All the while she jabbered and screeched so outrageously, that it seemed as though a thousand scurrilous tongues were wagging in her at once. The most remarkable part of it was that she remained fully conscious, and aware of what was said to her, and when she was reproved for her conduct, explained that it was beyond her power to talk and act any differently. She also asked that she be held securely, to prevent her from doing any actual harm. Later on she had a clear recollection of everything, even of her attempts to commit murder in its most horrible form, and this depressed her so greatly that I had to devote several days especially to her, until, in answer to my long and earnest prayers her distressing experiences were gradually effaced from her memory. Nevertheless, there still remained within her a demon which made itself distinctly heard and which announced itself to be, not the spirit of a deceased human being, but one of the prominent angels of Satan and the head of all sorcery. This demon declared that if it were forced to fall into the abyss, sorcery would receive a wound from which it would in time bleed to death. Suddenly toward midnight the girl uttered a series of screams of despair, each single one of which was maintained for as much as a quarter of an hour, and which were so powerful that they seemed to threaten to shake the house to pieces. Nothing more awesome can be imagined. In the meantime, what was inevitable, fully half the population of the village stood listening in terror to the din of the conflict, in the midst of which Catherine was seized with a fit of trembling so violent that her very limbs appeared to be in danger of being shaken from her body. Mingled with exclamations of fear and despair, the fiend's voice could be heard uttering remarks of defiance, challenging God to give some sign, and demanding that it be spared the ignominy of laying down its part like an ordinary sinner, and that it be allowed to go down to Hell with honors, as it were. There probably never has been another such shocking exhibition of mingled malice, despair, defiance and arrogance. The final critical moment, which cannot possibly be conceived by anyone not actually present as a witness, arrived at last. At about two o'clock in the morning the alleged imp of Satan, in a voice of which the human throat seemed scarcely capable, bellowed out, while the girl threw her head and shoulders backward over the back of her chair: "Jesus has won! Jesus has won!" words which could be understood as far as they could be heard and which made an indelible impression on their hearers. From this instant on the strength and power of the demon appeared to fail from moment to moment. It became more and more quiet and incapable of motion, and at last disappeared by imperceptible stages, as life ebbs away in the dying but not until about eight o'clock in the morning."

Thus ended the two years' battle.

What Blumhardt had experienced were the manifestations of the low and evil spirit-world through human mediums. In themselves, these were nothing new, but for him they were a novel experience. Had he not taken the part of these mediums who were in the Evil One's power, the same thing would have happened to them which happens daily to so many people whom, in our general complete ignorance of the subject we leave to their own devices. They would either have landed in an insane asylum, or would have put an end to their own existence. The inmates of our asylums are in large part the victims of the low spirit-world, and this same uncanny power also is often active in the case of suicides.

Theophila Dittus was a "deep-trance medium." How she came to be developed as such cannot be determined from anything appearing in Blumhardt's relation. It is quite probable that she had engaged in "table tapping" experiments and the like with her brothers and sisters, and that her innate mediumistic qualifications underwent a constant development in this way.

She would lose consciousness whenever her own spirit was forced from her body by strange spirit-beings which then took possession of her. At the egress of her own spirit she would fall down as though dead, and would be brought back into an erect posture by the spirit of some demon which had entered her body and made itself manifest there.

The powerful rapping sounds were produced by the od which Theophila, thanks to pronounced mediumism, surrendered to the spirit-world, and with which the latter brought about those resounding blows which seemed to be inexplicable to the observers. The greater the odic power which accumulated in the medium, the louder these blows became, and this odic power was reinforced by the masses of od radiated by the people about her. Since Blumhardt also, although he was unaware of the fact, was endowed with considerable mediumistic power, the manifestations of the spirit-world through the medium were stronger during his presence than they were in his absence. The phenomena of materialization and the appearance of light also were brought about by the demons with the aid of Theophila's mediumistic od.

Her sister Catherine was no deep-trance medium, but went into part-trances only. Consequently, her spirit was not entirely expelled from her body and could hear everything spoken through her by the strange spirit. She was able, therefore, to remember everything that had happened, even though she could not prevent the manifestations themselves, since she was completely in the power of the strange spirit-being.

Blumhardt gradually learned to distinguish between the different kinds of spirits. Above all, he became convinced of the important fact that a Divine control presides at the appearance of higher spirits and of spirits which though suffering, are well-disposed, so that everything proceeds in perfect order. This control determines which spirits are to be admitted. Hence the suffering spirits which had been granted access by the higher control did not obey Blumhardt in the beginning, when he tried to send them away without having given them any help. They had entered the medium at the orders of a superior authority for the sake of being instructed by Blumhardt and of being shown the way to God by him; they were therefore entitled to his instruction and it was his duty to grant their petitions. Unfortunately he did not recognize this duty until a late hour.

The instructive feature of these occurrences as regard Blumhardt was the undeniable fact that communication with the spirit-world exists. The events that took place before his eyes were no delusions, and cannot be relegated to the realm of fable by anyone, since they were enacted quite openly and could be confirmed by a large number of witnesses who had seen and heard what went on.

The reality of the occurrences was also the reason why the ecclesiastical authorities requested Blumhardt to present a memorial of the events.

At first Blumhardt could see only the undeniable facts of what took place before his eyes, and it was not until later that he learned to correlate certain items in this field. Of the eternal laws governing intercourse with the spirit-world he seems to have known nothing until the day of his death. For this reason he was unable to discover the way in which both the people of Israel and the first Christians were able to communicate with the good spirit-world. He did, indeed, experience in a harrowing manner the speech of evil and suffering spirits through human mediums, but the wonderful messages brought by God's high spirits through speaking mediums were denied him. For this also there was a good reason, for there is a time for everything that happens. Undoubtedly the conditions of the times in which Blumhardt lived were not suited to intentionally produced communication with the good spirit-world, and undoubtedly also, the attitude taken by his church toward these matters would have endangered his entire activities and might have cost him his position. As it was, he met with enough opposition on the part of this ecclesiastical superiors, when later on the good spirits began to manifest themselves to him and to his parishioners, as I shall relate presently. To have ventured further in this field, as, for instance, by holding spiritistic meetings, would without doubt have called forth the most energetic action on the part of the leaders of the Protestant Church against Blumhardt. Even God's spirit-world adapts its activities to the circumstances presented by the conditions of the age.

If Blumhardt had seen, and personally experienced, harrowing examples of the pouring out of the spirit of Darkness upon mankind, he was destined also to witness in a far more wonderful manner the pouring out of the Spirit of God upon him and his congregation, in a way which recalls the pouring out of the Divine Spirit during the first days of Christianity.

The first gift from above vouchsafed to Blumhardt for his whole parish and its surroundings after his faithfully fought battle against the Powers of Evil, were the spirits of repentance and change of heart. One by one all of the inhabitants came to him, impelled by some irresistable inner force, and confessed all of the sins of their lifetime. Inwardly guided by a spirit of God, Blumhardt could say, whether or not these sins would be forgiven. This was not a case of ordinary confession and absolution as practiced in the Catholic Church, but a cleansing from sin in consequence of a revelation brought by a spirit of God. Hence from that time on Blumhardt's motto was:

"Let us pray and hope for a new out-pouring of the Holy Spirit."

The spirit of healing also came to Blumhardt. The most severe diseases were cured by the laying on of his hands, by his prayers and by his presence. In this connection it became evident that most chronic diseases are the work of evil spirit-powers, as the Bible also teaches us. Once these powers departed from the patient, his recovery followed immediately. The miraculous cures effected by Blumhardt will be found described in Zuendel's book.

I shall close my presentation of the influence of the good and the evil spirit-world on Blumhardt's life with the following words, taken from one of his letters:

"If anybody should wish to find out whether everything that the Lord is doing for me is personal, or whether others can imitate me, I must admit that as a result of my battles I have acquired a personal something that not everyone can obtain out of hand. *At the same time I am convinced that what I have acquired must eventually become more commonly held, and that in general it is permissible to pray for a complete restoration of the original powers.* In my case I have for the present received proof of the fact only, that such a prayer may be offered. But unless the Heavens are opened, so to speak, to receive the prayer, it will not be answered, and it is a mistake to think that a mere renewal of faith will restore everything that man had in the apostolic days. No, those powers have indeed been revoked, and it will take a long time to recover them. Want of faith and defection from Christianity, dating back for more than a thousand years, have brought upon us the Lord's disfavor and have given preponderance to the powers of Satan. On this account we cannot make a new beginning out of hand; if we attempt it, we very soon meet with obstacles. You can see by the foregoing how widely I differ from the Irvingites who, ignoring the present state of the Christian world, expect that everything will be restored to them. The first thing that is needed is a new conversion of Christianity, and that of a much more sweeping character than what we witness on a small scale. In order that this may come about, we must fight harder, preach more according to the Scriptures, and pray more earnestly. If a spirit of repentance is poured out on a great scale, as I witnessed on a small scale in my community where this was followed immediately by the first signs of spiritual gifts, then other things will come, one by one, until we shall have returned to an apostolic age, in which, it is true, the real Anti Christ will re-appear."

This exposition of Blumhardt's is somewhat obscure and but partly correct. The truth of the matter is, that every human being, Christian or non-Christian, can get into touch with the good spirit-world if he is in earnest, and if he seeks this communication in the manner described in this book. The one thing that everyone derives from communication with good spirits is instruction as to the right path leading to God. What he learns is the truth. Whether or not any further exertions are made on his behalf by God's spirits depends in each case on whether the individual fashions his life in accordance with the truth imparted to him, and to what extent he does so. Whoever merely accepts the truth as it is laid before him by the spirit-world but fails to act accordingly, will receive no further gifts from above. On the contrary he will lose even what contact he had at first with the good spirits, which will cease communicating with him. But whoever receives the truth within himself and strives to reconstruct his inner life in conformity with it, will give evidence of the efforts of the spirits on his behalf such as we find among the early Christians, and in each case, to correspond with the individual's task in life. Even among the early Christians not everyone possessed the same gifts, nor were the several gifts bestowed for the sole purpose of benefitting their recipients, but to be used for the general good of all. The Apostle Paul constantly lays great stress on this fact. Today also the smallest community of pious and devout men and women will receive the same things from the spirits of God that were received by the first Christians. The only condition imposed is, that we shall strive with might and main for the good, and reject all evil.

Whether the group in question is large or small is a point which will never affect the activities of the spirit-world of God.

A picture of the manifestations of the evil and the good spirit-worlds similar to that presented in the case of the Protestant clergyman Blumhardt, is encountered in the experiences of the Catholic priest Vianey, of Ars.[1]

Jean Baptiste Maria Vianey lived from 1786 to 1840; hence a considerable part of his life falls within the lifetime of the clergyman Blumhardt. While the latter was exercising his beneficent functions in the German parish of Moettlingen, Vianey was living and laboring in the tiny community of Ars in France. Because of his limited talents, it had cost Vianey great exertions to qualify for the priesthood.

From childhood on he had devoted much time daily to meditation and prayer. This inward concentration which he continued to practice all his life, as did Blumhardt, brought about the development of his mediumistic gifts which is the pre-requisite for the influences exercised on people by the spirit-world. The same was true of Blumhardt.

But while the Protestant minister at first witnessed the demoniacal manifestations through the medium Theophila Dittus of his parish, and did not experience the influences of both the evil and the good spirit-worlds upon his own person until later, the curate of Ars was the only one through whom the spirits manifested themselves, no similar effects having been noted in the case of any of his associates or parishioners.

In other respects the experiences of both were the same. Blumhardt as well as Vianey witnessed the same kind of activities on the part of the demons, as well as on the part of the good spirits. Both received a powerful spirit of healing. Both had the gift of clairvoyance as regarded past, contemporaneous, and coming events. Both were able to read the inmost thoughts of people by clairvoyance. Upon the parishes of both pastors the spirit of reformation was miraculously shed and gradually extended its influence to far distant districts. Both became the goal of pilgrimages made by thousands of people tortured by the consciousness of a sinful existence, who went to confess their transgressions and to receive assurance of God's forgiveness. Both knew by inner inspiration, those persons to whom such assurance could be given.

---

[1] Joseph Vianey: Leben und Wirken des Johannes Baptista Vianey, Pfarrers von Ars. 1930. Published by Gebr. Steffen, Limburg a. d. Lahn.

The coincidence in all of these matters as regards these two men extends to the smallest details, enabling us to discover therein the workings of a Divine law. Finally, the laws according to which the demons revealed themselves were the same in both cases.

Let us now allow the facts taken from Vianey's life to speak for themselves, beginning with the activities of the demons revealed to him.

In his biography, the part which deals with the demoniacal influences is introduced with the following words: "It is not out of place here to say a word for the benefit of those who might feel tempted to have any doubts on this score, or to smile as they read what is related in the succeeding pages. They will not be the first to do so. In fact they will not form or utter a single opinion on the subject, which was not formed or uttered by the world during Vianey's lifetime, and which the clergy of his day expressed even more forcibly than did the laity. For scarcely had the rumor begun to spread that the curate of Ars was being persecuted by devils, when loud laughter burst forth from all the parsonages of the surrounding districts. Forthwith all of the "dear" colleagues of the curate of Ars explained to him that he was a great dreamer and that his brain was affected; that the Hell out of which his demons came, was nothing more or less than the kettle in which he allowed his potatoes to grow moldy. "Dear colleague," they used to tell him, "try to live like other people. Be more careful of your diet. Then your brain will get well and you will see nothing more of those devils."

Vianey, it should be explained, lived very modestly, sustaining himself almost exclusively on potatoes, which he cooked for himself at the beginning of the week and ate cold; it not infrequently happened that by the end of the week they had become moldy as well.

"So far from being a weak-minded simpleton who would be imposed upon by hallucinations, as his colleagues assumed, Vianey was by nature so little credulous, that at first he would not admit that it was devils which plagued him. It was not until he had sought in vain for an explanation of the peculiar noises which again and again disturbed him at night, that he recognized their origin and nature.

"One day he heard loud knocking at the door of his house. Opening the window, he asked: "Who is it?" There was no answer, and when the sound was repeated at the door leading to the stairway, he repeated the question. Again there was no answer. Inasmuch as he had in his parsonage certain splendid vestments which had been presented to him for his church, he thought that thieves had tried to break into his home, and considered it advisable to take precautionary measures. He therefore asked several courageous citizens to keep watch for him. They came accordingly and stood guard for several nights, hearing the same noises but discovering nothing definite. A watch which was set in the belfry was equally unsuccessful. Violent blows were heard, but nothing was seen. This naturally alarmed the watchmen, and even the curate became thoroughly frightened. One winter's night when he had again heard loud knocking at his housedoor, he sprang hastily out of bed, and went down into the courtyard, convinced that if human miscreants were concerned in the matter, they must have left their tracks in the new-fallen snow, thus furnishing a clue for their arrest. However he could see no one nor hear any further noises; neither were there any footprints in the snow. There was now no further doubt in his mind that he was being persecuted by Satan.

"From the day on which he became convinced that the nocturnal rioters were demons, he felt much less afraid.

"In the meantime the main efforts of the demons were obviously aimed to interfere with his pastoral activities by robbing his over-worked body of its nightly rest. All the measures taken by these imps seemed admirably designed to make it impossible for him to get any sleep. Generally Vianey heard one of those monotonous noises which are notoriously conducive to sleeplessness. Sometimes the sounds resembled those made in sawing or boring through a beam; again, as though a row of nails were being driven. Then he would hear the foot-falls of regiments of soldiers passing by his door; trampling as of a herd of sheep overhead; the hoof-beats of a horse galloping across the room; noises as though someone were drumming upon his table, as though a cooper were hammering metal bands on casks, as though every wagon in Lyons were being driven over his floor, or as though an uproarious meeting were being conducted in his courtyard in a strange language. The last mentioned nuisance continued for several nights in succession. On another occasion he heard the door being opened and someone calling him roughly by his surname. He was also subjected to a world or coarse witticisms, among which the most frequent was the epithet: "potato-feeder." Moreover his furniture was moved back and forth, and his curtains were pulled about with such force that he was surprised to find them whole in the morning." (pp. 66-70.)

Great also were the inward tribulations inflicted upon him by the evil beings for the purpose of driving him to despair.

We meet with the same thing in Blumhardt's case. Unfortunately, the descriptions contained in his memorial of the demoniacal influences to which he was subjected in person, have been deliberately suppressed in his biography, as I have already stated.

In Blumhardt's case as well as in Vianey's, the sole purpose of the demoniacal powers was to curtail, if not to destroy completely, the usefulness of these two men in their efforts to lead their fellow-creatures back to God. For this reason they tried to ensnare Blumhardt, through Theophila Dittus, in the, to him, unfamiliar field of the demoniacal, and after these efforts had failed, to confuse and discourage him by external and internal trials. With Vianey, their first attempt was aimed at dispiriting him and driving him to despair, through the instrumentality of the Catholic clergy of the neighborhood, which opened such a campaign of slander and insinuation against the poor curate of Ars and continued it for ten years, that anyone else must have succumbed to such odds. When this brought no results, the demons tried to undermine his health by depriving him of sleep, an effort from which they did not desist as long as he lived. It was only in the closing years of his life that he seems to have been no longer disturbed at night.

The similarity between these two men becomes even more striking when we compare the Divine aid they received from the good spirits. In this respect their experiences were identical.

On both their lofty Divine gifts were bestowed only after they had been severely tried in battle with the Powers of Evil and their human instruments. This fight must be fought by everyone who wishes to labor as an instrument of the Lord for the salvation of his fellow men and to acquire the Divine powers necessary for the purpose. Christ Himself had to fight his battle. His work in public, giving proof of the Divine power residing within Him, began only after He had been subjected for forty days and forty nights to the terrible assaults of the demons, and had resisted them successfully. And surely, the servant is no higher than the master.

The reclamation of souls through an inner mending of ways

which followed the outpouring of a spirit of repentance, took the same course in Blumhardt's parish as in Vianey's, and in both parishes alike, spread by degrees to the most distant regions. The first effect of spirits of repentance upon the hearts of men is to awaken within them an alarm over past sins and transgressions, and over the consequent drifting away from God. This alarm for themselves which is felt by people who have been touched by the spirit of repentance is so great, that they can find no rest until they have laid bare their inmost souls to a faithful servant of the Lord, and have heard his judgment. They are urged on by an unseen power, until they feel the Divine presence within them, and have received the assurance conveyed thereby that their sins have been forgiven. The sensation of happiness which then fills their hearts is beyond the power of human words to describe. Let the reader consult the lives of these two men if he would know the feelings of those who have been reclaimed from a life of sin.

Those souls which did not require his help were recognized by Vianey at the first glance. He used to ask them in a friendly way: not to take up his time, occasionally telling them:

"Go home and do not worry. You have no need of me."

The healing of ailing souls, which could not effect their own cure, was the main object of the curate of Ars. In his eyes the healing of physical ailments was of much less importance.

There were many to whom Vianey gave information concerning the lot of their departed dear ones in the Beyond, whenever he thought it conducive to their spiritual good to do so. He was able also to foretell the future by clairvoyance, and that, to such an extent, that it might be said that while during his lifetime nothing aroused so much interest as his battles with the evil spirits, after his death all the world began to speak of his predictions. These, in almost every case, related to the fortunes of individuals and not to public matters. To some of those who had reformed he predicted the imminence of their death; in other cases, he foretold this to the person's relatives, in order that they might be prepared for the event.

He also had mental pictures of distant happenings which concerned persons with whom he was engaged in conversation. One day, noticing a man in the crowd that was waiting to be admitted, he said: "Get back to Lyons as fast as you can. Your house is on fire," a message which proved to be correct. On another occasion Vianey ordered a peasant woman who had just confessed to him, to go home at once, telling her that a snake had crept into her house. The woman hastened home and searched the house all over, but found nothing. Finally it occurred to her to shake out her pallet, which she had laid in the sun to air; as she did so, she saw a snake crawling out of it. A young girl whom he saw standing in the church was directed by him to return home without delay, as her presence there was urgently wanted; upon her arrival, she found her sister, who had hitherto been in perfect health, lying dead. Once a woman, who had been given a bottle of an alleged miraculous remedy by a "sorcerer", came to Ars to confess her sins. After Vianey had listened to her confession he remarked to her: "You have told me nothing about the bottle that you hid in the bushes outside of Ars."

Even more frequent were his demonstrations of his ability to read the secret thoughts and feelings of others. This gift invariably manifested itself in the case of a particularly difficult reformation. It happened almost daily that Vianey left his confessional and beckoned to those persons who were the most pressed for time or the most unhappy, in order that they might be the first to receive his attention.

Among his visitors were some who merely came to test his powers. All of these left greatly crestfallen. One of them confessed a number of imaginary sins; after listening to him, Vianey remarked quietly: "You have indeed much guilt upon your conscience; but the evil which you have actually committed does not consist of the sins which you have just recounted to me, but of the following ones," whereupon Vianey, to the great dismay of the impostor, revealed all of the latter's past misdeeds.

Those who could not visit Vianey personally and were obliged to communicate with him by go-betweens or by letter, were healed, advised, consoled or reformed by him at a distance.

Every hitherto mentioned individual trait in the picture of the spirit-forces working through Vianey, appears also in kind and in extent, and, it might be added, identically, to the smallest detail, in the case of Blumhardt. As for which one of the two was visited by the greater number of people, who streamed to them in thousands and experienced in their own persons the miraculous workings of their powers, it is difficult to say.

Another manifestation which was shared by both was what might be called a miraculous replenishment of the food-supply. With Blumhardt it happened that owing to the great influx of outsiders who were hospitably received and lodged by his parishioners, a serious food-shortage developed. But a special blessing seemed to preside over the question of sustenance. One family which did not have enough food on hand for fourteen persons, managed to give forty-two people enough to eat without exhausting its larders entirely. In Vianey's case an even more remarkable miracle is reported, and vouched for by everyone in his parish. He maintained a home for poor children, and one day discovered that there were no provisions left except a few handfuls of grain in the corn-bin. With a heavy heart he made up his mind to send the children away, but before doing so, he offered one more prayer to God for help. On going back to the corn-bin he found it filled with grain to the top. All of his parishioners likewise came to see the miracle. The event caused great sensation throughout the entire district. In the end even the bishop visited the home and was shown the height to which the corn-bin had been filled.

If we compare these two men as instruments of God, we cannot fail to notice a very important point. We have before us two persons of radically different creeds: on the one hand, a Catholic priest, who venerates saints and relics, who attributes all cures to Saint Philomena, who celebrates Mass and regards confession as essential to the forgiveness of sins, who believes in transsubstantiation, and holds fast to all other teachings of his church; and on the other hand, the Protestant clergyman Blumhardt, whose creed is diametrically opposed to Vianey's; who categorically repudiates the adoration of saints and relics, the Mass and communion, the Catholic form of confession and absolution, Popery and everything connected therewith, as not ordained by God, but as the offspring of human errors. And yet, under the hand of God, both rank equally as instruments for the delivery of mankind from sin and from Satan, and for guiding it back to the Home of the Father. And both, in spite of the differences in the tenets of their respective creeds, receive the highest gifts which Christ promised to those who followed Him.

In one respect they are alike: in a profound faith in God and in their consequent reliance upon Him, as well as in their great love of God and of mankind. Before God, therefore, the religious denomination to which a man belongs is of no weight. He regards this only as as outer garment supplied to men, and as of no influence upon their spiritual personality, if this is imbued with faith, and with a love of God. He allows men to retain this garment, which is a patchwork of human errors, so long as it does not obstruct the task which has been assigned to mankind.

If the question should be asked why the good spirit-world did not enlighten these men as to the errors of their religious views and inform them of the truth, it can be answered without difficulty.

In the first place no such enlightenment was necessary, because the doctrinal errors in no way obstructed the work which God had assigned to both. They were called upon to persuade the people of their immediate neighborhood and those living at a distance to search their own hearts and to return to their God, something to which no objection could be found in either the Catholic or the Protestant creed.

But above all, the spirit-world could not have enlightened either man as to the errors of his religious doctrines, without making the fulfillment of the tasks by either a Blumhardt or a Vianey impossible. For had the Protestant clergyman Blumhardt received any new revelations, he must have altered his teachings accordingly, which would have placed him outside of the Protestant Church and thereby lost him his position as well as his sphere of activity.

The same thing is true to an even greater extent of the Catholic priest Vianey, for had he departed in only a single point from the doctrines of his church, his connection therewith would have been severed for all time.

Among Catholics the task of saving souls could be performed only by one who wore the robes of the Catholic faith, just as Blumhardt could hope for success among his co-religionists only as a representative of the Protestant creed.

Even as it was, the efforts of both were attacked without moderation by their own colleagues, although each of them was devoted to his church. How much more, then, would they have been antagonized, had they departed in one point or another from the doctrines of their respective churches?

In Vianey's case particularly there were no bounds to the attacks by his colleagues. As already mentioned, he was persecuted, criticized, slandered, abused, and made the object of suspicion by them for ten years, and was even threatened with physical violence. When the Catholic clergy of his immediate and more remote neighborhood saw their parishioners hastening to Vianey and paying more heed to his opinion than they did to those of their own priests, envy and jealousy were added to their hostile feelings. They spoke of him as the ignorant priest, who had barely been able to acquire a little Latin and had nearly been expelled from the seminary. Above all, the enthusiasm with which people spoke of the curate of Ars, caused the measure of hatred harbored against him by the other divines to overflow. He was slandered most shamelessly. Priests forbad their parishioners to go to Ars for confession, and threatened them, in case of disobedience, with barring them from the sacraments and denying them absolution even in the hour of death. Sunday after Sunday they thundered against the curate of Ars from their pulpits. Speaking of this in after days, Vianey once said: "The Gospel was given a complete rest in the pulpit, while everyone was busy preaching sermons against the poor curate of Ars." While some ridiculed his ignorance, others cast reflections on the life he was leading. He was the recipient of countless anonymous letters in which the most blackguardly charges, couched in the vilest language, were brought against him. The clergy even tried to incite the public against him. Mornings, on opening his front door, he would find it decorated with posters accusing him of having passed the night in the most shameful debauchery.

In his case as in Blumhardt's we find a repetition of the attitude taken by the Jewish priesthood toward Christ: "and the chief priests and the scribes heard it and sought how they might destroy him, for they feared him for all the multitude was astonished at his teaching." The popular sayings regarding "clerical jealousy" and that "one clergyman is hated by the rest as though he were the Devil," were amply confirmed in the case of these two men.

Even if the attacks made on Blumhardt by his colleagues never fell to the level of those delivered against Vianey, the former suffered his full share of trouble and persecution at their hands.

If such bitterness was shown in the fight that was waged against these two, in spite of their scrupulous adherence to the doctrines of their creeds, what would not have happened had it been possible to convict them of holding views in conflict with the teachings of their churches?

In selecting and preparing their instruments, even God and His spirit-world are guided by the condition of the times and by the religious atmosphere that prevails in the surroundings in which those instruments are destined to labor. Human opinions and errors are ignored by God's spirit-world, so long as they do not constitute a serious obstacle to the attainment of the goal it has set. Not a single one of Vianey's erroneous religious beliefs was corrected by the good spirits which appeared to him, because these errors in no way interfered with the task he had to perform. Only when, as a result of his mistaken views on bodily penance which he regarded as particularly acceptable to God, he undertook to mortify his body in this way, did the spirit-world intervene by means of its teachings. At that point such intervention was imperative, since any lowering of his physical powers would have resulted in a corresponding loss of effectiveness of his efforts. A commanding voice which he heard by clairaudience, reminded him of the real task that had been assigned to him. Speaking of this incident, Vianey says: "I do not know whether it was a real voice that I heard, or whether it was merely a dream; at all events, it caused me to wake up. This voice told me that it was more pleasing to God to save the soul of a single sinner than to offer untold sacrifices. This happened at a time when I had resolved to do penance for my own sanctification."

Vianey, the Catholic priest of Ars, was canonized by his Church. If it is at all within the power of man to canonize man, the Protestant clergyman Blumhardt is entitled to the same honor, for in point of character and effectiveness, and of the amazing gifts with which he was endowed, he was in no way his Catholic brother-clergyman's inferior.

The lives of these two men show, that the good and the evil spirit-powers are as actively concerned with mankind today as they were at any time in the past, and that their workings are subject to the same laws.

Spiritism in the Light of Modern Science

PRIOR to the time at which I learned of communication with the spirit-world, I had had no knowledge of the possibility of any such intercourse, having read neither books nor periodicals dealing with the subject. Similarly, throughout the period during which I was receiving the teachings recorded in this book from my ultra-mundane guides, I never came into contact with other spiritistic circles nor did I consult any spiritistic literature whatever. As long as I remained a member of the clergy, I devoted my full attention to the truths which were imparted to me week by week through the mediums, and which, more than anything else, caused a radical change in my religious views. My hours of study were devoted to the Scriptures, as I was eager to learn whether the new truths which were demolishing the structure of my previously-held beliefs, agreed with the teachings of the Bible. The Holy Writ was to be my touchstone. Moreover, the spirit-world was constantly urging me to compare my newly acquired knowledge with what is set down in the Bible. At our religious meetings the spirit which manifested itself, regularly took up the Bible and expounded its contents.

However, after a certain time, when I had absorbed the presentation of the truth and had acquired a firm conviction of the same, I was invited to make myself acquainted with present-day spiritistic phenomena, which I would have the opportunity of testing and interpreting in the light of the laws imparted to me. Should I witness anything that I could not understand, I could obtain the desired explanation by asking for it at one of the seances which I attended.

From the outset I resolved to test only those phenomena of whose genuineness there could be no question. At about that time, early in 1928, I heard of a scientific periodical issued with the co-operation of eminent scientists of almost all countries, and devoted to the discussion of occurrences which cannot be explained by any known natural laws. This periodical is entitled: *"Zeitschrift fuer Parapsychologie"*[1] (Magazine of Parapsychology). The word "parapsychology" signifies the science of things beyond the scope of the familiar laws governing psychic life.

[1] Zeitschrift fuer Parapsychologie, published by Oswald Mutze, Leipzig.

Securing the 1926 and 1927 series of this periodical, the earliest published, I used them as the material for my comparative study. The facts therein related are so thoroughly substantiated as to leave no room for doubt regarding their authenticity, and embrace all phenomena observed in the realm of spirit-communication. To be sure, the periodical confines itself to the statement of facts. As to how these are to be explained is something about which opinions differ widely. Regarding the existence of a spirit-world as the intermediary in these phenomena, modern science refuses to recognize this, and it is only very occasionally and with the greatest diffidence that a scientist will hint at the possibility of intervention on the part of spirit-beings. Instead, explanations are concocted which must strike any normally minded person as puerile.

Inasmuch as the "mediums" are the sources of the power used by the spirit-world for the production of the various phenomena, I shall, in the following pages, group the occurrences observed at the present day about the respective mediums, who are discussed in the publication in question, from which, also, the facts are taken, their correct interpretation being appended in the final part of each section.

Kluski, the medium of Warsaw. (Zeitschrift fuer Parapsychologie, 1926, p. 5-22.) F. W. Pawlowski, professor of anatomy at the University of Michigan, U.S.A., who gives an exhaustive account of his observations of the medium Kluski, writes as follows:

"The phenomena which I witnessed in Kluski's case were most extraordinary, and surpassed everything I had previously read and heard of such matters.

"The preliminaries that usually preceded a *seance* with the medium Kluski consisted of a minute examination of the room in which the test was held, and of all the articles contained therein. Windows and doors were locked and sealed, and strips of waxed paper, bearing secret marks and signed by the spectators were pasted over the crevices. If so desired and when no ladies were present, the medium appeared entirely naked.

"Almost as soon as the participants had taken their seats at the table and formed a chain, the medium went into a trance, upon which the phenomena usually made themselves evident at once. The chain was formed by hooking the little finger of each hand into that of one's neighbor. This allowed the observers to move the rest of the hand freely, as for writing, or for feeling of or touching objects, without breaking contact.

"The *seances* were held either in complete darkness or by the light of a red-lantern. In either case, luminous plates were provided on the table. The plates have a surface equivalent to about one square foot and are made of some light wood, having a handle something like that of a hand-mirror. One face of these plates is covered with a luminous composition.

"It is frequently unnecessary for the observers to turn off the white light, for as soon as the medium falls into a trance the white light goes out of its own accord and the red light is turned on. Habitual attendants relate that the going and coming of the light proceeds slowly and by stages.

"From personal experience and from first-hand testimony given by perfectly trustworthy observers, I can state it as a fact that the medium Kluski produces the following phenomena:

a. "*Rappings* or knocks which are characteristic, and represent something peculiar to themselves. I have often heard them and noted their peculiarity at once, without having my attention called to it by anyone else. I could distinctly hear, or rather feel, that they were not produced on the surface of the table or of the walls, but within the same. I mention this particularly, because I made several attempts to imitate the rappings produced by Kluski, but failed entirely to obtain the tone of the rappings heard at Kluski's *seances*.

b. "*Exhibitions of levitation* (maintaining the human body in the air without support). I did not witness this personally, but heard that it often occurs at Kluski's *seances*. Not only has the table been upset and lifted, but the medium himself as well as one or more spectators were raised several feet above the floor.

c. "Kluski's specialty is the production of partial, or, more often, of completely formed *apparitions or phantoms*. The partial materializations usually are those of heads. These materializations appear almost instantly either above or behind the medium, but still oftener behind or among the spectators, who are seated at some distance from him. After a few sharp, distinctly audible raps on the table or the walls, bright stars or sparks appear, rising above the table and floating upward toward the ceiling. These sparks, which have a bluish light, vary in size from that of a pea to that of a hazelnut, and often appear to the number of a dozen. They all move simultaneously and at considerable speed above the seats of the observers, flying in all directions and forming in groups or by twos. Some vanish, while others descend in pairs close to the spectators. Whenever they came within about sixteen inches of me, I could see to my great surprise that they were pairs of human eyes which looked at me. In a few minutes a perfectly formed human head appeared about such a pair of eyes, being clearly visible by the light of a hand which had also been materialized and the palm of which was luminous. The hand was raised above the head in order to see it plainly. All the while the eyes rested steadily upon the spectator, the face assuming a friendly, smiling expression. I saw a number of such heads, occasionally two at a time, flying like balloons from one spectator to another, and when entreated: "Please come over to me" taking the shortest route to the person making the request, often directly across the table and as swiftly as shooting stars.

d. "*Invisible phantoms, which, however, made themselves heard by foot-steps and the creaking of the floor-boards,* came and touched my face and hands and other parts of my body with their soft, living hands. The sensation of the touch of a living human hand was unmistakable. At the request of the spectators, these invisible phantoms will fetch articles from the different parts of the room in which the *seance* is being held, and in spite of the darkness, never make a false move, never collide with anything and never touch a spectator, not even when moving a heavy object like a bronze bust weighing thirty pounds, or when setting down an iron kettle filled with twenty-five pounds of melted paraffine.

e. "*Apparitions visible by red light.* These phantoms generally picked up a luminous plate and turned its back to the spectator, throwing the light upon themselves and going from one person to another, to give each one the opportunity of observing them close by. The light radiated by the plate was so strong that the pores and roughness of the skin of the phantom faces and hands could be distinguished. In the nose of one old man I could even see the sinuous tracing of the tiny veins. I could distinguish also the texture of the cloth with which the phantom was covered. These apparitions came so close to me that I could hear them breathe and feel their breath against my face.

"But the most impressive and convincing feature of these apparitions when they came toward us were the eyes and the faces with their lifelike expression. When questions were addressed to the apparitions the facial expression was always perfectly suited to the answer, while an amiable smile played constantly about their lips.

f. "*Of specters of animals* we saw chiefly squirrels, dogs and cats. On one occasion a lion appeared and on another, a large bird, either a falcon or a buzzard. I myself saw an animal of each of the first two mentioned species, which behaved quite as might have been expected, the squirrel hopping about the table, the dog running around it wagging his tail, jumping into the laps of the spectators and licking their faces. In short, he acted as any house-dog would. According to what was told me, the lion's demeanor was more threatening; he lashed his tail, striking it against the furniture and the startled observers, unable to control the brute, put an end to the *seance* by awakening the medium. The buzzard flew about, beating the walls and ceiling with his wings, and when he finally perched on the medium's shoulder, a flashlight photograph was taken of him, an apparatus already focussed upon the medium, having been held in readiness for the purpose.

"Within this class of phantoms should also be included the strange specter of a creature called the "pithecanthropos" by the members of the group. This apparition is frequently in evidence at Kluski's *seances.* Since it arrives only in complete darkness, a minute examination of it is difficult. It has the *appearance of a hairy man* or of a large ape, its face being covered with hair, its forehead fairly high; and its arms long and powerful; its behavior toward the observers is rough and boisterous. It tries to stroke their hands and faces, and in so doing generally breaks up the *seance,* or compels the spectators to do so, as they are unable to control the beast. I saw, or rather felt it only once, when it brushed against me, and noticed a peculiar odor which at the moment I could not define, but which others who were more familiar than I with the phantom, described as that of a wet dog. On the occasion mentioned it passed behind me, going to the lady at my side who was holding the medium's hand. It broke the chain and put an end to the *seance* by grasping the lady's hand and rubbing it against its face. This frightened her so, that she uttered a loud scream.

g. "*Many apparitions have luminous hands,* that is to say the palms of their hands shine in the dark. The light given off is white, slightly tinged with green, and is so strong that whenever the phantoms hold or pass their hands above their heads, faces or figures, every detail is shown as plainly as when luminous plates are used. They illuminate themselves in order to give the spectators an opportunity of observing them closely. They also turn their luminous hands or rather palms toward the spectators, so that the latter may be illuminated and, apparently, be observed by the phantoms in turn. On one such occasion I could see distinctly that the light was not altogether steady, but was constantly vibrating, showing different intensities, although the total amount of light thrown off by the palm remained the same throughout. I could also note especially bright sparks or rays running in zigzag courses by various routes from the base of the hand to the fingertips. At the same time the luminous palms diffused a powerful smell of ozone.

h. "One of the rarest, but perhaps one of the highest types, is *the phantom of an old man which is perfectly luminous by its own power*. I have seen it only twice. The apparition resembled a pillar of light, and, as I was told, is often seen by the Kluski Circle. The light radiating from it is so intense, that not only all the spectators, but all objects, near and distant, in the room, are illuminated by it. When I saw the apparition the palms of its hands and the region about its heart were more luminous than the other parts of its body. The phantom rose in the middle of the room, at some distance from us, the table at which we were seated standing near one corner, while the medium sat directly in the corner. The old man wore a high, conical headdress, and was clothed in a long robe which hung down from him in deep folds. He approached us with majestic strides, his robe swaying as he walked. His hands were engaged in making motions in the shape of triangles. At the same time he was speaking in a deep, solemn voice. He stopped behind me for about ten seconds, waving his luminous hands above us and speaking continually. He then withdrew to the far end of the room and vanished. His coming was accompanied by a wave of ozonated air which filled the room even after the *seances* had ended. The phantom is that of a very old man with a gray beard. His language was rather guttural, and unknown to anyone present, although between us we commanded probably twelve different tongues. To date no one has succeeded in identifying his language, or in discovering who the phantom is. Among the members of the Circle he is known as the Assyrian priest, a designation which fits his external appearance perfectly.

i. "*Paraffine molds* were made by the phantoms. As soon as they noticed the kettle filled with melted paraffine on the table, they would approach it with evident pleasure, and on request, would make complicated figures out of the paraffine. Sometimes they dipped their hands into the substance and allowed the glove-like molds so formed to drop upon the table. Whenever the phantom hand is luminous, it can be seen as it splashes about in the paraffine like a goldfish in a bowl. The glove-shaped molds were treated rather carelessly. On one occasion a pair of them fell from the table into my lap and from there to the floor. I called the attention of the others to the matter, asking them not to move their feet, lest the molds should be damaged. One spectator asked the phantom to pick up the molds and replace them on the table, which was immediately done. At the same time my ankle was seized and my leg pushed aside, to make room under the table where there were seven pairs of legs. The phantom required from half to three quarters of a minute to make a mold, whereas when I tried to do this myself, it took several minutes for the paraffine to cool sufficiently to be removed. Even then I found it impossible to strip the glove from my hand without breaking it; in fact I was unable to accomplish this with the coating of a single finger which I had dipped into the paraffine as far as the second joint.

"When I removed the paraffine from the plaster cast, by dipping it into hot water, I noticed a *number of hairs* floating in the water. They were of the kind that grow on the back of the hand and on that of the third finger-joint. Since I was quite sure that I had used perfectly clean water and a white porcelain bowl in conducting my test, I was greatly astonished at the discovery. I therefore examined all of the casts previously made, and noticed through the fine film of paraffine which surrounded one of them several bits of hair or downy matter embedded in the paraffine.

"One of the cases observed by me in this connection was especially noteworthy. In one cast the hand is doubled into a fist, the tip of the thumb projecting between the index and the middle fingers. In the test involving this particular case the phantom had been asked to do something complicated, unique and hard to imitate, but was left at liberty to do just as it liked. It had apparently reflected for a while as though trying to think of something appropriate. Then it had dipped its extended hand into the paraffine, and after having done so, had doubled it up. Before I filled this mold with plaster, I could see on the inside several irregularly shaped ribs of paraffine running through the hollow in the interior of the glove and supporting certain parts. They corresponded to the curved recesses between the fingers.

j. "Of *apports* I saw only few, and these were of small objects. I was told, however, that fairly heavy articles had been brought from distant rooms into that in which the *seances* are held. The most remarkable phenomenon of this sort was the disappearance of Kluski himself from the *seance* chamber which had been locked up and sealed. Greatly to their amazement, the members of the Society found him in a fairly remote room of the apartment, sound asleep.

k. "I was able to establish the fact that there was a considerable *fall in temperature* in the *seance-room*. I, as well as several other observers felt distinctly chilly toward the end of the *seances* lasting from one to two hours. The thermometers provided in the room showed a fall of temperature toward the end of the *seance* ranging from six to eight degrees Centigrade (10 to 15 degrees Fahrenheit). This is contrary to the usual experience since the temperature of a room, and especially of a tightly closed room, in which seven persons remain for a considerable time, generally rises, the more so as the room in question was only moderately large.

l. "As the phantoms made their appearance I saw something resembling *luminous smoke or fog* floating above the head of the medium like a small *cloud*. This cloud moved to one side and in a very few seconds became a human head, or else it would be extended vertically and become a complete human figure, which immediately began to walk about.

"The most astonishing and interesting part of these phenomena, and, in a way, their most important feature so far as I was concerned, was the *absolutely human behavior* of the apparitions. They acted precisely like guests at a party. As they passed around the table they greeted those persons with whom they were acquainted with a smile of recognition, whereas they studied any new faces attentively. The inquisitive look in their eyes is hard to describe. I could see from their efforts to understand our expression, our smiles, our questions and answers, as well as from their actions, that they were particularly anxious to convince us of the fact that they actually existed and that they were not illusions or hallucinations.

"Moreover, these apparitions are not always of life size. Toward the end of a *seance*, when the medium has become rather exhausted, or if he happens to feel indisposed before the *seance* opens, the phantoms do not appear in their full size, but smaller by a third or a half. When I saw a phantom of this kind for the first time, I thought it was that of a child, until on closer examination, I could tell by the wrinkled face that it was an old man or woman, though much below normal size.

"When such a shrinkage occurred, the leader of the Society would often say: 'Let us help the medium'. He would then beat time, while all the spectators *breathed deeply and regularly*. The effect was remarkable, for the shrunken figure of the phantom would instantly begin to grow, and in a few seconds would regain its full size.

"The phantoms which appear to Kluski belong to different nationalities and generally speak their native language. Nevertheless they readily understand remarks addressed to them in any tongue. They seem to have the power of reading the minds of others, for it is not necessary to utter any given wish or question; merely to think it is sufficient. It is necessay only to form the wish that a phantom should do some particular thing, in order to have such a wish granted, or, as the case may be, refused. In fact, phantoms occasionally refuse to do certain things, declaring that these are beyond their power, either at any, or at that particular time; again, they may promise to grant, or to attempt to grant, the request on some future occasion.

"Not all apparitions are able to speak. Many prefer to make themselves understood by rapping, a very tedious and lengthy proceeding, since the raps always correspond in number to the place of a letter in the alphabet.

"The voices are perfectly distinct and of normal strength, sounding like a loud whisper.

"The expression which animates the faces while the phantoms are speaking is very convincing. In one instance I could plainly see the look of expectation in the features of the apparition of a Turk who bowed before me saying: 'Chokyash Lehistan'. Seeing that I did not understand him, he repeated the words with an amiable smile. I still did not know what he was trying to say, but out of a feeling of admiration for his chivalrous nation, replied: '*Vive la Turquie!*' His pleasure at my remark was evident. He smiled with radiant eyes, folded his arms and disappeared. I wrote his words down on a pad and on the following day had them translated by a linguist, who told me that they signified: 'Long live Poland'."

Explanation of the foregoing facts. The experiences related as personal ones by Prof. Pawlowski in connection with the medium Kluski confirm in every respect what I had been told of the laws of spirit-communication, and especially, what is set down in the portion of this book relating to the odic force.

In nothing that takes place at the Kluski *seances* does the medium function in any way as a *thinking or acting person. He is simply and solely the source of power* from which the spirits that appear secure the od necessary for the manifestations. If the medium is unable to supply enough od, either because of his physical condition or because of a great drain on his strength due to the od already liberated, the phenomena take place either imperfectly or not at all.

The od was seen by Prof. Pawlowski as a *luminous smoke* or *cloud,* and again as *sparks* or *tiny flames.* Within these he saw pairs of eyes, and later, entire faces, which, in the measure as odic force increased, grew into complete figures.

It is the same thing that we find in the Bible in connection with the burning bush, the pillar of cloud and fire of the Israelites, the cloud resting over the tabernacle, the cloud on Mount Tabor, and the odic flames seen at Whitsuntide. All of these references occur in the Bible in connection with communications from the spirit-world, as has been exhaustively shown in the preceding chapters.

Regarding the accounts in the report quoted above of the growth of small apparitions to normal size, as soon as the participants at the *seance* began to breathe *deeply and regularly,* keeping time, this, after what has been said, will be understood at once. Not the medium alone surrenders od to the spirit-world, but also the others present, some of them liberating less, some more, especially those who have been attending such *seances* regularly. They are, in a manner, assistants to the chief medium. It is a fact, furthermore, that the liberation of od by those in attendance is greatly increased by deep and regular breathing; hence the art of breathing plays so important a part in the exhibitions given by fakirs.

That the temperature should have fallen toward the end of the *seances* instead of rising as might seem logical, is also due to natural causes. As was stated in the chapter devoted to od, it is only in its condensed form that od is perceptible to the human senses and can be used by the spirits for working on matter. It was further explained that the condensation of od is effected by means of cold currents according to the universally applicable law that *cold condenses.* Such cold currents must be used at an extra strength toward the close of a *seance,* because the warmth radiated by the persons present has an adverse effect on the condensation of the od. *It is these cold currents that cause a fall of temperature.*

Prof. Pawlowski is astonished at the human behavior of the incorporated spirits, into whose eyes and faces he could look, whose shapes he could feel, and whose heartbeats and voices he could hear. If, however, we bear in mind that these spirits are the same personalities that they were as mortals; that as spirits they possess the same organs as we, with the sole difference that *what is substance with us is ethereal matter with them,* we can readily understand that the heart of a materialized spirit beats audibly to us and that we can hear the breathing of the materialized lungs of the spirit-beings, which function precisely like ours.

By the same token, the various *individual members* that appear are simply the materialization of the respective *spirit-members.* The hands which were dipped into the paraffine until this cooled, were the materialized hands of a spirit, and had the same distinctive features that they had when that spirit inhabited its earthly abode. Hence the thumb and finger prints of a materialized spirit-hand are exactly the same as those of the corresponding human hand. Hence, also we find all of the other peculiarities which the spirit had when alive on earth, reproduced when it is materialized as a spirit, by means of the condensed od of a medium. That also is the reason why *the hairs on its hands and fingers* can be seen, if the spirit, as a human being, had patches of hair on these spots. Consequently it is quite natural that some of these hairs should have been found in the paraffine after it had cooled, for if a person whose hands are at all hairy dips them into hot paraffine, some of the hairs will fall out and remain in the same.

At this point it becomes necessary to insert a very important observation. The former physical peculiarities of spirits *are retained by them in the Beyond only as long as they remain at the spiritual level which they occupied as mortals. If, however, they progress in the Other World, their spirit-forms become finer and more beautiful and the defects and blemishes of their human shapes disappear.* Nevertheless, even spirits which thanks to their advancement in the Beyond have acquired a different and more beautiful aspect, are accustomed, when materializing at spiritistic *seances, to appear as they looked in their human form* which they are able to resume by artificial means. This is done by them only if they have *friends or relatives* present at the *seance*, and desire to be recognized by them. It is their way of establishing their identity.

The paraffine molds of which Prof. Pawlowski speaks could be made by the spirits only if the latter dipped their hands into the liquid mass and de-materialized or dissolved them completely or partially after the paraffine had cooled. In order to withdraw the hands without injuring the molds, a partial de-materialization, that is to say, a reduction of the thickness of the joints and a shortening of the fingers was sufficient. A hand-shaped mold could also be produced if, at the moment of immersion, the materialization had the *consistency of a dense mist.* The odic form of a spirit having this degree of condensation is even able to pass through solid matter. Therefore, a spirit-hand of a mist-like consistency can be withdrawn from the paraffine mold and leave this behind even *without being de-materialized.* Consequently when this happens the observer can see no change in the materialized spirit-hand.

A spirit therefore has the choice of three ways in which it can make and strip off such molds. It may either materialize its hand *solidly,* and re-dissolve it *completely:* again, it may dissolve the solid materialization only *partially,* reducing its thickness and length to the extent required, or, finally, it may use od condensed to the consistency of a heavy fog, in which case it can make the molds and take them off without changing the hand and without injury to the molds. By the last method the spirit-hand passes unhindered through the solidified paraffine, picks up the mold from the outside, and lays it on the table.

If in Prof. Pawlowski's opinion the spirits treated the molds rather casually and in one instance allowed them to drop to the floor, while in other respects their friendly and obliging manner commands his praise, his view reveals his ignorance of a very important matter. He seems not to know that it is not within the power of a spirit *to keep its hand materialized as long as it pleases.* Such materialization depends entirely on the od at the spirit's disposal and on the degree of condensation of that od. *But, as we know, heat dissolves od,* and in consequence the hot or very warm paraffine quickly destroys the materialization of the immersed spirit-hand, so that when the paraffine molds are taken from the bath, the degree of condensation is often no longer sufficient to allow the spirit to lay the molds down carefully. The molds are dropped, *not from carelessness* on the part of the spirits, *but for want of sufficient odic power and condensation.*

As for the materialization of the *spirits of animals* as well as of spirits of human beings, this is easy to understand if we remember that when an animal dies, its spirit leaves it in the same manner as a human spirit departs from its body. The sole difference between the spirits of animals and those of men is one of *degree of development,* not of kind. Animals are the incarnation of low spirits, while human beings are that of spirits which have already made progress upward.

The fact that animal spirits were materialized at Kluski's *seances* proves that these meetings are dominated by the low spirit-world, even if it happens now and then that spirits of the better class, like that of the "Assyrian priest" make their appearance there. These are as a rule the medium's guardian spirits, which endeavor to mitigate the evil influences as far as lies within their power. They cannot, however, accomplish much in that direction unless the medium and the observers of their own accord seek connection with what is good and lofty only, and reject everything low and mean. The greatest sufferer from the connection with the low spirit-world is the medium himself, and not alone morally but *physically* as well. The teachings which I received allude to the fact that the odic force taken from the medium by Evil, is not restored. Hence, as Prof. Pawlowski says, the medium Kluski *is completely exhausted after every seance,* and often *has to be put to bed before he recovers consciousness,* which occasionally does not return until several hours later. For this reason the medium under discussion prefers to hold *seances* not oftener than fortnightly, since otherwise his strength would be over-taxed.

Evil, once it has gained admittance to such a gathering, thanks to the faulty mental attitude of the medium and of the other participants, and has found its activities appreciated and welcomed by them, becomes rooted there. It does as it pleases, not as those who attend the meetings desire, and not infrequently perpetrates unmitigated mischief, at times creating scenes which can be terminated only by closing the *seance.* The situation is well described by the words of the poet: "The spirits I have raised, I cannot exorcise." Worst of all, *the medium's health is undermined little by little,* this being the reason why a great many strong mediums give out completely after a time, since during their *seances* much of their odic power is taken from them by the low and evil spirit-world, without being replaced. *Once a medium's odic power is gone, the phenomena cease.* Such mediums are then exposed to a new danger, to which many of them fall victims. Accustomed as they are to being highly regarded as mediums, they have not the moral courage to admit the loss of their mediumistic power openly, and try to conceal this loss by resorting to *trickery* and *deceit,* which they continue to employ until exposure follows. Exposures of this kind are then seized upon by the ignorant to brand the whole question of spirit-communication as a fraud and a swindle. On this score a heavy responsibility rests on all, who, when attending spiritistic meetings, fail to see to it that everything is done in the name of God, and that all evil is barred. If a meeting is regarded and conducted as an act of Divine worship, those who attend it have nothing to fear from demoniacal influences. *The forces of good are in control* and only that is admitted, which finds favor with God. The reader cannot, therefore, be warned too emphatically against spiritistic *seances held merely to provide a sensation or for scientific ends,* and not inspired by an endeavor to attain closer to God through the offices of the good spirit-world.

Again, the statements made earlier in this book regarding the smell of od, is fully confirmed by Prof. Pawlowski's observation, that the odor given out by the higher spirits was pleasant and sweet, while the od materialized into the great ape had the offensive smell of a wet dog.

Prof. Pawlowski's account concludes with the following remarks: "It is impossible for anyone to deny or to reject these phenomena, or to explain them by ascribing them to sleight-of-hand performances. I realize perfectly that it will be difficult for most people to believe them; that it is hard to conceive of the possibility of the coming into existence, within a few minutes, of living human beings, whose bones can be felt through their flesh, whose heart-beats can be heard and felt. . . I admit that all of these things are beyond our comprehension. We have been spoiled by the marvels of modern science. We believe only in natural happenings, presented to us in all their beauty; but we do not believe *in the secret of Universal Life;* in that *Divine secret* which is so carefully guarded from us. *To admit the possibility of these things would revolutionize our entire viewpoint of life and death as well as our entire attitude toward philosophy and science.*

"Science will recognize officially the great mass of experimental material already available and will lend its hand to the establishment of the truth, regardless of those moralists who see in the acceptance of psychic phenomena a menace to morality and religion. Intellectual cowardice is more or less excusable in moralists, whose narrow outlook is concerned more especially with matters of transitory interest, that touch the generality but fleetingly.

"But no student, no seeker after the truth, can afford to take such a stand. *In the end, truth will conquer and rule all things; it need not, however, be either feared or belittled.*"

Carlos Mirabelli, the Brazilian medium. (Zeitschrift fuer Parapsychologie, 1927, pp. 450-462). In 1927 there appeared in Santos, Brazil, a book entitled: "O Medium Mirabelli" containing a 74-page account of the phenomena observed in connection with a medium of that name. These phenomena occurred by daylight or at least by bright artificial light, at times in the presence of as many as sixty witnesses representing the leading scientific and social circles of Brazil.

Inasmuch as the relation of the occurrences includes the most amazing accounts as yet presented in this field, the editors of the "Zeitschrift fuer Parapsychologie" inquired of the Brazilian consul at Munich whether the persons cited in the book "O Medium Mirabelli" as witnesses of the truth of the aforesaid phenomena were known to him by name or reputation, to which the consul replied in an emphatic affirmative, adding that he was *personally acquainted* with fourteen of the witnesses named in the book, among them the incumbent President of the Republic, who had acted as the chairman of a board of arbitration, convoked to settle some question concerning Mirabelli. The consul furthermore named the Secretary of State, Reynaldo Porchat, Senator Muniz Sodre, and Olegario de Moura, professor of medicine at the University of Sao Paulo, and declared that if only these four men, who were not alone great scholars but persons whose veracity was beyond suspicion, vouched for a thing, it was not for him to express any doubts as to the correctness of their statement.

Mirabelli has been observed by 557 persons, including 452 Brazilians and 105 foreigners. Among them were 2 university professors, 72 physicians, 18 druggists, 12 engineers, 36 lawyers, 8 translators, 3 agriculturalists, 22 dentists, 5 chemists, 20 writers, 89 men in public office, 25 military men, 52 bankers, 128 merchants, 9 manufacturers, 18 journalists and 32 men of miscellaneous callings. Members of many religious orders also attended the *seances.*

Mirabelli is a universal medium, his odic power being adequate for all phenomena embraced by spirit-communication.

Mirabelli as a speaking medium. While in a state of trance, he speaks, besides his mother-tongue and several of the local dialects, German, French, Dutch, English, four Italian dialects, Czechish, Arabic, Japanese, Russian, Spanish, Turkish, Hebrew, Albanian, several African dialects, Latin, Chinese, modern Greek, Polish, Syrio-Egyptian, and ancient Greek. In his *normal state* he knows only his native language. While in a trance he delivers talks on subjects of which, in his ordinary human capacity, he knows nothing. These talks cover medicine, jurisprudence, sociology, political economy, politics, theology, psychology, history, the natural sciences, astronomy, philosophy, logic, music, spiritism, occultism and literature.

According to the medium's own statement, nothing that he utters while in a trance is evolved by him, his words being merely those of the spirits which speak through him and the names of which he willingly gives. He calls them his spiritual guides.

Mirabelli as a writing medium. To the present Mirabelli has written in 28 different languages while in a trance, setting down his words at a rate of speed which no penman in a normal state can equal. Thus in 15 minutes he wrote out 5 pages of Polish on: "The Resurrection of Poland"; in 20 minutes he wrote 9 pages of Czechish on: "The Independence of Czechoslovakia"; in 12 minutes, 4 pages of Hebrew on: "Slander"; in 20 minutes, a German composition on: "Greater Germany, Its Downfall and Restoration"; in 40 minutes, 25 pages of Persian on: "The Instability of Great Empires"; in 15 minutes, 4 pages of Latin on: "Famous Translations"; in 12 minutes, 5 pages of Japanese on: "The Russian-Japanese War"; in 22 minutes, 15 pages of Syrian on: "Allah and his Prophets"; in 15 minutes, 8 pages of Chinese on: "An Apology for Buddha"; in 15 minutes, 8 pages of Syrio-Egyptian on: "The Fundamentals of Legislation"; and in 32 minutes, three pages of hieroglyphics which have not yet been deciphered.

Mirabelli's mediumistic writing was done under the supervision of scholars who took the following measures to guard against fraud: the medium was led by two investigators into the *seance* room where his clothing and body were carefully searched. Paper and pencil were laid on a small table which had neither drawers nor shelves. Mirabelli, who is always in a state of great agitation before such *seances* seats himself in a chair in broad daylight. His examiners and the other participants form a circle around him and follow all his motions closely. The presiding member then calls for silence until the spirit-guide of the medium announces its presence.

The medium, now in a state of great ecstasy, begs in loud tones for Divine aid, and, still in a trance, begins to chant a hymn. His hand seizes a pencil, hurls it away repeatedly, grasps it again, and falls to writing feverishly. The pencil glides over the paper at lightning speed without stopping. While writing, Mirabelli turns his eyes upward and sighs, without any abatement of the speed at which his pencil travels. Then, with a radiant look, he gazes straight upward, allegedly at his guiding spirit hovering above him, which guides his hand while he writes and with which he converses affectionately. A secretary who stands beside the medium takes up the sheets of paper as they are covered, and puts them away in their proper order.

It sometimes happens that the medium's state passes from one of ecstasy to apathy, after which it undergoes still another change: Mirabelli seems quite beside himself, laughing, weeping, singing, shouting out names, answering questions, twisting about like an acrobat, spitting right and left without regard for anyone, assuming indecent postures, cursing, trying to beat out his brains, or to drink chemicals, frothing at the mouth and striking out in all directions. In the end he grows calm, and the *seance* can be concluded.

The manifestations just described should be explained before we proceed. The agitation of the medium before a *seance* opens is caused by the great number of spirits, good and evil, which crowd around him, knowing that he is about to write. They therefore press close to him in order that they may guide his hand, and a battle ensues between the good and the evil spirits. This is shown by his seizing, throwing away and resuming the pencil. If the evil power gets the upper hand temporarily, it uses the medium's body to commit the improprieties of speech and behavior mentioned above. The power of Evil is bent on accomplishing the physical and moral ruin of mediums serving the good cause. Mirabelli endeavors to attract only the good spirit-world and to serve as its instrument, as proved by his prayers for Divine assistance, but the fact of his also lending himself to *seances* held only to satisfy the scientific ardor of those who attend them and in many cases merely their craving for something sensational, is an error on his part which gives the evil spirit-beings a great hold on him.

Were he to confine his activities to religious gatherings exclusively, thus devoting his mediumistic talents to the cause of good, the forces of evil would have no power over him and the low and vulgar exhibitions which he makes of himself would never occur. Moreover, his mediumistic power would *remain unimpaired,* while as matters stand, it is to be feared that this will dwindle little by little if he continues to lend himself as a medium for wordly purposes. The weakening of his odic power by the evil spirits will assume such proportions in the long run, that he will fail utterly as a medium, losing his physical health entirely and possibly suffering an even worse fate. I shall ask the reader to compare Mirabelli's case with what is said elsewhere in this book concerning the influence of evil spirits on mediums.

The strength which the evil spirit-forces occasionally develop in opposition to the efforts of the good spirits is illustrated by certain events recorded in the Bible. When the high spirit, Gabriel had been sent to reveal the future to Daniel, the evil spirit, which had been made prince over the idolatrous kingdom of Persia "withstood Gabriel for one and twenty days, until Michael, one of the chief princes, came to help Gabriel" and delivered him from the attacks of the forces of evil. *(Daniel 10 : 13.)*

Mirabelli as a physical medium. At the Assis Pharmacy, Rua 15 de Novembro No. 9 in Sao Paulo, the panes of glass suddenly flew out of the show-cases while the medium was present. A skull which had been articulated came out of the laboratory, remained suspended in the air, opened and shut its jaws, threw various articles about, flew back and forth, and finally fell to the floor without breaking.

At a meeting held on a national holiday and attended by the medium and many other persons, they, as well as the people who did not take part at the meeting but who lived near by, heard the roll of drums and the blare of trumpets, playing a march. At the same time, glasses and bottles standing in the *seance* room were clinked without being touched by human hands, and gave out sounds that were perfectly harmonious, rendering a military march with wonderful musical skill.

Mirabelli played billiards without touching his cue, which made the strokes of its own accord. A skull moved its jaws, and a hat which had been placed upon it was raised as though in salutation.

All of these facts were confirmed by unimpeachable witnesses, the original affidavit stressing the point that all references to phenomena that are at all doubtful have been rigidly excluded.

At a well-attended *seance* in Sao Vicente the following things happened in the presence of the guests of honor, Drs. Mario Alvin and Annibal de Meneses, while Mirabelli, seated in a chair, was closely scrutinized by all present. The chair, still holding the medium, was suddenly moved out of place, without being impelled in any way by the medium's legs, as was definitely established. Mirabelli turned his eyes skyward, opened his arms, and sat as though enraptured. After he had prayed silently for some minutes the chair again moved with a sudden start and rose several centimeters from the floor. All the while closest attention was concentrated upon the medium's feet, arms and sides. The chair together with the medium continued to rise, floated to and fro, and finally reached an elevation of two meters above the floor. Another examination of the seance room was immediately made by those present. The duration of the levitation was 120 seconds actually timed, the investigators following the chair as it floated about in the air unsupported. It moved in one general direction and finally descended slowly back to the floor, landing at a distance of 2.30 meters from its original position. All the while the medium was in a trance and was speaking with different spirit-beings. Upon awakening, he could recall nothing of what had happened.

As has already been explained in the chapter on "Mediums" physical phenomena are usually the work of inferior, though not necessarily evil, spirits. Generally speaking, good spirits do not lend themselves to experiments like those referred to as Mirabelli's physical phenomena, described in the foregoing paragraph. By way of exception, they may participate in such performances if a Divinely willed purpose is involved, as, for instance, that of proving the existence of ultra-mundane spirits to a person seeking after God.

Mirabelli as an apport-medium. A revolver locked in a trunk, was apported from the residence Pinto de Queiros in Sao Paulo into that of a Mr. Watson, after the announcement had been made that this would be done. Furthermore, a picture was apported in broad daylight from Mr. Watson's home over a distance of several kilometers into the office of an insurance company, where it fell to the floor with a crash, causing immense excitement.

On another occasion, Mirabelli was at the da Luz railroad

station with several companions, intending to take a train for Santos, when he suddenly vanished. About fifteen minutes later a telephone message came from Sao Vicente, a town ninety kilometers away from da Luz, stating that the medium was present in Sao Vicente exactly two minutes after he had disappeared in Sao Paulo.

On the occasion of a session of the investigating committee held in honor of Dr. Enrico de Goes and attended by many scientists, Mirabelli vanished from the *seance* room without loosening the cords with which he was bound and without disturbing a seal on any of the doors or windows. He was found lying in a trance on a sofa in an adjoining room, singing a hymn.

These so-called "apports" come within the province of the dematerialization and re-materialization of matter. The latter is disintegrated and converted into od at one place, being thereupon transported through walls or closed doors in that state, and is recondensed into solid matter elsewhere. Several instances of the same phenomenon are recorded in the Bible; the prophet Habbakuk, who was brought from a great distance to Daniel in the lions' den; the disciple Ananias, who suddenly disappeared from one place and instantly re-appeared in a far-off city; the liberation of Saint Peter from prison, all of these things happened according to the same laws of disintegration and re-condensation of matter, as in the case of Mirabelli.

Mirabelli as a materialization medium. The materializations produced by Mirabelli are the most marvellous exhibitions of the incarnation of spirits witnessed in modern times.

What follows happened at a *seance* held in the laboratory of the investigating committee in Santos, over which Estanislao de Camargo, Alberto Riveira and J. F. Schmid presided. This *seance* which took place at nine o'clock in the morning was attended by many people of note. The room in which the test was *conducted* was situated on the ground floor and was eleven meters long by ten meters wide. The windows opening upon the street were faced with iron bars; the floor was composed of narrow strips of wood which had been examined one by one to make sure that they could not be manipulated surreptitiously. Everything was found to be in order, and it was definitely established that the only way of forcing an entrance into the room would be to break through its thick walls or its doors framed in stone.

Mirabelli, seated in a chair, turned pale, indicating the approach of a deep trance. His eyes bulged and he twisted about as though someone were trying to strangle him, while beads of sweat stood out all over his body. Suddenly three sharp raps sounded on a table which stood in the room, and a child's voice called out: "Papa". Dr. Ganymed de Souza who was present declared with great emotion that he recognized the voice of his little daughter who had died of the grippe in the capital. Everyone sat in tense expectation, and presently the shape of a girl appeared beside the medium. Almost beside himself, her father stepped out of the circle, spoke to his child, went close to her and folded her in his arms. Amid convulsive sobs he assured the others again and again that it was his own daughter whom he was holding, and that the dress worn by the apparition was the same as that in which she had been buried.

All the while, Mirabelli lay as though in death-agony, cowered in his chair, his complexion waxen, his muscles completely relaxed, his breathing weak and wheezy, his pulse barely perceptible.

Colonel Octavio Viana now rose to convince himself of the reality of the apparition. He also took the child in his arms, felt of her pulse, looked into her deep, fathomless eyes, and asked her several questions, which she answered rationally, although in sad monotones. Viana also was able to confirm that the vision was tangible. Dr. de Souza then recalled several childhood incidents in his daughter's life to the apparition, receiving replies which showed that his remarks were understood. *The apparition was photographed,* a copy of the picture being appended to the investigating committee's report.

After the picture had been taken, the child began to soar about the room, rising into the air and plunging about like a fish in its native element. The spectators had risen to their feet and followed the vision, which remained at a height within easy arm's reach. The medium meanwhile continued to imitate the child's motions with his forearms. She floated about in the air a few seconds longer, and disappeared all of a sudden, after having shown herself for thirty-six minutes by daylight and under unexceptionable conditions to a gathering of educated men, who testify that they saw before them a perfectly formed human being.

Dr. Ganymed de Souza thus lost his daughter for the second time, so deeply was he moved by what he had seen. The statement which sets out this occurrence is attested by the signatures of ten men holding the degree of Doctor of Science.

For some time after the medium had overcome the intense nervous strain caused by the demonstration described above, he continued to tremble and to give signs of great exhaustion. Even before he had regained his strength, violent blows were heard in a cupboard in which a skull used for purposes of study, was kept. The skull was being hurled about inside by an unseen force as though trying to break from its place of confinement. Someone present hastened to open the cupboard, when its door suddenly swung apart of their own accord and out shot the skull, rising into the air and chattering its teeth hideously. Dr. Ganymed de Souza was wondering to himself why the rest of the skeleton did not appear, when, as though in answer to his unspoken thought, the vertebrae of the neck began to form, followed in order by the bones of the chest and arms, the entire spinal column, the pelvic arch, the legs, and finally the feet, complete to the last bone. At this the medium, whose arms were held fast, erupted a mass of frothy saliva and, still seated in the chair, tried frantically to strike himself. All of his arteries seemed filled to bursting and throbbed violently, while his body diffused a sickening, corpse-like odor which was very annoying to the spectators and which impregnated the room to such an extent that not even the admission of fresh air served to drive out the smell.

The skeleton now got up on its feet and undertook to walk about the room with long, unsteady strides, occasionally seeming in danger of falling, but always regaining its balance. To assure himself that what he saw was real, Dr. de Souza touched the apparition and tapped its greasy bones. As he did so, he felt a nervous shock, and returned to his seat.

In the meantime the medium was squirming about in his chair to which he was held with difficulty, while the skeleton proceeded on its weird journey. Other participants, emboldened by Dr. de Souza's example, overcame their horror and got up one by one to touch this ghastly personification of death and nothingness. All of them were unnerved by the ordeal.

While the smell of decay was still much in evidence, the skeleton began to disintegrate in regular stages, commencing at the feet, until nothing was left but the skull which, though its teeth had ceased to chatter, continued to float in the air for some time, before it fell to the table and came to rest.

All this occurred at 9:45 a.m. by bright sunlight, under conditions as exacting as any that could be imposed by the police, and in the presence of numerous cultured persons, and extended over a period of twenty-two minutes.

While the spectators were still discussing the events related above, the medium again fell into a state of great excitement and declared that he could see the presence in the room of the figure of Bishop Jose de Camargo Barros, who had lost his life when the ship "Syrio" was wrecked. All conversation was quickly hushed and Mirabelli was again put under the prescribed supervision, conducted this time by the Messrs. Ataliba de Aranha and Odassio Sampaio. As the medium passed into a trance, the odor of roses filled the room.

Suddenly there appeared within the circle a fine mist on which all eyes were immediately fixed. The mist parted and became denser, gleaming like a golden cloud, out of which gradually, minute by minute, emerged a smiling apparition wearing the episcopal biretta and clad in the full insignia of office. Rising from the chair it announced its name: "Dr. Jose de Camargo Barros", in a clear voice which all could hear.

Rising from his seat, Dr. de Souza fearlessly took several steps toward the vision, face to face with which he stopped. The apparition smiled silently at the investigator, who now went closer to it, touching and examining it minutely by tapping its body and teeth and rubbing his finger over the gums to determine the presence of any saliva. He listened to the heart-action and to the breathing, applied his ear to the abdomen to assure himself that the bowels were functioning, looked at the finger-nails and eyeballs, to the veinlets in which he gave particular attention, and resumed his seat. There was no question in his mind that the figure before him was that of a man.

The other witnesses followed Dr. de Souza's example and were all shown an equal amount of consideration by the mysterious guest. Everyone was certain that this was no childish hoax that was being played on him, but that he was in fact face to face with a human being which possessed all of the organs of a normal human body. The bishop conversed with those present in pure, well-chosen Portuguese, and finally said: "Now watch me closely as I disappear." With this he went back to the chair of the medium who was still in a deep trance, while the spectators observed every motion, in order that they might lose nothing of the most interesting part of the phenomenon, namely the de-materialization.

On reaching the medium, whose trance continued unbroken, the bishop bowed over him, laying his hands on Mirabelli's head and regarding him for a while in silence, as all present gathered in a circle around the two figures. The bishop's body contracted spasmodically several times and then began to grow dim and to shrink in size. The medium, in a cold perspiration, was breathing with difficulty. When the vision had dwindled to a height of thirty centimeters, it vanished with incredible suddenness. Again the odor of roses filled the room, and Mirabelli slowly regained consciousness. A subsequent examination failed to yield any natural explanation of the occurrence.

At Santos where the headquarters of the Academy are situated a *seance,* the results of which are attested by sixty signatures, was held at half past three in the afternoon.

The first apparition seen was that of a woman who engaged in conversation with those present, and then vanished; a few minutes later a bell rose into the air and began to ring in silvery tones. Mirabelli woke from his trance and asserted that he saw a venerable figure clad in white linen and surrounded by an aura, standing by the table. Meanwhile, the bell in the air was ringing incessantly. Several spectators, seated somewhat apart, now rose and approached the circle proper which was formed by the investigating committee. Presently a sound was heard like that of a person's heels brought down firmly on the floor, whereat Colonel Soares and Dr. Octavio Moreira Cavalcanti announced the presence of the deceased Bezerra de Meneses, well remembered by all present as an eminent hospital physician. The apparition, turning to the spectators, spoke to them of himself and assure them that it was he himself who was with them. His language, and the positiveness with which he spoke, made a deep impression on all. His voice was carried all over the room by the megaphone, and several attempts to photograph the vision were successful.

Drs. Assumpcion and Mendonca now approached the shrouded figure and subjected it to an examination which lasted for fifteen minutes and furnished evidence that they had before them an anatomically normal human being, possessed of all of its natural organs. All of the scientists who were present vouch for the correctness of this conclusion.

After the incorporated spirit had shaken hands with the spectators, it announced that it was about to depart and soared off through the air like a flying machine. The feet vanished first, followed by the legs and the abdomen, while the chest, arms and head still remained visible. Dr. Archimedes Mendonca who, like all the rest, had watched developments with the keenest interest, stepped within arm's reach of the portion of the body that remained in a materialized state, and tried to grasp it, but instantly fell to the floor unconscious while the vision vanished entirely. When Dr. Mendonca regained his senses in an adjoining room into which he had been carried, he declared that he had felt a sticky mass between his fingers before he swooned away.

On waking, Mirabelli was greatly exhausted. His fastenings were found to be intact, as were the seals on the doors and windows.

The report of the investigating committee contains thirty-four illustrations, of which the first three show the conditions under which the test was carried out, the manner in which Mirabelli was tied, and the supervision exercised by the committee. A particularly remarkable photograph is the one showing Mirabelli dressed in white, in the midst of the fourteen members of whom the committee was composed. His forearms are de-materialized, nothing being visible of the left one and only a faint blur of the right. Most interesting of all, however, are the eighteen photographs of the spirit incarnated, most of them showing the materialized figure and the medium together on the same plate. In a few instances the apparition alone was photographed; in several others, the incarnated spirit is seated at the table with the medium and the persons conducting the test, and looks for all the world like a living member of the committee.

As the editor of the "Zeitschrift fuer Parapsychology" aptly remarks: *"In the face of the testimony of so comprehensive a body of witnesses and in the face of so thoroughly conducted an investigation, we have not the right to ignore, without further ado, this new and overwhelming mass of evidence of the genuineness of mediumistic phenomena."*

On going over the report relating to the phenomena produced through the medium Mirabelli, we are able, in the light of the laws governing od, as set down in this book, to understand them all without difficulty. Everything follows in accordance with immutable laws, whether the phenomena occur in Europe, America or any other continent, or whether they happened in ancient times or recently. The appearance of the three men to Abraham, the materialization of the angel Raphael to Tobias, the materialization of Christ after His resurrection, and countless other materializations of spirits, were brought about by the same laws as were the materializations recorded in the case of Mirabelli. The only difference between the former materializations and the last-mentioned, lies in the fact that in the case of the materialization of the high spirits of God we are not informed of the source whence the od was drawn, whereas in regard to the materializations which took place in Brazil, Mirabelli, as a medium, was the chief source of that power, assisted by the participants at the *seances* most of whom were undoubtedly mediumistically gifted to such an extent that they could contribute their own od without entering into a trance. Elsewhere, mention is made of the important fact that when the higher spirits are called upon to deliver messages to mankind at God's behest, the od necessary is placed at their disposal in unlimited amounts, so that they shall not be dependent on human mediums. Nevertheless, the laws according to which they manifest themselves remain the same.

Mirabelli's speaking and writing in the numerous languages foreign to him and his discussions of the wide range of subjects enumerated, are the work of the various spirit-beings which employ him merely as an instrument. The apports are brought about by the fact that the spirit-world, with the aid of the medium's odic power, produces the currents required for disintegrating matter and for recondensing the same. The materialization and dematerialization of the spirits are effected by means of the application of those same currents and by means of the utilization of the medium's od and his physical substance. Unfortunately the German version of the Brazilian report fails to state the amount of weight lost by the medium during the period of materialization of the spirits. The stunning shocks suffered by those who touched a phantom in the act of being disintegrated, proceeded from the odic currents by which the *disintegration* was effected. Had anyone attempted to touch *a materialization in the process of formation* his experience would have been the same. After materialization is complete, these currents are turned off, and the apparitions can be touched with impunity.

The presence in the materialized spirit-beings of all the organs of the human body is explained by the fact that a spirit possesses these organs in spirit-form. It has only to condense them with the aid of human od to the extent required, in order to make them visible in the material shape of a human body. Indeed, the same process took place in the case of Mirabelli himself, when he vanished out of the *seance* chamber, through its closed doors, and was found later, lying in another room. His disappearance from a room that was closed was possible only by virtue of the dissolution of his material body into an odic one, which was re-materialized in an adjoining room into solid matter, in the same manner and according to the same laws as in the case of the materialization of the spirits.

The fragrance of the od of the higher spirits in contrast with the smell of decay noticed in the presence of low spirits is sufficiently accounted for by the facts related concerning the smell of od in connection with the dissertation on that force.

Clairvoyance at a deathbed. (Zeitschrift fuer Parapsychologie, 1927, pp. 475-476). A contributor from San Francisco relates the things he witnessed for five hours by the bedside of his dying wife. His story is as follows:

"I have never had a satisfactory solution to the riddle as to whether I was subject to an illusion, or whether I had suddenly become clairvoyant during the last five hours which immediately preceded my wife's decease.

"Before I begin the relation of this incident, I wish to state for the benefit of the reader that in my case neither alcoholic beverages, cocaine nor morphine enter into the question and that I am not at all highstrung nor imaginative. On the contrary, I am generally called cold-blooded, calm and collected, and exceedingly skeptical regarding everything appertaining to spiritism.

"As all my friends know, my wife passed away on Friday, May 23rd, 1902, a quarter of an hour before midnight. A few of my closest friends had come to my house and were present, together with the physician in the case and two experienced nurses. I sat by the bedside, holding the patient's right hand in my own, and in this way two hours passed without any visible change. The servant came in to announce that supper was served, but no one seemed inclined to avail himself of this opportunity of partaking of food. At about half past six o'clock I urgently begged my friends to eat something, as there was no telling how much longer our vigil might last, whereupon all of them finally left the room.

"A quarter of an hour later I happened to glance toward the door and saw three separate, well-defined, *layers of cloud* drifting into the room. Each cloud seemed to be about four feet long and six or eight inches thick, the lowest one being about two feet above the floor while the others moved over it at intervals of approximately six inches.

"My first impression was that some of my friends were standing outside of the bedroom door, smoking, and that the smoke of their cigars was blowing into the room. With this in mind I jumped up to express my indignation at their conduct, but there was nobody near the door, nor could I see anyone in the hall or in the adjoining room.

"Overcome with wonder I looked back at the clouds. These floated silently toward the bed and enshrouded it completely. As I stared into the mist, I saw at the head of my dying wife a female form about three feet high, transparent but having the appearance of a bright mass of shining gold; it was the shape of a woman of so sublime an aspect that I cannot find words to describe her fittingly. She was wrapped in a Grecian garment with long, wide, sleeves, which hung down loosely. Upon her head she wore a radiant crown. Thus she stood motionless in her full splendor and beauty, her hands raised above my wife, seeming to bid her welcome with a cheerful and serene expression, and radiating peace and repose. Two other figures in white knelt beside my wife, apparently leaning against her. Still other shapes, more or less distinct, floated over the bed.

"Above my wife, but connected with her by a cord of od, hovered a nude white figure, apparently her odic body. For some time this remained perfectly still; then it shrank in size until it was barely eighteen inches tall. The odic body was complete, with perfectly formed limbs. While shrinking in volume as described, it beat about with its arms and legs as if struggling to get free and escape. For a long time it twisted back and forth, until it seemed exhausted; then it grew quiet, increased to its former size, and recommenced its struggles.

"This vision, or whatever else it may have been, was before me uninterruptedly for the entire five hours that preceded my wife's decease. Occasional interruptions that occurred, as when I spoke with my friends or closed my eyes and turned my head aside, failed to affect the mirage in the slightest, for as soon as I looked back in the direction of the deathbed, I would see the spirit-shapes again. Throughout these five hours I had a strange feeling of oppression, as though a heavy load were resting on my head and limbs, while my eyes felt heavy and full of sleep. During the entire time my sensations were so peculiar that I felt as if I were going out of my mind, and said more than once to the physician: "Doctor, I am going crazy."

"The fatal moment came at last. There was a sound of gasping; the odic body writhed to and fro, and my wife's breathing ceased. To all appearances she was dead, but a few moments later she began to breathe again. After she had drawn her breath twice, everything became quiet. At the instant of her last breath the connecting cord broke and the odic body vanished. The clouds and the spirit-shapes also disappeared immediately, and, strange to say, the sensation of heaviness that had weighed upon me left me all of a sudden. I was my own self again, cold-blooded, calm and self-possessed, and from the instant of my wife's death was perfectly capable of making all the arrangements necessary for looking after her remains and for laying them away in their final resting-place.

"I must leave it to the reader to judge whether I was the victim of a hallucination brought on by grief and exhaustion, or whether perhaps my mortal eyes had been privileged to catch a glimpse of the spirit-world in all its happiness, repose and peace."

The deathbed scenes related above were no hallucinations; they were real. However, in order that the dying woman's husband might be able to see the spirit-shapes, two prerequisite conditions had to be fulfilled.

In the first place it was necessary for him to have a mediumistic sense of clairvoyance, even if, as happened in his case, this sense had not been developed. In the second place, enough od had to be present in the room to allow the spirits to make their shapes visible by means thereof.

The source of the od is to be sought primarily in the dying woman herself, for at the time of death, the od is liberated from the body. Her husband also was able to liberate od by virtue of his mediumistic disposition. The sensation of oppression, sleepiness and exhaustion that rested upon him during those hours was caused by the surrender of his od, and consequently disappeared when the od he had liberated flowed back into his body, after the spirits had ceased to be visible.

Here too, the od was seen in the form of clouds which enfolded the whole deathbed and from which the figures of the spirits were subsequently formed. The husband's inability to see *clearly all* of the figures floating above the bed was due to the fact that the amount of od on hand was not sufficient to allow all the spirits present to show themselves with equal distinctness.

Spirits from the Beyond surround *every dying person.* Generally they are those of deceased friends and relatives, or the guardian spirits which watched over and protected that person during his lifetime.

Many dying persons themselves can see these spirits by clairvoyance, for at the time of death the soul is already partially released from the body, and hence is endowed with the power of spirit-vision. It recognizes the spirits of those who have gone before that are present at the deathbed, and calls them by name.

It is the duty of these spirits not only to escort the dying into the Beyond, but to assist in freeing their souls from their bodies.

Whenever a number of spirits are gathered for a definite purpose, they are under the orders of a leader. In the case before us, this leader was the beautiful female figure which the husband saw floating above his expiring wife's bed. She supervised the work which her subordinate spirits were called on to perform with the dying woman.

The naked white figure which the husband saw struggling above his wife's body, was her odic body. The writhing of this body, which was a perfect image of her own, was due to the exertion made by the spirit of the dying, enclosed in the odic body, to break the odic cord which still held it to the physical body, after the rest of the odic body had already made itself free. The husband himself saw this odic cord plainly. Such cords are fairly strong by nature, and are not easily broken.

Special Instances of Clairvoyance. (Zeitschrift fuer Parapsychologie, 1926, pp. 22-25). In an article which appeared in the publication mentioned, Professor Oesterreich discusses several instances of clairvoyance observed by Dr. Pagenstecher, a physician living in Mexico, in connection with his patient, Maria Reyes de Z., and subsequently investigated and confirmed by Mr. Prince, an American. Professor Oesterreich's account is as follows:

"The phenomena studied by Pagenstecher and Prince covered primarily clairvoyance and psychometry. Their investigations in this connection gave thoroughly convincing results, to the striking nature of which alone it was due, that Pagenstecher, a product of the materialistic school, became convinced by his own observation of the existence of such phenomena. On one occasion he recounted his experiences before the Association of Physicians of

Mexico, whereat his colleagues shook their heads, and probably more than one of them began to feel doubts as to Pagenstecher's sanity. Nevertheless, a committee was formed, whose members subsequently confirmed the correctness of his observations."

What, then, were the facts discovered in the case of the clairvoyant, or rather, the clairsentient Maria Reyes de Z.?

a. When in a certain condition, she had the same sensations as those felt by Dr. Pagenstecher who would sit facing her. At such times she felt as though she were enfolded within his organism, but she had this feeling only so long as Dr. Pagenstecher stood or sat in front of her at a distance not exceeding three meters.

b. On these occasions she would see a multicolored radiation and a luminous band which connected her with Pagenstecher.

c. When given a piece of a meteorite, she had the sensation of flying through space, passing alternately through hot and cold regions, and of falling into bottomless depths.

d. She was handed a letter, and although its writer was unknown to her, she sensed and described the scene of the sinking of a ship, and drew as accurate a picture of the person who had written the letter as she could have, had she stood beside him on the deck of the foundering vessel. She also had the sensation of sinking into the ocean and of rising to the surface again. The letter sealed in a bottle, had been picked up at sea.

The explanation of the incidents related above may be found in the chapter dealing with the laws of odic force.

Od is the carrier not of physical sensations only, but of all phychic ones as well. Inasmuch as the spirit of a living being is the bearer of its odic force, all of the thoughts and feelings of the spirit are expressed in corresponding vibrations of the od. At the same time the odic vibrations of a living being are influenced not alone by the thoughts and moods of its own spirit, but also by the odic vibrations of another living being whose odic radiation it re-receives. If, therefore, "clairsentient people" as they are called, come into close enough contact, in any manner, with the odic radiation of other persons, they will also absorb the latter's sensations. This is the law underlying the ability of certain people to "fall in with" the feelings, the character, the sentiments and the ways of others.

If therefore the sensations of the clairsentient lady in question followed those of Dr. Pagenstecher, it was because his sensations were transmitted by his odic radiation. In his case the radiation had an effective range of only three meters, and was not powerful enough at a greater distance to influence the odic vibrations of the clairsentient subject of his experiment. Under such circumstances a clairsentient person is in a state resembling a partial trance, in which his spirit is to some degree separated from his body.

The multicolored band of od seen by the lady, connecting her with Pagenstecher, was his odic radiation passing over to her. The fact that all odic radiations are colored has also been brought out in the discussion on od, since color depends on odic vibrations, as is true also of tones, odors, taste, response to the sense of touch, and all other similar od-borne indications of life. All of these matters are intimately correlated.

Meteorites also are living things, each one possessing a spirit, as does every other object in existence. Hence a meteorite has odic vibrations peculiar to itself, which, as it flew through space, were influenced by the odic vibrations of the heavenly bodies there, as well as by its fall into immeasurable depths. All odic vibrations of a living being leave impressions upon its od analogous to those left on a phonograph-record by the notes of a singer, with the result that they can always be reproduced thereafter.

The same process that takes place in material form in the case of a phonograph-record obtains ethereally in the case of the sensing of past events by clairsentient persons when they come into close enough contact with the odic record of a living being, whereby the same vibrations, and hence the same sensations, are produced in their own od as those which are borne on the record in question.

This explains the clairsentient medium's ability to see the fate and the appearance of the writer of the letter, on board of the sinking ship. It should be added, however, by way of further explanation, that the odic record of a spirit resembles not only a phonograph-record but also a photographic plate, and that, in consequence, it will reproduce not only the sensations, but also the image of the person from whom the odic radiations emanated, since the image too is produced by odic vibrations. In a similar manner our most recent inventions seek to make it possible for us to see the persons with whom we are talking over the telephone. These inventions also are based on oscillations which, in physical processes, occur in considerable material condensation, and in spirit-processes in an etherealized form.

In the case of Pagenstecher and his clairsentient medium, there was an average loss of weight of a hundred grams. This is easily accounted for, since every surrender of od is attended by a loss of weight, which in the case of Pagenstecher was due to the fact that he radiated a large amount of od to the medium, while in her case a corresponding loss was caused by receiving and mentally recording the odic impressions, all work, mental as well as any other, involving a certain consumption of od. It is like playing a phonograph-record, to do which we require a certain amount of power, in order that the disc may move fast enough to reproduce the notes recorded upon it.

All work performed by human beings involves the liberation of a given amount of od, which in turn means a loss of weight. If we weigh ourselves before working, and again afterwards, we find that our weight has decreased in proportion to our exertions, mental or physical, although there may have been no evacuations in the meantime. Even magnetopaths, who treat their patients by magnetization, and in so doing give off part of their od, undergo a corresponding loss of weight during the process.

The foregoing furnishes an explanation of all phenomena connected with clairsentience, regardless of the form of their occurrence.

PART FOUR

Messages from the Spirit-World Concerning the Great Problems of Religion

Introductory Remarks

"And they will be all instructed by God."
John 6 : 45.

THE teachings received by me relating to the laws governing spirit-communication with the material Creation, as well as all my personal experiences in that connection, shed so much light on events related in the Bible which theretofore I had not been able to understand, that all obscurity was dispelled. Moreover, I was enabled to understand many things that I heard or read of afterwards, concerning occurrences of an extraordinary nature.

However, *the great religious problems* were what concerned me most of all. I was a clergyman, and had devoted my whole life until then to imparting the teachings of my creed to my co-religionists. Hence it was but natural that I should be primarily interested in discovering whether all of the religious doctrines that I had so far believed and taught were true, or whether among the tenets of my church there were any which were at variance with the truth.

Although I could scarcely have foreseen that such discrepancies would prove as numerous and as wide as I subsequently found them to be, I was prepared for some such discovery from the first.

In later years I read that the Catholic Church itself and the writers among its adherents had issued insistent warnings against "spiritism" in general and against the so-called "revealed spiritism" in particular, that is to say, precisely against that which any earnest seeker after the truth is most particularly desirous of learning. Obviously, anyone who like myself, conducted spiritistic meetings as he would conduct Divine service, was not concerned with obtaining strikingly interesting spirit-phenomena, which is the aim of ordinary spiritistic *seances,* but with getting into touch with the good spirit-world which had instructed the people of Biblical times.

It was from this spirit-world that I hoped to learn the truth concerning the most important questions of life. *I wanted to be enlightened about the interrelation between the Here and the Beyond.* Everything else was of minor importance.

Looking at the question from the standpoint of the "churches," I could indeed see reason enough for the warnings they had uttered against spiritism as practiced by me, as well as against "revealed spiritism" for, once we grant the possibility of men being initiated into the full truth by direct communication with God's good spirits, the foundations of the churches begin to totter. What with their conflicting doctrines, the churches will then be in danger of losing their adherents, for men will no longer have to depend on the clergy in their search after the truth, but will, through their communication with God's spirit-world, learn of the direct road to the source of truth, as it was learned by the people of Scriptural times.

The root of the opposition on the part of the churches to spiritism in general and to revealed spiritism in particular is the instinct of self-preservation. The conflict waged by them is the same as the war declared by Herod in the defence of his kingship when the birth of Him, who was to be the King of the Jews, was announced to him.

But the war of the churches upon Divinely ordained spirit-communication will be as futile as was Herod's war upon Him Whom God had sent.

The truth, that the good spirit-world can communicate with men and enlighten them concerning the great and important problems of the Beyond, independently of any church, will in due time prevail with mankind, while as to the churches, it will be said: "For those who sought the child's life are dead." *(Matthew 2 : 20.)*

That which the churches of today are preaching to the ignorant multitude is not the truth, and differs widely from the answers given by God's spirit-world to the questions put to it, regarding God, His Creation and its ultimate fate, Redemption, Christ and Christ's life and work; regarding the Church and the sacraments; regarding Heaven and Hell: and regarding the origin and purpose of the Universe.

God

"Can you discover the deep things of God? Can you reach the Almighty's range of wisdom?" *Job 11 : 7.*

"YOU ask that I enlighten you concerning God, but what can I tell you that you would understand? You do not understand even the lowest creatures about you; you do not understand yourself even. You cannot comprehend the smallest stone by the wayside, nor the most insignificant worm of the fields. You are utterly ignorant of the most commonplace objects that meet your eye, and yet you ask me to teach you about the Supreme Being, to give you understanding of something purely spiritual! That is impossible, seeing that you lack all conceptions required to enable you to grasp these mighty truths. "For the corruptible body presses down the soul, and the earthly tabernacle weighs down the mind that muses upon many things. And hardly do we guess right at things that are upon earth, and with labor do we find the things that are before us: but the things that are in heaven who has searched out." *(Wisdom 9 : 15.)*

"There is only one thing that each of you can reason out for himself by logical thinking: *There must be some Cause for the existence of everything in Creation.* Precisely as it is impossible to conceive of a clock without assuming the existence of a clock-maker, it is impossible to conceive of the greatest and most accurate timepiece of all, the Universe, without assuming the existence of a great Master-jeweler who built this timepiece with its billions upon billions of wheels, all of them so perfectly geared and running so accurately, that the astronomers of today can calculate what the exact relative positions of the various wheels will be thousands of years hence.

"The Creator of this timepiece, whose greatness surpasses the grasp of the human mind, is known to you as God. It should, therefore, be obvious to everyone that a God must exist, for "only the fool has said in his heart: There is no God." *(Psalms 14 : 1.)*

"But *as to the nature of God,* that is something which I cannot explain to you, any more than I can explain the *Cause of the Divine existence.* It would be like trying to explain the calculations of a planet's orbit to a four-year old child, who would naturally lack all knowledge of astronomy and mathematics and of all the principles, formulas and equations involved. If it takes even your greatest astronomers years to calculate the orbit of a single star, a person unfamiliar with the first inklings of science would be driven mad, if it were attempted to teach him something utterly beyond the reach of his understanding. In the same way you would be driven out of your senses if I were to try to fill your mind with ideas which are quite incomprehensible to you and which your understanding could not assimilate. You yourself would be forced to admit: "Such knowledge is too wonderful for me; it is far, far beyond me." *(Psalms 139 : 6.)*

"There is little I can tell you concerning God that you do not already know.

"Your own reasoning teaches you that God is a creative spirit, endowed with a will, which orders all things sagely, and similarly, you are convinced of His omnipotence, wisdom and greatness, so far as the human mind is capable of grasping the same. The Scriptures enlighten you further as to the way in which He rules the world, as to His wonders and His love and mercy for His creatures. All that I can do is to offer you a more precise interpretation of the truths to be found in the Holy Writ relating to God, and to call your attention to *erroneous ideas* contained in the teachings of your various creeds as to God and His attributes.

"*The fact that God is a spirit* is one thing on which all religions agree, and for which you have the word of Christ: "God is a Spirit: and they that worship him must worship in spirit and truth." *(John 4 : 24.)* A point on which they do not agree, however, is whether or not this spirit has *shape*. Many people think that shape is associated with matter only, but not with spirit. This is a mistake. Material forms are images of spiritual forms, and since all material things have form and shape, so, too, have all spiritual things, and so also, has God. In fact there is nothing but what has shape, in either the material or the spiritual world. Beauty is perfection of form, a statement which is equally true of the realm of the ethereal. God is the perfection of beauty, and hence, also, the perfection of shape.

"God as an integral, thinking and planning being, is a *personality,* and there can be no such thing as a personality, an "ego" without form or shape.

"God as the highest spirit differs from all created spirits, and difference is possible only where distinguishing features exist. Again, features can exist only where there is shape and form.

Inasmuch, then, as God has shape, He can be seen by the other spirits. All who go to Him, will see Him face to face, as He is. For this reason Moses begged God to travel *in person* with the people of Israel: "And he (Moses) said unto Him: if Thy presence go not with me, carry us not up hence." *(Exodus 33 : 15.)* And again Moses besought: "Show me, I pray Thee, Thy glory . . . And He said, Thou canst not see my face; for man shall not see me and live." *(Exodus 33 : 18.)* God therefore has a figure and a countenance, and can be seen by spirits, though not by human eyes.

"Inasmuch as God possesses shape and personality, He is not *omnipresent* in the sense in which you understand the word. It is true that He is aware of all things and of all events through the force that emanates from Him, for everything in existence owes its being, its perpetuation and its functions solely to the force disseminated by God. "In Him we live, move and are." Through His power He maintains contact with everything that exists; nothing can escape His notice. *But as a personified spirit He is not everywhere.* You unconsciously admit as much in the opening words of the prayer: "Our Father *which art in Heaven.*" The Lord looketh from heaven; he beholdeth all the sons of men; from the place of his habitation he looketh forth upon all the inhabitants of the earth. He that fashioneth the hearts of them all, that considereth all their works." *(Psalms 33 : 13.)* "God looked down from heaven upon the children of men, to see if there were any that did understand, that did seek after God." *(Psalms 53 : 2.)* And regarding God's habitation we read: "There is a river, the streams of which make glad the city of God, the holy place of the tabernacles of the Most High. God is in the midst of her; she shall not be moved. . ." *(Psalms 46 : 4.)*

"The many references in the Scriptures relating to God are not figurative or allegorical, but literal, with the reservation that what you accept in a material sense, should be accepted in a spiritual one as applying to God. God's throne and God's habitation exist in fact. God is able to visit all parts of the Universe in person. The Bible records the literal truth when it tells you: "And he left off talking with him, and God went up from Abraham." *(Genesis 17 : 22.)* You are, of course, familiar with the many passages in the Bible in which mention is made of the coming and going of God.

"I cannot even begin to tell you how wonderfully God has

planned the government of the Universe, for this far exceeds the limits of human comprehension. You probably cannot picture to yourselves *that spirits of God stand watch over each living being and that they report on whatever happens.* Hence nothing can take place without being known to God, and for this reason you speak of God as being *omniscient.* In this you are right, although in one respect you exaggerate His omniscience, perhaps through fear of detracting from His greatness. You teach, namely, *that God also knows how men will act of their own free will at some future time, but in this respect you are misinformed.* God knows everything that has taken and is taking place. He knows the past and the present. He knows men's thoughts, and as for the future, He knows those destinies which He Himself has planned for His creatures. *But He has no foreknowledge of those future events which men may shape by the exercise of their free will.* He does not know beforehand what a creature of His will do of its own will in all circumstances. *For this reason He tries His creatures.* To do this would be superfluous and to no purpose if the outcome of the trial were known to God beforehand, and God does nothing without purpose.

"Again, any foreknowledge on God's part of actions within the control of his creatures would have to be predicated on laws making future decisions compulsory, and hence eliminating the exercise of free will. *To assert that something shall depend on the free exercise of will, and yet be predestined, is in itself a contradiction.* Anything of which God had a definite foreknowledge, would necessarily happen, for even God's knowledge *is subject to eternal laws,* and hence, the law that two and two make four applies to God as well as to every other spirit. *In the absence of anything which might serve as a basis, there can be no knowledge nor foreknowledge, not even on the part of God,* for even He is bound by the axiom: "Nothing exists without a reason." If God knew to a certainty how his creatures were going to act of their own free will in future situations; there would have to be a reason for His knowledge, and the only possible reason would be, that God so forcefully influences the exercise of that free will, that only one course is left open. This, however, would eliminate any freedom of choice on the part of His creatures.

"Ignorance of future decisions freely made by His creatures, *does not indicate that God is in any way imperfect, but is the necessary outcome of the freedom of will,* the greatest gift God could have bestowed upon His creatures. Just as there are many things which God cannot do because they are self-contradictory, as, for example, not even He can make two and two equal five, so He cannot create a free agent whose future actions He can foresee with absolute certainty, in which case those actions would be bound to occur. Freedom to decide, and being forced to decide in a certain way, are two things which conflict inherently, and absolute certainty that an event will take place *invariably presupposes that it must take place*. This is an axiom that none of your theologians can refute, let them write what books they will to prove the contrary. Their conclusions are fallacies which serve only to bewilder mankind. They are utterly in the wrong when they assert that for God there is only a present, and not a future, and that everything that is going to happen, even the voluntary actions of His creatures, is an accomplished fact in His eyes, and therefore known to Him. No more than a house which you may be planning to erect is already built, are the events of the future accomplished facts with God. I might add in conclusion that the very idea of freedom of choice means that there is a question whether the events dependent on such choice *will occur at all, and if so, just how they will occur*.

"You know that I am telling you the truth in this, as I have done in all else. You have had plenty of proof of the fact that I am a truthful spirit. For this you have my oath, taken in the name of the Almighty, the true God. When I tell you that God has no foreknowledge of the voluntary actions of men, I am not detracting from His greatness; it is you who would dishonor God by teaching the contrary and thereby picturing Him to men in an odious light, for there are many people who deny the existence of God because they cannot conceive of a deity capable of creating beings, knowing them *with absolute certainty*, to be predestined to everlasting misery. Among other things which you teach, incorrectly, as it happens, is the doctrine of eternal damnation. According to this doctrine, then, God has created millions of human beings with the full and unalterable assurance that they are to be everlastingly damned. Such a God would not be a God, but a monster. Not even the most degenerate human father would knowingly send his child to unending torment, and yet you are asked to believe that your Heavenly Father, with His infinite love, is capable of a degree of barbarity which in a human father would be unthinkable!

"Read the Scriptures! They teach that God sends His trials in order to learn how men will act when put to the test, and what course they will choose. "For the Lord your God proves you, to know whether you love the Lord your God with all your heart and with all your soul." *(Deuteronomy 13 : 3.)*

"When God spared certain nations from falling into the hands of Joshua, thus allowing them to survive, His reasons for so doing are given in the Bible as follows: "Now these are the nations which the Lord left, *to prove Israel by them,* even as many of Israel as had not known all the wars of Canaan . . .: namely the five lords of the Philistines, and all the Canaanites, and the Sidonians, and the Hivites. . . And they were left, *to prove Israel by them,* to know whether they would hearken unto the commandments of the Lord which he commanded their fathers by Moses." *(Judges 3 : 1-5.)*

"Of King Hezekiah, who did that which was right in the eyes of the Lord it is told: "Howbeit in the business of the ambassadors of the princes of Babylon, who sent unto him to inquire of the wonder that was done in the land, *God left him, to try him, that he might know what was in his heart." (2nd Chronicles 32 : 31.)*

"In the Psalms you will find: "His eyes behold, his eyelids *try, the children of men.* The Lord *tries* the righteous; but the wicked and him that loves violence his soul hates." *(Psalms 11 : 4, 5.)* And in the Proverbs: "The refining pot is for silver, and the furnace for gold; but the Lord *tries* the hearts." *(Proverbs 17 : 3.)* Finally in the Book of Isaiah you read: "Behold, I have refined thee, but not as silver; I have chosen thee in the furnace of affliction." *(Isaiah 48 : 10.)*

"The tribulations of Job as related in the Bible were only *a test by which God sought to learn* how that righteous man would bear himself toward the Lord in the hour of greatest adversity.

"All trials to which men are subjected by the Lord would be mere farces, *if their outcome were known to Him in advance.*

"Obviously, God Who knows the hearts of His creatures full well, can *foretell very closely* what course they will decide upon, and we spirits also have this faculty to a great degree. Even you mortals, if you know the character of a fellow-creature, are able to *predict with reasonable certainty* how he will behave and decide in any given circumstances. But all of this is *mere conjecture,* and is not the point at issue. I was speaking of *an infallibly certain foreknowledge of a course of action which is determined by the exercise of free will,* and such unerring foreknowledge is possessed by no spirit, nor even by God Himself. Hence God could not foresee that some or a great many of the spirits He had created would forsake Him, and naturally could not know in advance which of them would do so. He knew only that there was a possibility of such defection, by reason of the fact that the spirits were free to act as they might choose.

"Had God had the positive foreknowledge, as your doctrines teach, that beings which He had created would abuse their liberty of action by deserting Him, He would not have called them into existence at all but would have created only such of whose loyalty no question could ever arise.

"There are two other grave errors in the conception of God entertained by your creeds, and of these I shall speak very briefly, because they will be discussed at greater length on another occasion.

"You teach of the union of three persons in one Godhead, maintaining that there are three Spirits, each of which is a true Deity, but which, when united, are one God as to substance. This is a piece of human fallacy and is an absurdity. There is no union of three persons and no Trinity in the sense in which you teach. *God is an individual person. Only the Father is God.* All other holy spirits are God's *creatures.* None of them is the Father's equal.

"Furthermore, you teach of a God Who inflicts *eternal punishment* and you teach of an *everlasting Hell.* Hell is not everlasting. God is Love. He does not condemn any creature eternally. All those who have incurred the guilt of deserting Him, will ultimately return unto Him. That is the truth, as I shall prove to you on another occasion.

God's Creation and Its Vicissitudes

" . . . but Thou hast ordered all things in measure and number and weight. For Thou canst show Thy great strength at all times when Thou wilt."
Wisdom 11 : 20, 21.

"GOD is a spirit, and everything created by Him is spirit. It was in His image that He called into existence spirit-beings in numbers so vast, that no figures devised by man can even begin to express them.

"*In what manner* the infinitely great and almighty God created the spirit-world is something that you as a mortal could not understand were I to try to explain it. A knowledge of this is not necessary to man and is of no value to the good of his soul. It is sufficient for him to know how he stands with regard to God's Creation, in order that he may learn why he was placed on earth and what tasks he has to fulfill during his stay there. To teach you these things is the purpose of what I am about to tell you of the Creation.

"God did not create the world at one stroke. God is the great Architect who, with strict observance of laws conceived with infinite wisdom, builds up little things into large ones, simple things into complex, and, out of a single seed, produces the tree with its millions of seeds; who builds up the family, not by calling into existence parents and children simultaneously, but by first creating the parents and endowing them with the power of reproduction, so that in time the family may grow through the birth of the offspring, and that, out of this family new ones may arise without limit.

"In a similar manner God proceeded with the creation of the spirit-realm. Every law which you find on earth, exists in the spirit-world also. I have told you this repeatedly and insistently and shall emphasize it once more, because it is the basic truth underlying all knowledge of the Beyond, whether you believe it, or whether you reject it with a smile of incredulity.

"Thus you may shake your head in unbelief when I tell you that the law which prevails in Nature on earth, with all living things, namely, that of *reproduction by the union of the male and the female,* must and does apply to the same extent in spirit-creation. For matter is merely the incarnation of the ethereal, and hence merely *another state of spirit,* for which the spirit-laws are not abrogated, but applied in a way which is adapted to matter. Just as in material creation there are males and females in every species, so too there are male and female spirits in the spirit-creation. Among spirits there are as many males as there are females, a female spirit being allotted to each male, according to God's law. They are invariably perfectly mated, and find their greatest happiness in mutually supplying each other's limitations and in faithful collaboration in the task which God has assigned to them.

"Such spirit couples which were created for each other are known as 'duals,' a term intended to express: 'two who belong to each other.' These are the matches that were made in Heaven. None but God, not even the 'Son of God' known to you as 'Christ,' is exempt from the union of the male with the female. To all created spirits the words of the Bible apply: 'Male and female created He them,' and 'Be fruitful and multiply.'

"Christ is the highest Spirit which the omnipotent God could create. He is in every way God's most perfect image, so far as any created spirit can possess the Creator's perfection. Hence Saint Paul rightly calls Him 'the image of the invisible God, the *first-born* of all creation.' *(Colossians 1 : 15.)* Christ is therefore not God, as is so generally taught today, but the first created 'son of God', and, as such, His highest and most perfect Creature.

"Following Christ, six further spirits, also called 'Sons of God' came into being, but these owe the existence of their spiritual bodies to the first-created Son and are His inferiors in power, greatness and glory.

"The second 'son of God' was he whom you call 'Lucifer' — the 'Light-Bearer' — next to Christ the greatest of created spirits and subsequently a rebel against God. Still another of God's seven sons is met with in the story of Tobias in which the great celestial spirit which had accompanied the young Tobias in human form made itself known to the youth's family with the words: 'I am Raphael, one of God's seven sons.' *(Tobias 12 : 15.)*

"Save for the first created Son of God, the entire spirit-world was brought into existence not by *direct* Divine creation, as was

God's first-born Son, but was called into being through that Son upon Whom God had conferred creative power. Hence Saint Paul writes in his epistle to the Colossians: 'for in him (Christ) were all things created, in the heavens and upon the earth, things visible and things invisible, whether thrones or dominions or principalities or powers; all things have been created through him, and unto him; and he is before all things, and in him all things consist'. *(Colossians 1 : 16, 17.)* Just as the whole human race has the source of its *corporeal* existence in the first man, so the whole spirit-world owes its *physical* existence to Christ; and as men have inherited *only their corporeal bodies* from their first ancestor through many generations, while their spirit is united with their body in every instance without any collaboration on the part of their procreators, so the celestial beings owe their *spiritual bodies* to the Firstling of celestial creation, to the first-born Son of God, while their spirits, as coming from God, are always joined by Him to their spiritual bodies. After what I have already told you of the difference between 'celestial' and 'terrestrial' bodies, you will know how to distinguish between the two. In ultra-mundane beings the body exists in spiritual form, a subject to which Saint Paul alludes in his first epistle to the Corinthians: 'There are also celestial bodies and bodies terrestrial: but the glory of the celestial is one, and the glory of the terrestrial is another. . . If there is a *natural* body, there is also a *spiritual* body . *(1st Corinthians 15 : 40-44.)* The spirit receives its shape in what is called the 'odic body', being itself a spark of the Divine fire which shines according to the lodging in which it is housed. I am now speaking metaphorically only, but there is no other way of presenting the facts relating to things spiritual to you mortals, than by employing incomplete metaphors.

"As in terrestrial creation you have the most widely divergent kinds and orders of living organisms, high and low, although each one is perfectly designed to fulfill its functions, so too there is a wonderful variety of kinds and orders among the spirits which God has shaped into individuals endowed with celestial bodies. In your Bible, you yourselves distinguish between cherubim, seraphim, archangels, dominions, powers and principalities.

"The spirit-world created through Christ and united with Him in a communion, formed a wonderful *living organism* in which all spirits were members of a spiritual community, although they differed in kind and perfection. Like the members of a terrestrial body, which, though having different shapes and functions, yet constitute an organic whole in which no member is superfluous while none is independent of the others, the spirit-creation formed a spiritual body of which Christ was the head, the members being composed of the other spirits. In a well-ordered kingdom on earth the king, as the head of the country, together with his ministers and his officials high and low, and the mass of his subjects, constitutes a single great family in which everyone works for the common good, upon which, in turn, depends the welfare of the individual. The same was true of the great family of the spirits. Every spirit had its allotted task, great or small, but together they all formed one great and glorious unit, in which no spirit was superfluous and in which no spirit worked for itself alone, but in which all collaborated with each other at the wondrous task to be fulfilled by God's Creation. It was intended that they should share in the labors of God, and, consequently, in the happiness and beauty of Him Who had called them into existence, in the glory of God and of Christ, their King whom God had anointed.

"Hence Saint Paul in his epistles constantly refers to the 'secret of the body of Christ'. 'For even as we have many members in one body, and all members have not the same office: so we, who are many, *are one body in Christ,* and severally members one of another. And having gifts differing according to the grace that was given to us. . .' *(Romans 12 : 4-6.)* 'We must be faithful to the true doctrine and in time through love make all creatures spiritual members of him who is our spiritual head — namely Christ. For through him the spiritual body is fitly put together and joined into one structure in which each member has its duty to perform according to the strength with which it is endowed as a part of the whole. Thus each member helps to build up the spiritual body until the spiritual edifice of Christ is completed, resting on a foundation of love'. *(Ephesians 4 : 15, 16.)* 'Christ is the Head for which the whole spiritual body is knit and held together by its joints and sinews, and thus grows, as God ordained'. *(Colossians 2 : 19.)*

"This great communion of spirits is also referred to by Saint Paul as the 'church'. *(Colossians 1 : 18.)* 'He has put all things under his rule and has made him the supreme head of the church, the 'Church' being his spiritual body which he restores in its entirety by re-uniting with himself all parts of the universe'. *(Ephesians 1 : 22-23.)*

"The 'church' is therefore the communion of spirits loyal to God under the rule of Christ. The word 'church' signifies the 'rule of the Lord'. Whoever pledges his allegiance to this rule and consequently, to God, belongs to the 'church'. The true meaning of the word 'church' has therefore nothing in common with your worldly churches and religious denominations, which are the work of man, conceived in human error, and, like all of man's handiwork, ephemeral.

"What Saint Paul describes as the spiritual body of Christ was *a literal fact* in the spirit-creation. All spirit-beings brought into existence were members of the great spirtiual organization and were subject to Christ, its Head. They were, however, under no compulsion, enjoying perfect liberty and being free to follow their own will in all things. All of them were truly devoted to Christ, God's Regent and their King, and through Him, to God. This great spiritual family was closely united in the bonds of love. Christ's rule as God's regent was not that of a despot, but one of brotherly guidance; it was the protecting hand of the strong extended to shield the weak.

"In view of their freedom of action, which was the highest gift conferred upon the spirits by the Creator, it was possible for them to refuse obedience to the laws of the King whom God had set over them, for the words of the Bible: 'Even on his heavenly servants he cannot rely; his very angels he convicts of error', *(Job 4 : 18)* and 'Even on his angels God cannot rely, the very heavens are stained to Him' *(Job 15 : 15)* are true of every created spirit, save only of the first Son of God. And yet, the *spirits are holy* so long as they recognize the authority over them of God and of Christ, *and do not by apostasy, secede from God's kingdom.*

"Unhappily the defection of a large part of the spirit-world from God came about through rebellion against Christ. It was not, as you teach, *a direct rebellion against God Himself,* but against the Regent appointed by Him.

"This was the first revolt, which took a course more human than you could imagine. It was an exact counterpart of the revolutions you have on earth. In your own uprisings, it is not the physical bodies of the revolutionists which lay the plans and attempt to carry them out, but their minds. And if you follow the origin and history of human revolutions in all their details, you will get a very faithful picture of what happened during the first revolt in God's spirit-world.

"All revolutions are planned well in advance. They do not come suddenly. They usually originate with some ringleader who wins as many adherents as possible to his cause, unfolds his plans to them and promises them high offices and places of influence in the event of success. Those so initiated next go to work, carefully at first but gradually more openly, on the great mass of the people, without whose help no revolution is possible. This mass of so-called *partisans,* who do most of the vociferating and shouting in human revolutions generally know nothing of what it is all about. They join the movement because others do, and shout because others shout. They are, therefore, less guilty than the *ringleaders* who considered their plans with all of the consequences thereof beforehand, and carefully prepared for all eventualities. These know exactly what they are doing and hence, even when judged by human laws, are subject to the greater penalties, whereas the mass of their followers are judged and dealt with much more leniently.

"*The ringleader* in the revolt in God's spirit-kingdom was *Lucifer,* the 'Light-bearer', the second son of God, and after Christ, the highest and fairest spirit in Creation. What was his aim? He was ambitious: *he wanted to be the supreme ruler,* being unwilling to occupy a second place, subordinate to a superior. He wanted to step into Christ's place and to reign in His stead. He wanted to usurp his Brother.

"This plan did not come to him suddenly; it matured gradually within him, until his determination became fixed and found consummation in the sin which eventually besmirched this high spirit.

"God did not interfere to stifle the revolt in its birth and to prevent it by force as He could have done. He leaves His creatures free to act as they choose, just as among men He does not intervene when they begin to plan a crime and prepare for its execution. So He allowed Lucifer and his *fellow ringleaders* to proceed and did nothing to hinder them from trying to corrupt the higher and more influential spirits and to mislead the masses of the partisans with promises. It was the supreme test to which God desired to put the whole created spirit-world, leaving it free to decide whether it would remain true to Christ as its lawful King, or whether it would desert to Lucifer.

"One of the partisans, of whom there were many in all ranks of the spirits, was a prince known in your Bible as Adam, the name he bore as a human being. Of these princes there were many in God's spirit-kingdom, each of them, like Adam, the ruler of numerous subjects. Not a few of the princes became ringleaders to help Lucifer in his preparations for the revolt. Others, of whom Adam was one, merely supported the movement, seconded by the greater or smaller contingents of their adherents.

"The moment arrived when Lucifer and his party considered themselves strong enough to usurp the control of the spirit-kingdom, the more so as a large part of Michael's forces was ready to throw in its lot with them. As is also true of your revolutions on earth, great efforts had been made to win over the army to the side of the rebels. In this, Lucifer had succeeded to a great extent. God had maintained these forces, which were, in a sense, a standing army provided against any possible future need, as you also keep standing armies as a safeguard against sudden emergencies.

"When the war broke out and the spirits had made their choice whether to fight for or against Christ, God intervened. The hour of trial was over; covert and open treason had become a fact, and the punishment was at hand. Prince Michael received orders to overthrow the rebels with the legions which had remained loyal, and, armed with the might of God, he obeyed. Fearful was the fate which overtook the one-time Light-bearer and his chief henchmen. They were driven into the deepest spheres of Creation, into darkness and horror of which you can form no conception, not even were I to attempt to describe them. The darkness which you know on earth may give you a faint idea, for, as you know, darkness comes on with the waning of light and becomes ever denser as the light continues to fail. Darkness therefore *owes its being* to the withdrawal of light, but of what it *consists* is beyond your comprehension. You do know, however, that a mixture of all colors produces white and that all colors are contained in the light-ray; you know moreover that black is merely the absence of all colors. Translate these human observations of yours into the exile of the fallen spirits from all contact with light and consequently with all color, and you may form an idea of the impenetrability of the gloom to which they were consigned, even if you cannot conceive of its full measure.

"The Scriptures contain frequent references to this war of the spirits and to the overthrow of the evil ones. Christ Himself says: 'I beheld Satan fallen as lightning from heaven'. *(Luke 10 : 18.)*

The Apostle John had a vision of the battle of Michael and his legions with Lucifer: 'War broke out in heaven; Michael and his angels assailing the dragon and the dragon and his angels offering resistance. But they could not prevail nor could they maintain any place in heaven'. *(Revelation 12 : 7, 8.)* Saint Peter writes: 'Even the fallen angels were not spared by God, but were driven down to hell, into the caverns of darkness, there to remain until they have repented of their ways. . . . *(2nd Peter 2 : 4.)*

"The account of the spirit-creation and of the secession of part of the spirit-world as contained in the original Bible was very similar to the description I have given you. Subsequently however it was deleted.

"In considering the defection of a great part of the spirit-world, men may well ask: How was it at all possible for spirits, high in rank and enjoying perfect happiness, to fall? The reason in the case of these spirits was the same as that which so often leads your own souls astray: the craving for more. He who has much, always wants more, and he whose power is great, desires to see it augmented, even at the risk of losing everything at one stroke. Do you not see the same thing exemplified in the great events in the history of mankind, and in a small way in everyday life?

"Ezekiel, in his lament voiced at God's behest, over the king of Tyre, pictures in stirring words the reason for the king's apostasy from God at the time of the great revolt of the spirits under Lucifer, in which he had taken a subordinate part and had been overthrown in consequence: 'Thou sealest up the sum, full of wisdom, and perfect in beauty. Thou wast in Eden, the Garden of God; every precious stone was thy covering, the sardius, the topaz, and the diamond, the beryl, the onyx, and the jasper, the sapphire, the emerald, and the carbuncle, and gold: the workmanship of thy tabrets and of thy pipes was in thee; in the day that thou wast created they were prepared. Thou wast an anointed cherub that covereth: and I set thee, so that thou wast upon the holy mountain of God; thou hast walked up and down in the midst of the stones of fire. Thou wast perfect in thy ways from the day that thou wast created, till unrighteousness was found in thee. By the abundance of thy traffic (with Lucifer) they filled the midst of thee with violence, and thou hast sinned: therefore I cast thee as profane out of the mountain of God; and I have destroyed thee, O covering cherub, from the midst of stones of fire. *Thy heart was lifted up because of thy beauty;* thou hast corrupted thy wisdom by reason of thy brightness: I have cast thee to the ground; I have laid thee before kings, that they may behold thee. By the multitude of thine iniquities, in the unrighteousness of thy traffic, thou hast profaned thy sanctuaries; therefore I have brought forth a fire from the midst of thee; it hath devoured thee, and I have turned thee to ashes upon the earth in the sight of all them that behold thee . . . thy fate is awful. . . *(Ezekiel 28 : 11-19.)*

" 'Thy heart was lifted up'. These words best express the reason for the defection of the spirit-world. 'I want to rule, not to serve', brought about its downfall.

"*What, however, was the fate of the great mass of the rank and file?* They were far less guilty than were the ringleaders, and since God's punishments are always commensurate with the offense, He could not, in justice, commit them together with Lucifer to the pits of darkness.

"God dealt very leniently with them, condemning them to a relatively light penalty. He did, indeed, cast them out from their former glory, but only to transfer them to a sphere which, if you could see it, you would regard as Heaven. It may not have been comparable to the splendor which they had enjoyed in God's kingdom, yet it answered your conception of *Paradise,* for the sphere to which the followers were transported was the Scriptural "Paradise" even though it was not situated on earth, as you incorrectly assume, *for at that time, material creation had not yet come into existence.* The Scriptural account of Paradise with its rivers, trees, flowers, and fruits, has led you to think of it as being on your planet, as you do not know that everything you have on earth in *material form,* is also to be found in *spiritual form* in the ultra-mundane spheres. There too are shapes, habitations, rivers, trees, bushes, flowers, fruit, food and drink, gold and jewels, mountains and valleys, music and song, fragrance, color and tone. You will find this statement of mine confirmed in many passages of the Scriptures, where there are descriptions of the City of God with its walls and towers, its running waters and its blooming flowers and every treasure that gladdens the heart. You look upon these things as imagery. *They are no imagery, but facts.* Did not Christ Himself say: 'In the house of my Father there are many dwellings. If there were not, I would have told you. And because I am going there now, I will have a place prepared for you, and when I am there and prepared a place for you I will come back and take you with me, that you also may be where I am'. *(John 14 :*

2-4). And again: 'You have my solemn assurance, that I shall not offer again a drink of the fruit of the vine, until that day in which I drink it in God's spirit-world and indeed in a form as yet not known to you'. *(Mark 14 : 25.)* And in the Old Testament did not the angel Raphael tell Tobias: 'I eat invisible food and drink something invisible to human eyes'. *(Tobit 12 : 19.)* Finally, does not the description of the fallen cherub given by the Prophet Ezekiel, expressly mention the beautiful garments set with jewels and embroidered with gold, in which that spirit was clothed before its fall? Have I not told you, when speaking to you of od, that every spirit possesses an odic body for its spiritual body, and that your terrestrial bodies are merely the condensed odic ones? The most perfect state of od is therefore not one of condensation into matter, but ethereal. It is not the material, but the spiritual body that is the more beautiful; not material but spiritual gold that has the greater value, gold and jewels, in both material and spirit form being nothing more or less than marvellously prepared od, which in one case is present in its condensed, and in the other in its uncondensed state. This may be hard for you to understand since you are accustomed to thinking in terms of the materialistic, having no true conception of an ethereal state about which you were taught nothing in your younger days. But clairvoyants, whose spiritual vision enables them to see the ethereal, can understand perfectly what I have told you. They can also comprehend the description of Paradise with its trees, herbs, fruits and rivers as applying to a *spiritual sphere.* In your own case, what you experience, see, and hear in your dreams, is not perceived by you physically, but appears to you in spiritual form and shape.

"Such was the spiritual sphere of Paradise into which the rank and file of the rebels were sent, not altogether as a *penalty, but to try them once more.* It was an act of justice and kindness on the part of God to give these spirits one more opportunity to redeem the transgression of which they had been guilty through weakness. They were mere followers, who had sinned not out of malice, but because in a moment of weakness they had yielded to the tempter's blandishments. They had outwardly renounced their allegiance to Christ's authority, but at heart they were still divided between Christ and Lucifer, as is the case even today with so many people. In a way, they were carrying water on both shoulders, but God, with justice, demanded that they choose one way or another, even with regard to their inner sentiments. By transferring them into the paradisaic sphere He therefore put them into a 'neutral zone' where they could make up their minds at their leisure. To make their choice would have been easy enough, had they still retained their mental faculties to the extent to which they possessed them while dwelling in God's kingdom. This, however, was not the case, for as I told you when speaking to you of od, every act of insubordination to God on the part of a spirit is attended by a change in its odic body which becomes clouded, losing its purely ethereal nature and undergoing a certain condensation. This not only impairs the intellect, but deprives the spirit of all recollection of its previous existence. Consequently, the spirits in the paradisaic sphere were unable to recall the splendor in which they had lived in God's kingdom before their fall. Could they have done so, the test to which they were submitted in Paradise would have been impossible, for had they possessed any consciousness of their past happiness, and compared it with their actual lot, their choice would have been made without a moment's hesitation. But they remembered nothing whatever of the splendors they had forfeited, nor of the spirit-war which had been fought, nor of their own treasonable attitude in that war. They were aware only of their existence at the moment, just as you mortals are aware only *of the life you are actually living* and have no recollection of any previous state of existence, most people believing that their present appearance on earth as human beings is also their first one. Of their erstwhile dwelling with God, of their banishment from God's kingdom in consequence of a revolt, and of the subsequent incarnations on earth of their spirit, they know nothing. Only a few have a dim consciousness of having lived before.

"The test provided for the spirits in Paradise consisted in a prohibition laid upon them by God, the purpose of which they could not understand, and which the Bible pictures as a certain fruit, to eat which they were forbidden. This prohibition extended to all who, like Adam, had followed in the wake of the revolution, who dwelt in the same sphere with him and who were clothed in a similar odic body.

"These spirits were the object of particular concern to the loyal hosts of Heaven as well as to the sinister Powers of the Abyss, the former seeking to persuade them to remain steadfast and to observe God's command, the latter sparing no pains to convince the spirits that it would be to their advantage to ignore the same, by dangling alluring prospects before them. It was the same battle that rages today about every man. On the one hand he hears the insinuations of Evil, counseling the violation of the Divine laws and picturing sin in an advantageous light, and on the other, the inner voice of conscience, warning and admonishing him not to yield to temptation. It is for him to decide, which of the two he will follow.

"Men, whenever they wish to attract the great mass of the people to their cause, seek first of all to win over persons of standing in the community, and such, whose judgment and course of action are likely to be the deciding factor with the masses at large.

"Such also was the case with the hosts that dwelt in Paradise, among whom Adam, once a high prince in Heaven, stood out prominently by virtue of his great intellectual qualifications. It was therefore natural that his attitude toward God's prohibition would decide the course to be taken by the other spirits in Paradise. For this reason, Evil was primarily concerned in bringing about his downfall, making use, for the purpose, of a female spirit, the same one which had been allotted to Adam as his dual, and which is known in your Bible as 'Eve'. Eve fell a victim to the temptations of Evil, and in her downfall, caused Adam's as well. Their example was followed by all the spirits dwelling in the sphere of Paradise.

"By this second fall, Adam and the other followers of the revolt became the prey of Evil, and fell almost to the level of Lucifer himself. Driven from the sphere of Paradise, they were hurled into the darkest depths and thenceforth Lucifer was lord over them. In his own realm he was an autonomous ruler. It is true that he was still subject to the might of God, and hence not entirely free to do as he chose, but God did not restrict his authority over those who had voluntarily become his subjects. It was the terrible consequence of the justice meted out by God that Lucifer was allowed to call his own all those who had seceded to him. For such, there was now no escape. Even if they repented of their desertion to the standard of Evil, their retreat was cut off. They had indentured themselves to the Ruler of Hell for all time. That is the acknowledgment of indebtedness to which Saint Paul refers in his epistles as an 'insuperable obstacle' to the salvation of the fallen.

"Things are no different in your temporal States. Whoever becomes the subject of a country must yield obedience to its authorities. Without their permission he may not leave its boundaries, and if the country in question goes to war with another, he is never allowed to join the enemy. The same thing is true of Lucifer's realm: it is in a constant state of war with the kingdom of God, and hence it was out of the question that Lucifer would allow a vassal of his to return to that kingdom.

"Let me cite another example: whoever volunteers for service in the Foreign Legion is held to the terms of his enlistment. He may regret his step a thousandfold; he may weep over and lament the hardships he has to endure, but it will avail him nothing. He is under a harsh discipline that knows no mercy. He must stay, for if he tries to desert he will be overtaken and recaptured by the legionaires, after which his lot will be harder than ever. There is no bridge to carry him back to that home and country which he left of his own accord.

"Satan's dominions are a Foreign Legion of this sort. For those who had entered it, there was no retreat, no bridge spanning the gulf that lay between the Foreign Legion of Darkness and God's kingdom. Not until later was this bridge built in the Redemption through Christ, Who, in the parable of the rich man and the beggar Lazarus, causes the same truth to be uttered through the words of Abraham: 'And besides all this, between us and you there is a great gulf fixed, and they that would pass from hence to you may not be able, and that none may cross over from thence to us.' *(Luke 16 : 26.)*

"By way of a third illustration, consider the fate of a soldier who deserts his own side in wartime and goes over to the enemy. However bitterly he may repent of his desertion subsequently, and much as he may long to be back in his native country, he will not be released.

"I have now taken you to that point in my teachings at which you are shown two antagonistic realms, separated from each other by an unbridged gulf: the realm of those who had departed from God, or the 'Kingdom of the Dead', and the Kingdom of God; the realm of Darkness, opposed to the Realm of Light; Lucifer's kingdom against that of Christ; on one side Lucifer, on the other, Christ.

"Nevertheless, God loves all His children, even those who were driven from their Father's home because of their own transgressions. Since He had created them through His Son, and had incorporated them as spiritual members with the spiritual body of Christ, He was desirous that these severed limbs be reunited to His Son's spiritual frame. 'And they also, if they continue not in their unbelief, shall be grafted in: for God is able to graft them in again'. *(Romans 11 : 23.)*

"However, this regrafting of the limbs broken from the tree of life, this re-incorporation of the severed members with the life-giving organism of Christ's body, was possible only if *freely desired* by the apostate spirits. It was of their own free will that they had joined the rebels, some as ringleaders, others as partisans in the revolt. If the partisans, when again subjected to trial in the sphere of Paradise, had fallen a second time, it had been by their own free choice, and by their own free choice must they raise themselves anew and return to the house of the Father.

"This did not seem possible. Out of hand, the return of Lucifer and his chief henchmen was considered out of the question, for arrogance that has been humbled turns into sullen spite, which had rather remain unhappy than to confess itself beaten.

"The rank and file, those spirits which had been deluded into joining the revolt, were still animated by sentiments very different from those entertained by their leaders, yet even they saw no hope of being saved from the Pit. Where no hope of salvation exists, the will to achieve it is absent, and where the will is lacking, no effort is made to prepare the way to salvation.

"Even if these spirits had possessed the will to escape, they would have faced an impassable obstacle in the shape of Lucifer's control over them, which even God, after He had granted it, could not curtail.

"But God's ways are wonderful, and His wisdom finds means to achieve every end. 'But thou sparest all: for they are thine, O Lord, thou lover of souls'. *(Wisdom 11 : 26.)*

"Therefore, after the defection of the spirits, He determined upon a plan by which He would recover those who had forsaken Him.

"God's plan of salvation is the great secret imparted to Saint Paul and to the other Apostles by spirits which Christ had sent them, but even the apostles did not dare to reveal this plan in its entirety to the early Christian communities, to which indeed the greater part of the plan would have been incomprehensible. In their case it had to be left to the spirits of God, speaking through mediums, to instruct these communities little by little in the whole truth, much as I am instructing you at this moment.

"You too will find it difficult to grasp the full truth of God's plan of salvation. Mortals cannot, as Saint Paul told the early

Christians in his epistles, digest solid food, but must at first be fed with milk, as infants are fed. The truth in its full grandeur and in its entirety is an intellectual food, fit only for those whose minds have acquired their full strength. A selection of truths which are easily understood is the 'milk' which is given to those who are undeveloped in the faith and its truths.

"What I shall give you hereafter will not be milk, but meat, as indeed there was much meat in what I have already related to you. I shall not content myself with *merely apprising* you of the truth concerning the great questions of the Beyond. I want, rather, that you should gather *a thorough knowledge of the fundamental correlation of the individual facts from my teachings, for the inquiring mind is satisfied only by an understanding of the underlying causes of events.*

God's Plan of Salvation

> "And yet, what we say as true wisdom, although it is such only in the eyes of those who are ripe to receive it; not the wisdom of this world or of its rulers, who are far from being wise. We proclaim the mysterious plan conceived by God in His wisdom, a plan which was hitherto lain hidden, but which was perfect by God, before time began in order that we might be led back to glory."
>
> *1st Corinthians 2 : 6, 7.*

"AFTER the revolt of a great part of the spirit-world, God determined upon a plan for saving the unfortunate beings which had fallen into the Abyss, and for bringing them back into His Kingdom. His clemency would be extended first of all to the less guilty, those countless hosts which had deserted Him when they were subjected to trial in the sphere of Paradise. Only after these had been saved, would their corrupters, Lucifer and his lieutenants, be allowed to return to the house of the Father.

"God is just. Those who had been misled were guilty of weakness only, but those who had led them astray had sinned with premeditation, and since their offenses had been fundamentally different, so too would be their punishment, and so too would be their respective roads of escape from the Abyss.

"God's first step toward salvation was the creation of spheres of progress or amendment, disposed in stages after laws incomprehensible to you and conceivable only to the infinite wisdom of God. In his letter to the Ephesians, Saint Paul hints at these steps by which spirits may ascend out of the darkness toward God, by Whom they were created in order to insure the execution of His decree providing that all would once more be reunited with His Son. At this point the original text of the Bible makes use of the metaphor of the erection of a house with its several stories. If you will apply this metaphor in a spiritual sense you will more easily understand what I am about to tell you of the spheres of amendment for the fallen spirits.

"What you call "Hell" is the lowest stage into which they sank. But even Hell has its spheres of progress through which a spirit may climb upward by a change of heart, until it reaches the lowest of the *terrestrial* spheres. These begin in the lower forms of animal life and advance through the stages of rocks, plants, herbs, flowers, and the higher beasts, arriving at last at the highest of animals known to you as "man". Such terrestrial spheres exist not on your earth only, but also on the other heavenly bodies. There are, therefore, many stages parallel to those on your earth. Moreover, the terrestrial stages exist not only in material shape as you see them in animals, plants and minerals, but there is also a corresponding *spiritual shape*, and, in consequence a spiritual animal, plant and mineral kingdom embracing all orders and species of living beings, which in the spirit-kingdom are clothed in *odic bodies*, the counterparts of the *material bodies* which you see on earth.

"Spirits, parted from their material bodies by corporeal death, enter into the respective parallel spirit-spheres where they remain until they are reincarnated by rebirth on earth. Spirits which have not progressed are reincarnated in the same stage as often as may be necessary to fit them for reincarnation in a higher one.

"Each stage of advance required a special act of God to permit of the desired physical shaping of the spirits, and to this end He created the odic shapes of pairs of spirits corresponding to the shape in question and endowed with the power to reproduce the body peculiar to that stage. The spirits themselves are incorporated in the bodies thus procreated, according to fixed laws which prevail in the spirit-world.

"You mortals cannot indeed understand "how" these processes came about, any more than you really understand the processes of Nature which go on all around you, although you witness them daily with your own eyes.

"Your science concerns itself with the problem of descent, particularly with that of the descent of man from the apes.

"There is no such thing as physical descent of a higher form from a lower one. Plants do not produce animals, nor do the lower animals produce the higher forms. Every form of life breeds true to kind, although within each species there are many races, the individual belonging to races of the same order being mutually capable of reproduction among each other.

"Man belongs to the order of the apes. He is the highest race of this order, and you are correct in saying that the ape is the lowest stage of humanity and that man is the highest of the apes. Man is, therefore, the highest animal on earth. Nevertheless, he has not descended physically from the ape, in spite of the fact that in point of physical development, the ape most closely resembles him.

"Before the *first incarnation* of the spirit of man in the human body, that spirit inhabited the body of an animal, and is therefore the same spirit rising through the different stages of Nature in constantly increasing perfection.

"These stages undergo no physical changes. They are the same today that they were milleniums ago, even if, in the course of the ages, certain orders died out because spirits were no longer incarnated in them. For this reason God created other and higher forms incarnating in them those spirits which had previously inhabited the extinct species, which had served as intermediate stages in the evolution upward. When they disappeared and the higher forms took their places, the spirits in question were compelled to wait until the replacement had been effected.

"So it is that you find to this day the remains of extinct species of plants and animals that lived in former ages.

"*There is no retrogression of the spirit from one stage of progress to a lower one* even though a spirit may remain at the same stage for a long time. As I have already told you, a spirit which, when its body dies, has not progressed during its incarnation, must be reincarnated again and again until it is fit to enter the next higher stage. That is true of man also; if, during his life on earth he has made no advance on the road leading to God, he must go through life again as a human being. Every life is an examination: whoever fails to pass, must try again until he succeeds. That is a Divine law which applies with equal force to all Creation: there is nothing capricious about the ways of God.

"When I tell you that a spirit does not retrograde into a lower stage, the reason is, that although it may have degenerated in one respect it will have advanced in another, so that a balance is struck. Here too you can see the working of a Divine law.

"Of the ages that elapsed from the days of the fall of the spirits to that on which the first fallen spirit was fit to be incarnated in human shape, you can form no conception. "One day is with the Lord as a thousand years, and a thousand years as one day." *(2nd Peter 3 : 8.)*

"Of all these facts Christendom of today is ignorant, and they run counter to your own previous ideas. But why conceal the truth from you even if you may find it beyond belief and because it may be scoffed at by your fellow men? You have the opportunity of inquiring into these truths during the spirit-communications at spiritistic services, and if you do so you will find my statements confirmed in every particular.

"Unfortunately the important facts which I have revealed to you have been deleted from the Biblical account of the Creation, until scarcely any of them have been retained. This account says nothing of the creation of spirits by God, nothing of the revolt and secession of the spirits, nothing of the spheres of progress, nothing of the shaping of the odic bodies of the fallen spirits into their various stages, and nothing of the incarnation of those odic bodies into earthly substance. Your Biblical story of the creation of the world describes an original and entirely independent creation, quite unconnected with the creation of the spirits and their fall.

"The original Scriptures contained all of these facts, but when they were revised later, the Powers of Darkness were at work to deprive men of the knowledge of the links in the chain of God's plan of salvation and to withhold from them the consolation of knowing that *ultimately everything will return unto God.*" "This is good and acceptable in the sight of God our Savior; who would have all men to be saved, and come to the knowledge of the truth." *(1st Timothy 2 : 3.)* It was for the very purpose of leading everything back to God, that the material world was created.

"The Powers of Darkness were, of course, much better served by the doctrine of hopelessness and despair, and by the belief in an "eternal Hell" of which your poet has written the dreadful words: "All hope abandon ye who enter here."

"Such sentiments were far more acceptable to the rulers of Hell than was the belief in a merciful God, Who may, indeed, be angered, and punish with just cause, but Who, at last, will forgive His children and call them back to Him. The conception of a Deity has been debased by the doctrine of "eternal damnation" designed only to inspire terror. What is more, that doctrine added to the difficulty of carrying out the plan of salvation conceived by a God Who sent to sinful and suffering humanity this message of all-forgiving affection: "Can a woman forget her infant, forget to pity her babe? Yet even were a mother to forget, never will I forget you." *(Isaiah 49 : 15.)*

"Many passages in your Bible have shared the fate of the paintings by the old masters placed upon the walls of some of your ancient churches. In later times, so-called "church decorators" came and daubed their commonplaces over the masterpieces, so that if today you remove the outer layer of paint carefully from the walls, the ancient pictures are once more revealed, leaving the beholder enraptured over the great painter's art.

"In the same way the truthful picture presented by the original Bible was defaced in later times. Erring mortals revised the Biblical accounts, omitting what they could not understand or adding their own mistaken explanations. Their successors "improved" further upon the previous work, supplementing and abridging at will. In this way was not only the truth crowded aside, but many things crept into the Scriptures that tend to make a travesty of the word of God. One of your poets coined the phrase: "Books have their vicissitudes," and unfortunately this is true of the Bible also. Much that it should contain has been eliminated, and much of what it does contain should never have been admitted, because it conflicts with the truth.

"The various "churches" which refuse to acknowledge this fact and persist in regarding your version of the Scriptures as "authentic" are serving the cause of God but poorly. In fact they are doing that cause more harm than good, for even the least intelligent reader of the Bible, and of the account of the Creation in particular, must realize that much of it must be inaccurate, to say the least.

"The falsifications introduced into the Old Testament called forth the protests of God Himself, voiced through the prophet Jeremiah, as witness the passage: "How do ye say, we are wise, and the law of the Lord is with us? But behold, the false pen of the scribes has written falsely. The wise men are put to shame, they are dismayed and taken: lo, they have rejected the word of the Lord and what manner of wisdom is in them?" *(Jeremiah 8 : 8, 9.)*

"Elsewhere in the Holy Writ the truth has suffered at the hands of translators who have rendered certain words and phrases of the original text so inadequately as to distort their real meaning beyond recognition.

"From what I have said you can see the reason for the great obscurity and the many misstatements to be found in the story of the Creation as you have it today. Only occasional references retain a faint glimmer of the truth. It is true that some of the stages of the evolution of material creation are indicated, but these are not consistent with facts, in point of number or of sequence.

"The same is true of the Biblical version of the creation of the first human beings, a passage in which the creation of spirits is hopelessly confused with their first incarnation in the human body.

"In the first chapter of the Bible you are told that God brought man into existence as the last act of Creation, after the earth, plants and beasts had already been made. Then follows the statement: "And God created man in his own image, in the image of God created he him; male and female created he them. And God blessed them: and God said unto them, Be fruitful, and multiply. . ." *(Genesis 1 : 27.)*

"It is perfectly true that the two spirits which were the first to be incarnated as human beings and which, as such, bore the names of "Adam" and "Eve", had been formed by God and in God's image previous to their apostasy. It is also true that He had created them male and female spirits, and had blessed their union. This, however, did not happen after the earth with its plants and animals had been made, but at the time of their creation as spirits. Anything made by God in His image must perforce be a spirit, for God is spirit, and spirit only, and hence, not substance. Therefore, whatever He creates in His image must likewise be purely ethereal, and not partly ethereal and partly material, as is the case with mortals.

"The rest of the Scriptural account of the creation of man contains contradictions even more flagrant, for a few lines further on you are told that God made man out of clay, and, moreover, only the male, at a time when there was no other living thing on earth, whereas, according to what went before, man is said to have been made *after* all other life had been created. Thus, according to the second statement, God placed man upon a barren earth, and not until then did He create the Garden of Eden into which He "put the man whom He had formed." Still later, it is said that God caused this "Paradise" as you call it, to grow up in trees bearing luscious fruits of all kinds, and that He put the man into the garden to dress it and keep it. Inasmuch as there was no living thing on earth to endanger the garden, it is hard to understand the need for such keeping. Every single sentence contradicts the one which precedes it!

"Compare this picture with the facts as I shall relate them! You now recognize in Paradise that spiritual sphere into which God, after the revolt of the spirits, sent the least guilty of the rebels, partly as a punishment, partly to try them once more. Within this Paradise grew the spiritual tree of the knowledge of good and evil; this was nothing else than God's commandment, which had been given for the purpose of proving the spirits in this sphere and the significance of which they did not grasp. The observance or the violation of this commandment or rather, of this prohibition, would show whether the spirits in the sphere of Paradise were prepared to take sides with God, or whether they had fully determined to join Lucifer. Should they respond to this test by obeying God, the commandment would become for them the tree of life in God's glorious kingdom; should they disobey, it would become a tree of death. They would be driven from Paradise into the realm of Lucifer, and on that day, the day of their spiritual "death", their severance from God would be complete. "For in the day that thou eatest thereof thou shalt surely die." *(Genesis 2 : 17.)*

"Now you will understand why Adam was commanded to keep Paradise, namely, to protect himself and others against succumbing to the temptation to sin by disobeying God. Now you will also understand what the Scriptures mean by saying that after the expulsion from Paradise of the spirits which had shown disloyalty, they were prevented from returning thither by Cherubim "and the flame of a sword." The die had been cast: they had given their allegiance to the Ruler of the Pit. Henceforth the spheres of Darkness were to be their lot; they had no further claim upon the fields of Paradise, which will remain closed to those fallen spirits until the day on which they are once more admitted to them as a step Heavenward, on their return to God. Then they may reenter the spiritual Garden of Eden, and from it ascend to that glory out of which they were once driven because of their own sins.

"The mocking remark said by the Bible to have been uttered by the Lord on this occasion is also the reverse of the truth. By the Scriptural account, God, at the moment when countless hosts of His children were being driven into the unspeakable woe of utter exile from His kingdom, exclaimed: "Behold, the man is become as one of us, to know good and evil; and now, lest he put forth his hand, and take also of the tree of life, and eat, and live forever, therefore the Lord sent him forth from the Garden of Eden. . ." *(Genesis 3 : 22.)* These are the words of a fiend, not those of an infinitely benign God, and as a matter of fact they were spoken by Satan in mockery of the deluded spirits. On the contrary, God wished that even after their fall, those spirits would reach out after the tree of life, in obedience to His will and in an effort to return unto Him.

"But the Powers of the Abyss are intent upon preventing the spirits which were the first to benefit by God's clemency, shown by the creation of the spheres of regeneration, from extending their hands toward the tree of life and from returning to God. Could Lucifer have had his way, those stages would never have been created and no material world would ever have existed. He would then have been able to exercise his despotic sway over those spirits without restraint and without having to fear the loss of a single one of his subjects.

"Furthermore, I must take exception to the way in which the creation of the first woman is described.

"As told in the Scriptures, God resolved to give to the first man a helpmate in his isolation. To this end He is said to have formed out of the ground "every beast of the field and every bird of the heavens; and brought them unto the man," in order that he might find a helpmate among them. "But for man, there was not found a helpmate." Then God is said to have caused the man to fall into a deep sleep, during which He "took one of his ribs, and closed up the flesh instead thereof, and the rib, which the Lord God had taken from the man, made He a woman, and brought her unto the man." *(Genesis 2 : 21, 22.)*

"As you know, this story has been made the butt of ridicule, especially among the irreligious. It is a sad thing to see the act of creation so grossly misrepresented and converted into a laughing-matter for mankind. In this instance also, Evil has turned the fair image of truth into a repulsive caricature, through the instrumentality of its human agents and with the view of converting the conception of a sublime and all-knowing Deity into something ludicrous, since to make a thing an object of ridicule is to forge the deadliest weapon for its destruction. God did not prevent this distortion of the truth, as indeed He never intervenes in misdeeds contemplated by man. Seekers after the truth, and the righteous generally, always had means at their command to allow them to discriminate between the true and the false in the altered versions of the Scriptures, being free to communicate with the good spirit-world from which they could learn the truth at all times.

"What, then, is the true story of the creation of the first pair of human beings?

"Adam was the first spirit to reach the point at which he could emerge from the higher orders of beasts and be incarnated in the form of man, although his incarnation did not proceed in the manner incorrectly related in the Bible. God did not fashion a human figure out of clay and blow life into its nostrils, thus making man a living soul. On the contrary, the formation of the first man proceeded according to the identical laws which still apply today in the materialization of spirits.

"This is a subject in which I have already instructed you at length, so that you know that nowadays the od of so-called "materialization mediums" is required for converting the spirit-forms into matter.

"This same law was applied by God in the incarnation of the first human spirit. Since, naturally, no human materialization mediums were available to supply the required od, God took the od of the earth, and, incidentally, in a composition which corresponded to that of the human body. The odic mixture was the same as that by which the formation of the human body through growth, takes place today. In the words of Saint Paul: "But God gives to the plant its body as he pleases, to each according to the seed. Neither are the bodies of all living creatures alike. The body of man is unlike that of the four-footed beast, as this again is unlike that of a bird or a fish." *(1st Corinthians 15 : 38, 39.)* The preparation of the od for the incorporation of the first man was undertaken by God's spirit-world.

"The body of the first man whom you call "Adam" was therefore literally taken from the earth, although not in the manner in which you have heretofore believed. No figure was fashioned out of clay, but the ethereal members of that human spirit were covered with a material garment, with the aid of the condensed od of the earth, and that same body of Adam, formed as I have described, was again dissolved into earthly od after his death. It had been taken from the earth in the form of od, and in the form of od it was returned to the earth. That is the law which rules all material creation.

"The first man who thus came into existence was the only one of his kind. As your Bible quite rightly says, he was lonely, surrounded as he was by nothing but plants, and by the beasts of the earth, and longed for the hour when another spirit should have progressed to the point at which it could be incarnated in human form. He therefore looked about among the higher animals to find one which at its death would be considered worthy in God's sight of being advanced to the human stage. Your Scriptural account hints at this when it tells you that God brought all the beasts unto the first man, so that he might choose a helpmate from them.

"The day came at last on which another spirit had reached the human stage. This time it was a female spirit, the same one which had been Adam's consort in God's kingdom and later, in the sphere of Paradise, where it had been the first one to disobey, and in so doing had caused Adam to fall likewise.

"As her guilt had been the greater, so too had been her punishment. Her ascent from the depths had therefore been slower, and she did not reach the level of human existence as soon as did her male dual spirit.

"The story of the incarnation of this female spirit as given in the Bible of today gives a faint inkling of the truth.

"The incarnation of "Eve" as the first woman is called in your Bible took the same course as do all spirit-materializations. In her case it was no longer necessary that God should take the od of the earth, since a materialization-medium, namely Adam, was available. The possession by Adam of unusual mediumistic powers is to be ascribed to the circumstance of the materialization of his own body by the spirit-world, with which he was in constant mediumistic contact.

"Just as today the materialization of a spirit is possible only when the materialization-medium is in a deep trance, so was it in those times. The deep trance into which Adam went is referred to in the Bible by the words: "And the Lord God caused a deep sleep to fall upon the man, and he slept." *(Genesis 1 : 21.)* This was a mediumistic sleep, in which Adam's spirit left his body. As is the case today, the od of the materialization-medium is not sufficient to effect complete materialization and must be supplemented by substance drawn from the medium's body in dissolved form, so, in materializing Eve, the spirit-world dissolved a part of Adam's physical substance and used it to fashion Eve's body. This proceeding gave rise to the Biblical account of the removal of one of Adam's ribs: "and he slept: and God took one of his ribs, and closed up the flesh instead thereof: and the rib which the Lord God had taken from the man, made he a woman. . ." *(Genesis 2 : 21, 22.)*

As a rule, the materialization of spirits lasts for a limited time only, after which dissolution again takes place and the physical substance lent by the medium is returned to him. However, in the case of Eve, *permanent* materialization was aimed at, and for this reason, none of the od nor the part of the physical substance taken from Adam could be restored to him. Hence the spirit-world had to make his loss good, which it did by drawing upon the od of the earth, as it had done when it first formed Adam's body. This is indicated to you by the Bible in the words: " . . . and he took one of his ribs, and closed the flesh instead thereof."

"In this way was formed the first pair of human beings, from whom the whole race of man was to descend by reproduction.

"In physical reproduction, the germ alone, out of which the offspring's body is to grow, is transmitted. The spirit is united with that body only moments before birth, in conformity with laws unknown to you. The life of the child within its mother's womb originates with her. It is her blood which circulates through the child's body and sets its organs in motion as soon as they become partially ready to function, which generally happens in the fifth month of pregnancy. This movement of the child's organs while it is still in the womb is necessary, to accustom them by times to the part which they will have to play, and is not, therefore, produced by the child's spirit, which is not embodied until later, but to the mother. It is a process similar to that used in breaking in an engine after it has been finished and assembled: at first it is set in motion by outside power, before being allowed to run under its own. It must be broken in before it is ready for service, and the same thing applies to the bodies of terrestrial living beings.

"God's omnipotence and wisdom are nowhere more evident to thoughtful minds than in connection with the great natural secret of the coming into the world of a new human life, the same thing being true, of course, as regards all other living creatures. In all instances it is fallen spirits which are incorporated in bodies produced by procreation, in conformity with the laws of God conceived with such wisdom that your human understanding could not grasp this Divine secret, even were I to try to explain it.

"Adam and his wife had sons and daughters. *(Genesis 5 : 4.)* The brothers took their sisters as wives, so that when you read in the Bible that Cain, after slaying Abel, fled into another country and "knew" his wife there, this does not mean that he became acquainted with her in the ordinary sense of the word, or that there were in existence people not descended from Adam and Eve. According to the usage of the Hebrew tongue, the word "to know" also connotes having sexual intercourse; hence, as you are told: "and Cain knew his wife; and she conceived, and bore Enoch." *(Genesis 4 : 17.)* The same words are used in speaking of Adam: "and the man knew Eve, his wife; and she conceived and bore Cain." *(Genesis 4 : 1.)*

"Thus all of mankind is descended from the first pair of human beings and constitutes the highest terrestrial stage of progress in the ascent of the fallen spirits. This was the frontier of Lucifer's jurisdiction, and *before the Redemption, this was the point beyond which no spirit was allowed to pass.* Being lawfully Lucifer's subjects, none could escape from his rule, since he was unwilling to waive his right of sovereignty even in the case of those spirits which had repented of their misdeeds and longed to return to God's kingdom. *The surrender of this right had to be forced upon him by a Redeemer,* prior to Whose coming all human spirits would be obliged to remain in the human sphere, either as corporeally existent human beings, or as spirits in a sphere of the same level as that of mankind.

"Beyond this lay the great gulf dividing Lucifer's kingdom from that of God. To bridge this gulf, a victory over Lucifer must be achieved. As to how the Redemption was conceived and carried out I shall tell you presently.

"Once Redemption had been accomplished, God contemplated the creation of the spirit-spheres through which the spirits of men could, after their earthly death, ascend to the sphere of Heaven step by step. To create such spheres before the Redemption would have served no purpose, since none of the fallen spirits could have reached them, and through them attained to Heaven.

"In this connection I will call your attention to another matter of great importance, namely, that before the Redemption there lived a great many people who were the incarnation *not of fallen spirits,* but of spirits from Heaven to whom God had granted permission to be born as human beings, in order that they might help others to attain the true faith in God and thus prepare themselves for redemption. Of these spirits which lived in human form were Enoch, Abraham, Isaac, Jacob, Moses, Joshua, Caleb, most of the prophets, Mary, the Mother of Jesus, and many others whose names do not figure in the original Scriptural documents. After their death on earth, these spirits returned to God's kingdom, since, having taken no part in the secession from God, they had not fallen under Lucifer's jurisdiction.

"As for the spirit-spheres which had been provided for in God's plan of Salvation and through which, by that plan, the souls of men were to ascend to God after the Redemption, these are *thirteen* in number. I need not describe each in detail. What you, as a mortal, can understand of this subject has already been told to you personally in the many communications imparted through mediums for your enlightenment, by spirits from the several spheres. From their manner of appearance and from their speech you were able to form an idea of their lot in each sphere, as well as of the general appearance of the spheres themselves.

"You have seen those suffering souls which after death went into the lowest of the thirteen spirit-spheres, and in them you have learned the meaning of Christ's words: "Cast him out into the outer darkness; there shall be the weeping and the gnashing of the teeth." From them, also, you learned the meaning of those words of the Bible: "The dead know nothing." Those spirits, severed from God and condemned to spiritual death as a result of their unbelief during their life on earth, knew nothing. They were ignorant of their identity as human beings, of their former place of abode, and of the significance of the horrors which they were experiencing in the darkness and which rendered their lot so wretched.

"You could also see that as the spirits rose into higher spheres their consciousness broadened and their attitude toward God became less refractory. You were able, likewise, during these communications to distinguish the different light-effects pertaining to the individual spheres, the colors ranging from the deepest black of the lowest stage, through all hues, to the most radiant white of the uppermost sphere. The thirteenth sphere is of a white too dazzling to be endured by mortal eyes. This is the color that prevails in the sphere inhabited by God's pure spirits, or that which you call "Heaven".

"From what you have seen of the spirits of the lowest spheres you will have gathered how hard it is for them to struggle upward from their lamentable state, since their ascent within those spheres is possible only if they will turn to God. But you yourself have witnessed the rebellious attitude taken by these very spirits toward any thought of God, and in their case it is a great act of clemency on His part to allow them to reassume human form with the least possible delay, for as human beings it is easier for them, from what they see of God's Creation and learn from their own reflections or from the precepts and example of others, to acquire a belief in God, than it would be in those low spirit-spheres.

"Most human spirits must go back to earth repeatedly, seeing that their lives there again and again leave much to be desired and cause them to fall back instead of fitting them for the higher stages in the Beyond. Consider the lives of most men. Are they not wholly centered on worldly matters? How many ever even think of God? How many firmly believe in Him and live righteously? Ever since the Power of Evil introduced money into the world it has an instrument which gives it an unrestricted dominion over the majority of mankind.

"The time which the spirits of the lower spheres must spend in the Beyond before they are re-incarnated in human form varies in each individual instance. It is determined in part by that spirit's transgressions during its last preceding stay on earth. God is just, and every sin must be atoned for, but He is also charitable, and never punishes His creatures beyond their deserts.

"The spirit-communications from which you learned what you know of those thirteen spheres came through mediums of the most *widely varied types*. The purpose of this was to convince you of the truth of these communications, for had you received the accounts of all the spirits through one and the same medium, you might have thought that they proceeded from his subconsciousness. As you know, your up-to-date science is always ready to resort to the word "subconsciousness" when asked to explain anything in this field for which it cannot account on purely human grounds, and which it is unwilling to attribute to the working of spirits.

"The creation of the thirteen spirit-spheres was the last act in God's plan of Salvation, and before it could be effected, a far more difficult problem had to be solved. Of what avail were the stages of progress from the deepest infernal spheres to the highest terrestrial—the human—stage, and of what avail were the thirteen spirit-spheres contemplated for the further ascent to the level of God, so long as Lucifer refused to release any of the spirits which had deserted to him, and so long as he insisted upon exercising his sovereignty over them, as a right which God had conceded?

"Who, indeed, could force Satan to waive his rights over those, at least, who longed to return contritely to God? It is true, God Himself could have done so, but from a sense of fairness He had conceded that right to Lucifer, and for the same reason He was now unwilling to withdraw it.

"Only a spirit willing to enter the realm of the Prince of Darkness and to expose itself to the rigors of his tyrannous rule would have the right to do battle with him. The same situation holds good in your international law, when a nation which is oppressed and harassed by its rulers, rises against its tormentors in an effort to shake off their yoke.

"But it must be a spirit which would not, by deserting God, become subject to Lucifer, and thus fall irretrievably into his clutches.

"It must be a celestial spirit which, after assuming human shape, would invade Satan's dominion in body only, for every incarnated being is exposed to the influence of the Powers of Evil. Hence Evil has so great a hold over all earthly creatures, even over those which are not evilly minded. The most righteous of men daily experience the influence of Evil over them, and often stumble under its impulse.

"Thus the undertaking would be a great act of daring on the part of the celestial spirit which would venture upon it. Born, as it was to be, in human form, it would necessarily, as a mortal, remember nothing of its previous existence in Heaven. It would therefore be ignorant of its own identity as well as of the mission for the performance of which it had been incarnated, and would be tempted by the Evil One to sin. Moreover, God would not give it any greater spiritual aid than He gave to others, for this would have offended His sense of justice. It would have to earn whatever special Divine aid might be needed for solving its task, by repelling all advances of evil, and hence would receive such assistance only in the measure in which it withstood such attacks. That is true of all men. On the other hand, as the measure of Divine aid increased, the assaults by the Powers of Evil would grow in violence. God permits temptation commensurate with the power to resist it; children must not be as severely tempted as are adults; shoulders able to bear only half a hundredweight must not be called upon to carry twice that amount.

"By the same token, the celestial spirit that was to assume human form would not be exposed in childhood to the evil influences with which it was to be brought into contact at maturity. Only after it should have discovered its identity and the purpose to be served by its incarnation was Hell to be permitted to unleash its full strength. Then the life and death struggle was to begin, a war to be waged by that spirit as a mortal *defensively*, against the attempts on the part of Evil to induce it to abandon God. It must be a war ending in the bodily martyrdom of the incarnated celestial spirit, provided it remained steadfast unto death, since it is the recognized procedure of the Forces of Evil, when their light and intermediate artillery fails to reduce a fortress, to bring up their heaviest batteries in the shape of physical torture, and thus to compel surrender. For this purpose they never lack human instruments and helpers.

"If, in the face of the greatest torments of mind and body which the spirit could suffer as a mortal at the hands of the Powers of Hell and their human agents, it remained faithful and true to the last breath, then indeed it would have earned the final measure of Divine aid and strength which can be granted to any spirit. Armed with this Divine power it could, after its earthly death, enter upon a *war of offense* against the Powers of Hell, which as a mortal it had been able to meet in defensive combat only. Its victory over Lucifer was then assured, since the warring hosts of Heaven would be at its disposal.

"Then indeed there would be a war like that which had raged in Heaven when Michael and his legions overthrew Lucifer with his satellites.

"This time, however, the war was to be fought in Hell, which the celestial redeeming spirit would invade, in order to overcome Lucifer on his own ground. It was not intended to deprive the latter of his sovereignty over the apostate spirits or to condemn him to utter impotence; the victor was to content himself with merely *curtailing* Lucifer's previous authority, for theretofore he had exercised it not only over those who were with him at heart, but to an equal extent over others who had deserted to him deliberately, it is true, but who now repented of their step and longed to be discharged from Satan's Foreign Legion, in order that they might return to the house of God. By the victory of the celestial spirit, Satan was to be forced to release the *penitent* spirits from his despotism, retaining the right, however, to employ every means of corruption, as before, in order to bring about another change of heart in them and to bind them to himself anew. But no longer might he keep them under his scepter *by force* as he had done in the past. He was to be compelled, as it were, to retire his frontier guards from the bridge to be built by the Redeemer, so that no spirit desiring to return to its homeland would be forcibly prevented from so doing.

"Should the Prince of Darkness consent to this limitation of his rights, which, as the vanquished, he was bound to do, and should this limitation be embodied in the terms of the treaty of peace, its observance by Satan would thenceforth be *obligatory,* since God Himself was to be the omnipotent and just guarantor of that treaty, even Hell being subject to His might and helpless against His arm.

"The consequences of such a peace would in the end be disastrous to Lucifer and his kingdom, for by it, he would lose his subjects one by one, and in the end, be in the position of a captain whose entire forces have deserted to the enemy and who, when at last reduced to utter helplessness, has nothing left but to admit defeat, and surrender.

"In the same way, Lucifer, after having been abandoned by all, would ultimately recognize his impotence before God and be forced to tender his submission.

"This, then, would be the day on which under God's plan of salvation there would be no more separation from Him, no "death". On that day all limbs broken from the tree of life would be regrafted to it, woe and wretchedness would be no more, and all the tears shed in such numbers by His erring children on the long road of their wanderings, would be dried by Him. That was to be the day on which the kingdom of God would once again shine in the full glory which it had before the fall of the spirits, and on which all of His children, who had returned home, would resume the places which once had been theirs in their Father's house.

"Even Lucifer, the last and most penitent of all to cross the bridge built by his Conqueror, would again be the glorious Light-Bearer of old, by the side of his brother, Christ, whose love and benign rule he had so contemptuously spurned, and the Heavens would resound with peans of joy.

"Such was the plan of Salvation conceived by God after Lucifer and his angels had fallen, but it was revealed by Him only to His first-created Son and to a few of the holy spirits of Heaven, one of which was to declare itself ready to undertake, *when called upon,* the dangerous mission of being born of woman, and as a human being, vanquishing the Prince of Darkness. All knew what it meant to assume the human shape. All knew that as human beings they would incur the risk of being *overpowered themselves* by the very foe they had set out to conquer, and that, in this event, the coveted Salvation could not be accomplished. They knew, too, that a defeat of that spirit sent to earth as a redeemer, would make necessary the sending of a second, perhaps to be followed by others, until the effort was successful. Nevertheless, every one of the high heavenly spirits eagerly volunteered to undertake the venture.

"However, Christ, as the highest of created spirits and as God-appointed king over the spirit-world, begged to be the first to be allowed to make the attempt. It was against Him that Lucifer had revolted, and it was on His account that the great secession had come about. It was on His account also that the gulf between the kingdom of God and that of Darkness had opened, and for these reasons He felt that He, and no other, should build the bridge across that gulf to enable all of God's wayward children to make their way home.

"God consented to the incarnation of His Son, to take place when the fallen spirits, in their ascent through the spheres of progress had reached the highest terrestrial stage, that of man, and had thus advanced to some extent, and when, as men, they had given evidence of a desire to return to God.

"The plan was kept secret from all other spirits of God's kingdom as well as from the Powers of Darkness, in order that Hell might have no opportunity of thwarting it. Had the Forces of Evil known the true purpose of the human birth of the Son of God, had they known that His desperate struggle against the assaults of Evil, and His agonizing death were pre-requisite to his victory as a spirit over Lucifer, they would never have tempted Him, and would have done their utmost to prevent, instead of bringing about, His death upon the Cross.

"Only after Christ had died a redeemer's death would the time be ripe to reveal to all Creation God's plan of salvation in its full, inconceivable grandeur, for then its revelation could no longer do harm, but only good. The outer structure of the edifice of salvation being finished, it would be safe against destruction. The completion of the inside work would rather be hastened by proclaiming the plan, for this completion would lie in the fact that the spirits which had forsaken God would now return home over the bridge which the Redeemer had prepared for them.

"Every part of God's plan of salvation that might be revealed to mankind as an anchor for its hopes was to be found in the original Bible, including the truths concerning the creation of the spirits, their revolt, their fall, the creation of the spheres of regeneration as the means for a gradual ascent from the Pit, and the coming of a great, God-sent Envoy as Deliverer. Except for the announcement of the Messiah to come, everything has been expunged from the sacred writings of the Old Testament little by little. Mankind no longer understood these truths, and what men do not understand, they as a rule regard as folly and dismiss from their minds.

"This was true also in the days of Christ. Whatever lay outside of peoples' daily experience or conflicted with the creed inherited from their ancestors, could not be brought home to them then any more than it can today. For this reason Christ did not devote Himself to expounding the foregoing truths at length, but confined His teachings to proclaiming the truth concerning God, the fulfillment of the Divine will, and His own mission on behalf of the Father. Everything else He left to the truth-bearing spirits which He intended to send to visit mankind.

"But even after God's spirit-world had arrived in the role of teachers, only men who had made progress in the knowledge of the truth were able to comprehend the Divine plan of redemption. For the others, it was a diet too hard to digest. There were even many Christians who considered Saint Paul beside himself when he preached on the subject, *(2nd Corinthians 5 : 13)* and when Paul spoke before King Agrippa in the presence of the governor Festus, about the revelations which he had received, Festus said with a loud voice: "Paul you have lost your wits. Too much study is making you mad." *(The Acts 26 :24.)*

"You also, when you lay my teachings before your fellow men will be told that they are absurd fancies, and that you have gone out of your mind. It has been the fate of the truth in all ages to be branded as untruth and folly, while at the same time palpably incorrect doctrines as to the Beyond are thoughtlessly accepted as true, are preached broadcast and raised to the rank of religious creeds.

"What I have told you of the Divine plan of salvation you will find confirmed in every detail on a later occasion, when I shall disclose to you Christ's whole doctrine in due sequence as revealed to the faithful, partly by Christ Himself, partly by the truth-bearing spirits speaking through the Apostles and through mediums. Then we will also draw a comparison which will be most instructive to you, between the real teachings of Christ and the Christianity of today.

Christ — His Life and His Work

> "There is for us Christians but one God, the Father, from Whom all things are and to Whom we shall all return, and there is but one Lord, Jesus Christ, through Whom all things came into being and through whom we shall return to God."
>
> *1st Corinthians 8 : 6.*

"WHAT think ye of Christ?" This question was written in letters of fire before my eyes from the day on which I had resolved to join the ministry. It was to be my duty, henceforth, to proclaim not only Christ's teachings to my co-religionists, but also the truth concerning His person, His life and His work.

Who was Christ? Who had He been before He became a man? Was He God, or only a Son of God? Was He, born of woman, a man like ourselves in mind and body? Was He begotten and born like all other men? As a child, was He obliged to acquire knowledge, as are all children? Was He compelled to come, step by step, to a recognition of God, and to travel the same road travelled by all seekers unto God, in order to learn God's ways and God's will? Was He exposed to the temptations of evil, and to all of the fateful consequences attendant upon His choice, as happens to all of us daily? Was it possible that He, like the rest of mankind, might succumb to those temptations? Could He, perchance, like millions of others, be induced by the Powers of Evil to forsake God? And if He had been sent to redeem humanity, wherein did the redemption lie? What was the explanation of all these correlated questions?

Consequently, after I had convinced myself at the spiritistic meetings that God's spirits speak to men through mediums, as they had spoken to the early Christian communities, my first thought was to beg for full enlightenment on these problems concerning Christ. My request was granted, to the smallest details, and that knowledge thenceforth constituted the most precious possession of my soul.

In what follows, I shall repeat the truths regarding Christ, His life, and His work of Redemption, as they were imparted to me by the spirit which taught them:

"You are in search of enlightenment as to the person of Christ, His birth as a man, His life, sufferings, and death as a man, and as to the truth relating to Redemption.

"A few of those questions I have already answered by telling you of God's Creation and its later history, as well as of His Plan of Salvation.

"At that time you were told that Christ is the highest of the spirits created by God and the sole one to be created directly; that the rest of the spirit-world came into being through Christ, and, together with Him, formed a great spiritual community or kingdom with Christ as its Head, as God had willed. In this kingdom Christ was therefore in a sense God's viceroy. Christ Himself was not God, but only the first of God's sons, and owed His power, and His glory and His kingdom to God. He was but one of God's creatures and as such, not eternal like God. It was against Christ's reign that the revolt of the spirits headed by Lucifer was directed. After the defection of a part of the spirit-world and its fall into the spheres of the Abyss, Christ volunteered to bring back the fallen spirits to God's kingdom in accordance with the plan of Salvation which God had conceived.

"Christ's work of redemption was begun immediately after the apostasy of the spirit hosts had occurred. It was Christ Who created the stages of regeneration of which I told you in detail in the course of my teachings on God's Plan of Salvation. Thereby Christ became the creator of the whole material universe, which forms the ladder for the ascent of the fallen spirits from the Abyss to the heights of God's kingdom.

"From the earliest days, after those spirits had risen to the level of human existence, Christ became the leader of mankind, and strove to turn men's thoughts, which ever tend toward evil, Godward. As opposed to Him, the ruling powers of Hell did their utmost to maintain their sway over men. This led to a mighty struggle between Christ and Lucifer over the spirits incarnated as human beings, a conflict which forms the main theme of what has been preserved to you in the writings of the Old Testament.

"In this conflict Christ was supported by the good spirit-world under His command, many of the spirits volunteering to become mortals, in order that they might, by preaching the truth and by setting the example of righteous living, lead men unto God.

"One of the celestial spirits whose incarnation on earth was permitted was Enoch, who proclaimed to his contemporaries the true God and the right path to a knowledge of Him. Moreover, he particularly taught them of communication with God's spirit-world with which he himself was in daily contact, for in his day, almost all were given to communicating with evil spirits and had been led into idolatry of the most abominable kind and into all manner of depravity.

"Unfortunately the result of his efforts was not lasting. The power of evil was so strong that the nations of those times became addicted to abominations of which you of the present age can form no conception. The highest of the infernal spirits made use of human deep-trance mediums not only for speaking, but also for purposes of propagation, for just as the spirit of a medium can use his body for that purpose, so a strange spirit can enter that body and, through it, propagate, the corrupt female world of the times considering it an honor to be thus mistreated at the idol-worship. You will find confirmation of this in the Bible, in the passage relating that the "sons of God came in unto the daughters of men, and they bare children unto them." *(Genesis 6 : 4.)* The term 'sons of God' refers to those spirits which had taken a leading part in the revolt against Him. These are the same spirits of which Job says: 'Now it came to pass on the day when the sons of God came to present themselves before the Lord that Satan also came among them'. *(Job 1 : 6.)* In this case also it is only the apostate sons of God to which the passage refers, for Satan, as you know, was the second son of God. As rulers of the kingdom of Darkness, these sons of God are not free to do as they like, but remain subject to God's sovereignty, and are, at times, called to account by Him.

"The efforts of Christ and his world of good spirits to influence a race of men who had become corrupted almost without exception, were fruitless. It was therefore imperative that the whole existing generation be wiped out and replaced by a new one. The destruction was brought about by the Flood, from which only one family, that of Noah, was saved to perpetuate a better race of men.

"However, very shortly after the passing of the Deluge, evil once more raised its head among Noah's descendants, as witness the cities of Sodom and Gomorrha and the family of Lot. The more widely mankind spread out, the more zealously did men serve the Devil by idol worship and unrighteousness.

"In order to accomplish His end in spite of the terrible sway of evil over humanity, Christ strove, long before His incarnation, to win over at least a small fraction of mankind to the cause of God, a fraction which was to be the bearer of the faith and of the hope of salvation for later generations. It was to be the yeast with which the whole mass of humanity would ultimately be leavened, the mustard seed, which in time would grow into the great tree of the true religion and the search unto God, and gather all mankind under its sheltering boughs. Once this tree had attained a certain growth, the 'fullness of time would have arrived for the Redeemer to descend to earth as the Son of man, to complete the last part of His mission of salvation. Not until then would it be worth while to build the bridge by which the righteous spirits could cross from Lucifer's realm into the kingdom of God, even as you do not build bridges unless the number of persons likely to use them warrants their construction.

"The first to be chosen as the leavening and the mustard-seed of the faith and of the hope of redemption, was Abraham, a man of unshakable loyalty to God. Christ communicated with him, at times directly, at times through His spirits, since Abraham himself was an incarnated celestial spirit.

"His devotion to God was soon put to a severe test, as is the case with all to whom God thinks of entrusting a particularly important mission.

"When you build a railroad bridge to be used by freight and passenger trains, you, also, test its bearing-capacity before opening the bridge to traffic. If it fails to meet these tests it is strengthened, and if, even then, it proves unsafe, it is condemned, and a new bridge is built. Even so, God proceeds in the case of mortals selected to fulfill tasks of importance to His kingdom. If their power to endure fails under His tests, and if His efforts to strengthen them are futile, they are put aside as unfit, and others are taken in their places. It often happens that people otherwise fit for God's great ends must be discarded because of disqualifying defects for which they themselves are responsible, but which they persist in retaining. Many are called, but few are chosen.

"Fearsome indeed was the test to which Abraham was put when he was commanded to sacrifice his son, for 'he that loveth his father or mother, his brother or sister, his son or daughter, or his friend' more than God, is not worthy of performing God's great work.

"Sorely tried though he was, Abraham proved steadfast, and was rewarded with God's promise: ' . . . because thou hast done this thing, and hast not withheld thine only son, in blessing I will bless thee, and in multiplying I will multiply thy seed as the stars of the heavens, and as the sand which is upon the seashore, . . .

and in thy seed shall all the nations of the earth be blessed'. *(Genesis 22 : 16-18.)* By the seed mentioned in this promise is not meant Abraham's human progeny, for even had this embraced all the nations of the earth it would not have equalled in numbers 'the stars of the heavens and the sand which is upon the seashore. However, God does not exaggerate, and what He says is always literally true. Abraham's seed was spiritual and would ultimately embrace all of the fallen spirits, in the sense that his faith in God and his devotion to Him would little by little extend to all who had forsaken God. Indeed, it would not have proved a blessing to Abraham had he had a countless human progeny which eventually might fall into evil ways. As a matter of fact, in later days whole generations of Abraham's descendants forsook the true religion and turned to the worship of idols.

"Abraham's human seed of the second generation, Jacob and his sons, were led into Egypt, where they were to settle in the fertile land of Goshen, there to become a great nation, isolated from the idolatrous inhabitants of Egypt, and free to uphold the true faith.

"But long-continued worldly prosperity always endangers a nation's faithfulness to God, Who therefore permitted the Hebrews, as Abraham's descendants had come to be known, to be savagely oppressed by the Pharaohs and to be held in rigorous servitude by them.

"It was not God Who instigated Pharaoh to pursue this course, but the Powers of Evil which had realized that the Hebrew nation, as the bearer of the true faith, was a dangerous weapon in Christ's hands and might be used by Him against themselves. Hence, its destruction was determined upon, and since this end was not being accomplished by the forced labor which the Hebrews were compelled to perform, the demoniacal powers suggested their extermination to the Pharaoh by the simplest and at the same time the most effective method. Every Hebrew man-child was to be killed at birth. As a justification for this measure, the Powers of Hell had filled the King's mind with the thought that the Hebrews within his dominions, having already waxed strong in numbers, might become a source of danger by allying themselves with the enemies of Egypt. Evil well knows how to attack men, and the rulers of men in particular, at their weakest point, which, with a King, is always a fear that his throne is in peril. Hence Pharaoh fell a ready victim to the insinuations of the Evil Ones, and began the slaughter of all of the newborn Hebrew male infants. According to Pharaoh's plan, this measure would have resulted in the extinction of every Hebrew man within a comparatively short period, and when this had been brought about, the Hebrew women having become the wives or slaves of Egyptians, would have been absorbed by that race and, like it, have fallen into idolatry. Thus at one blow all the efforts of Christ and His spirit-world to provide for human upholders of the true religion would have been nullified.

"But once again it happened, as it happens so often in Nature and in the lives of men, that the very force which was intent upon doing evil, promoted the cause of good, for the moment at which a nation is driven to desperation by the slaughter of its children on the part of the authorities, is also the most favorable moment for persuading that nation to leave the scenes of its sufferings.

"There was still another and yet more potent reason why it was high time for the Hebrew nation to be led out of the land of the Pharaoh's. During the four centuries of their sojourn there the Hebrews had gradually drifted toward Egyptian idol-worship, until not a few of the members of that race were participating in the pagan rites. This grave danger to the religion of the Hebrew people could be obviated only by an exodus from Egypt, and the present moment was the most propitious one that could be imagined for the purpose, since the massacre of their infants was making the sojourn there a living inferno for the Hebrews.

"To conduct so numerous, and by nature unmanageable, a people out of the land, was a task which called for a great human leader, hence Christ selected one of His heavenly spirits for the purpose, and caused it to be born in human shape. The spirit so chosen was Moses. As the son of Hebrew parents, he was saved from death by Pharaoh's daughter, who saw to it that he was instructed in all of the sciences of the times, thus equipping him, as a mortal, with whatever learning he would be called upon to display as the head of a great nation.

"When he had grown to manhood, Christ spoke to him from the burning bush and appointed him as the leader of 'God's people'. Moses was called upon to perform, first of all, two tasks, one of these being to reveal himself to the enslaved Hebrews as God's envoy, charged with the mission of leading them forth from Egypt. His second duty was to persuade Pharaoh to allow the Hebrews to leave his realm.

"Superhuman power was conferred upon Moses by Christ, for

the execution of both of these missions, but the evil spirits, seeing their plans thwarted, appeared in the theater of war in full force, making use of the Egyptian sorcerers as their instruments.

"Then began the greatest battle among spirits, ever fought on earth. On one side was ranged Christ with His good spirit-world, and Moses as His visible champion; on the other, Hell with its retainers, the Egyptian magicians. With the aid of God's spirits standing invisible beside him, Moses performed the greatest miracles which the world ever saw before the coming of Christ and by which he hoped to convince both the Hebrew people and Pharaoh of the Divine nature of his mission. By these signs which took place before their eyes, God's people were to be moved to render obedience to Moses as their leader, and Pharaoh was to be induced to allow those people to depart.

"At first, and for the purpose of counteracting any effect Moses might produce upon Pharaoh and the people, the evil powers accomplished miracles equal to his, but before long their efforts began to fail the magicians themselves were forced to admit: 'This is the finger of God'.

"Never had such materialization of spirits been witnessed as that which took place in this battle. On the part of Moses, a good spirit, disintegrating his rod, changed it into a serpent; the same thing was done for the sorcerers by the evil spirits. Entire hosts of spirits were materialized as frogs at Moses's command, and at the command of the magicians, low spirits did the like. Moses turned the waters of the river to blood, with the aid of God's spirits, and with the help of the infernal powers the same miracle was performed by the magicians. God allowed the wicked to exert their powers to the utmost of their ability, in order that, in the end, He might have the opportunity of showing His full omnipotence, and thereby, above all, of fortifying the faith of the Israelites, since this was a life and death struggle in which the Hebrews, as God's people, were the stake. Israel was the first-born of the true faith; should it fall a victim to Hell, a long time must elapse before another nation fit to take that part could arise.

"Christ, God's First-born, fought against the first-born of Hell, on behalf of the first-born human upholder of the faith and of the hope of salvation. Christ was the victor. God's destroying angel smote all of the first-born in the land of Egypt, and thus forced the decision. Pharaoh and his people were seized with fear, and at the insistence of his subjects, he allowed the Hebrews to depart. Travelling in a pillar of cloud, Christ led the fugitives, and out of that cloud He spoke to Moses, protecting the people from the pursuing hosts of Egypt. The good spirit-world divided the waters of the sea, and made the waves as a wall on the right hand of the people and on their left. Putting their trust in Him Who spoke from the pillar of cloud, the children of Israel walked upon dry land in the midst of the sea, receiving their first baptism unto Christ, with full faith in the 'Angel of the Lord', who was none other than Christ Himself. God and Christ led Israel through the desert; it was at Their behest that the good spirit-world brought forth water from the rock and prepared manna. Hence Paul says, rightly: 'for I would not, brethren, have you ignorant, that our fathers were all under the cloud, and all passed through the sea; and were all baptized unto Moses in the cloud and in the sea; and did all eat the same spiritual food; and did all drink the same spiritual drink: for they drank of a spiritual rock that followed them: and the rock was Christ'. *(1st Corinthians 10 : 1-4.)*

"God and Christ, as well as the good spirit-world, gave to the people whatever advice and instruction were necessary. It was God Himself Who issued the Commandments on Mount Sinai.

"The long sojourn in the desert was necessary in order that the people might be proved, to show whether their faith and belief in God were strong enough to enable them to face the perils which would threaten them on the part of the pagan inhabitants of the country that later was to come into the possession of the Israelites. It was imperative that they preserve their religion intact, since otherwise, all of the work of the past would go for nought.

"Still another menace to their faith, against which provision had to be made, was the greed for worldly belongings and the excessive love of material wellbeing, which ever tend to drive men into the arms of evil.

"Christ resorted to every measure which would obviate, or at least diminish this danger, taking radical steps to cure His people of these failings by enacting legislation by which the Israelites, as the Hebrews eventually came to be known, were obligated to the payment of tithes. Furthermore, they had to offer their first-fruits, or to redeem these with some other offering, and in addition, they were called upon to make numerous sacrifices of beasts and fruits such as burnt-offerings, meal-offerings, peace-offerings, sin-offerings and trespass-offerings, for which only unblemished gifts were accepted. When harvesting, they were forbidden to reap wholly the corners of their fields or to gather the gleanings of the harvest, which they must leave for the poor and the sojourner, and every seventh year they might not till their land, but must let it lie fallow. Every fiftieth year they must 'return every man unto his possession, and every man unto his family'. Finally, the taking of interest was forbidden, thereby forestalling usury at the outset.

"Should the people of Israel observe these statutes, the danger of their being ruled wholly by worldly considerations and breaking faith with God out of love for Mammon, would be brought within reasonable limits.

"The other danger which threatened the faith was therefor far greater: this was the idolatry of the nations with which the Hebrews would be brought into contact in the so-called 'promised land'. Their idol-worship was all the more dangerous, because, like all of its kind, it consisted of tangible communication with the evil spirit-world.

"The realm of the spiritual possesses a mystery of its own in human eyes, and all mystery exerts an irresistible attraction on men. Ghost-stories are the ones to which you listen with the greatest attention, and wherever anything mysterious and spectral actually or allegedly happens, the crowd will invariably gather.

"On this account the Israelites had, already in the past, been allured by the mysteries of the Egyptian idol-worship. Saint Paul refers to this in writing to the Corinthians when he says: 'Ye know that when ye were Gentiles, ye were led away unto those dumb idols, howsoever ye might be led'. I need scarcely add that the Israelites did not content themselves with merely looking at images, for lifeless stone and wood attracted the people of those times as little as they attract men today. The allurement lay in the actual communication with the low spirit-world. The speech by spirits through images and human mediums, and the performance by them of other marvellous feats were the factor that attracted people. It was here that they were told so much that was mysterious; that they received answers to their questions relating to their worldly prospects, and that they heard alleged predictions as to the future, something that all men welcome eagerly. Added to this, they were told things highly gratifying to their human passions, for here vice was elevated to virtue, while virtue was branded as vice. Whoever once became addicted to this kind of spirit-communication found it difficult to desist from the habit.

"As the leader of God's people, Christ took two measures to guard his wards from relapsing into idolatry.

"One of these measures was to give them the opportunity of communicating with good spirits, as a substitute for the form of spirit-communication which had been forbidden by Him. He gave to the Israelites the tent of testimony, the breast-plate of judgment, and the good mediums known to you as 'prophets', as I have already related to you at length in my previous teachings.

"As the second measure He commanded them, in the name of the Lord, to exterminate certain nations into whose country they were destined to migrate. Of these nations there were six which had fallen into such idolatry and abomination that their reformation seemed impossible, while on the other hand there was every reason to fear that should they be allowed to live, they would corrupt the Israelites who had settled among them.

"The command to exterminate these peoples has led many of you to look upon the God of the Old Testament as a cruel Deity and to maintain that the writers of those portions of the Scriptures were incapable of conceiving of a Christ-like Divinity, since otherwise they would never have attributed such cruelty to the will of God. In this they are mistaken. One and the same Christ preached the conception of God which you find in the New Testament, and commanded the destruction of the peoples which I have mentioned. In one case as in the other, Christ appears as the Savior. By consenting to the extermination of those peoples, He preserved them from sinking still further into idolatry and depravity, and indeed gave them the opportunity of working their way, in a new existence, out of the depths to which they had fallen. The underlying motive was the same as that for which, in earlier times, the human race was destroyed by the Deluge and for which the cities of Sodom and Gomorrha were laid waste.

"To this motive must be added the even more important one of preserving religion among God's people. When men make war, they do not hesitate to shoot anyone who tries to induce a soldier to desert, a measure which you accept as perfectly justified. Was not God equally entitled to the right of ordering the death of those who were about to instigate His chosen upholders of the faith to desert their colors and to go over to the Powers of Darkness? Again, it was through God's people that the hour of the redemption of all mankind was to be prepared; was Christ, then, to stand idly by while this work, difficult enough at best, was being ruined by those who were enemies of God and instruments of Lucifer?

"You mortals become very tender-hearted when God's wisdom and justice demand the destruction of utterly wicked and irretrievably depraved people, lest they corrupt millions of others and in order that they themselves may be brought back into the path of salvation. Remember, also, that it was God Who did these things, the Master of Life and Death, He Who had showed these people unmerited forebearance, even though they had committed everything abominable in His sight at their worship, going to the length of sacrificing their own children as burnt-offerings to their images. *(Deuteronomy 12 : 31.)*

"When making war upon other peoples the Israelites were commanded to conduct themselves humanely. 'When thou drawest nigh unto a city to fight against it, then proclaim peace unto them'. *(Deuteron. 20 : 10.)* They were forbidden even to injure fruit-trees when laying siege to a city and were commanded to build their siege-works of the wood of trees bearing no edible fruit.

"Moses received his first foretaste of the danger of idolatry on the occasion on which his followers began their worship of the golden calf. Soon afterwards, also when they approached the land of Moab, 'the people began to play the harlot with the daughters of Moab; for they called the people unto the sacrifices of their gods; and the people did eat, and bowed down unto their gods'. *(Numbers 25 : 1, 2.)* The harlotry here alluded to was part of the pagan ritual and was demanded by the demons through the mediums as particularly pleasing to their gods. It formed an important part of the religious ceremonies, as it does among all heathen races.

"Armed with the weapon of idolatry and its attendant abuses, the Powers of Evil in the days that followed did much harm among God's people and thereby, to the work leading up to the Redemption. Whole generations of the Lord's chosen race subsequently forsook the true God, almost without exception, a transgression for which terrible vengeance was later exacted from them. Christ on His part sent the prophets, in an effort to win them back to the good cause, these prophets, the mediums of the good spirit-world, being hard put to it to maintain a successful fight against the influence of the demons' mediums, or Baal's prophets. Most of the true prophets were incarnated celestial spirits, although in their life as mortals they were quite as much exposed to evil as was the rest of mankind, but thanks to their efforts they succeeded in preventing, at least, the complete eradication among the generations which were to follow of the belief in the true God and in the Redemption.

"The time finally came when a great part of humanity was ripe, at all events insofar as its desire went, to accept a belief in Christ's act of redemption, and to cross the bridge which He was destined to build over the gulf dividing the realm of the Abyss from the Kingdom of God. Countless human souls stood waiting, eager to cross.

"At last the fullness of time had come when under God's plan of salvation, the Redeemer was to appear.

"Shortly before Christ was born upon earth, He sent a herald to prepare for and proclaim His coming. This herald also was a celestial spirit, Elijah, the same spirit which at a time when idolatry was at its worst, had gone upon earth on Christ's behalf and had fought victoriously against the tools of the Forces of Evil. After accomplishing his mission he had been taken back to Heaven without having suffered the pangs of earthly death. Now, as Christ's precursor, he was born as a mortal for the second time as the son of Zacharias, and bore the name of 'John'.

"Even before John's birth the incarnation of God's Anointed was foretold. The archangel Gabriel who had announced to Zacharias that he was to be the father of a son who would be the forerunner of Christ, was entrusted also with the message of the coming of the Redeemer.

"Gabriel was sent to a virgin named Mary, living in Nazareth, who had been chosen to be the Mother of the Savior.

The Human Birth of Jesus.

"Generation and birth within God's Creation follow immutable laws. The union of the sperm of the male and the female is in every instance imperative, *a law to which there is no exception.*

"Human propagation can therefore come about only if the germ of the male unites with that of the female. Hence no discarnate spirit, celestial or infernal, can beget offspring without employing the human body and the human sperm.

"You interpret the Biblical account of the conception of Christ as though a spirit from Heaven had begotten the Child in the virgin's womb without the aid of a human body. This is an incorrect interpretation and gives countless people, believers and unbelievers, good ground for denying, or at any rate for doubting, the way in which the Son of God became a human being. Here we have an instance in which the marvellous and the unusual, although at the same time the normal, borders closely upon the unreasonable, and hence the incredible.

"I will tell you the whole truth of the matter, for I know that you can understand it.

"When a deep-trance medium's spirit has left his body and a strange spirit has entered, that spirit is capable of using the organs of the body in precisely the same way as they can be used by the medium's own spirit. Consequently a strange spirit, good or evil, which occupies the body of a male medium, is capable of begetting offspring with a woman. Did I not, when speaking to you of the idolatry of ante-Deluvian times, particularly call your attention to the carnal intercourse had by the evil spirits with the daughters of men, by whom, according to the Bible's own testimony, they had children? If this is possible for evil spirits, should it not be equally possible for the good ones? If the fallen sons of God could beget children through human mediums and so corrupt mankind, ought not the true sons of God be able to do likewise on behalf of mankind's salvation?

"Now you will understand the human origin of Christ without the need of any further explanation from me. The human medium was Joseph, to whom Mary was betrothed. Spirits of God had already repeatedly announced to Mary through Joseph, as their medium, the coming of the Redeemer. Such spirit-messages were nothing out of the ordinary; on the contrary, the Jewish people were thoroughly familiar with communication with the spirit-world. This is evident from the account in the Scriptures of the appearance of the angel to Zacharias, who when he left the temple was not able to speak, by which the people knew that he had been visited by a messenger from God. *(Luke 1 : 22.)*

"Hence Mary was not alarmed when it came to pass that a spirit entered Joseph as its medium and brought her the Divine tidings, but she was greatly troubled at being addressed as being 'highly favored', by which it was indicated that she would become a mother. This was beyond her comprehension, as she had never had relations with any man and therefore had no reason to expect motherhood. But 'the angel answered and said unto her, A Holy Spirit shall come upon thee, and the power of a Most High shall overshadow thee; wherefore also the holy thing which is begotten shall be called the Son of God'. The spirit then told what was about to happen, although this is a point on which your Bible is silent. It announced that as soon as it had left the medium's body, a very high Spirit from Heaven would enter the same, and by this Spirit she would become a Mother by the law which obtains throughout Nature. And Mary replied: 'In my own eyes, I am a servant of the Lord. Let it be with me as you have said'. *(Luke 1 : 38.)*

"After Gabriel had departed out of the medium and before Joseph had awakened from his mediumistic sleep, Christ Himself entered his body and through Him Mary conceived under the same law that governs conception in all women. His spirit entered the body of the embryonic Child during thelast momentsof the Mother's pregnancy, or at that stage at which the incarnation of a spirit occurs with all mothers, through the entry of that spirit into the infant organism.

"That such was the way in which Christ was begotten was well known to the early Christians, to whom it was revealed in the same manner as that in which I am revealing it to you. They knew, therefore, that the mortal body of Christ was begotten by Him through Joseph as His medium, by which I mean that the Holy Spirit which, according to Gabriel's message was to come upon Mary, was Christ Himself, Who wished to perform in person everything that He held necessary to achieve the Redemption. It was by Him that the most difficult preparatory work had been taken in hand at the outset, by Him that God's people had been chosen as the upholders of the faith, by Him that they had been led, taught, admonished, warned and chastised, and by Him that the high spirits of Heaven had been sent to earth as prophets. The last step was the begettal of the mortal vesture into which He was to pass after a few months within His Mother's womb, in order that, by being born as a mortal, He might mingle with mortals as one of them.

"As soon as Joseph had awakened from his deep trance Mary related to him the things that had happened. It was a hard test to which he now found himself subjected. Was he to believe what his betrothed had told him? Like all other men, he was but human. Evil thoughts assailed him fiercely. The Powers of Hell had but one end in view: to incite Joseph to doubt Mary and to cast her off, for under the Jewish law, a virgin betrothed who was found to have relations with another man, was stoned to death. Evil sought to inspire him with the belief that Mary had deceived him, and that she was now making use of the pretext that a spirit of God had used Joseph's body while he was in a mediumistic state. There was nothing in the way of distrust, jealousy and bitterness to which men are subject by reason of disappointment, that the Evil Powers neglected to instil into Joseph, and under their onsets it seemed as though the burden placed upon him was more than he could bear. At times 'he was minded to put his betrothed away privily'. Privily, indeed it must be, for Joseph, being a righteous man, was unwilling, in the absence of positive proof that he had been deceived, to denounce a fellow-creature for an offense the penalty for which was death. On the other hand, he was not ready to make his betrothed his wife as long as any lurking misgivings persisted. Mary's sole defense was, that God would reveal the truth to him in one way or another, for she, also, suffered unspeakably under his suspicions. Then, during that very night, an angel of the Lord appeared to the clairvoyant Joseph, bidding him not to fear. This ended the conflict within him.

"I realize that this truth, — and it is the truth, — will appear entirely too human and too much in accordance with the everyday laws of Nature to convince you puny mortals. It is not marvellous and mysterious enough to satisfy you. The human act of procreation is something debasing in the eyes of many, who, as it were, blame God for making it a part of the order of things. To their way of thinking, God is wanting in chastity. Wretched beings that you are, to so misjudge the most wonderful laws enacted by God's omnipotence and wisdom, as exemplified in the procreation, the prenatal life, and the birth of a child! Christ, the highest of created spirits, did not find it beneath Him to beget His own earthly tenement in conformity with the eternally fixed laws of propagation, in order that He might dwell and suffer among you. Even though the truth regarding His human paternity may not be miraculous enough to suit you, for Him everything was miraculous that happened according to the sacred laws given by His Heavenly Father, of which the Preacher says: "I know that, whatsoever God does, it shall be forever; nothing can be put to it, nor anything taken from it; and God has done it, that men should revere him'. *(Ecclesiastes 3 : 14.)*

"That reverence is something which unfortunately you do not feel, and for this reason you account for the incarnation of Christ by means of ingeniously concocted theories, which, because of the alleged miracles they involve, are full of contradictions, and furnish good grounds to the skeptics for deriding the first step which had to be taken in order that He might assume the shape of man.

"Had the incarnation of Christ not followed the laws of human propagation, He would have differed fundamentally from other men, and Saint Paul could not have said of Him that He was 'born according to the flesh'. His body would not have come into being from human seed. Christ became as one of you, even as regards the generation of His mortal vesture by the human germ.

"Now, at your request, I shall speak of certain doctrines of the Catholic Church which touch the subject I am discussing. As you were formerly a priest of that church it is natural that you should be particularly eager to learn which of its doctrines are true and which are false.

"The Catholic Church teaches that the Mother of Jesus was free from *'original sin'*. This is true, but not for the reasons advanced by your former church. Like certain other mortals who lived before her and who had been called upon to perform the work of the Lord, Mary was an incarnated celestial spirit. The same was true of Enoch, Abraham, Moses, Elijah, and others of whom I have spoken. It was true too of John, who foretold the coming of Christ and in whose shape Elijah returned to earth. In Mary, therefore, there was incarnated, not one of those spirits which had forsaken God, but one which had remained loyal to Him. The sin of that desertion, of which all other terrestrial beings are the heirs, did not rest upon her. That is the 'original sin' from which she was free.

"On the other hand the Catholic doctrine that Mary as a mortal was devoid of all sin, even of the most venial, is utterly false. There is no mortal who has no human failings as you call them, but these have nothing in common with *that sin* from which Christ meant to redeem the world, namely, the sin of having rebelled against God. *That is the real sin.* All others are human frailties from which not even Mary was free. Nevertheless, she remained true to God, as did also Moses, that high spirit from Heaven, in spite of the fact that as a man he transgressed on more than one occasion, and was punished by not being permitted to enter the promised land.

"Again the Catholic Church is wrong when it maintains that Mary *remained a virgin* even after the conception and the birth of

Christ. She was, thereafter, as little a virgin as is any woman who has conceived and given birth to a child.

"Only before Christ's conception was she a virgin; it was not intended that the Redeemer should be born of a mother who had conceived and borne other children before Him. That is the meaning of the words of the prophet: 'Behold, the virgin shall conceive and shall bear a son'.

"It is furthermore contrary to the truth for the Catholic Church to assert that no more children were born to Mary after the birth of Christ. On what grounds do you assume that after the birth of her First-born, she was willing to waive her right to be a mother, or that Joseph was ready to waive his rights as a husband and a father? The fact that Christ had brothers and sisters who were born after him can in no way detract from His personality, nor from His life, His teachings and His work.

"The references in the original texts of the New Testament to brothers and sisters of Jesus allude to His own, *flesh and blood* brothers and sisters, and not 'kinsfolk' as the Catholics try desperately to prove. Had 'kinsfolk' been in question, they would have been called such, and not 'brothers and sisters', or do you suppose that the language of those days had no word equivalent to your word of 'kinsfolk'? You surely cannot maintain this seriously, for in the story of the visit of the twelve-year-old Jesus to the temple, it is related that His parents had sought Him 'among their *kinsfolk* and acquaintance', whence you see that where *kinsfolk* are meant, the Evangelist finds the word to express the idea. When somewhat later the same Evangelist writes: 'And there came to him his mother and his brethren . . . *(Luke 8:19)*, he is surely not trying to convey the meaning that these were merely kinsmen who happened to be with His mother, nor were the people who told Him: 'thy mother and thy brethren stand without, desiring to see thee'. Matthew and Mark likewise relate that Christ's 'mother' and His 'brethren' had come to speak to Him; do you believe that all three Evangelists used the word 'brethren' when they meant 'kinsfolk', in which case that was the word which they could and should have used? Any such assumption is foolish.

"Furthermore, in telling of the appearance of Jesus in His native village of Nazareth, Matthew records: 'He went on to his home city Nazareth and preached in the synagogue there. His words impressed his hearers so deeply that they asked of one another: From where has this man all this wisdom and the power of his eloquence? Is he not the son of the carpenter? Is not his mother's name Mary, and are not his brothers named James, Joseph Simon and Judah? Do not his sisters also live there? How has he come by all this'? *(Matthew 13 : 54-56.)* Can any rationally minded person contend that this enumeration of the father, mother, brothers and sisters of Jesus refers to kinsfolk only? Just as the allusion in this case is to the real father and mother of Jesus, so too His real brothers and sisters are meant. What purpose could be served by calling over the names of His kinsfolk? The inhabitants of Nazareth were astonished at His works and His teachings, and asked each other, as you would under similar circumstances: 'Whence has He all these things? His father, the carpenter, is a man like the rest of us. Mary, His mother, is a simple, unpretentious woman, and His brothers and sisters are nothing out of the ordinary, for his brothers James and Joseph, and Simon, and Judas, live among us and we see them every day, but we have never discovered anything unusual in any of them, and as for His sisters, all of them live in this village and are no different from any of the other women of Nazareth. How does it happen that of all the family, Jesus is the only one who is so wonderfully gifted?'

"The contention that the expressions: 'brethren' and 'sisters' as used here, refer to 'kinsfolk' only, is too trivial to be advanced by anyone without an ulterior motive. You can see in this an instance in which one untruth must be supported by another. The Catholic Church has taken the unreasonable stand that Mary remained a virgin in spite of the fact that she bore Jesus, a position which would, of course, be utterly untenable in the face of an admission that she afterwards gave birth to other children. On the other hand, there are many references in the Bible to the brothers and sisters of Jesus, and since this conflicts with the doctrine of Mary's perpetual virginity, it becomes necessary to transmute these historically established brothers and sisters into 'kinsfolk'. Otherwise, the dogma of Mary's perpetual virginity, and with it, that of the Papal infallibility, would fall to the ground.

"The birth of Jesus took its course like any other human birth, as regards both the Mother and the Child. The newly-born Infant was nursed, cared for and eventually weaned, as are all children.

"The message of the angels to the shepherds and their salutation of the Redeemer of mankind Who had appeared, the presentation of Jesus in the temple, the coming of the Wise Men of the East, all happened exactly as it is related in your New Testament.

These Wise Men were Divine instruments and were highly gifted with mediumistic powers. At home they were the dispensers of the true faith, and through their communication with the good spirit-world they had been initiated into many of the truths relating to the salvation of mankind. The same spirit-world which had announced the birth of the Savior to the shepherds, brought to the Magi also the tidings of the happy event which had already been foretold to them as impending, by messengers from God. They were now invited to set out in search of the Child in Whom the Son of God was incarnated. The name of the place at which the Child lay was withheld from them, but they were told that the gleam of a light would go before them to guide them on their way. Not only the Wise Men, but everyone else saw this light, which appeared as a bright star moving before them and leading them as Moses and the people of Israel had once been led by the pillar of cloud.

"Their journey took them first to Herod in Jerusalem. This was an act of God, by which that temporal prince was to be apprised of the human birth of Him Who was to rule the world, and in order that the fate of the children of Bethlehem might be fulfilled, as had been foretold by the prophet. Here again the forces of Anti-Christ gave evidence of their activity by inspiring Herod with fear for his throne and thus driving him to perpetrate the slaughter of the children, in order that the new-born Herald of the truth might perish.

"The Magi did not reach Bethlehem until *after* the presentation of Jesus in the temple, His parents having returned thither from Jerusalem with the intention of resting a few days before resuming their journey to Nazareth. It was immediately after their arrival in Bethlehem that the Wise Men found them, and after the latter had set out for home, the parents of the Child also prepared to continue on their way, when a messenger from God appeared to Joseph warning him to flee into Egypt with his wife and child, as Herod, who on first learning of the birth of a new King of the Jews had determined to destroy him, was now on the point of carrying out his design.

"After the Babe had emerged from the years of infancy, His childhood was like that of other children. He learned to walk and to speak, and in time began to play, like the rest. On occasions, He misbehaved, as all children will. With the passing of His boyhood His understanding developed, and inasmuch as He was the incarnation of the highest of created spirits, He was also endowed with intelligence of a high order. Nevertheless, He had to learn things from the beginning as does everybody, even the most brilliant minds. As a child He came to know of God exactly as you yourself did, namely, by what He learned from His parents and teachers. He listened to sermons on God in the synagogue of His native village, and discussed them with His elders, of whom He asked for explanations of the things which He had not understood or which had impressed Him as being untrue.

"As a boy, moreover, He was assailed by those temptations which come to all children of men and which are sent of a strength in keeping with youth's powers of resistance, temptations which He overcame in the measure as His knowledge of evil increased with the advancing years. Nevertheless, there were times when He erred and was guilty of failings due to human weakness, as is the case with the best of children. With every victory over temptation the Boy received from God greater inner strength and knowledge of the spirit, but as His power of resistance grew, the Forces of Evil were permitted to increase the violence of their assaults upon Him. It is so with every mortal, and no exception was made in favor of the Boy Jesus, for it is a law that applies to all men alike that they gain in ability to resist sin with every victory over temptation, while, on the other hand, Evil is left free to proceed with more vigor than ever, with the result that the whole life of a God-fearing man is a constant battle with the Hostile Powers. 'War is the lot of man upon earth'!

"As the Boy grew in years, the numerous errors of the Jewish faith professed by His parents caused Him many an inward struggle. All of these had been introduced in the course of time by the Jewish Church in the form of manmade doctrines and alleged amendments to the Divine commandments.

"When He had reached the point of being able to read and understand the original texts of the Old Testament, He began to question the interpretations given to Him by His Jewish instructors, but whenever, in His youthful enthusiasm, He expressed these views to His elders, He was severely rebuked. It was these convictions conflicting with the Jewish religious doctrines which at the age of twelve He laid before the priests in the temple at Jerusalem much to their amazement, putting questions to them and replying to theirs out of His own wisdom.

"Undoubtedly He was in this respect what you call a 'child

marvel', such as you find in all branches of human endeavor. This Boy was a 'child marvel' in His knowledge of God's ways of salvation. But He was human, like all others. *At first He did not know who He was, nor what mission He was destined to fulfill as a mortal.*

However, soon after He had reached the years of discretion, He began to exhibit great mediumistic powers. These consisted of the gifts of clairvoyance and clairaudience, which, from small beginnings, rapidly attained great perfection, enabling Him to communicate with the spirit-world, to see the spirits as a clairvoyant, and as a clairaudient to hear the words spoken by them. This gift with which the adolescent youth was endowed was nothing new; it had been possessed by many others before Him, but in the case of this Envoy of God it was developed to the highest degree attainable by man.

"Through His communication with the Divine spirit-world He was taught, while on earth, everything which He needed for the execution of His task, for in these matters He, as a mortal, was as ignorant as all the rest. Recollection of His previous state as the highest of God's spirits he had none, because in every instance, the incarnation of a spirit in a material body destroys all memory of the past.

"Therefore, the things that Christ preached while He was on earth, were taught to Him by the spirit-world, as Moses was taught, by inquiring of God in the tent of testimony, all of those things which he later proclaimed to the people.

"Thus Jesus passed from boyhood, through adolescence, to manhood, and as He grew older, His wisdom increased, not only in the way in which this is the case with all people as they mature, but chiefly by reason of the teaching which He received from the Divine spirits. Hand in hand with this went the growth of His goodness, or, as your Bible expresses it: 'Jesus grew in wisdom and became day by day dearer to God and to men'. *(Luke 2 : 52.)*

"It was real progress and not merely a gradual disclosure of Himself, as your former religion maintains. As a mortal, Christ was not originally perfect, a thing which is impossible for any spirit incarnated in human form, since all matter is inherently base and full of imperfections. Even a spirit which enters, pure and flawless, into the garment of flesh, must, during its life as a human being, fight its way step by step toward perfection, through the debasing influence of evil.

"The weaknesses and failings of every human body react upon the spirit which it houses and which, however perfect, must constantly wrestle with them and can never quite free itself from them during its earthly existence. This is a part of human nature from which not even Christ was exempt. To His last breath He was compelled to fight against these failings and more than once succumbed to them in His battle with Evil. In the garden of Gethsemane even this mighty Conqueror turned faint and weak praying that the Father might let the cup pass away from Him, yet adding: 'Nevertheless, not as I will, but as thou wilt'. He knew that it was the Father's will that He must suffer, and His outcry reveals the weak, imperfect mortal, whose nature, being human, quails and rebels at the thought of an agonizing death. A perfect being would have said: 'Father, send whatsoever torments thou wilt and deemest best. I will endure them'. He would not have said: 'Let this cup pass away from me'. And it was human frailty which spoke from Him from the Cross, when He uttered the plaint: 'My God, my God, why hast thou forsaken me?'. This cry would never have been uttered by a human being perfect in every way, but such human beings do not exist. If they did, mortals would no longer be what they are, and the material body would cease to be.

"Saint Paul has recorded this truth in his Epistle to the Hebrews, in words which may offend those who regard Christ as a Deity, and hence deny the possibility on His part of sin or of rebellion against God. The passage in question reads: 'In the days of his stay upon earth, Christ, amid loud lamentations and many tears sent up fervent prayers to Him, Who could save him from the spiritual death of apostasy, and was heard because of his piety. But although he was a Son of God he also had to learn through the sufferings that lay before him, and only after he had attained perfection did he become the author of the salvation'. *(Hebrews 5, 7-9.)*

"In these words you will find confirmation of everything I have told you, to the smallest particular.

"In my explanation of God's Plan of Salvation I called your attention to the very important fact that even the highest of created spirits is exposed by incarnation to the danger of being overcome by Evil and to being persuaded to desert God. This danger threatened Christ Himself Who was fully aware of it. On more than one occasion He was on the point of succumbing to the assaults of Satan, as Saint Paul intimates in the passage I have quoted by saying that Christ had called upon God amid loud lamentations and many tears to save Him from death. That it was not corporeal death from which He prayed to be saved is evident from the fact that Paul expressly says, that Christ's prayers were heard, and that God saved Him from the death which He so greatly feared. Did God then save Him from earthly death and its terrors? On the contrary; that was a cup which Christ was compelled to drain to the dregs, and therefore it must have been death of another kind from which Christ was saved in answer to His prayers. As you know, the word 'death' in almost all passages of the Bible, and above all, where it is used in the epistles of Paul, signifies 'spiritual death' or the abandonment of God. This was a danger at which Christ trembled even before He knew that He was fated to die on the Cross; such was the fierceness of Satan's assaults upon Him. Your Bible says nothing of Christ's daily battles with the Powers of Hell which spared no effort to break His will-power and thus to force Him to forsake God. From the fact that He raised His voice in tears to God praying for help as Satan and his hosts bore down upon Him, and that He trembled for fear that He might not prevail against Hell for long, from all this, you may gather that it was possible that even Christ might forsake God. Had there been no such possibility, He would have had no occasion to tremble before Hell's onset; still less, to call to be saved from death 'with strong crying and tears'. Furthermore, Satan, who knew exactly what manner of a foe he had before him in Christ, would have known better than to take the field against Him with all his forces, had he seen no prospect of victory. It is for this reason that he never directs his attacks upon God Himself, but against His creatures. If Lucifer, the highest but one of created spirits, had deserted God, why should not the highest of them all do likewise, particularly when, in the shape of a weak mortal, it found itself face to face with the Infernal Powers. Satan knows full well what he is doing, and undertakes nothing that does not offer at least a fair prospect of success.

"The further fact that Christ had human weaknesses and failings is indicated by Paul in the same passage, for he says that 'Christ, though he was a Son of God, yet *learned obedience* by the things which he had suffered'. Thus Christ, as a mortal, had to learn obedience. Not even He, on every occasion, gave heed to the appeals to His better nature which came from without and within, but the penalties which He as a man suffered for even the most trifling act of disobedience, *taught* Him obedience little by little, when He stumbled. It is only he who is never weak that never stumbles.

"It is precisely this that constitutes Christ's wonderful merit, that although He was the Son of God, He was compelled to battle with the human frailties and short-comings which He shared with other men, and in spite of which He held out against the Infernal Powers. He was called upon to sustain their most savage attacks, directed against Him as a vulnerable antagonist who, terrified at the threat of defeat, cried out to God in prayer. He therefore knows from experience how helpless you mortals feel in your feebleness. 'For in him we have, not a high priest unable to feel for us in all our failings, but one who in the face of temptation all about him felt as we feel, and yet did not commit the sin of apostasy'. *(Hebrews 4 : 15.)*

"The word 'sin' is used here not to designate transgressions due to human infirmities from which not even Christ was free, but with reference to the iniquity which severs us from God, the sin whose wages is death. Christ was never one of the fallen spirits, and even as a mortal did not allow His loyalty to God to waver. The 'mortal sin' as the Apostle John calls it, was something of which He was never guilty, but in other ways He became as all men, even as to their infirmities, and like them, there were times until He achieved perfection, as proved by His consummate act of submission: — His death upon the Cross.

"The public appearance as a preacher of penitence of John the Baptist was destined to be a decisive event in the life of Christ Who until then had not known that He was the promised Messiah. When, however He went in search of John who hailed him before the people as the Lamb of God 'that taketh away the sin of the world' He knew Himself, and was confirmed in His knowledge by the voice of God saying: 'This is my beloved Son, in whom I am well pleased'.

"The moment had now arrived for the Divine spirit-world to reveal to Christ His mission in life. He was told that He was the highest of created spirits, God's First-born; that it was His mission to proclaim the Divine truth; that He must stand firm against the attacks of Satan who would do battle against Him to 'the utmost and bring about His death upon the Cross, as the

Prophets had foretold. But only after His earthly body had died upon the Cross and His Spirit had departed from it, did Christ learn wherein the final victory over Satan lay.

"Hell recognized in Christ the Son and Emissary of God, Who was to lead humanity Godward by His teaching and Who was to be ready to die for the truth, but of the true connection between Christ's Crucifixion and a victory over Hell, not even Satan was aware. Had he been so, he would neither have tempted Christ, nor brought about His death. As it was, he sought only to render Christ, in Whom he saw only a herald of the truth, harmless, as speedily as possible. Should he be unable to induce Christ to forsake God, he hoped to discredit His teachings by preparing for Him a malefactor's death as the surest way of attaining that end. In this he reckoned upon the fact that men would naturally expect that a Son of God, such as Christ proclaimed Himself to be, would be endowed with Divine power sufficient to prevent so ignominious an end at the hands of His enemies. If He failed to prevent this, His teachings would be condemned. Such was the way in which Satan reasoned.

"Christ now knew Who He was, as well as the nature of his task, but before beginning with the execution of the same His powers of resistance must be tested, as had been those of all men who had previously served God as His instruments. He must prove Himself equal to His momentous, far-reaching Mission. It was to this end that the Spirit led Him into the wilderness.

"Here it was that He was called upon to face a terrific onset on the part of the Powers of Hell. No helper stood beside Him. No word of human consolation from His mother, His brothers or sisters, or His friends, could reach Him, at the very time when, torn by the conflict within His soul, He yearned for the sympathy and support of a friendly human heart. All this was denied Him in the wilderness; instead, he heard the howling of wild beasts, and His clairvoyant eyes saw shapes from Hell before Him, coming and going without cease. He could hear them enticing, promising, threatening. Every form of appeal to which men are amenable was employed against the Son of Man, for Satan has his specialists in every field of evil. Among them were spirits of despondency and timidity, and spirits of doubt, seeking to shake His belief in Himself as the Son of God, and in His Divinely assigned mission, and to drive Him to despair of Himself. Again, there appeared spirits of hatred, intent upon embittering Him against a God who would drive Him forth into the desert to suffer. There also came the spirits of a sinful life of pleasure, drawing the most enticing pictures of human ease and enjoyment in contrast to the dreary waste about Him.

"The parts which these various spirits had to play were skillfully assigned. The ablest of them were the spirits of doubt which appeared upon the scene again and again. How, argued they, could any God send His Son into a desert to suffer hunger and unspeakable torture of the soul? After all, was not everything that He had heard from the allegedly good spirits, was not the utterance of the Baptist, was not the voice of God speaking to Him by the Jordan, merely a part of a great delusion? Was not His Sonship of God a great hallucination, to which He had fallen a victim?

"This was the point upon which Hell centered its main attack, seeking to destroy within this Son of Man His conviction that He was the Son of God. Once this end was accomplished, Satan had won the battle, for whoever loses faith in his mission, casts it aside.

"For forty days and forty nights this remorseless persecution was continued against a victim who stood helpless and defenseless, trembling at every limb from emotion and from physical exhaustion, brought on by hunger and sleeplessness. The desert offered no nourishment; Christ fasted, indeed; not voluntarily, however, but because there was no food. Nothing but sand and rock, as far as the eye could reach.

"Nevertheless, all the specialists of Hell labored in vain to overcome this fever-racked Jesus of Nazareth, in spite of the fact that what with bodily fatigue, hunger and thirst, He was at last no longer able to stand. Again and again, amidst tears, He cried to His Father for help, in order that He might be spared the mortal sin of desertion, and be given the strength to hold out victoriously against the assaults of the Evil Powers.

"Finally, on the very last day, when the other infernal powers with all their arts of seduction had failed to make headway against their tormented victim, the Prince of Darkness arrived in person. He, too, is a specialist in some branches and in particular as a worker of infernal miracles. As such he now stood before the famishing Jesus and said: 'Thou callest thyself a Son of God. If this be true, thou needest not suffer hunger. Command that these stones become bread. That, however, is beyond thy power, deluded man, and because of thy obsession, thou must die here of starvation. Thou art not able to work miracles. Thou never wert, and never wilt be, and yet thou imaginest thyself to be a Son of God! Look upon me! I am a son of God, Whom I have left, and Who in His cruelty leaves thee to suffer thus. I can work miracles, and turn these stones into bread, which I will give thee to eat. Thou wilt see that I am able to do this. Abandon Him, Who has abandoned thee to die of hunger! Worship me, and the choicest viands on earth will be thine.'

'Get thee away, Satan, I want not thy bread, nor would I want any could I make it out of these stones. I await the magic word that cometh from the mouth of God. That word will come at the hour appointed. By it I shall have food, and shall live'.

"Satan, however, was not so easily discouraged.

"So be it! he replied, 'If thou wilt work no miracle in my presence, nor accept the bread that I offer thee in pity, thou mayest choose another way to convince thyself whether thou are indeed a Son of God, for that thou art not, I would gladly prove to thee, and rid thee of thy delusion. Behold the pinnacle of the temple; I will take thee thither and do thou cast thyself down, for it is written, He shall give His angels charge concerning thee and on their hands they shall bear thee up. Make the trial, therefore. Thou knowest that I will not help thee, since it is my purpose to prove to thee that thou art not of the Sons of God, and I am certain that the fall will dash thee in pieces. Nevertheless, thou shouldst make the trial. Not even God may demand of thee a blind belief that thou art His Son. Unless thou art willing to put thy Sonship to but one single trial, thou must confess thyself lacking in understanding. If it be that thou survive thy fall unhurt, even I will believe in thee. But if thou perishest, be thankful that death hath relieved thee quickly of the deceit with which thou hast been beguiled, rather than thou shouldst waste thy life in such madness, to die at last, disappointed, and reviled by mankind'.

"Tortured though He was by weeks of suffering, Satan's Victim controlled Himself with a mighty effort and replied steadily:

'I will not make trial of the Lord. Not in this way will I seek to prove that I am His Son. In His hands I leave the proof. He will not fail me, as thou too shalt find'.

"At this speech Lucifer, the second, the fallen, son of God, quailed for a moment before his elder brother, the loyal. His sorcery availed him nothing against One Who would accept no miracles nor presume to perform these on His own account.

"Not even then did Satan lose hope; he had still another lure to offer that in the past had always given brilliant results: the world was his, for everything material is under his sway. He could give the kingdoms of the earth to whomsoever he pleased; whether to the Babylonian, Nebuchadnezzar, or to the Roman, Tiberius, or to the Nazarens, Jesus, was for him to decide. All those to whom he had made such a gift heretofore, had become his vassals and had obeyed his orders. The kingdoms of the earth in all their entrancing splendor, passed as in a film before the fevered eyes of the Son of Man. 'All these things will I give thee. If thou desirest them all, they shall be thine; if but one, thou hast but to choose. But thou must bow down to me as thy overlord. In the kingdoms which thou hast seen, I am, and will remain supreme. But thou shalt be next in power'. 'Get thee hence, Satan, for it is written, Thou shalt worship the Lord thy God, and him only shalt thou serve'.

"Satan had lost the battle. In the days which had passed he had felt certain of his victim Whose prayers for help to the Father he had overheard and Whose signs of fear he had witnessed, and that at a time when only Lucifer's subordinates had been engaged. Now he had come in person to reduce a fortress which seemed ready to yield to an assault and into which hunger had entered as his ally. He found that he had been mistaken: spiritual weapons and bribes had no effect upon this mortal. One implement of warfare remained untried; one before which all men tremble and grow pliant, namely, physical tortures, of which he resolved to use the most excruciating. To inflict these there was no lack of human minions, from the learned to the ignorant, from kings to peasants; authorities temporal and spiritual. In the end he could not fail; he need only bide his time, and await the most favorable moment. Therefore, as your Bible tells you: 'When the devil had vainly exhausted his artifices and wiles in tempting Jesus, he withdrew from him to bide his time'. *(Luke 4 : 13.)*

"It was these terrific onsets of Evil upon Jesus which Saint Paul had in mind when he wrote that Jesus had 'offered up prayers and supplications with strong crying and tears unto him that was able to save him' from the mortal sin of abandonment of His God.

"As you see, God does not bestow His precious gifts without exacting something in return; those who receive them must prove themselves worthy by standing severe trials. Even Christ as a man was compelled to earn painfully the strength which He would need for the mighty task before Him. He received nothing for the asking, but whenever He had fought victoriously with Evil, He was rewarded by an access of Divine power. The heavens opened and God's spirits flocked about Him, and so it was after the battle in the desert. '. . . and behold, angels came and ministered to him'. *(Matthew 4 : 11.)* They also gave Him earthly food, after His fast of forty days. Now that the stones were turned into bread by Divine intercession, Jesus accepted it, giving thanks to God. When it had been offered to Him at the instigation of Satan, He had felt constrained to refuse it.

"After this first trial which He had met triumphantly, Jesus began His career of teaching the multitudes, collecting about Him a few men known to you as the Apostles, who though poor and obscure were willing to accept the truth. It had been His intention to initiate them into the mysteries of the Redemption but presently He found that even they were the weak product of their times and unable to endure more than a portion of His doctrine.

"The first step to be taken by Jesus was to convince not only His disciples, but the people as well, of the Divine nature of His mission. He must reveal Himself and His intentions, and prove His word with the aid of Him Whose emissary He proclaimed Himself to be.

"The same had been true of Moses, whose mission was in every respect the counterpart of that of the Messiah, whose coming he predicted in the words: the Lord thy God will raise unto thee a prophet from the midst ot thee, like myself'. *(Deuteronomy 18 : 15.)* Moses had been sent by the Lord to lead a people out of the land of bondage into the Promised Land; the bond slaves were the Israelites; their taskmasters, the Egyptians under Pharaoh.

"Those whom Christ came to deliver from bondage were all the spirits which had fallen from God; their taskmasters were the Powers of Hell, under Lucifer.

"Before Moses could succeed in solving the problem before him, two things had to be done. First, he must persuade his people to agree to leave the land of their bondage and to accept him as their leader. Next, and far more difficult, he must compel the Egyptians and their king to allow the Israelites to depart, for that Pharaoh and his subjects would not part *willingly* with the cheap labor of their serfs, male and female, went without saying.

"In the same way the redemption through Christ depended in the first place upon His success in persuading the fallen spirits, which, having reached the level of incarnation in human form, were groaning under the bondage of Evil, to declare themselves ready to abandon its ways. With this accomplished, there remained the harder task of compelling Lucifer's government to surrender all those of its subjects who desired to return to God.

"With Moses as with Christ, the task involved two clearly defined steps.

"As regarded Moses personally, it was incumbent on him above all to remain firm before Pharaoh, and to allow himself to be diverted from his God-given mission neither by threats nor by blandishments, lest God's plan come to nought by reason of his lack of purpose. The people of Israel, on their part, must do their share by declaring themselves willing to leave and by holding themselves in readiness for the journey. It then rested with God to grant them a decisive victory over Pharaoh and to consummate their deliverance. The manner in which this was to be achieved did not concern either Moses or the people; that was for God alone to decide.

"So too it was with Christ. He had nothing to gain by telling the people how the redemption was to be accomplished. It was His duty only to proclaim to them that the hour of their deliverance was near; that they must strive to make themselves worthy of the gift, and that it was He Whom God had sent as their Savior.

"On His own part, He must beware of succumbing to the Princes of Darkness who left no stone unturned to induce Him to forsake His God and to abandon His Divine mission. Like Moses, Christ must guard against being vanquished by the foe whom He had come to conquer. If He could hold out in His entrenchments against the assaults of Evil, it was for God to determine how the defense could be turned into a successful attack, for obviously, as a mortal, Christ could not wage an offensive campaign against spirits. The most that mortals can do is to defend themselves against the attacks of the Evil Powers when these attempt to lead them astray by means of insinuations, suggestions, temptation and intimidation, or by apparitions, as well as with the aid of human agents. Hence Christ could advance for an attack upon Satan only as a spirit, and only after His earthly death. Not until then could it be said of Him that 'He had descended to Hell'.

"As I have told you, the possibility existed that Christ, the man, could be overcome by Satan; had this happened, the Prince of the Lower World would have numbered the first Son of God also among his vassals. In that event, God would have brought about the incarnation of another of the highest of the celestial princes to accomplish the work of redemption which, because of human infirmities, His First-born Son had failed to perform.

"You may shudder at the thought that Christ could have fallen before Satan's attacks, and yet this is a fact. You mortals do not even faintly appreciate the love of your Heavenly Father, Who did not spare His First-born, but Who, for your sake, risked losing Him as He had lost His second son. Nor can you picture to yourselves how desperate was the battle which Christ was forced to wage against all of Hell, in order that men might be redeemed.

"The least of the devils can bring about your desertion of God in a very few moments. The victory is his, for the offering of a handful of money, earthly fame, or sensual pleasures. But Christ, your oldest Brother, was assailed by all of Hell's forces led by Lucifer in person, not once and for a few instants only, but again and again throughout the whole span of a human life. Column after column of those sinister warriors advanced, day in, day out, upon the Son of Man, resorting at last to the most fiendish physical torments, until their victim, bleeding upon the Cross, died, indeed, in the body, but did not waver in His loyalty to His God. Satan had proved powerless against Him, yet He, against Whom the full forces of Hell were marshalled, was as human as you are, and was in every way like you.

"This, then, is the true picture of the Redeemer, and such was the way in which He performed His mission.

"Like Moses, who had to make himself known to the Israelites as Divinely sent and prove his claim by means of miracles, Christ owed it to the people to tell them Who He was, and to accredit His mission of redemption by similar means.

"Who was Christ, and what did He profess to be? 'I am Christ, the Son of the living God'. Such is His testimony of Himself, substantiated by the words of God: 'This is my beloved Son, in whom I am well pleased'. Christ was therefore the *Son of God*, and claimed to be nothing more. He was not the Deity. Not once did He say: 'I am God'. Not once did He assert that

He was God's equal in any respect. Never does He weary of repeating explicitly that He can do nothing by His own power, that His words are not His own, that His miracles owe nothing to Him. It is the Father Who has sent Him; from Whom He has derived His teachings; from Whom He has received the power to heal the sick and to raise the dead. Whatever He does is as the Father wills, and at the hour appointed by the Father.

"Just as a viceroy may act only in the name and on behalf of his sovereign by whom he was appointed, and only within the limits of authority delegated to him, so is it with Christ. Even if a ruler confers full powers upon his lieutenant, the latter cannot call those powers his own, for he is merely the ruler's dependent and can be relieved of his place at any moment. Thus Joseph was set over all the land of Egypt by Pharaoh who 'took off his signet ring from his hand and put it upon Joseph's hand, and arrayed him in vestures of fine linen . . . and said to him 'without thee, shall no man lift up his hand or his foot in all the land of Egypt'. Nevertheless, it was not Joseph, but Pharaoh, who had been, and continued to be, the sovereign head of the State. Joseph was merely his governor, even though he was invested with full regal powers. He did not hold these by virtue of his own right, but by voluntary bestowal on the part of the king, who could restrict or withdraw them at pleasure, or confer them upon someone else.

"This is the simplest way of illustrating the relations of Christ to God. God is Lord and Creator of all things, not excepting His Son. God is *of Himself*, eternal, omnipotent, omniscient. Not so His Son. Upon Him the Father has conferred the government of Creation, and foremost of all, the task of redemption. But the Son has nothing *by virtue of His own initiative*, neither His existence, nor His viceregal office, nor His power. Everything was conferred upon Him by the Father. Although in Heaven the Son be arrayed like unto His Father and act with Divine authority, nevertheless, it is not He Who is God, any more than it was Joseph who was the monarch of Egypt.

"This fact is so clearly brought out in the Holy Writ that it is surprising to find that people could ever have regarded Christ as God's equal, in the face of God's solemn declaration: I am the Lord thy God. Thou shalt have no other gods besides me .

"Not even those Christian denominations which revere Christ as the Deity and would make Him the equal of His Father in all things, dare assert that He ever said: 'I am God', but base their contention upon the fact that He called Himself the Son of God. They argue as did the high priests, the scribes, and the Pharisees, of whom the Bible says: 'Because of these words the Jews sought more intently than ever to take his life, holding him guilty not only of profaning the Sabbath, but also of making himself equal to God by calling God his true father'. *(John 5 : 18.)*

"Christ did not defend Himself against the charge of having called God His own Father, for He was a Son of God in a sense which was not true of the other Sons of God, the Divine spirits. He was not only the highest of created spirits, but the *only one* whose celestial body had been called into existence by God. Of the others, the *spiritual part* was God-created, whereas their celestial bodies owed their existence to His First-born Son. Christ was therefore not only God's First-born, but the only one whose *whole being* was by *direct Divine creation*. He was alone of His kind. He was His Father's *'sole offspring'*.

"In another respect also He was the Son of God in a sense which applied to Him alone. Upon Him, and upon no one else, had God conferred the rule over creation. It was the same position as that held by Joseph in the kingdom of Egypt, under Pharaoh.

"In this particular, then, the Jews were right: Christ did call Himself a Son of God in a specific sense. He was *the* Son of God.

"But against the charge brought by His Jewish enemies, that He made Himself equal with God, Christ defended Himself vigorously. Again and again He protested that He was not from Himself, and that by His own power He could do nothing. No one who makes such an admission freely lays claim to the attributes of a Deity, a conclusion so obvious that not even the high priests and the scribes could have failed to see it, but although they understood well enough what Jesus meant by the phrase 'the Son of God', they professed not to, for they were seeking a ground for His death and could find none better than to assert that Christ was making Himself equal with God by calling Himself His Son. Once they were committed to this pretext, they must adhere to it at all costs; nothing that Christ could have said in refutation would have been of any avail.

"It is true that Christ had full authority on earth and in Heaven, but not from Himself. As Joseph held his power in Egypt by the grace of Pharaoh, so Christ derived His power from His Father. Neither Joseph nor Christ was the sovereign master.

"The Father alone, and none besides Him, is God. The power resides in the Father exclusively, and in no other being. At His own pleasure the Father can delegate this power to any spirit, in and through which He performs His works. That power which was conferred upon Christ, could have been conferred by the Father upon any created spirit other than His First-born Son, and the great miracles worked by Christ could have been performed by any other man had God given him the necessary power. Christ Himself says frankly that the things He had done could be done by any one who believed in Him. 'He who believes in me, shall have the power to do the same deeds that I do, and even greater deeds'. *(John 14 : 12.)* Belief in Christ is belief in God; not, however, because Christ Himself is God, but because He is the promulgator of God's teachings. 'The doctrine that I have taught is not my own; it was my Father, who sent me, that directed me what I should teach and in which words I should present my doctrine'. *(John 12 : 49.)*

"Between the Father and Christ there prevails a perfect unity of love, a unity to which each of God's creatures can attain and for which Christ prays to God on behalf of His disciples. '. . . that they may be one, as we are one. I, united with them, and Thou with me, so that they may attain to the highest perfection of unity'. *(John 17 : 22, 23.)*

"You see how illogical it is for your former religion to base its contention of the Divinity of Christ upon the phrase: 'I and the Father are one', in the face of the fact that the same oneness that exists between them is promised to all who believe.

"If you will study those of Christ's utterances in which He describes His relations with His Father, you will see the impiety of referring to Christ as God; of picturing Him as the giver whereas He is but the recipient Who can give to others only those things which He Himself receives from God. The same sacrilege with which the Jews charged Christ when they falsely asserted that He made Himself God's equal, is committed today by the people who today raise Christ to a level with the Deity, in spite of the fact that He Himself spurned any such pretensions.

"Christ's contention concerning His own person, concerning the source of His doctrine and the power which He possessed was, therefore, that He had received each and everything from the Father. From Himself He had nothing. *He is not God.*

"There were things which God withheld, even from Christ,

and which He reserved to Himself. Witness Christ's answer to the mother of the sons of Zebedee: '. . . but the places at my right and at my left are not mine to give, for they will be bestowed upon those to whom they are allotted by my Father'. *(Matthew 20 : 23.)*

"Again, nothing is known by the Son of the Day of Judgment, the knowledge of which is the Father's alone: 'The day and the hour of fullfillment are known to no one, neither to the angels of heaven, nor to the Son, but to my Father alone. *(Matthew 24 : 36.)*

"Nor was Christ allowed by God to evade the agony of death upon the Cross. Hence His prayer in the garden of Gethsemane that the cup be permitted to pass, was not answered.

"Christ's own family as well as the Apostles and those of the people who believed in Him, saw in Him nothing more than a 'prophet — 'God's emissary'. It is true that His mother knew that in Him was incarnated one of the 'Sons of God' for this had been revealed to her by the angel, before Christ was born. But she was also aware that He was human and that He had human infirmities. His conduct in public and the doctrines preached by Him did not meet with her approval. She had known that His creed differed materially from the doctrines held by the Jewish religion, but to see Him proclaim His views openly to the multitudes distressed her sorely. She had pictured to herself His mission on earth in a very different light, and when she heard that Jesus in His sermons had spoken strongly about the spiritual guides of the Jewish people and had publicly branded as false many of the tenets of her ancient faith, she, in company with her other sons, sought to restrain Him, and even tried to compel Him to return to His parental home, believing that in this way she could allay the ill will that His actions had aroused among the high priests, scribes and Pharisees. 'And when his family heard it, they went out to lay hold on him: for they said, He is out of his mind'. *(Mark 3 : 21.)* 'At that time, not even his brothers believed in him'. *(John 7 : 5.)*

"That His mother and brothers should have discountenanced His conduct in public is easy to understand. They believed that the doctrines of the Jewish religion were true. Their ancestors had lived and died in that faith, and the fact that now an own son and brother should preach publicly that this faith embodied many errors, was more than these simple and inexperienced people could bear. Whatever they were told by their own clergy was final so far as they were concerned. Moreover, they lived in fear of their fellow men. They were pointed at as the relatives of a man who was assailing the faith of his fathers. They had frequently to listen to criticism of themselves on that score by the head of the synagogue of their native village. Their business interest suffered. Hardest of all to bear was the news that the supreme ecclesiastical council had excluded Jesus from the synagogue, and had threatened to do the like with all those who adhered to Him or acknowledged Him as the Messiah. 'For the Jewish leaders had already agreed, to put a ban on all who might acknowledge Jesus as the Messiah'. *(John 9 : 22.)*

"The Jewish priesthood warned the people against Jesus and His doctrines, resorting freely to slander as a weapon, and alluding to Him as a 'false prophet', 'a man possessed of the devil', 'an agitator', 'a wine-bibber', 'a profligate', who passed his time in the company of wayward women and sat down at table with publicans and sinners. There was no expedient so low that they did not avail themselves of it to render harmless Him Who was a menace to their hold over the people. They could not endure to see the great mass of the people accepting as a religious truth something that differed from what they themselves preached. It was to them that the people owed obedience. What the clergy did not believe, the people *must* not believe, under penalty of being damned. 'Is there a single one among the leading people or the Pharisees who has been brought to believe in him? Not a man; it is only the common herd which understands nothing of the law. Curses on it'! *(John 7 : 48.)*

"It is the old, old hymn, intoned by the clergy of all denominations, as soon as it sees its influence on the people threatened by an evangelist of the truth.

"You too will become better acquainted with that melody than you have been in the past, as soon as you have made public the truths imparted by me, when you will witness a repetition of everything that took place in those days. The servant is not greater than his master, and you will be called a renegade priest, a false prophet, a madman, a man obsessed of the devil, a degenerate. Even your friends will heap reproaches on you, and tell you that you should have left well enough alone, and that what was good enough for the rest of the cloth, was surely good enough for you also. But be not afraid! Trust in God! What have you to fear of men? And on the other hand, by disseminating the truth you will be of great benefit to many. More than one member of the clergy even on reading your book will become convinced that it contains the truth, even though they may not be disposed to admit this openly. Things were no different in the days of Christ. 'Nevertheless, among the leaders of the people many believed in Jesus although they dared not admit it openly for fear of being put under the ban by the Pharisees, for they loved the glory that is of men more than the glory that is of God'. *(John 12 : 42, 43.)*

"Even the Apostles on more than one occasion felt doubts as to their Master, for they also had formed a different conception of the Messiah. Not until the day when Simon Peter gave utterance to his conviction: 'You are the Messiah, the Son of God of our Saviour', *(Matthew 16 : 16)* did His Apostles know that in Jesus of Nazareth the 'Son of God' had come upon earth. This conviction, however, had not been reached by Peter by reason of Christ's words and acts nor by any process of reasoning of his own, but by virtue of a revelation from God. '. . . this was not revealed to you by men, but by my heavenly Father'. *(Matthew 16 : 17.)*

"As to the manner in which the Divine revelations reached Christ I have already intimated this to you, but I wish to go into the subject more fully because it is essential to an understanding of Christ's life and work, and in order to make it clear to you that in this particular the experiences of Christ offer nothing altogether new or previously unheard of.

"You have only to recall the way in which God had conveyed His revelations and commandments to His instruments in the past. How did He communicate with Abraham, Isaac and Jacob? With Moses and Joshua? With the judges, kings and prophets? With Zacharias, Mary and Joseph? In precisely the same way He now communicated with Jesus who in this respect was not favored above those who had preceded Him as Divine instruments and emissaries. God caused the spirit-world to enter into communication with Him as with all the others, and through it He revealed all things that Christ required for the fulfillment of the task before Him.

"The prerequisites for communicating with the spirit-world were the same with Him as those which apply to any other person. It was but natural that His mediumistic gifts were of the highest, for He was the highest and purest of spirits incarnated in human form, ever created by God. The ability to concentrate, and to 'submerge the spirit' of which I spoke to you in connection with the development of mediums, was possessed by Christ to an extent never attained by man before or since. Moreover, no other human medium has ever possessed a physical od as pure as that of Christ. In Him then the prerequisites for communicating with the Divine spirits existed to a degree which no other mortal can hope to attain.

"The problem given to Christ to solve on behalf of the kingdom of God, was the greatest ever assigned to a mortal, hence it was necessary that God send Him spirits in abundance, not only as regarded their numbers, but also with respect to their strength and ability.

"Among them went spirits of fortitude, to infuse new strength into Him when His own began to fail in the battle with the evil powers. Often these spirits were accompanied by those of hope, joy, and peace of soul. Again, militant angels from Michael's Legion came to His side, when Satan marshalled his legions in full force, and when the fury of their assaults threatened to be more than human strength could bear. Spirits of truth and understanding instructed Him as to the best way of bringing the word of God before the multitudes or of answering questions concerning Himself or His teachings. Spirits of wisdom taught Him how to solve individual problems, but all this assistance came only after He had exhausted His own resources without avail. With Him as with all other mortals the motto holds good: 'God helps those who help themselves'. If you would arrive at a goal, use your own strength first, and if this does not suffice, God will intercede with the aid of His spirit-world. God does not heedlessly distribute favors and success. He demands that everyone exert himself to the utmost, and this He demanded of Christ also.

"When the sick required His attention, spirits of healing came to His rescue whenever His own native healing powers proved inadequate to cure the diseased od of the patient, although in many cases these powers sufficed to bring about the desired end without the help of the healing spirits.

"Nevertheless, Christ did not cure everyone who appealed to Him, for there are cases in which sickness is a punishment sent by God, to be suffered by the patient for a period commensurate with his offense. Christ's power of clairvoyance and clairsentience enabled Him in every instance to tell whether or not the suppliant's plea should be granted. Moreover, a belief in God and in Himself as God's envoy was exacted by Him in every cure which He effected.

"Not in all cases was the cure permanent, for many individuals relapsed into their former ailment as soon as they lost their faith in God and in Christ, the main purpose of His healing being to bear witness to the truth of His message.

"In connection with 'raising the dead', I am compelled to say something that may surprise you. In all cases so referred to, both those mentioned in the Old Testament and those ascribed to Christ, the spirits of those who were thus raised had not actually passed into the Hereafter. No one who has actually died can again come to life; his spirit can never again take possession of the body from which it departed at the moment of corporeal death. This is a Divine law which admits of no exceptions. His race on earth is run, without recall. Only by rebirth can his spirit ever again take human shape.

"All individuals recalled to life by Christ were those whose spirits had indeed emerged from their bodies but still remained connected with the same by a slender band of od. This was so feeble, that the spirit could not have returned to the body either by its own efforts or by virtue of any human assistance, and that, in consequence, death would have ensued very shortly by the rupture of the odic band. In the case of Lazarus, this had already become so weak that the vitality which could be conveyed to his body was insufficient to prevent the setting in of decay. Hence, neither the odor which accompanies that process nor the livid spots which appear at its inception are infallible symptoms of final decease.

"The fact that the 'dead' so raised were only cases of suspended animation is clearly indicated by the words of Christ when He raised the daughter of Jairus: 'The girl is not dead, but asleep'. *(Matthew 9 : 24.)* These words have been explained as a jest, but Christ did not jest in such matters, least of all when He was engaged in proving the Divine character of His mission to the people. In the case of Lazarus also He calls the attention of His Apostles to the fact that death had not taken place, for on hearing of the man's sickness, He said to them: 'This sickness will not end in his death, but will serve to glorify God'. *(John 11 : 4)*, and when, as his friends thought, Lazarus had died, Jesus said again: 'Our friend Lazarus is fallen asleep; but I go, that I may awake him out of sleep'. But when once more His Apostles failed to understand Him, Christ, seeing the uselessness of further explanations which in any event they would have misunderstood, said:

'Lazarus is dead'. This was perhaps not a strictly accurate statement of the condition of Lazarus, but it was the only one that He could use, for at the time Lazarus was already in his tomb, and people thought of him as being dead. Had this really been the case, Christ would not have said a few days earlier: 'This sickness is not unto death', nor could He, after the entombment, have used the words: 'Our friend is fallen asleep'. On both occasions Christ stated the truth, since Lazarus was dead not in reality, but to all appearances.

"Nevertheless, nothing that I have said detracts from the merits of the case, for what Christ did could not have been accomplished by any human power, but only through the power of God. This is true of every instance in which Christ recalled the dead to life. Human power was of no avail, and the Divine spirits interceded, accomplishing whatever was needed to allow the return of the spirit into the body. Christ, by clairvoyance, observed the work of the spirit-world, and at His word, the spirit was reunited with its body and the seemingly deceased arose.

"It does not occur to you mortals that such things are done in accordance with Divine laws. This is true not only of the raising of the dead, but of all other miracles performed by Jesus. When He turned water into wine, this task also was accomplished by the Divine spirit-world, and for this reason not even He was able to bring about the transmutation instantly, as His mother wished. His 'hour was not yet come', because the spirit-world had not completed the necessary work, for time is required, even by spirits.

"It is because you do not understand these processes that you fail to grasp the meaning of certain words found in the Bible which, in consequence, have been incorrectly rendered into your several languages. Thus your version of the Scriptural account of the raising of Lazarus contains a sentence which must impress you as utterly incomprehensible: 'Seeing her weeping, and that the Jews who were with her, were likewise in tears, Jesus was so moved with indignation in the spirit and troubled himself'. *(John 11:33.)* Why indeed should Jesus be moved with indignation and trouble Himself at the sight of the weeping sister and friends of a man who had died? On the contrary, the original text reads: 'A shivering passed through his spirit and he was shaken', for when spirits come near you and allow their powerful odic radiations to act upon you, you too feel a sensation of shivering and actually begin to shake. The sensation is an agreeable one in the presence of good spirit-beings, and unpleasant when it originates from the proximity of evil ones. It was the sensation produced by the nearness of good spirits which passed through Christ on this occasion; the powerful odic radiations of the spirits about Him, infusing Him with their strength, by virtue of which He consummated the work of the spirits with the summons: 'Lazarus, come forth'.

"To raise the dead was something that Christ could undertake only when He had been assured by messengers from God that such was the Divine will, for all signs which bore testimony to the power of God were manifested solely when they were of special service in promoting the aggrandisement of the kingdom of God or the sanction of His Emissary and the latter's teachings.

"In public Christ never mentioned His connection with the Divine spirit-world, of which He spoke only when compelled to do so. Thus He replied to the Jews who reproached Him with casting out demons with the aid of Beelzebub: 'But if I drive out the demons with the help of one of God's spirits, then indeed the spirit-world of God has already come to you'. *(Matthew 12 : 28.)*

"Associated with the gift of clairvoyance in its highest form which was peculiar to Jesus, was His ability to recognize the mental state of persons and to read their thoughts. In all times there have been people similarly gifted, although your age has no understanding of this matter and above all, does not realize that here also there are involved certain eternal laws governing these phenomena.

"Even in the case of Christ these laws applied in every particular, and were taken into account by Him in the sense that He always selected the time and place for communicating with spirits with a view to securing the conditions most favorable for the purpose. He Who counselled His adherents to withdraw to their inner chambers for prayer, Himself sought shady hillsides in the cool of the dusk and the night, for light and warmth and the noises of the day exert an exceedingly adverse effect upon the formation of the od required for communicating with the spirit-world. Hence He preferred the solitude of the woods and gardens, and the darkness and coolness of the night.

"Furthermore, all predictions of the future made by Christ had been learned by Him from the messengers sent to Him by His Father.

"You have been in the habit heretofore of regarding Christ's miracles and prophesies as evidence of *His Divine nature.* This conclusion is entirely erroneous. You confuse the Workman with His implement. The Workman is God. His *visible implement* may be any being whatsoever, while His *invisible implements,* are the Divine spirits assigned to that being. A little reflection on your part would enable you to discover this fact for yourselves. When you, personally, used to preach on the 'Divinity of Christ' and tried to prove this by means of His miracles and prophesies, did it never occur to you to draw a comparison between Him and God's emissaries who had preceded Him? Did not they perform miracles similar to those performed by Christ? Were the miracles accomplished by Moses any less wonderful than those which Christ performed ? Were the transformation of a rod into a serpent, and that of water into blood, the killing of the first-born of Egypt, the passage of the Red Sea, the flow of water, caused by the stroke of a rod and many other signs given by Moses of less account than the transformation of water into wine, walking upon the waves or conjuring the storm? If, then, you cite the acts of Jesus as evidence of His Divine status, you are bound to concede the same character to Moses. Were not the sick healed and the 'dead' raised by many mortals who were Divine instruments? Then these mortals also are entitled to be regarded as Divine, as are Joshua, Elijah, Elisha and other great prophets, not to mention the Apostles, since they performed miracles equal to those performed by Christ, and according to His word, 'greater works than these shall they do'. You can cite not a single miracle performed by Jesus which has not been performed in the same or in a similar manner by other mortals acting as envoys of God. You misunderstand completely God's purpose in bringing these miracles about. You do not pause to think that God must establish His instruments as such by the performance of the unusual, before He can expect humanity to recognize them as Divinely appointed.

"In the fulfillment of their mission, all of God's envoys have suffered greatly at the hands of men. Every one has had his Calvary. They have been the vessels from which radiated the Divine truth and light, a light which mankind, lying in the bonds of darkness, could not endure, as being too bright for eyes afflicted with sin. Men turned from the light and sought to destroy the human vessels which served as lamps. So it has always been; so it is today, and so it will remain while there are human eyes sore with sin, which ache when the light of the truth is turned upon them. The Evil Powers, and all mortals enslaved by them, hate this light and its bearers, and do their utmost to encompass their destruction.

"How desperate, then, would be the efforts on the part of Evil to break the power of the greatest Light-Bearer Who ever came upon earth! How painful the road that Christ had to travel!

"His inner sufferings at the hands of Evil were hidden from human eyes, and therefore nothing is said about them by the Bible beyond the very casual account of His temptation in the wilderness. Yet the onslaughts made upon Him there by Satan were so savage, that any one of the earlier Divine emissaries would have abandoned God, if He had allowed the Powers of Hell to proceed against him with the same vigor as He permitted them to assail Christ. Moreover, the bodily tortures which Jesus had to undergo until His last breath were such, that His predecessors could not have held out against them, the less so as they had to be borne in addition to mental suffering equally severe.

"It is true that the sufferings of Christ had a higher significance than did those of any other of the Divine prophets. For them, death spelled the fulfillment of their tasks, if they had remained true to God. For Christ, however, the end of His earthly life marked only the fulfillment of a portion of His mission, the more important part of which was still to be completed thereafter, by gaining a victory over the Prince of Darkness. His crucifixion was a condition precedent to that victory, not indeed, crucifixion in itself, but His ability to endure it without faltering in His loyalty to His Master. He might, indeed, while yet alive upon the Cross, have lost faith in God at the last moment, and gone over to the Enemy. Had He done so, He would have died upon the Cross nevertheless, but defeated and apostate. Until that moment, He had stood upon the defensive against the terrific hail of missiles that Hell poured upon Him; had He yielded, all would have been lost. The effort at redemption would have failed and Christ would have been a prisoner of the Prince of Darkness.

"If, on the other hand Christ held out against the most dreadful anguish of soul and body inflicted on Him by the Infernal powers, the moment of His death on earth would mark also the beginning of the second part of the War of Redemption. He, Who as a mortal, had stood on the defensive against the Powers of Hell, would now, as a spirit, advance to attack them in order to render His victory complete. To force the decision He would descend into Hell. 'He also descended into the lower parts of the universe'.

"However, I shall dwell a little longer upon the first stage of this war, the most important that was ever fought, and pass in review those hours of Christ's human suffering which you call the Passion, seeing that humanity appreciates far too little the unspeakable anguish which this Divinely-sent Bearer of the Cross was forced to endure in order that men might be saved.

"On the evening before His death Jesus was in the guest-chamber of a house, in company with His disciples. The feast of the passover which He was observing with them was also His farewell feast, but who among you can measure and realize the anguish of His soul? He knew from the Divine spirit-messengers that all preparations for His arrest and speedy execution had already been made. He knew that one of His disciples had had dealings with the high priests and for a traitor's reward of thirty pieces of silver had declared himself ready to deliver his Master to them. And at that very moment, the traitor was lying at table with Him. They were not seated about a long table, as you think, and as they are shown in your paintings, but were reclining upon the skins of animals, elevated, at the head by bolsters, gathered in groups of three about low taborets, their left elbows resting on the bolsters, their right hands serving to convey the food before them. At the same taboret with Christ reclined John and Judas, John to the left, his head close to his Master's breast, and on His right, Judas, who dared not meet his Master's eye and was anxiously awaiting the moment when he could leave the chamber without attracting attention.

"The Master's heart bled on seeing before Him His traitor in this youth, whose terrible end He foresaw. 'It had been good for that man if he had never been born'. As He looked upon him, Christ's eyes filled with tears, for His heart was filled with love for even this lost brother. In His mind arose a picture of what within a very few hours was to be a reality: Judas, despair in his soul, standing, rope in hand before the tree on which he was to end his own life, and beside him Lucifer, ready to take the spirit of him who he had led astray, into the Pit. Terrified at the vision, the Master trembled.

"As for the other Apostles, would they stand by Him and console Him in the hour of His martyrdom? The events that the next twelve hours were to bring forth passed before His mind's eye. He could see them all fleeing in terror for their own lives, and Peter, shaking with dread before a maid, denying all knowledge of his master with oaths and curses. He saw the devils crowding about the door of the guest-chamber, ready to seize upon His disciples as they went out, and in this very night fill their minds with doubt of their Master, in order that they might offer no support or help to One Who was doomed to die. 'Satan hath asked to have you, that he might sift you as wheat'. Why had Satan desired this? Only now it had been divinely revealed to him what he had at stake in this war. God's sense of justice did not permit Him to conceal any longer from Lucifer the fact that the battle which was now to open between him and Christ was to decide the sovereignty of Hell over the fallen spirits. God had revealed to Lucifer that Christ, should He remain steadfast throughout the death-agony which was at hand, would thereafter as a spirit advance to an attack upon Hell at the head of the celestial legions; that he, the Prince of Hell would be overcome and would be deprived of an essential part of his sovereignty. At this news, Satan trembled; then, appealing to that sense of the Divine justice which on one occasion had given him absolute sovereignty over the fallen spirits, he demanded that God observe strict neutrality in the decisive battle which was impending. What Satan asked was, that God withdraw His hand entirely from Jesus, leaving Him not even any human support, while allowing Hell to have a free hand. Should God accede to these demands, Lucifer hoped that by doing his utmost, he would succeed in breaking the spirit of this Jesus of Nazareth at the last moment, and in driving Him to despair of His cause.

"God granted the terms asked by Satan with the sole exception of reserving to Himself the right to strengthen Christ's purely physical vitality. Had He not done so, Christ would have died in the garden of Gethsemane, and His martyrdom would never have reached consummation.

"At Lucifer's desire, all the mental and physical anguish on earth, crowded into a few short hours, was to be concentrated upon his antagonist, coincidently with an attack to be launched upon Him and His followers by the entire infernal hosts. For Jesus, alone, betrayed by one of His disciples, deserted by the others, denied any Divine aid against the forces of Hell, Lucifer hoped to prepare an end worthy of a Judas.

"After Judas had left the guest-chamber, and even as Jesus gave to His Apostles the wine and the bread symbolical of His approaching death, His heart was bleeding from a thousand wounds. He was human, as you are, and had no advantage over other mortals during this hour and those which were to follow. On the contrary, He lacked even those things which are most men's, to fortify and console them in the hour of suffering.

"Picture Him now, going out into the dark of the night to the garden of Gethsemane. The night is no man's friend, least of all his who is overwhelmed with sorrow. His disciples, on whom the evil spirit-forces are already at work, walk silently beside Him, in dread of what is to come. Under the burden of His mental torments, He too is silent.

"At the remote spot in the garden, chosen by Him as the place in which to offer prayer for strength, Lucifer is in wait with his ablest assistants, ready to break down their intended victim's spiritual resistance by their united efforts. This is the very opportunity which God has conceded to the Prince of Darkness.

"Human words would fail to portray the terrors of the visions held up by Hell to its victim in this brief hour. As once the same Lucifer, when he tempted the Son of Man in the wilderness, had shown to Him the kingdoms of the world in all their splendor in order to cause His fall, so now and to the same end he exhibited to Christ all that is fearful and detestable in mankind, causing to pass before His eyes pictures of blaspheming, sinful humanity in its full viciousness and corruption, in a steady succession of hideous pictures. Next he showed to Jesus the supposed 'fruits' of His years of endeavor among the Jews as God's people, pointing mockingly to His disciples, one of them actually approaching at the head of a multitude, the others fast asleep near by, with never a word of comfort for their Master and unwilling to sacrifice a single hour of sleep for His sake. 'And wouldst thou die to prove thy gospel, for such as these?' Lucifer's mocking voice sounded in His ears, 'for such as blaspheme thy Father and will condemn thee as a fool if that thou givest thy life for this perverse generation. And hast thou taken thought what thy end will be?' Before the clairvoyant eyes of his trembling victim there now passed the scenes of the suffering in store for Him; His capture, the flight of His disciples, Peter's denial, the roar of the multitude which but a few days earlier had hailed His entry into Jerusalem and which now thirsted for His blood, the death sentence, the flagellation,

His captors' brutality, the crown of thorns, Calvary, the Crucifixion, — everything painted in its most terrifying aspects, in order that He might give way to despair and abandon His resistance. All the while the spirits of hopelessness and desperation were driving the maddest of thoughts into the mind of this victim of theirs whom all had forsaken. His pulse throbbed, His whole body was shaken with fever, His heart threatened to burst. The terror of death seized upon Him, drops of blood oozing from His pores and trickling to the ground. Through it all, His disciples were sleeping peacefully.

"The meager outlines preserved by your Bible of the story of the Passion of Jesus fail utterly to convey to your minds the anguish of soul and body suffered by your Redeemer. Indeed, many of the worst tortures are not even mentioned in the Bible. Thus, nothing whatever is said there of the frightful hours which He was compelled to spend in the underground dungeons of the courthouse, fetid and swarming with vermin, into which the soldiers had thrust Jesus after they had scourged and mocked Him and crowned Him with thorns, and after they had rubbed salt into the countless deep gashes left by the lash upon His lacerated body and had bound His hands, lest by removing the salt He might find some relief from His unspeakable torments.

"Never did man endure such torture as did this Son of God incarnated. Through its human tools, Hell did its worst, for in Him it recognized its greatest foe who could ever appear on earth. But not even the physical sufferings which it prepared for Him could equal those which His soul had to endure; moreover, both forms of torment, mental and bodily, were applied to Him simultaneously. Add to this that to the last He was without any human consolation, and, what was still harder, without any Divine aid. God had withdrawn His protecting hand and had left Him helpless to the devices of Hell. The cry uttered by Jesus as He hung dying upon the Cross: 'My God, my God, why hast thou forsaken me?' reveals in full the mental agony which He felt on finding Himself forsaken by all in this hour of supreme physical suffering. Satan should never be able to allege the excuse that his failure to reduce this mortal to submission was due to the help received by his victim from external sources. He should be forced to confess that he had met his match in an unaided human being, who, in spite of the most excruciating torments of mind and body, could not be driven to desert His God. *(Matthew 27:46) (Mark 15:34)*

"The Biblical account, according to which the mother of Jesus stood by the Cross, accompanied by John, is incorrect. Even this consolation was denied Him. Not one of those dearest to Him was near, at the Crucifixion. They could not have borne the sight, as where, indeed, can you find a mother who would look on while her child was being crucified? Again, you go so far as to assume that Mary was *standing* by the Cross throughout; had she been present at all, she would surely not have remained standing, but would have fallen unconscious. Hence it is also untrue that Christ exclaimed from the Cross: 'Woman, behold thy son!' and to the disciple: 'Behold thy mother'. He did, in fact, speak similar words to Mary and John as He was being led from the court after Pilate had pronounced the death-sentence and while His mother and John were clinging to Him in anguish until they were torn away by the soldiers. His mother had been present at the trial, as had the disciples, and had never lost hope that it would end in His favor, for there constantly recurred to her mind the story of Abraham, whose son was spared from sacrifice at the last instant, even as the knife with which he was to be slain was being bared. To this day there has not been a mother who would not attend a trial in which her child's life hung in the balance, nor on the other hand is there a mother who would go to witness the execution of her own offspring.

"To see His mother on the verge of swooning from agony and terror cut Jesus to the soul, and all He thought of was to spare her any further sight of His own suffering. He therefore begged John to take her to his home until everything was over, and spoke lovingly to her, urging her to go with John and to implore God for strength in this hour of tribulation, and telling her that the things which He must now suffer were as the Heavenly Father had willed and that after three days she would see Him again. *(John 19:25-27)*

"John willingly acceded to his Master's request and took the mother, pierced by a thousand sorrows and keeping to her feet only with the utmost effort, to his home; not permanently, as might be gathered from the text of your Bible, but for the time being, to remove her from these harrowing surroundings. At that home also foregathered others, who had remained faithful to Jesus. Some time later, when it was fair to assume that the crucifixion had been carried out, some of them, among whom was Mary Magdalene, went to a spot whence the site of the execution could be seen, and returned to relate the death of Jesus. *(Mark 15:40)*

"His mother staid at the home of John only so long as she lingered in Jerusalem. In the end she returned to Nazareth, the home of her other children and her own. Naturally, she often revisited Jerusalem to see the Apostles, in particular John, as long as they continued their sojourn there.

"As during His life Christ had been confirmed as God's envoy by signs, so was He in the hour of His death. The sun's light failed for three hours, and a darkness came over the land, not by reason of natural causes but as a sign from God. At the moment when Jesus gave up the ghost, the veil of the temple was rent in the midst, as a token that the wall dividing the realm of God from that of Satan had been shattered by His death. The earth shook and the rocks were rent, but the story recorded in your version of the Gospel of Saint Matthew that the dead had arisen from their tombs and had been seen by many in Jerusalem is a falsification of one of the original, accurate texts, which reads: 'The veil in the temple was rent in two from the top to the bottom; and the earth did quake; and the rocks were rent; and the tombs were opened; and many bodies of those who had fallen asleep were cast forth. Many, who had come from the holy city, did see the bodies lying there'. This text which is accurate, therefore records what naturally would, and did happen, namely that the tombs carved into the rocks were opened by the earthquake shocks and that the bodies were cast out upon the surface, and were, of course, in plain sight of the many who had come from the city to witness the crucifixion and who would have to pass close to the shattered tombs.

"Here you have merely another of the many instances of the falsifications introduced in the past into the Sacred Texts, for very particular reasons. The false doctrine had been set up that the earthly bodies of men will be resurrected on some future day, and in order to sustain this doctrine with passages from the Bible, this particular passage, in addition to others, was distorted by altering the original text which read: 'The bodies of those who had fallen asleep were cast forth', into: 'Many bodies of the *saints* that had fallen asleep were *raised*'. The word 'saints' had to be interpolated if only for the reason that it would never do to say that the bodies of the *unsaintly* also had been raised at the death of Christ. Still greater a difficulty remained to be overcome in falsifying this passage, inasmuch as the Church holds that there could have been no resurrection prior to that of Christ, Who was the first of the dead to arise. Hence it was necessary to insert the sentence: 'after his resurrection they entered into the holy city and appeared to many'. They who committed this falsification did not pause to consider that it had already been expressly stated that the bodies were raised on Good Friday, or three days before Christ's resurrection and whether they appeared to the people of Jerusalem on that same day or on Easter Sunday in no way enters into the question. Besides, where did these bodies which allegedly had risen on Good Friday pass the intervening days? Where were they after Easter Sunday? Did they return to their tombs and if not, where did they go? It is strange that not one of the other three Evangelists speaks of this resurrection on Good Friday, and as a matter of fact, Matthew did not say the things that are attributed to him, as you have seen from my explanation.

"Christ was dead. His earthly death had released His spirit from its material vesture. As a mortal He had withstood all the onslaughts of Hell and had thereby performed the first part of His Messianic mission successfully. He had not been conquered by Hell. Nevertheless, this alone did not insure His victory over the Enemy whom He had repelled, for in a battle between two opponents, he who acts wholly on the defensive, is not truly the victor, even if he succeeds in defending himself against the other's attacks. In order to claim a victory he must overpower his antagonist and force him to acknowledge himself beaten.

"This was true of Christ as well. As a man He had repelled all the attacks of His mighty opponent; He had done all that man can do. Now, however, that He was freed from the flesh, He could, as a spirit, advance upon His enemy, the Prince of Darkness, and descended into Hell relying upon the all-conquering Divine power, which as a mortal He had earned by His loyalty to God, Who now sent to Him the Heavenly hosts as His comrades in arms. Now began a struggle like that which had occurred when Lucifer with his adherents had battled with the Heavenly Legions in the days of the great Revolt of God's spirit-kingdom. The present battle was waged in Lucifer's realm and was a duel between him and Christ, as well as a general engagement between the legions of Heaven and those of Darkness. This mighty conflict raged until it had invaded the lowest depths of Hell into which Lucifer and his followers had been forced to retreat. Then, when the defeat of the Powers of Hell was no longer in doubt, many of those who had formerly served it but who, nevertheless, repented of their disloyalty to God, went over to the side of the Heavenly hosts and fought with them against their former oppressors. The number of those who thus deserted grew from moment to moment.

"When Lucifer saw that all was lost he begged for mercy. He who in the desert had tried to tempt the Son of God by offering Him the kingdoms of the world, now stood quaking before Him Whose faith in His Sonship of God he had then sought to undermine and trembled at the thought that this same Jesus of Nazareth intended to deprive him of all his sovereign power, and that the moment had arrived when he himself with all his followers would be doomed forever to the Pit of Darkness. He was but too familiar with the prophecy which foretold that the time was coming when he, as the Prince of the kingdom of the dead would be hurled into the uttermost depths, shorn of all his power and deprived of his sovereignty over God's fallen children.

"Christ however disclosed to him that he was not to be deprived of his sovereignty entirely, but that this was to be restricted to apply to those of his subjects who were whole-heartedly devoted to him, but that any who desired to leave his kingdom and to return to God must be released unconditionally. They were no longer to be regarded as his subjects. He might, if so disposed, bind them to himself by artifice and guile, but not by force, as heretofore.

"Satan accepted these terms. He had no other choice, and had, in fact, expected much harder conditions. The title by which he held his sovereignty and which God Himself had once issued to him was changed to suit the wishes of his conqueror, Christ, and God, in Whose name the Victor made terms with Lucifer is the just and almighty Protector Who warrants the exact observance of these peace-stipulations. To His power everything, even Hell, is subject. His commands must be obeyed even by those who are His enemies.

"Thus was concluded the mighty task of redemption. In all of its important aspects, God's Plan of Salvation had been realized. The gulf that yawns between the Realm of Darkness and the kingdom of God had been spanned by a bridge which could be crossed freely by all who desired to leave Satan's Foreign Legion and to return to their old home in the land of God. No sentinel in the service of Hell could prevent them from passing the frontier.

"Surrounded by His triumphant hosts, Christ returned from Satan's stronghold to the sphere that once had been the Paradise, and the cherubim who had since stood on guard at its entrance lowered their flaming swords in salute to their Lord and Master and His victorious spirit-legions. In Paradise a halt was made until the day on which, with Christ at its head, the great procession re-entered the portals of Heaven.

"During this time, however, neither Christ nor His host of spirits had been idle. Their stay in Paradise must be utilized to spread throughout all Creation the news of the Redeemer's triumph and to urge all who were minded thereto that they begin their homeward journey. Especial pains were taken to seek out the countless sufferers in the lower spirit-spheres in order that they might be instructed, admonished, cheered and consoled, and incited to arouse themselves to set out upon the road to the Father's house which Christ had laid open. Christ Himself was foremost in counselling these unhappy spirits and in seeing to it that as many as possible of them should take the homeward path without delay. This is indicated in the words of Saint Peter: '. . . in which also he went and preached unto the spirits in prison, that aforetime were disobedient, when the long suffering of God waited in the days of Noah, while the ark was a preparing. . .' *(1st Peter 3 : 19, 20.)*

"Materialized in human form, Christ appeared to those who had been closest to Him in life and had borne much sorrow with Him and on His behalf: His mother, the Apostles and His friends.

"The day arrived on which He returned to the spirit-hosts which were awaiting Him in Paradise, after He had said farewell to His friends on earth and had assigned to each his task. This was the day of the Ascension, on which, as a conquering hero, He led His army back into the kingdom of God.

"From the time at which the Redemption was achieved by Christ it has been free to those who have fallen from God to make use of the opportunity thus offered to them. Satan's prison-camps have been thrown open by Christ's victory, and their inmates are free to leave; whether or not they avail themselves of the opportunity, rests with them.

"Christ has indeed built the bridge, but whether it is used in returning home is left to the decision of each individual, who must not shirk the hardships attendant upon the journey. Consider what the prisoners taken in the World War were ready to undergo after peace had released them from their captivity, wandering from the furthest steppes of Siberia with bleeding feet, week after week, in their efforts to make their way back to their native land.

"The prisoners of Satan must do likewise if they would find their way back to God. Christ will be beside them ready to help them to overcome the hardships they will face in their wanderings. His messengers show them the way, strengthen, cheer and console the travellers, and raise to their feet those who have stumbled and fallen from exhaustion. But the homeward bound traveller may not turn back and re-enter the ranks of the enemy by deserting God; if he does, the longer it will be before he can again come to the resolution: 'I will arise and go to my Father'. But every one, without exception, will see the day on which he can no longer appease his hunger for peace and happiness with the husks of evil, and will resolutely set out on the homeward path.

"For some, the span of a single human life will be sufficient. Others must suffer for hundreds, and still others, for thousands of years, sundered from God in their race for the gold of happiness which they seek in the counterfeiters' dens of iniquity, and led by Satan's will-o'-the-wisps from one delusion into another. It is by their own fault that they must pass through repeated incarnations, and that they were so slow to find the Road of Light which the loving care of their Father and of His Son, the Redeemer of the fallen, has built for them.

Christ's Teachings and Modern Christianity

> "See to it, that no man captivates you by means of so-called science or by the foolish and vain theories grounded on the traditions of men; for they have their source in the evil powers that rule the world, but have nothing in common with the teaching of Christ." *Colossians 2 : 8.*

DURING the first spiritistic *seance* which I attended, I had asked of the spirit which was speaking through the medium: "Why is it that the teachings of Christ no longer seem to exert any influence upon the people of today?" and had been told in reply that we no longer possess Christ's precepts in their pristine purity and clearness, but that in the course of time, many human errors had crept into the Christian religion. Later on, I received a detailed exposition, in which the true teachings of Christ were compared with the doctrines of the Christian churches of today, and particularly with those of the Catholic faith, of which I was a priest. On that occasion I was told as follows:

"At what point in a brook do you find the purest and clearest water: near the source or near the mouth? Most assuredly, near the source, for as the spring-water flows on as a streamlet, it loses its coolness, and with it, its purity and clearness. Turbid rills, coming into it from either bank, mingle their waters with its current. Further down it receives the drainage from human habitations, human and animal refuse, and waste from mills and factories. It no longer refreshes, and those who must drink its waters to quench their thirst, do so only when forced to and when no spring-water is to be had.

"The same may be said of the truth. Taken at its source, it is a refreshing, life-infusing draft, but when drawn from the stream which has been flowing for a distance through the lowlands of human error and worldly passions, its purity and coolness are gone. The admixture of untruth and error has given it an ill flavor. The thirsty truth-seeker drinks of it with inner repugnance, and only when denied the clear water of the fountain head of truth.

"The teaching of Christ met with a fate like that of the water from a spring which, as a brook, flows by the haunts of men. It also was defiled when it flowed through human channels. The evil that is in men, and the Powers of Evil which surround them, have so sullied and rendered unpalatable Christ's pure precepts, that they have lost their life-giving power.

"The source of all truth is God, a source to which man cannot ascend in his terrestrial shape. He must therefore depend upon the bearers of the truth who draw from that source. These are God's spirit-messengers, and only they are admitted to that source. Only they possess the clean vessels in which the truth can be brought fresh and unsullied to mankind.

"The first and the greatest of truth-bearers was Christ *as a spirit,* in the days preceding His incarnation. It was He Who, partly in person, partly through His subordinates in the spirit-world, brought the first draft of truth to humanity. Hence the active intercourse with spirits in the case of the sick and exhausted world of the time of the Old Testament. Hence the coming and going, in the early days of the Christian era, of truth-bearing spirits, constantly drawing upon God's fountain-head and bringing the water of truth, at Christ's behest, to the parched souls of men.

"It is, therefore, one of the fundamental precepts of the true Christian faith, that men cannot promulgate the truth out of their own consciousness. They can do so only as instruments of God's spirit-world.

"Even Christ *as a mortal* could not of His own volition ascend to the source of the truth. As a man, He had no more inherent knowledge of the truth than had others. What He had known in the days when, as the first-created spirit He abode with God, had been obliterated from His memory by His entry into a material body as completely as the knowledge of a previous existence is obliterated from the recollection of other men, although the time was, when they too had abode with the Father. The property of substance by which the recollection of a previous existence is wiped out, exerted the same action upon the incarnated Christ that it exerts upon every other spirit incarnated in human form.

"Thus Christ after His incarnation was dependent upon the spirit messengers sent to Him by the Father, as He acknowledged when He said: 'You shall see the heaven opened, and the angels of God ascending and descending upon the Son of man'. *(John 1 : 51.)* He was but God's envoy, and had no advantage over the Divine envoys who had preceded Him, for they, too, had been instructed by God's spirits. Neither Enoch, Abraham, Moses, nor any of the Old Testamentary prophets uttered things evolved in their own minds, but all, in the words of Saint Peter 'preached the gospel by *a holy spirit* sent forth from heaven'.

"Christ repeatedly assures His hearers that He speaks not of his own knowledge, but only as He had heard from the Father. It was the Father Who directed Him as the occasion required, by means of His spirit-messengers 'constantly ascending and descending above the Son of Man' '. . . then you will know, that I do nothing of myself but only speak as my Father has taught me'. *(John 8 : 28.)* '. . . I speak to the world only those things, that I have heard from Him'. *(John 8 : 26.)*

"The same fountain-head of truth from which Christ had drawn was to serve all those who came to spread His gospel after Him. The first of these would be the Apostles, who were not merely to repeat the words which they had heard Christ utter, as they interpreted them, since it is a common human failing to quote inaccurately when called upon to repeat what someone else has said. Of a hundred listeners to the same speaker, no two, when asked to repeat his remarks, will agree precisely as to his words or his meaning. Hence the Apostles were to be instructed anew by the spirits of the truth, concerning those things that Christ had spoken to them as a man, in order that His words might suffer no distortion from their erroneous interpretation. They were to receive from God's spirits confirmation of the teachings proclaimed by Christ, as well as certain new truths which He had withheld from them, either because under God's plan of Salvation these truths could not be announced before the Redeemer's death, or because the Apostles themselves were not yet qualified to receive, and hence, to understand them.

"You will find this statement of mine confirmed in Christ's own words: 'Then will I ask the Father, and He will give you another helper, who will be with you henceforth. That helper are the spirits of truth'. *(John 14 : 16.)* 'I have yet many things to say to you, but you cannot bear them now. Howbeit, when the spirits of truth have come, they shall guide you into all the truth'. *(John 16 : 12, 13.)* '. . . after me will come the helper, holy spirits, whom the Father will send in my name, to teach you whatever else there may be and to recall to you what I have said'. *(John 14 : 26.)* According to these words, then, the spirits of truth had a twofold task before them. First, it was their duty to *bring to the remembrance* of the faithful all that Christ, while on earth, had told them, and to confirm its truth. After that, they were to continue the teaching which Christ had begun, and to proclaim those further truths which He had purposely withheld for reasons which I have already stated. Moreover, the spirits of God were to be with the faithful forever, since, what with the power of evil and the weakness of man, the fear of error was ever present. The living must not be dependent upon the religious traditions of their ancestors, for such human traditions would bear no warrant of truthfulness, nor could those, to whom they would be handed down, be expected to be able to know what part of them was derived from God's well-spring of truth and how much was attributable to human error.

"Thus after Christ's corporeal death, God's messengers arrived constantly as spirits of truth, according to His promise. The Apostles continually call upon them when exhorting their hearers to faith. Saint Paul's writings especially, abound in references to these messengers. 'The things that I have said and preached I did not lay before you in the winning words of human wisdom, but it was God's spirit-world and God's power, that spoke through me, so that your faith should rest not on the wisdom of men, but on a divine power . . . but to us, God has revealed them through his spirit-world. . . Now the spirits which we have received are none of the evil spirits, which rule the world, but spirits coming from God, that we may know the things that God in his grace has bestowed upon us. Of this we preach also, not in the words taught by human wisdom, but in words which are taught to us by God's spirits; thus we deliver the message of a spirit in the same words in which the spirits gave it to us. True, a worldly-minded man does not accept things brought by a spirit of God, for he looks upon communication with God's spirit-world as madness; neither is he fit for an understanding of such matters, because only those, who understand the laws, by wnich spirit communication is governed, can form a proper judgment'. *(1st Corinthians 2 : 4-14.)* '. . . you are an epistle of Christ, written by us as servants of Christ, not in ink, but in a spirit of the living God'. *(2nd Corinthians 3: 2-3.)* 'Let me say to you, brothers, that the gospel which I preached, is not the word of men. I neither received it from men, nor was it taught to me by men, but it came to me through a revelation of Jesus Christ'. *(Galatians 1 : 11, 12.)*

"Not only the Apostles received their teaching from God's spirits, but also the 'mediums' who were to be found in every community. As you already know, they were called 'prophets'. Saint

Paul writes that the mystery of Christ 'hath now been revealed unto his holy apostles and *'prophets'* by a spirit of God. *(Ephesians 3 : 5.)* It was through these mediums as the instruments of the good spirits that the faithful could at any time ascertain, whether a doctrine was true and how it was to be understood. Hence Paul writes to the Philippians: "if in any matter your belief should differ, that also God will make clear to you'. *(Philippians 3 : 15.)* They had the privilege of inquiring of God at their religious gatherings, and were answered by His spirits speaking through the mediums.

"Speaking of the earlier prophets as well as of those who preached the gospel in his own day, Saint Peter says that they 'preached the gospel by a holy spirit, sent forth from heaven'. *(1st Peter 1 : 12)* to which he adds in another epistle: '. . . no prophecy of scripture is of private interpretation, for no prophecy ever came by the will of man: but men spoke from God, being moved *by a holy spirit'. (2nd Peter 1 : 20, 21.)* The word 'prophecy' which occurs so often in the Bible does not mean, as you believe, the prediction of an event to come, but all speech by a spirit of God through a human medium.

"In the Old Testament God exhorted men to seek the truth of Him: 'Inquire of me'! — and revealed the truth through His spirit-messengers. By His own confession, Christ, as a mortal, received the truth from spirits of God. He promises His Apostles that they too shall learn the truth from the spirits of truth. The Apostles testify that this promise of Christ was fulfilled, and that they received their teachings from God's spirits.

"But whence does Christianity of today draw the truth? Can the ministers of the various Christian denominations say of themselves that a spirit of God is speaking from them? Can they testify, as did Saint Paul, that they 'speak not in words which man's wisdom teacheth' . . . but that they have the mind of Christ?' They can not. They are in the employ of their churches, whose respective creeds they studied under human instruction at schools, seminaries and universities. What they absorbed there was 'man's wisdom', professorial wisdom, with all of its errors, and that is what they preach to their congregations. Of spirits as messengers from God and as heralds of the truth they know nothing. In their eyes it is, to use one of Saint Paul's terms, foolishness, to expect any further teachings from a spirit of God at this late day. According to modern ideas, no further teachings are needed. In their opinion, such teachings may have been necessary in the days when men were supposedly much more ignorant than they are in your enlightened age. A man like Moses may have felt that he must communicate with God's spirit-world and to 'inquire of God' in order to learn the truth. So also the great prophets, Christ Himself, as well as His Apostles, but nowadays all that is considered as old-fashioned and as a thing of the past. To be sure, you have made great progress in science, you can all read and write, and have millions of books to which you can refer. And in addition you have no end of learned theologians, doctors of divinity and professors. They can surely tell you what the truth is.

"As a matter of fact it is precisely these doctors and professors of the 'sacred theology' who are responsible for the introduction of those doctrines against which Saint Paul utters these words of warning: 'See to it, that no man captivates you by means of so-called science or by the foolish and vain theories grounded on these traditions of men; for they have their source in the evil powers that rule the world, but have nothing in common with the teaching of Christ'. *(Colossians 2 : 8.)* 'Wishing to be regarded as versed in the law although they do not understand the meaning of the terms which they use or the things of which they speak with so much assurance'. *(1st Timothy 1 : 7.)* 'These are they who make separations, sensual, having not a spirit of God'. *(Jude 19.)*

"The spirit-world of God has long since been eliminated from the Christian creeds; the heads of the churches have exiled the holy spirit. But wherever spirits of God have been forced to yield, spirits of another nature presented themselves, like those of which Saint Paul writes to Timothy: 'God's spirits declare expressly, that in times to come, many will fall away from the faith and, turning to spirits of deceit, will spread doctrines inspired by demons'. *(1st Timothy 4 : 1-2.)*

"Into the places of the good spirits stepped the Powers of Evil, whose chief concern it is, to obscure and to reverse the truth, an end which they seek to accomplish by playing upon every human weakness, such as vanity and arrogance of learning, or the greed for power, distinction, money and luxury. All of these motives are utilized by them to tamper with the truths of God's wisdom, love and mercy, and to forge these into chains with which the heads of the churches manacle their poor, inexperienced adherents and render them subservient to themselves.

"The root of all evil is greed, — the love of money. Even in your Christian churches money plays an important role. Satan knew what he was about when he made a bait of money in the field of religion. He knew that this was the surest way of binding the spiritual leaders fast to error. He knew that none of them would be unduly ready to give up a well-paid position for life as the servant of a church, even after they had recognized the erroneousness of the doctrines they had been preaching.

"Thus it came that since the time when communication with God's spirit-world as the sole road to the truth was dispensed with, errors of the most varied and far-reaching nature have crept into Christianity. Century by century conditions grew worse. Truth after truth was contaminated by error and rendered unpalatable. And what has been the result? *Today you have before you a Christianity split into a hundred parts, into countless creeds each one of which proclaims a separate truth and each one of which contends that its doctrines alone represent the true teachings of Christ.* Do you wonder that a Christianity so adulterated and disfigured has ceased to exert an influence on mankind? Restore to humanity the faith of the early Christians! Remove from its shoulders those spiritual burdens imposed by manmade dogmas and out of motives of ambition; let men have access once more to God's messengers of the truth, and you will be amazed to see how much influence true Christianity can have, even on the people of today.

"The Catholic Church seeks to explain this breaking up into so many Christian 'sects' as it calls them, by the fact that all other Christian denominations have fallen away from it, the only true faith and the one which alone leads to salvation, but I shall show you that even the Catholic Church retains scarcely any part of the Christianity of Christ and His Apostles.

"It has, true enough, succeeded in finding a human substitute for the Divine spirits so much in evidence in the early days of the Christian era, by introducing the doctrine of the 'Papal infallibility'. This solved the problem of the truth in the simplest way, for thenceforth Christ would be spared the labor of sending the spirits of truth to erring humanity as He had promised. He would likewise be relieved of His promise to be with the faithful, even unto the end of the world', now that there was a 'Vicar of Christ' on earth, since the presence of a vicar renders the appearance of his principal unnecessary.

"Under this doctrine of an 'infallible vicar of Christ on earth', the source from which the Divine truths could be derived was placed wholly into the hands of erring, sinful mortals, to the exclusion of God's messengers, thus opening the door to human caprice and the lust for temporal power. You may claim that the Papal elections are held under the guidance of the 'Holy Spirit', but you cannot cite a single instance in which a Pope was chosen to office by a Divine spirit, nor has it ever happened that a Divine spirit, speaking through one of the electors present, has announced who was to be chosen for that office, as was done by God's spirits in the early Christian churches whenever an elder or a bishop was to be ordained. Consider the whole history of the Papal elections; were they not at times conducted in a manner positively diabolical? Was not intrigue of all kind and even armed force, resorted to, in order to place the tiara upon the head of adherents and favorites of certain families? Were not a succession of Popes instruments of Hell in their actions and their daily lives, rather than 'vicars of Christ'?

"In order to evade this issue you have resorted to the strange expedient of distinguishing between the Pope as a man and the Pope as the 'vicar of Christ', maintaining that even the most evil of men, as soon as he becomes Pope, represents Christ and acquires infallibility. This means that he can be a tool of Satan and at the same time the representative of Christ! Could there be any greater blasphemy of Christ and of God? Would any human being allow his greatest enemy to act as his representative for an hour? Assuredly not. Would God and Christ allow it? Would God entrust the highest gift that is His to bestow to a laborer in the field of salvation to a servant of Hell? Common sense should teach you that this is impossible. God's spirits bring their gifts only to the righteous, and remain with them only while they retain their righteousness. This is demonstrated by the history of Saul. As long as that Divinely favored monarch remained obedient to God, he was in daily communication with the Divine spirit-world and could 'inquire of God' whenever he felt the need of enlightenment, invariably receiving his answer from the spirits of truth. When, however, he broke faith with God, this communication was instantly interrupted. His inquiries addressed to God remained unanswered, and in the place of the Divine spirits, evil spirits took possession of him. At a stroke he was deprived of his gifts.

"No wicked man can ever be the holder of God's sacred gifts, not even if he is the Pope. It follows that among the Popes, the wicked ones at least could never have been infallible, and since you have no means of knowing whether a Pope, or indeed any man, is at heart friendly or hostile to God, you can never be sure whether a Pope's doctrines are true or erroneous.

"God alone chooses those among men to whom He sends His spirits of truth, and no human choice can establish a mortal as the bearer of the Divine tidings. Not even Christ selected His Apostles according to His own judgment, for it is expressly stated in the Acts that He selected them through a holy spirit'. It follows that God cannot make the gift of infallibility contingent upon any office held by the grace of man, as is the Papacy.

"Consequently, also, the interpretations given to many parts of the New Testament in support of Papal infallibility, are wholly erroneous. Among the passages so cited are the words addressed to Peter by Jesus: 'Thou art Peter, and upon this rock I will build my church; and the gates of Hell shall not prevail against it. I will give unto thee the keys to the kingdom of Heaven; and whatsoever thou shalt bind on earth shall be bound in heaven: and whatsoever thou shalt loose on earth shall be loosed in heaven'. *(Matthew 16 : 18, 19.)* From these words you deduce that Peter, the man, was the foundation of the church of Christ; that as the leader of that church he could not err, and that moreover he had been invested with the power to bind and to loose the members of the church; that this power had descended upon his successors, the Popes of the Church of Rome, who, in consequence, it is claimed, had the same gifts and powers that once were Peter's.

"These deductions are mere fallacies.

"It was not Peter the man to whom Christ referred as the rock upon which His church was to be built, but the faith which Peter had professed. *Peter's belief in Christ* as the Divinely-sent Messiah is the eternal, everlasting rock against which Hell cannot prevail, — *not the person of Peter,* who very soon afterwards was utterly vanquished by Hell as he proved by thrice denying his Master, thus proving how little dependence God can place upon men, and that no institution for the saving of souls can rest upon them. It would be a house built upon sand. One thing only endures: truth, and the faith in the truth conveyed by the spirits of God, as they, too, had revealed to Peter the truth that Christ was the Messiah, for as Christ said: 'Flesh and blood has not revealed it unto thee, but my Father who is in heaven'. It was because Peter had received this revelation from the Divine spirits that he believed it and in this belief he stood upon unyielding rock, for God's spirits do not lie. Whoever does as Peter did, stands upon the same rock upon which Peter rested his faith; whoever is ready to receive the Divine truth from the hands of God's messengers and to believe in it, belongs to the church of Christ. *It is a church of the spirit,* recognizing no membership as that term is understood by the organized religions of mankind. It knows of no bishops and priests, with the broad powers assumed by the clergy of the Catholic church. It knows of no infallible Pope. *Christ has no vicar on earth.* Among the adherents of the church of Christ are people of every creed in the world.

"This spiritual church of Christ can never be overcome by Evil, for it is the source of the truth, and truth is unconquerable. It derives its doctrines not from men, — not from Popes, bishops or priests, — but from spirits sent by God.

"The *'keys to the kingdom of Heaven'* which Christ promised to give to Peter because of his faith, are the Divine truths. By means of them he was to 'bind and to loose' by passing them on to those who lay bound in the chains of error. Whoever rejected those keys by opposing truth with unbelief, would be bound closer than ever to his error, but the bonds of those who eagerly accepted the proffered key would be loosed. The power to bind and loose applied to terrestrial existence and in particular, to the life in the Hereafter.

"The same metaphor of the 'keys to the kingdom of Heaven' is used by Christ in speaking of the spiritual leaders of the Jewish people of His day, who, by the false doctrines which they preached, had given to the Jewish people keys with which the doors of the kingdom of Heaven could not be opened. The right key, which was offered by John the Baptist and by Christ Himself and which the people were ready to receive, was torn from his hand by the Jewish clergy, drawing from Christ the exclamation: 'Woe to you, scribes and Pharisees, hypocrites that you are! You closed God's spirit-world to others. You yourselves do not enter, nor will you let those enter who would'. *(Matthew 23 : 13.)*

"The words: *'Feed my lambs, feed my sheep',* which Christ after His resurrection addressed to Peter, are also interpreted by you as indicative of preference. This is not the case. Peter had thrice denied his Master under oath, and according to all human standards it was to be expected that Christ would dismiss the unfaithful disciple from His service and relieve him of his apostolic office. Peter himself fully expected this, remembering Christ's words: '. . . whosoever shall deny me before men, him will I also deny before my Father who is in heaven'. This would have been the natural course for men to take under the circumstances, but Christ had mercy on the repentent Peter, and was willing to permit him, in spite of his breach of faith, to lead his fellow men to the pastures of truth on an equal footing with the other Apostles. Christ's question to Peter, thrice repeated: 'Lovest thou me?' was intended to remind Peter of his thrice repeated denial, and to bring home to him God's infinite goodness in overlooking the past and retaining him as an evangelist of the faith and as an instrument of the Divine spirits.

"You may see how mistaken are the interpretations given by your former Church, of the passages in question, and that these cannot be construed to support a preferential status for Peter or the doctrine of the Papal infallibility. That Church has long since fallen a victim to Hell, which is also the author of that doctrine, for inasmuch as most of the doctrines of that Church are wholly erroneous, Hell is intent upon perpetuating them among men as long as possible. This end is best achieved by means of the coercive measure of the infallibility, for the Church, having taught its errors under the sanction of infallibility, cannot now retract them. To surrender them would be to commit self-destruction.

"Your Papal doctrine is a succession of untruths. Thus it is historically untrue that the Bishop of Rome is the direct successor to Saint Peter in the Apostolic office, for the bishops of the first Christian churches were not elected as such by their fellowmen, nor appointed by the Apostles, but were appointed exclusively by the manifestant Divine spirits. If it occasionally happened that an Apostle or the disciple of an Apostle ordained someone as bishop, this was done only after a Divine spirit had announced the name of the person to be so ordained. Moreover, no bishop is another's superior nor has any Apostle any greater powers than have his fellows. 'Whatsoever they were', says Saint Paul, 'it makes no matter to me: God accepts not man's person'. *(Galatians 2 : 6.)* At the same place he relates how on one occasion he had opposed the Apostle Peter vigorously and had reproached him before the entire community with departing from the true gospel.

"Had it sufficed for God to reveal the gospel to Peter as the first infallible Pope, the early Christian churches would have had no need of the visits of the Divine spirits, since in Peter they would have had an infallible source of the truth. Moreover, why was Saint Paul not sent to Peter in order that he might receive the truth from him? The distance between them was not great. Why was he taught by Christ Himself, according to his own words?

"I shall now lay before you in their broad outlines certain individual doctrines of the gospel of Christ, comparing them with the doctrines of modern Christianity and in particular with those which you have heretofore preached as a member of the Catholic clergy. In so doing I shall fulfill the wish which you have long cherished, and shall at the same time demonstrate the falsity of those doctrines which depart from the teachings of Christ and which are held by other Christian churches.

1. Christ taught a *unipersonalist God,* the Creator of Heaven and Earth. He knows of no triune God of Whom the Catholic and other Christian denominations teach. Only the Father is God. None other is His equal, neither the Son, nor what you call the 'Holy Ghost'. After His resurrection, Christ said: 'I ascend unto my Father and your Father, and *my God* and your God'. *(John 20 : 17.)* 'My Father who gave me the sheep is above all, and no one can snatch anything out of the Father's hand'. *(John 10 : 29.)* According to those words, the Father is *above all.* If this is true, there is nothing equal to Him, and He is *greater than the Son,* a truth which Christ confirms with the words: '. . . for the Father is greater than I'. *(John 14 : 28.)* Also, whenever Jesus was addressed as 'good Master', he would reply: 'Why callest thou me good, since no one is good save *God alone'.*

"Inasmuch as God is above everything, He can confer power upon whomsoever He will, as He did to His Son, Whom He invested with the fullest powers. 'Thou hast given him power over all creation in order that all creatures which thou hast entrusted to him may have life hereafter'. *(John 17 : 2.)*

"That Christ is not God I proved to you by the Scriptures and in greater detail, when I taught you concerning His life and His work.

"The truth that only the Father, but not the Son, is God, is furthermore sustained by the teachings of the Apostles. Thus Paul writes: '. . . there is no God, but one. For although there may be such as are called gods in the heavens and on earth — and indeed there are many such 'gods' and many such 'lords' —, there is for us Christians but one God, the Father, from Whom all things are and to Whom we shall return'. *(1st Corinthians 8 : 4-6.)*

"Furthermore, Paul calls the Father the 'God of Jesus Christ'. 'That the God of our Lord Jesus Christ . . . may give unto you a spirit of wisdom'. *(Ephesians 1 : 17.)* According to Paul also, Christ's appearance will come at the will of Him 'who is the blessed and only Potentate, the King of kings, and Lord of lords; who only has immortality, dwelling in light unapproachable. *(1st Timothy 6 : 15, 16.)* If the Father alone has immortality, the Son has not. If the Father is the only Potentate, the Son cannot be such, and hence cannot be almighty by virtue of His own power. It follows that the Son is not God, but is, as He calls Himself and as the Apostles unanimously proclaim Him to be, the 'Son of God', less than the Father, Whose creature He is.

"The entire Bible, both the Old and the New Testaments, recognizes only *one God in one person.* The Father is God, and He only. Not one of His Sons, neither the First-born nor any of the others, is God.

"It is because you have raised Christ to the rank of God that you find insuperable difficulties in understanding His personality, His life, His sufferings, and His death. You are prevented by your misconception, from accepting His clear statement of His relation to the Father in its true sense, namely that of a Divinely created Being, albeit the highest, to its Maker.

"The result has been the most absurd theories invented by your theologians, for the purpose of bringing the undeniable facts in the life of Jesus as well as His own words, into harmony with His alleged Divinity. They have reconstructed the person of Jesus, claiming that in Him as a man there were present two spirits: one Divine, the other human. Hence Christ is alleged to have possessed a twofold intellect and a twofold volition, Divine and human; nevertheless, both spirits are regarded as having constituted but a *single personality.* This is sheer madness. Every spirit possesses an independent personality, and not even God can fuse two spirits into a single personality, any more than He can fuse two human beings into one; omnipotent though He be, since it is inherently contradictory that two should be equal to one. Common sense should tell you that if Christ had been God, He would not have cried out from the Cross: 'My God, why hast thou forsaken me'. Could God forsake Himself, then? When furthermore it is related in the Scriptures that Christ was raised from the dead by the hand of the Father, what need was there of the Father's help if Christ Himself was God? After His death upon earth, had He not divested Himself of all human limitations, becoming a God, and as such, in every respect His Father's equal according to your doctrine? If so, He had the same power as His Father, and possessing that power, why need He have depended upon that held by another? These contradictions are irreconcilable. And again, how, do you explain the fact that Christ does not once assert: 'I am God, my Father's equal in all things', and this despite the fact that on innumerable occasions He spoke of His relation to God. Is it reasonable to assume that He never once spoke the truth and admitted that He was God? On the contrary, he calls Himself only the 'Son of God', and protests that He is dependent upon the Father for all things. He solemnly declares: 'And this is the life eternal, that they should know thee *the only true God,* and him whom thou didst send, even Jesus Christ'. He is but God's envoy; He is not God. Paul calls Him the Firstling of creation; He was, therefore, created by God and hence God's creature, and is no more God than are His fellow-creatures.

"Inasmuch as nothing could be found in the New Testament to support the false doctrine that Christ is God, resort was had to the forgery of several Scriptural passages in order that the desired evidence might be forthcoming. Several of these I shall cite.

"In his Epistle to the Romans, Saint Paul writes: "Willingly would I be banished from my fellowship with Christ in the place of my brothers, men of my own race according to the flesh, who are Israelites. Time was, when they were God's people. They witnessed the glorious deeds of God; it was with them that He made His covenant; it was they to whom He gave the law, the true form of worship, the promises. Theirs are the patriarchs and from them in his mortal body sprang Christ, for which the allruling God be praised forever. Amen'. *(Roman 9 : 3–5.)* In this passage as elsewhere in his epistles, Paul voices his heartfelt thanks to God for the fact that the Messiah is sprung from a race of which he himself is one, but the text has been altered to read: 'and of whom is Christ concerning the flesh, who is God over all, blessed for ever'. By means of this falsification, the Messiah has been accorded the status of a Deity.

"A similar case of misrepresentation occurs in the Epistle to Titus *(Titus 2 : 13.)* '. . . looking for the blessed hope and appearing of the glory of the great God and of our Savior Jesus Christ'. In this place Paul speaks of the glory of the great God, the attainment of which is the aim of all material creation, and also of the glory of our Savior, Jesus Christ, through which we shall arrive at God according to the Redeemer's words: '. . . no one cometh unto the Father, but by me'. Thus Paul here distinguishes between the glory of the Father and the glory of Christ. The sense of this passage also has been distorted by its current rendering: '. . . looking for the blessed hope and appearing of our great God and Savior, Jesus Christ. . .' This version is intended to convey to the reader the impression that Christ is the great God for Whose appearance we must look.

"Of course, alterations of this sort will immediately attract the notice of anyone who is familiar with Saint Paul's Epistles and who knows the sharp lines of distinction which that Apostle draws in all of his writings between the person of Christ and the person of God, referring to the Father as the 'God of Christ', and to Christ as the 'Lord' appointed by God; teaching that God will put all His enemies under the Son's feet, the last enemy to be abolished being Lucifer, the Prince of Death; and that when all things have been subjected unto Him, then shall the Son also himself be subjected unto Him, that God may be all in all. *(1st Corinthians 15 : 27, 28.)*

"Paul's salutation always runs: 'Grace to you and peace from God our Father and the Lord Jesus Christ. He never says 'God the Son'. If therefore there is any part of your present Bible which can be construed into something else than the truth that only the Father is God, then the fault lies either in the translation, or in a falsification of the Greek text from which that translation was made, and in some cases in a combination of both. Of this last you will find an instance in Paul's letter to the Philippians *(2 : 5, 6)* in the passage which reads according to your version: 'Have this in mind in you, which was also in Christ Jesus: who, existing in the form of God, counted not *the being on an equality with God* a thing to be grasped, but emptied himself, taking the form of a servant'. The unaltered text read: 'Have this in mind in you, which was also in Christ Jesus; who, although in form like unto a God, counted it not a thing to be grasped to humble himself before God, but emptied himself, taking the form of a bond servant'. It is true that the celestial body of Christ as a Spirit resembled a God, and that all spirits on seeing Him for the first time think they are seeing God — so gloriously has God endowed His First-born. The original text has been crudely falsified by substituting the words: 'the being on an equality with God', for the words: 'to humble himself before God'.

"Inasmuch as I have just had occasion to use the words 'resembling a God', I shall make mention of the opening passage of the Gospel of Saint John, also cited in proof of the Divinity of Christ. 'In the beginning was the Word, and the Word was with God, and the Word was God'.(*John, 1 : 1*)

"First and foremost the text should read: '. . . the Word was *a* God'; and not: 'the Word was God' for at this passage John uses the term 'a God' as it was applied in his day to all who were God's special instruments and who as His envoys stood in particular communication with Him. The same usage was employed by God when speaking to Moses, Christ's prototype, to whom He said on that occasion: 'And he (Aaron) shall be thy spokesman unto the people; and it shall come to pass that he to thee shall be a mouth, and thou shalt be a God to him'. *(Exodus 4 : 16.)* Christ, also, when reproached by the Jews with making Himself the equal of God by calling Himself the 'Son of God' retorted with the question: 'Is it not written in your law, I said, Ye are gods? If he called them gods, unto whom the word of God came (and the scripture cannot be broken), say ye of him whom the Father sanctified and sent into the world, Thou blasphemest; because I said, I am the Son of God?' What Christ intends to express in these words is: 'How can you accuse me of wishing to make myself God's equal by calling myself His Son? Even if I had called myself a god, I would not have committed blasphemy, for those who have heretofore appeared as God's envoys were called gods, because they came to proclaim the Divine word. With how much better right, then would not I call myself a god, since to me has been entrusted the greatest task ever assigned to a Divine emissary! But I purposely refrain from calling myself a god, in order to prevent any misinterpretation of the word, and call myself what I truly am, the Son of God'. So, also, we find in the writings of Saint Paul: 'For though there be that are called gods, whether in the heaven or on earth; as there are gods many, and lords many; yet to us there is one God, the Father, . . . and one Lord, Jesus Christ. . .' *(1st Corinthians 8 : 5, 6.)* Paul here indicates that Christians should not continue to use the term 'god' in its improper sense, but should speak of God only when meaning the true

God, the Father, and that Christ, and He only, should be known to them as the 'Lord'. They might not therefore speak of Jesus Christ as 'God'.

"Another falsification is found in the Epistle of John, the passage in question reading in its correct version: 'We know that the Son of God is come and has given us an understanding, that we know him that is true, and we are in him that is true, even in his Son, Jesus Christ. It is he that is true, and eternal life'. *(1st Epistle of John, 5 : 20.)* In addition to other inaccuracies which this passage contains, its last sentence has been altered to read: 'This is the true God, and eternal life'. What John teaches here is the same as that which was uttered so often by Christ and by the Apostles, namely: God is He that is true, but the Son also is true, for He utters His Father's words, teaching only as the Father has directed Him. In everything that He reveals He is therefore as true as is the Father Himself, hence those who are in communion with the Son are thereby also in communion with the true God. And since God has granted to His Son eternal life, the Son also is eternal life for those who are in communion with Him.

"The doctrine that three persons are united in one Godhead finds its main support in the grossly falsified passage in the Epistle of John, the correct version of which reads: 'For there are three that bear witness, the Spirit, the water, and the blood: and the three of them are in accord'. *(1st John 5 :8.)* To this has been added the spurious sentence: 'And there are three who bear witness in Heaven, the Father, the Word, and the Spirit, and these three are one'. That this entire last sentence is a spurious interpolation is a fact of which your Catholic theologians are well aware. Nevertheless it is retained in the Catholic editions of the Bible, although certain other Christian denominations have eliminated it.

"Except for the passage I have mentioned, there is not in the entire New Testament even the most far-fetched evidence to support the doctrine that what you call the 'Holy Ghost' is a Deity equal to the Father. The term 'Holy Ghost' as used in that part of the Scriptures refers to the good spirit-world as a whole. God is a Holy Ghost. He is the highest and most sacred of *all* spirits. The Son of God is a Holy Ghost; He is the highest and most sacred of all *created* spirits. The princes of Heaven like Michael, Gabriel, Raphael, and many others, are holy spirits. All of the celestial legions are holy spirits. So too was Lucifer before his fall, and so too were all men as well as the entire material creation.

The great misunderstanding that has arisen from the term 'the Holy Ghost', is due to inaccurate translations of the Greek texts of the New Testament, for wherever the words '*a* holy spirit' occur, they have been translated for some unknown reason as '*the* holy spirit'. This is all the more surprising, since the translators were men who had a command of the Greek language and who knew well enough how strictly the distinction between the definite and the indefinite article is observed in that tongue of all others.

"You yourself while at school studied Greek, the language in which the New Testament has come down to you, and you will probably remember enough of what you learned then to be able to confirm my statement by referring to the Greek version of the same. I shall cite only a few passages out of many.

"Let us take the Gospel according to Matthew. In its very opening lines it is stated that Mary was with child of *a* holy spirit, not of *the* Holy Spirit. A few lines further down you find: 'that which is conceived in her is of *a* holy spirit', not of *the* Holy Spirit, as though there were but one.

"If you will now turn to the Gospel according to Luke you will find the same thing. Here also the text should read: '*A* Holy Spirit shall come upon thee and the power of *a* Most High shall overshadow thee', and not, as your rendering has it: '*The* Holy Spirit shall come upon thee and the power of *The* Most High shall overshadow thee', for it was not *the* Most High, but one of the most high spirits of God Whose power overshadowed Mary. So also in the preceding lines with reference to the birth of John, the correct reading is: 'He shall be filled with *a* holy spirit, even from his mother's womb'. This also is true of the passage referring to Elizabeth which should read: 'She was filled with *a* holy spirit', as well as of that relating to Zacharias, which should read: 'He was filled with *a* holy spirit'. Christ says: 'But if I, by *a* spirit of God cast out demons. . .' *(Matthew 12 : 28)* and John the Baptist declares: 'There comes after me . . . that shall baptize you in *a* holy spirit. *(Mark 1 : 8.)* In the first lines of the Acts it is related that Jesus had chosen His Apostles by commandment of *a* holy spirit, and in the second chapter, that on the day of Pentecost all those who were gathered were filled with *a* holy spirit.

"When explaining the 12th and the 14th Chapters of the First Epistle to the Corinthians I called your attention to this far-reaching error of translation which has led to the belief that there is but one holy spirit, a Divine person, forming one Godhead with the Father, as your former faith teaches.

"Wherever the original Greek texts read 'a' spirit, one of many is meant. You therefore distort the meaning entirely by substituting: *'the'* holy spirit. There are certain passages, it is true, where reference is made to 'the' holy spirit or to 'the' spirit, but in those cases the term either connotes a distinction between the spirit and matter, as in the sentence: 'The spirit is willing, but the flesh is weak', or else the reference is to the Spirit of God, namely God Himself, or to spirits of a certain kind such as the 'spirit of light', the 'spirit of truth', the 'spirit of comfort' and others. This does not mean that there is only one spirit of each kind, but is merely an instance in which the singular is employed in place of the plural. You have the same usage in your modern languages, for when you say to a sick person: 'I will get *the* doctor, 'you do not mean to imply that there is only one physician in the world, and when you speak of the farmer having had a prosperous year, you are referring to all farmers collectively. So too you use the terms: 'the' workman, 'the' lawyer, 'the' artist, you mean all those who are engaged in the respective callings.

"When therefore Christ says: 'I will send the spirit of truth', He means *spirits* of truth, for as you already know, the Divine spirits are assigned to various callings according to their respective tasks. There are spirits of protection, spirits of battle, spirits of strength, spirits of wisdom and innumerable others. A spirit of truth has tasks of a very different nature to perform than has a spirit of Michael's legions, and hence possesses different qualifications. Neither one can take over the work of the other. Every spirit has its definite calling, and is gifted accordingly. Similarly, Lucifer has marshalled his hosts according to their specific work. He too has his fighting forces, his spirits of lying, of despondency, of avarice, pride, envy, revenge, lust, and of every other vice. The different kinds of spirits, good or bad, are specialists in their various callings and are well qualified to influence those on whom they work, either for good or for evil within their respective provinces.

"As you see, the doctrine of a triune Godhead is not only contrary to common sense, but is entirely unsupported by the Scriptures.

"Yet, although only the Father is God, while the Son and all the other spirits are His creatures, nevertheless a most intimate harmony and unity obtains between the Father, the Son and the good spirit-world, a harmony of will and deed. The Father's will is also the Son's, and that of the spirit-hosts under His command. God is the master and owner of all creation, spiritual and material; everything belongs to Him. The management of creation has been conferred upon the Son, in a way similar to that in vogue among men, as when a factory-owner places the management of his factory in the hands of his oldest son and puts the entire working force under his orders. In cases of this kind the son in question receives his instructions and orders from his father, upon whom he remains dependent in all things, since the father continues to be the master and owner of the factory, while the son may act within the instructions received from him. But so far as the workmen and employees are concerned, the son is the 'master', whose orders they must obey, and whatever wants they wish to make known to the father as the owner of the factory must go through the son as his agent and representative. Translate this example taken from human experience into the relation existing between God and His Son, and all utterances of Christ upon that subject will at once be clear to you. He has been given all the authority over creation required as His Father's lieutenant. This He holds, not by virtue of His own power, but as a gift from His Father. Everything is subordinate to the Son, subject, however to the Father's will. Whatever the Father desires to perform in the universe, He does through the agency of the Son, and only through the Son can the Father be reached. Hence, as Christ says: '. . . no one comes unto the Father, but by me'. The Son receives His Father's directions, and those which are not to be executed by Him personally, are transmitted to the spirits best fitted for the task in question, who perform it at the direct command of the Son and at the indirect command of the Father. This also is the meaning of the words which were addressed by Christ to the Apostles when He sent them forth, and which are somewhat incorrectly repeated in your Bible: 'Go you therefore, and make disciples of all nations, baptizing them in the name of the Father and of the Son, in a holy spirit'. *(Matthew 28 : 19.)* The mission on which Christ sent the Apostles had been assigned to Him by the Father; consequently, the Apostles were acting indirectly in the Father's name, but inasmuch as they had been sent directly by the Son, it was in His name that their mission was carried out, and since this could be done only with the aid of the power of one of God's spirits, it was said to be performed 'in a holy spirit'. The spirits which the

Apostles needed for their tasks were assigned to them by Christ Himself. They are therefore constantly invoked by the Apostles in their preachings, who emphasize that the truth has been revealed to them by a holy spirit. So it is in everything that you do, that is pleasing to God — you are acting in the fulfillment of His will, and consequently in the name of the Father; but the will of God is revealed to you through the Son, so that you are acting also in the name of the Son; and the power which you need is lent to you by a holy spirit. Hence you are performing your task in a holy spirit.

2. There is little to be found in the New Testament concerning *God's Creation and its vicissitudes,* for the facts relating to the creation of the spirits, to the defection of a part of the spirit-world under Lucifer's leadership, to the Divinely created spheres of progress by which the fallen spirits are led Godward, to the investiture of the spirits in matter, were things which the people of those times found as difficult to understand as do the people of today. The Epistles of the Apostles likewise have little to say upon the subject which lends itself but poorly to instruction by means of letters, and could be brought home to the faithful only by oral message.

"Nevertheless, Paul at least hints at these truths in several passages of his writings, even if you fail to discover them because they no longer fit in with your religious views. Thus he writes: 'For the earnest expectation of the creation waits for the unveiling of the sons of God. For the creation was subjected to vanity, not of its own will, but by reason of him who subjected it, in hope that the creation itself also shall be delivered from the bondage of corruption into the liberty of the glory of the children of God. For we know that the whole creation groans and travails in pain with us. And not only so, but ourselves also, who have the first-fruits of the spirit, even we ourselves groan within ourselves, waiting for our adoption, to wit, the redemption of our body'. *(Romans 8 : 19-24.)* In this passage Paul says that the *whole* creation is waiting to be delivered from the bondage of corruption, meaning thereby the stones, plants, flowers, animals and men. Such 'earnest expectation' is possible only where a spirit exists in the state of incarnation, hence throughout creation there are spirits, clothed in matter of various sorts. They are the rebellious spirits, which in the beginning resided in glory and splendor as God's obedient children and as His holy spirits, but which later became disobedient and were therefore exiled from their Father's house. But exiled though they be, they remain God's children to this day. They long to return to the home of their Father and strive to rid themselves of the vesture of substance in which they are clothed, as during the birth-pangs a child struggles to escape from the confines of its mother's womb. Those spirits were not subjected to that garment of flesh by their own will, but by reason of the will of God, Who so clothed them in His mercy, in order that by trial and purification they might prove themselves worthy of being saved. All material beings long for such salvation, even though they may not know the way to it nor the end in view, and pine for the day on which, purified and freed from the bondage of corruption, they shall once more be called the children of God. This longing abides, foremost of all, in the righteous, for although, as was the case with the early Christians, they may be in daily communion with the spirit-messengers from their Father's home and from them have received the first-fruits and a foretaste of the kingdom of God, they are still far from having attained to that kingdom so long as they still live in the flesh.

3. *The upward evolution in Nature* is indicated by Paul in his epistle to the Ephesians, in which he says: '. . . making known unto us the mystery of his will, according to his good pleasure which he purposed in him unto a dispensation of the fulness of the times, *to sum up all things* in Christ, the things in the heavens, and the things upon the earth. . .' *(Ephesians 1 : 9, 10.)* There are however, many things upon earth besides men, who form only a small fraction of what exists thereon. If, then, God purposes to sum up *all things* upon earth in Christ, it follows that in all things there are spirits which in the evolution ordained by God progress steadily, until they return as pure spirits into that great community under Christ to which they belonged before their fall.

"The fact that everything, not mankind alone but all the rest of creation, is included in God's Plan of Salvation, is apparent from the following passage in Paul's epistle to the Romans *(11 : 25-32):* 'For I would not, brethren, have you ignorant of this mystery, lest you be wise in your own conceits, that a hardening in part has befallen Israel, until the *fullness* of the Gentiles be come in; and so *all Israel* shall be saved. . . For God has shut up *all things* by reason of their disobedience, for he purposes to have mercy on all'.

"I have given you this passage as it should be. If the last sentence in the translation before you runs: 'For God hath shut up all unto disobedience, that he might have mercy upon all', it is because the translator has made two mistakes. First, he has written 'all' whereas the Greek text says: 'all things'. Secondly, he has said: 'God hath shut up all unto disobedience', when he should have said: 'God hath shut up all things by reason of their disobedience', meaning that all things were clothed by Him in matter which corresponds to the various stages of progress. God shuts up no one unto disobedience; on the contrary, He desires the return of all who were once exiled from His kingdom because of their disobedience. The Israel of the millenniums that had gone before was the people to whom the pure faith had been revealed and who were to spread this faith to the other nations of the earth, acting as a leaven of truth. Had Israel accomplished this duty faithfully, it would have been the first to reenter God's kingdom after the Redemption had been consummated, but the greater part of Israel showed itself unworthy of the high mission with which it had been charged. Consequently, the first to be saved will be the non-Israelites, the very ones who in the past had known nothing of God, and only when 'the fulness of these be come in', will those be saved who had once possessed the true faith, but who had failed to observe its precepts. 'The first shall be last'. But all, without exception, will be saved.

"The reference to the course followed by God's work of redemption, in Saint Paul's first Epistle to the Corinthians is brief but clear: 'For as in Adam all died, so also in Christ all shall be made alive. But each in his own order: Christ the first fruits; then they that are Christ's, at his coming. Then comes the rest, when he shall deliver up the kingdom to God, even the Father; when he shall have abolished all rule, and all authority and power. For he must reign, till he has put all enemies under his feet. The last enemy that shall be abolished is '*death*'. For, He put all things in subjection under his feet. But when he says, All things are put in subjection, it is evident that He (namely God) is excepted Who did subject all things unto him. And when all things have been subjected to Him (God), then shall the Son also himself be subjected to Him that did subject all things unto him, that God may be all in all'. *(1st Corinthians 15 : 22-28.)* Thus all things will return to God which had been separated from Him and had been subjected as spiritually 'dead' to the Prince of the death of the spirit. Christ will lead back all things to God, for was He not the first to return from Hell, the realm of the Prince of Death, after having descended thither and vanquished Lucifer on his own ground? His was the first resurrection from the spiritually dead. As time passes, all who have died in spirit will follow Him, as they learn to know and to love God, but 'each in his own order', which depends upon the spirits themselves. Those which hasten and apply themselves to seeking unto God and to living as He would have them live, will come before those that give no thought at all to a return or show but little zeal. Everything depends upon their own initiative. He who fails repeatedly in his examinations will be late in reaching the goal. This is true of life on earth, as well as in the Hereafter. The last of all to return unto God will be the Prince of Death himself, Lucifer. Paul calls him 'death', for he is the cause of the exile from God's kingdom and hence, of spiritual death. He is the 'murderer from the beginning', guilty of the spiritual death of all those who are parted from God, and of having done his utmost throughout millions of years to prevent the return of his subjects to the Realm of Life in God. He is therefore the personification of separation from God, the *personification of death.* Thus when you read in the Revelation of John *(20 : 13):* 'And death gave up the dead', the meaning is, that Lucifer, the Prince of Death, was forced to give up the spiritually dead that were in his kingdom. As to what I said, that the order of the return of the fallen spirits depended upon the free will of each, I must qualify this statement by adding that *Lucifer himself* is the only one who cannot return to God until the last of his dupes has arrived at that goal. He cannot do so, not even if he were to attempt it by reason of a change of heart, nor may he, even if he should be the first to see the error of his ways, urge any of the fallen spirits to reform or even aid it with his advice, for the purpose of hastening his own return to God thereby. That is the just doom which rests upon him as the one-time ringleader, and which he cannot mitigate.

"The redemption of all of the fallen, even that of Lucifer, is the glad tidings not only announced in the Epistles of Saint Paul, but shown to the prophets of the pre-Christian era in their visions. It is that to which the Revelation of John alludes in the words: 'But in the days of the voice of the seventh angel, when he is about to sound, then is finished the mystery of God, according to the *good tidings* which he declared to his servants, the prophets'. *(Revelation 10 : 7.)* If it were true that there is an eternal Hell as is taught today, wherein would lie the gladness of the tidings which God had promised at the completion of His Plan of Salvation? A completion which involved the eternal damnation of countless spirits would assuredly be no day of gladness, but a day of terror for all creation. What then would become of the redemption of all, preached so insistently by Saint Paul? What of the fulfillment of God's promise given through the mouth of the Prophet Isaiah: '. . . unto me every knee shall bow, every tongue shall swear. Only in the Lord it is said of me, is righteousness and strength; even to him shall men come; and all they that were incensed against him shall be put to shame?' What, further would become of the fulfillment of all the passages of which I had previously spoken to you? All of God's enemies will be put in subjection under His feet by Christ, not by force, but by a merciful love, against which not even Lucifer can hold out forever. God forces no fallen spirit into subjection; had He wished, He could have done so long ago, for even Hell must obey His omnipotent will, and if Hell ever humbles itself before Him, it must do so of its own free will in contrite acknowledgment of His justice, love, and patience.

"A doctrine to which you cling with astonishing tenacity although it was unknown to the early Christians is that of an 'eternal Hell'. This is a bogey which you seem unwilling to surrender. Do you perhaps imagine that you can accomplish more with poor humanity by preaching a barbarous untruth, than by preaching love and mercy? What pains you give yourselves to find support for this untruth! You say that a so-called 'mortal sin' must entail eternal punishment, seeing that it is an unforgiveable affront to God. That is a wholly mistaken, manmade idea. No creature can affront God unforgiveably and thereby incur unending punishment. The lower the standing of him who affronts you, the less attention you will pay to his insults. What is a miserable creature as compared with its Creator? A mere speck of dust! Your insults do not even touch God; they hurt not Him, but yourselves. Again, if a mortal sin were an unpardonable affront to God, it could not be forgiven on earth; on the other hand, if according to your doctrine, it can be forgiven in men, why should it not be forgiven the spirits of the Hereafter? They are, after all, the same spirits, whether they inhabit a mortal body or whether they have become separated from it by death on earth. The 'ego' with all its mental attributes, is the same in the Here and in the Hereafter. Hence a change of heart may occur in spirits in the Beyond as well as it can while they reside on earth.

"Proof that the tortures of Hell are everlasting is sought by invoking the Bible, by citing the word 'eternal' which is used in your translations of the New Testament in connection with punishment in the Hereafter. Let us see what the word is in the original Greek texts, translated by you as 'eternal', for the proof lies, not in your renderings, but in the sense of the word as it occurs in the original. It so happens that wherever your translators of the Scriptures use the word 'eternity' or 'eternal' the Greek text uses 'eon'. You have adopted this word to designate long periods of time, and this is correct, for in Greek the word 'eon' never signifies 'eternity' or the idea of anything everlasting, but merely an indefinite lapse of time. Antiquity was an 'eon', the Middle Ages were an 'eon', the Modern Age is an 'eon'. By the Romans, an 'eon' was regarded as equivalent to a hundred years.

"An 'eon' is therefore a period of time the limits of which are elastic. Even a man's lifetime is sometimes so designated. Never, however, can it be used to describe eternity, nor can the adjective derived therefrom be translated as 'eternal', the correct equivalents being 'time' and 'temporary'.

"I shall first call your attention to the interesting circumstance that in many passages of the Bible the word 'eon' and the corresponding adjective have been correctly translated as 'time' and 'temporary' because in those particular places the word 'eternal' would be nonsensical. Only when punishment in the Hereafter is involved, have the translators used that word, indicating clearly that they were influenced by denominations which preach eternal damnation.

"Let us consider a few of the numerous passages in the Bible in which the word 'eon' can be translated only as 'time' or something pertaining to time. Thus it is said that blasphemy against the Spirit shall not be forgiven, either in this 'eon' or in that which is to come. In this passage 'eon' has been correctly rendered, the translation reading: '. . . it shall not be forgiven him, neither in this world (or age), nor in that which is to come. Inasmuch as there is only one eternity, you cannot rationally refer to 'this eternity' and the 'eternity that is to come'. In the parable of the sower, it is said that some of the seeds were choked with the cares of this 'eon' which again has been correctly translated as with the cares of this 'life'. Here also the rendering of the word as 'eternity' would be obviously meaningless. The same is true of the parable of the tares among the wheat, in which Christ explains that the harvest would be at the end of the 'eon', which you have rendered as the 'end of the world', or the 'consummation of the age'. In this passage the word 'eon' occurs twice, both times in a limitative sense. Finally, I shall quote a passage from Saint Paul's Epistle to the Corinthians: 'We speak a wisdom not of this 'eon', nor of the rulers of this 'eon' . . . but we speak God's wisdom in a mystery . . . Which God foreordained before the 'eons' unto our glory'.

"From these passages which could be multiplied manifold you may see that the word 'eon' does not mean 'eternity', but an age of limited duration. Whence then do you derive the right to translate a word as 'eternal' when referring to damnation, if elsewhere you have rendered it as referring to a transitory stage? It would almost seem as though you took a particular delight in the thought of an everlasting Hell.

"According to your translation, Christ has said: 'It is good for thee to enter into life maimed or halt, rather than having two hands or two feet to be cast into the eternal fire'. What you here designate as the 'eternal' fire is also only a fire which will last throughout an 'eon' and hence be temporary; strangely enough, the original text did not even contain the word 'eon' in this passage, but read: 'into the hell of fire'. Similar spurious alterations have been committed elsewhere. Thus your present Bible says: 'Depart from me, ye cursed, into the eternal fire . . .' whereas the authentic version was: 'Depart from me, ye cursed, into the outer darkness'. I hope I have convinced you with my explanations, that there is no authority in the Bible to support your inhuman and untrue doctrine of an everlasting Hell.

"The duration of the punishment meted out to the various spirits depends upon the spirits themselves. The longer they persist in their rebellious attitude, the longer their exile and the longer the penalty attached thereto. Not even God knows when the individual spirits will come back to Him, since their return depends upon their own free will, and as I have told you, all decisions at which spirits are free to arrive, lie outside of the scope of God's foreknowledge of events.

"Again, what you have incorrectly translated as the 'eternal life' by a mistaken rendering of the word 'eon' is merely a life in the 'eons' or 'ages' to come. How long this life may last depends upon yourselves. If you remain faithful to God, that life will be, in truth, eternal. But who can tell whether in the future there may not be another rebellion of the spirits, in which you will again take part, as you did in the first revolt under Lucifer? Spirits in Heaven have the same freedom of choice now as formerly, and the possibility of a misuse of that freedom is as much a fact as it was at the time of the first revolt. Whether or not there will ever be another is something that even God does not know for the reasons which I have already indicated to you.

"You cannot, therefore, speak of an 'eternal' reward, any more than you can speak of an 'eternal' punishment.

"Wherever the Bible refers to the 'fires' of Hell, it does so symbolically of the excessive pain suffered by those condemned to that place. You too speak of a burning pain without having reference to actual fire. The tortures of Hell are beyond your conception. Christ says: 'For everyone shall be salted with fire', for as salt permeates everything, so does agony permeate the spirits of the damned, — but He adds: 'Salt is good. . .' So too the tortures of the spirits are in reality good for their salvation, however cruel the proceeding may seem and however incomprehensible to men, as not in accord with God's mercy. And yet the tortures of Hell are merely an evidence of the love of God. A mother, who subjects her child to the surgeon's knife in order that it may be cured of a dangerous illness, acts under the impulse of maternal love and is driven to expose her child to pain because there is no other remedy. Similarly, the disposition of the spirits of the Pit can be cured only by the pains which they have to endure; no other way exists. But to all, even to the most hardened, the hour will come when, by their tortures, they will be brought to see the error of their ways and will arise and go to their Father.

"It is because Christianity of today has no true conception of the great story of the Universe that it is so helpless in all the most important questions relating to the Hereafter. For the same reason it is unable to explain either the origin of the human soul, nor the sin of the revolt against God which rests upon that soul, nor the purpose of material creation. Its doctrines in regard to all of these questions are wholly erroneous.

"4. Whenever enlightenment is sought of the Christian denominations of the present age as to the *origin of the spirit of man,* the answer is: 'The human spirit is created by God at the moment of conception. It is, nevertheless, burdened with the so-called 'original sin', because the ancestor of all mankind sinned in Paradise and his sin has descended upon all of his progeny'.

"The exponents of such a doctrine do not stop to consider its absurdity. They do not pause to think that everything created by God comes forth from under His hand pure and flawless, and that the contamination of a spirit can be due only to some fault incurred *personally*, and, consequently, that if the human spirit were created by God at the instant of conception, it would be entirely pure and spotless. In this case there could be no question of any 'original sin', for why should Adam's descendants be punished with the bondage of sin and exile from God's kingdom because of their ancestor's fault? And that, by a God who once said: 'The soul that sins, it shall die: the son shall not bear the iniquity of the father'. *(Ezekiel 18 : 20.)* In the face of this, Adam's descendants cannot be punished by God for Adam's fall, in which they took no part. As a matter of fact, they themselves fell — as I have already told you — by following the example set to them by Adam as a spirit, thereby like him incurring banishment from God's kingdom with all of its dire consequences'.

"It is true that the spirit of man bears from birth an iniquity which you call the 'original sin'. But it is false to assert, as you do, that the human spirit comes into existence only at the moment of human conception and that it bears an iniquity of which it has not itself been guilty.

"In the light of your false doctrine as to the origin of the human spirit, how do you seek to explain all the suffering that exists on earth? Do you imagine that God has brought forth His creatures to suffer through life and allows them to die in agony if they had never been personally guilty of any wrong? Think of the millions of children who die amidst suffering every year! What have they done to deserve such a fate? Have they by any chance so affronted God during their life on earth as to merit such a punishment? They were incapable of sinning, being unable to distinguish right from wrong. Would an infinitely good and just God torture innocent infants? Wherein, then, would lie His goodness, and above all, His justice? Not even the most brutal human father is so cruel and unjust as to maltreat a child which has done him no harm. Could God be capable of such a monstrosity? You may offer what explanations you will; you cannot explain away the hideous injustice that has been done to these children, assuming the correctness of your doctrine. The same thing may be said of the lot of humanity generally. But when you learn that your spirit came into this life bearing the iniquity of a former existence, the mystery of your lot on earth is solved in an instant. Then you are made aware of the great revolt against God in which the spirits of mortals once participated, as well as of previous incarnations in human form, and of the commission therein of sins for which the present life must make atonement. If you will bear this in mind, you will be less often tempted to exclaim in the hour of deep distress: 'What have I done to deserve this'? If, in reply to this question, God were to show you a picture of your entire past, you would be struck speechless with horror.

"Moreover, in the light of your new knowledge you will be able to understand many parts of the Holy Writ which have heretofore been obscure. Thus you can, by your own efforts, solve the apparent contradiction contained in the Old Testament which in one passage says: 'The son shall not bear the iniquity of the father', and in another: 'For I will visit the iniquities of the fathers upon the children, upon the third and upon the fourth generation'. If God visits the sins of the fathers upon their children, it is not by allowing innocent children to suffer for their father's sins. That would be manifestly unjust. He does, however, incarnate in the sinful father's children spirits which have independently incurred a painful lot, and whose lot serves as a punishment to the father also. Now since a father seldom survives beyond the fourth generation of his descendants, this punishment is visited upon him unto the fourth generation.

"Again, how, in the face of your doctrine that the spirit of mortals comes into being at the moment of conception, do you explain the sentence from the Bible: 'God is able of these stones to raise up children unto Abraham'? You may say that God in His omnipotence can turn stones into human beings, who, nevertheless, would not be children of Abraham, for human beings could become children of Abraham only by way of procreation and as his descendants through a line of human ancestors. But how can stones become Abraham's children through procreation? All your theological learning will not enable you to answer this question, but when you know that spirits exist in stones, as they do in all other matter, the explanation is obvious. Then you will realize that God is able to divest the spirits so incorporated of their garment of matter, and incorporate them in the bodies of those children that come into being as descendants of Abraham according to the established laws of procreation.

"The same thing is borne out by the words of Christ: 'I tell you that, if these shall hold their peace, the stones will cry out'.

(Luke 19 : 40.) Obviously, stones cannot cry out unless they are the abode of spirits.

"5. Just as you have established a false doctrine as to original sin, your *entire conception of sin as a whole* is erroneous.

"The Bible draws a distinction between the sin of 'departing from God' and the sins of the faithful committed by reason of human infirmities.

"In the first Epistle of John occurs a passage, the explanation of which has offered you great difficulty and which reads: 'If any man see his brother sinning a sin not unto death, he shall ask and shall give him life even to them that sin not unto death. There is sin unto death: not concerning this do I say that he should make request. All unrighteousness is sin: and there is sin not unto death'. *(1st John 5 : 16, 17.)* John thus draws the distinction here between sin unto death and sin not unto death, and, what may strike you as quite incomprehensible, tells you that you need not even pray for those who have committed a sin unto death.

"The sense of these words is best explained by means of an example. Every soldier, on joining the colors, is required to take the oath of enlistment. Now it often happens that soldiers commit offenses for which they are punished by disciplinary measures, without therefor ceasing to be soldiers of their respective countries. There is, however, one sin which terminates a man's career as a soldier of his country and the punishment of which is death: desertion to the enemy in time of war. He is pronounced dead by the home authorities; from a military point of view, he has 'sinned unto death'. No mother's plea will avail to wrest a pardon from the Government of her country for her renegade son, seeing that he is no longer under the jurisdiction of his own Government but has entered that of a hostile state, to whose laws he is henceforth subject. That State will not surrender him, even if he should be willing to return, which, naturally, he has no desire to do. Hence any appeals for mercy addressed by his mother to the home Government are to no purpose whatever.

"Apply this example to your relations toward God. As mortals who acknowledge Him, you are subjects of His kingdom and even if, erring pilgrims that you are on earth, not a day passes on which you do not commit some trespass great or small for which you are duly punished, you do not on that account cease to be His subjects. If, however, you turn your back upon God by abandoning your belief in Him, by denying Him or by living as though there were no God, you are guilty of desertion. This is the sin by which you sever yourselves from Him and go over into the camp of the evil, godless, powers. You abandon your allegiance to God completely, exactly as a deserter abandons his allegience to his own sovereign. In the eyes of the kingdom of God, you are legally dead, having committed the 'sin unto death'. Of what avail, then would be the intercession on behalf of such a deserter by a fellow man? The traitor cares nothing for God and has no desire to return to Him, and, in order that your prayers might be granted, God would have to force him to do so. This He cannot do, because He has bestowed on all men the gift of freedom of will, and hence never employs force to compel the decisions of His creatures. It is left to the free determination of everyone to work out his salvation.

"The first treason was the great revolt of the spirits led by Lucifer. That was the first 'sin unto death'.

"6. *The Resurrection of the Dead* is therefore the return of the spiritually dead spirits from their exile into the kingdom of God. It is the homecoming of onetime deserters. For their permission to return and for their deliverance from constraint on the part of the ruler of the enemy's country, Lucifer, they are indebted to the Redeemer, Who by His victory over the hostile potentate secured the release of all those who sincerely repent of their ways and long to return to God. Christ was the first to descend to the dead inmates of Hell without being one of the number that had revolted against God. He also was the first to ascend to Heaven from thence. It had not been possible for any of the fallen spirits to do this before Him. Spirits, once they had entered Hell, were powerless to escape therefrom. Christ's ascent from the lower parts of the earth was the first 'resurrection of the dead', to which frequent reference is made by Paul in his Epistles, as in that to the Ephesians, in which he writes: 'Now, this, He ascended, what is it but that he also descended into the lower parts of the earth'? *(Ephesians 4 :9.)* By these Paul means the spheres of Hell, which, as I have told you, lie below the terrestrial spheres. To the Colossians he wrote: 'Having despoiled the principalities and the powers, he made a show of them openly, triumphing over them in it'. *(Colossians 2 : 15.)* The powers and principalities to which Paul refers are those of Hell, against which Christ fought, aided by the celestial legions after His descent, and which he overcame, forcing Lucifer, their prince to surrender those of his subjects who desired to escape from his rule. This fact is indicated in the same Epistle by the words: 'Having been buried with him in baptism, wherein you were also raised with him through faith in the working of God . . . and you, being dead, . . . you, I say, did he make alive together with him'. *(Colossians 2 : 12, 13.)* The Colossians to whom Paul's Epistle is addressed had also formerly been spiritually dead and subject to Lucifer, but in time they learned to believe in Christ and in the kingdom of God. By their faith they gave their allegiance to the Savior and shared in that kingdom, together with Him. Although it is said here of Christ that He was raised, this does not mean that He had been spiritually dead, but that He had visited the realm of those who had died in spirit and had, for the time being, gone beyond the boundaries of God's kingdom. In consequence He was, during His stay in Hell, spiritually dead to all appearances although not so in reality. God 'raised Him from the dead' insofar as He gave Christ power to overcome the forces of the realm of the dead, and thus brought Him back into the kingdom of celestial life.

"The 'resurrection of the dead' has therefore not the slightest reference to *the resurrection of the physical body.* There is *no resurrection of the 'flesh'* of which the catechisms of the various Christian creeds teach. These, in the early centuries of our era did not speak of the 'resurrection of the flesh', but of the 'resurrection of the dead', to convey the consoling message that all those who were dead in spirit, not excepting Lucifer, would ultimately come home to God. The false doctrine that the terrestrial bodies of those who had died would come back to life, is of later invention and is responsible for the alteration of the expression, in spite of the fact that Paul explicitly has given you the true doctrine in the words: 'It is sown a natural body; it is raised a spiritual body'. *(1st Corinthians 15 : 44.)*

"*Not even of Christ was the natural body raised.* Like the physical bodies of all mortals it had been created from the od of the earth and like them it returned to earth, with this exception, that it was not redissolved into terrestrial od by way of decay, but by dematerialization effected by the spirit-world. Similarly, the bodies of men like Enoch and Elijah had been dissolved into od. From the od of the earth are created all human bodies and into the od of the earth they are ultimately dissolved. This is a law which admits of no exceptions.

"To the Christians of today the 'resurrection of the dead' means the making anew of the physical body, and Christ's resurrection on Easter Sunday is regarded by them as the reunion of His spirit with His body which had lain in its grave for three days. These are wholly mistaken ideas, for, to repeat it once more, Christ's resurrection from the dead merely signifies His return from the realm of the spiritually dead, His return from Hell, into which His Spirit had descended. The Apostolic catechism expresses this correctly in the words: 'Descended unto Hell, on the third day risen from the dead. . .'

"The term 'resurrection of the dead' confuses you as it does, because the word 'death' means to you only the cessation of life on earth, and 'the dead' only corpses, graves and churchyards. You do not consider the usage of the language of the Bible, according to which 'death' means severance from God, and 'the dead', those who are so severed.

"To this misunderstanding the incorrect translation of certain Biblical passages has contributed liberally, as in the case of the Book of Job *(19 : 25, 26)*: 'I know that my Redeemer lives and at last he will stand upon the earth. Then shall I see God, though my skin is destroyed and my body without *flesh*'. These words have been completely distorted into the opposite meaning in the version: 'I know that my Redeemer lives and will at least *raise me from the dust, when I shall be covered with this my skin and in my flesh I shall see God*'.

"Another falsification, attributed to Saint Matthew, which speaks of the dead having risen on the day of the Crucifixion, whereas in reality it is related that an earthquake had cast bodies from their tombs, has already been pointed out to you.

"I should also mention a passage from the Gospel of Saint John *(5 : 28) reading:* 'For the hour comes, in which all that are in the *tombs* shall hear his voice, and shall come forth'. The word 'tombs' as here used signifies the same thing that Saint Peter calls 'prison' when he writes in his Epistle: 'In which also he went and preached unto the spirits in prison', *(1st Peter 3 :19)* and again: 'For God did not spare the angels when they sinned, but cast them into dungeons, and committed them to pits of darkness'. *(2nd Peter 2 : 4.)* That the word 'tombs' as used by John in the passage I have cited cannot mean places of interment, is sufficiently indicated by the words of Christ: 'The hour comes, *and now is,* when the dead shall hear the voice of the Son of God', for if the reference had been to graves, the resurrection of the dead would have begun then and there. What Christ meant by his words was the spiritually dead in Satan's dungeons, whom he intended to redeem on the occasion of His descent to Hell that He had in view, insofar as they might give heed to His voice.

"Furthermore, the fact that Christ after His death upon earth appeared to His followers in *material form* has led you to the erroneous conclusion that His spirit re-entered His former physical body. In reality He made Himself visible in the same manner in which all spirits do so, namely by the materialization of His spiritual body. Had not many spirits done this before Him? Did not three spirits, completely human in form, appear to Abraham, eating with him as Christ ate with His disciples after the Resurrection: Did not the archangel Raphael for many weeks accompany young Tobias, eating and drinking with him, until Tobias was convinced that he was dealing with an everyday man? Was it therefore anything unprecedented, that Christ should have shown Himself after His death to His disciples, and that He should have spoken with them or partaken of food and drink in their company? You have similar cases of materialization today. Evil spirits, also, are able to materialize themselves in the same manner.

"The true meaning of the 'resurrection of the dead' was made clear to the Apostles and the faithful by Divine spirits only after the Ascension, for whenever Christ during His stay on earth spoke to the Apostles upon the subject, they were unable to understand Him. 'And they kept the saying, questioning among themselves what the rising again from the dead should mean'. *(Mark 9 :10.)* Concerning the views of the Jewish priesthood of the day as to the 'rising of the dead', the Acts tell you: 'For the Sadducees say that there is no resurrection, neither angel, nor spirit; but the Pharisees confess both'. *(Acts 23 : 8.)*

"For his ability to return from the kingdom of the dead in spirit to the kingdom of God no one need place his dependence upon any human institution, be this an organized religion or a clergy, as claimed by the denominations of today and in particular by the Catholic church. He who has strayed from God may at all times communicate in spirit with God, the Father, and from Him receive pardon and strength to live righteously, without the aid of human intermediaries.

"7. Your former religion, on the contrary, teaches the necessity of the so-called *Sacraments* as the means of achieving salvation, and since these sacraments can be dispensed only by priests ordained by bishops, the Catholic Church possesses in that doctrine a perfect means of holding its followers to its organization, since according to its precepts, no one can attain unto God save through the mediation of a member of the priesthood.

"As you read the New Testament you will be struck by the fact that there is not one single word in the gospel of Christ and of His disciples on which the sacramental doctrine of yours can be based. Your sacraments, as interpreted by you, are institutions of human origin, as I am about to prove to you.

a. First and most important of the sacraments in your eyes, is that of *baptism.* You contend that baptism *per se,* or entirely independently of the attitude of the infant baptized, converts the same from an enemy of God into one of His children, by the effacement of the so-called original sin as well as by that of all personal sins. Hence you go so far as to baptize infants so young that they are utterly unaware that the rite is being performed. This shows a complete misconception of the significance of baptism, which, in the early days of Christianity, was merely an external rite emblematic of an attitude of mind. Baptism, therefore, wrought nothing new, as you preach, but was merely an external manifestation of the sentiments of him who received it. Thus the baptism administered by John was a public acknowledgement on the part of those whom he baptized, that they were ready to accept his gospel and to mend their ways. The essence of the rite lay in *its administration in public,* so that all men might know who those were that had been baptized.

"You may perhaps think that an attitude of mind requires no outward sign, but you mortals often deceive yourselves as to your own real sentiments and become quite sure of them only when called upon to manifest them in public. Then you frequently find that what you had considered the good within yourselves is not as great as you had imagined it to be.

"Among the multitudes that went out to hear the Baptist preach there were many who had *thought* that they were experiencing a change of heart, but when they were faced with *baptism in public* their courage failed them. The fear of man in them was stronger than the fear of God; they dreaded the taunts of their fellow men, and in particular, those of the Jewish priesthood which had not acknowledged John as Divinely sent. Because of this fear they therefore declined baptism. Had they not been faced with the choice between accepting or rejecting this *outward manifestation,* they would never have realized that as a matter of fact they were not yet ripe for the kingdom of God, for no dependence can be placed upon him who because of worldly considerations refuses to stand up in public for what he knows is true and right, and to accept all the worldly consequences of his action. He is of no service to the cause of God, for the things of the world mean more to him.

"It was for this very reason that Christ accepted baptism from John: He too wanted all men to see that He was making Himself a sponsor for the truth of the Baptist's gospel.

"As a sign of the acceptance of his gospel, John chose baptism by immersion. He might indeed have chosen any other symbol, but immersion in water was the most beautiful one indicative of the purpose of his preachings. He taught the cleansing from sin by virtue of an abandonment of previous evil-mindedness, and as the neophyte was cleansed physically by immersion and, in a manner, emerged from the water as a new being, so the acceptance of the truth would cleanse his soul and enable him as a new man to lead a life of obedience to God.

"It was because of the symbolic nature of the rite that Christ retained baptism with water as an outward sign of the acceptance of His gospel.

"You of today can form but little conception of the consequences drawn upon themselves by the early Christians by reason of the acceptance of baptism, in token of their conversion to Christianity. By it the Jewish converts exposed themselves to hatred and persecution on the part of their former co-religionists and particularly on the part of the Jewish priesthood. They were insulted in the streets, dragged to prison, stoned. The story of Paul and the fate of Stephen shows you the fanaticism with which the Jewry of the times persecuted those of their race who had become Christians. Their persecution by the Gentiles was equally savage. The pagan religion was that of the State, the worship of the gods, the festivals held in honor of the idols and the sacrifices offered to them being prescribed by law. It was therefore considered as a most serious offense against the State and its ruler, to fail in attendance at such acts of worship and sacrificial ceremonies, and was punishable with death and confiscation of property. On the other hand, no Christian could continue to lend his presence to such occasions, although he knew that if he were denounced, he must be prepared for the worst. The horrors that attended the persecution of the Christians by paganism are but too well known to you.

"How many so-called Christians of today do you think would be willing to accept a baptism involving such consequences to their lives and property? Yet he who lacks the courage to testify to his faith in the face of such sacrifices, is no true Christian.

"Baptism was therefore not regarded as dispensing inner grace, but as a mere symbol that the neophyte was ready to accept all consequences attendant upon the open confession of his belief.

"What, then, is the logical deduction? First and foremost, it follows that *the baptism of infant children is of no value,* since they are utterly incapable of recognizing the truth or of expressing a belief therein. For this reason the Christians of the earlier centuries never dispensed baptism to children, and hence, also, Christ commanded His Apostles that they should *first preach* the gospel and only *thereafter baptize* those who were ready to accept it. The second conclusion is the utter falsity of the doctrine of those Christian churches which teach that baptism purges a child of the original sin and that the souls of children who die unbaptized are forever lost. A cleansing from sin can be effected only by a determined effort to abandon the ways of evil, and not by any action that comes from without.

"Paul relates of some of the Christians of his day that they caused themselves to be baptized on behalf of persons who had already died. This was merely an exhibition of a neophyte's excess of zeal. No one can be baptized in another's place. Everyone must work out his own salvation, for in this there can be no substitution of persons. Nevertheless, the intentions of these converts were good: they merely sought to signify, that the deceased, were they alive, would also have accepted Christ's teaching and would have allowed themselves to be baptized in testimony thereof. It was a gesture of love for the departed.

"b. The second sacrament recognized by your Church is that of *'confirmation'*, on the occasion of which the bishop lays his hand upon the confirmed, whom he anoints and for whom he then offers a prayer. It is held that by virtue of this act the 'Holy Spirit' comes upon the confirmed, as it descended upon the Apostles on the day of Pentecost.

"It is true that Christ promised that after His resurrection He would send His Father's spirits to the faithful, but He did not make their sending contingent upon any ceremonies conducted by a bishop. The messengers from God were promised to all who were worthy to receive them, and even if there is, in the Acts, a reference to the laying on of the hands in connection with the outpouring of the Holy Spirit, the interrelation between the two things was quite different from the construction placed upon it today. The Elder laid his hand upon the person newly baptized or converted, in token of his admission to the community, and since the elders possessed mediumistic power to a high degree, the odic power of mediumistically gifted neophytes was so greatly increased by that act, that the messages of the spirits were frequently communicated through these neophytes. For this, a state of trance, properly speaking, was not necessary, the influence of the spirit-world being often the same as that which you have seen in the case of so-called 'inspirational mediums'. Persons under the spell of this influence uttered words of prayer or glorification of God, a manifestation known to you in connection with the early history of Christianity as 'praying in the spirit'. Frequently also they spoke words of admonition or advice which moved their hearers profoundly. Furthermore, the laying on of the hands was performed in the case of those to whom some special task had been assigned on behalf of the community, to signify that they were to be regarded as instruments of God after having been appointed as such by the Divine spirit-messengers.

"If therefore the Apostle Paul warns his fellow-worker Timothy to 'lay hands hastily on no man', he has two things in mind: one of these is, that Timothy must not assist anyone to become a medium unless he has first made sure of his disposition and loyalty to the faith, lest the medium should later devote his powers to evil ends and thereby cause serious harm to spiritual welfare of the community. The second reason is, that no one should be sanctioned by the laying on of hands as an instrument for a given mission unless specifically assigned to that mission by a Divine spirit. A person on whom the power of healing had been bestowed could be employed only as a healer, and not, for instance, as a teacher, a duty for which he was neither called nor qualified. 'Are all apostles'? asks Paul in his Epistle to the Corinthians, 'Are all prophets? are all teachers? are all workers of miracles? have all gifts of healings? do all speak with tongues? do all interpret?' *(1st Corinthians 12 : 29, 30.)* And when Paul admonishes Timothy to 'stir up the gift of God which is in thee through the laying on of my hands', he is referring to the gift of teaching, for, under the direction of a Divine spirit Timothy had been commissioned by Paul, through the laying on of hands, to teach the gospel of salvation and had been sent forth on that mission, but because of the many difficulties which he had encountered in the performance of his mission as a teacher, he had become listless and despondent.

"If you will compare the workings of the spirits in the early days of the Christian era with the doctrines on the subject that obtain today, you will see how widely in this matter also you have strayed from the truth. The Spirit of God will not submit to being dispensed by mortals through outward gestures and according to human whim. It comes, without the intervention of bishops and episcopal rites, to those whose inner lives have rendered them worthy of it and who desire it with heart and soul. The Spirit of God 'bloweth where it listeth', not where man listeth that it should blow.

"Before Christ brought redemption, the spirit of darkness pervaded all mankind, exerting thereon its sinister influence. This you can see from the many cases of mental obsession recorded in the Scriptures in connection with the cures effected by Christ. In other cases the victims suffered physical injury at the hands of the evil spirits; thus you read in the Gospels of people who had been struck dumb, deaf, blind, or epileptic under their influence. At times it was a single demon that fell upon his victim, at other times a host of demons. 'My name is Legion; for we are many', was the admission of one of them.

"Even if the majority of men were not so palpably affected by the Powers of Evil as were those who suffered bodily torments at the hands of demons, nevertheless even in their case the influence of evil was such as to prevent them from seeing the truth and the path of righteousness, and to harden their hearts.

"However, not even the Redemption has wrought any change in the influence of the evil spirits upon those people who by reason of their lack of faith continue, voluntarily, to expose themselves to such influence. Satan exerts his power, now as then, upon all *who belong to him at heart.* In this present age also there are many cases of persons possessed of demons, incorrectly classed by you with the mentally deranged whose madness is due to a diseased condition of the brain.

"The power of evil over those who return to a faith in God and to obedience to His word was broken by the Redemption, but even they must continue to fight, and require, as Paul says, 'the whole armor of God, that they may be able to stand against the wiles of the devil. For our wrestling is not against flesh and blood, but against the principalities, against the powers, against the world-rulers of this darkness, against the spiritual hosts of wickedness in the universe'. *(Ephesians 6 : 11, 12.)*

"c. The third sacrament recognized by the Catholic Church is known as the *'Eucharist'*. Other creeds call it the 'Communion'; Paul refers to it as 'the Lord's Supper'. This also has been converted in the course of centuries into something quite different from that which Christ intended that it should be.

"Sacrificial feasts were common features in the religious rites of both Jews and pagans, and constituted an essential part of their ceremonies. Animals were slaughtered in consecrated places, their blood was poured out to the deity in whose honor also certain parts of the flesh were burned, while the rest was eaten by the worshippers at a communal feast. Not only animals, but fruit, bread, wine, oil and the like were offered in sacrifice. A part of these things was destroyed in honor of the deity, the rest being consumed as an act of devotion. The portion which was burned or poured out to the gods served, as you know, to prepare the power-current required for spirit-communications.

"But even the part which was consumed by the worshippers was regarded as sacred and as sanctified by the gods. The eating and drinking of the sacrificial remnants was a *symbol* of inner communion with the deity itself, for just as the consecrated food and drink became united to the body of him who consumed them, so the participants at the feast were supposed to become united to the deity as instruments to perform its wishes. Such was the significance of the sacrificial feasts held by Jews and pagans alike.

"The feast of the Passover of the Jews on the anniversary of the exodus from Egypt was emblematic of their wish to remain in communion with the God Who had manifested Himself to them through Moses, their savior, and to abide by His commandments for all time. It was therefore the symbol of their redemption from the bondage of Egypt under the leadership of Moses as their God-given leader.

"Christ was the great Emissary of God, foreshadowed and foretold by Moses, and destined to lead mankind out of the bondage of Satan, the Pharaoh of Hell. On the eve of the day on which He was to consummate the deliverance of mankind by His death and His victory over Hell, He celebrated in the company of His disciples the same feast that had once been celebrated by Moses on the eve of the deliverance of the Jewish people. This feast was intended to have a twofold significance: His impending departure from earth by the death of His body, and His intention to remain united with His followers in spirit.

"In token of these things He selected bread and wine. Taking the bread, He broke it, and gave it to His disciples with the words: 'This is the symbol of my body which is given for you. This do in remembrance of me'! As He now broke the bread into pieces, so upon the day to follow was His earthly body to be broken in death and divorced from life.

"Likewise He took a cup of wine and let all drink thereof, saying: 'This cup is the new covenant in my blood, even that which is poured out for you. As often as ye do drink of it, remember me!'. As the wine flowed from the cup, so on the day of His death was the blood to flow from His body.

"In its essence, however, this meal was symbolical of the spiritual communion which Christ meant to maintain with His followers despite the fact that He would be parted from them on earth. As the bread which He distributed to the disciples had been a single loaf, and as the wine which they drank had been a single cupful, so the disciples were to constitute thenceforth but a single unit in spirit with Christ as well as among themselves. It was for this unity that Christ prayed so fervently and touchingly on this evening. He admonished them to preserve their love for their Master in their hearts and by it to remain united with Him in a spiritual body of which Christ would be the head and they the members. This they were besought to remember as often as they came together in order to repeat the meal in memory of the one of which He had partaken with them in farewell. Nor must they forget that it was a feast of love which their Lord and Master had held with them and that only those might take part in the observance of this meal who were united with God and men by bonds of love. Whoever does not feel this love in his heart is not fit to receive the rite commemorative of love, for whosoever harbors within him hatred, enmity, anger, envy and other forms of spite against his neighbor would be guilty of the greatest hypocrisy by receiving communion. It would be an insult of the most flagrant kind to Him Who instituted this rite in commemoration of His love, wherefore all who contemplate receiving it should search their hearts, to know whether they truly love the Lord and their neighbors, since otherwise the communion would be a mockery of Christ.

"That is the real significance of the Lord's Supper and of its observance in commemoration of Him.

"What, however, has been done to this rite in the course of the centuries? The doctrine has been established that Christ, by virtue of the words which He spoke in the act of distributing the bread and the wine, had converted the bread into His actual body and the wine into His actual blood; that therefore the bread and the wine had not been mere symbols, but that the bread had turned into Christ's living body and the wine into His living blood, although the transsubstantiation was not perceptible to the human senses. It is further asserted that the same transsubstantiation takes place even today, whenever a priest pronounces the words of Christ over the bread and the wine.

"This is perhaps the most preposterous doctrine which the human mind has ever been asked to accept. It would signify that on the occasion of the Last Supper in the guest chamber at Jerusalem Christ's person had been present twenty-three-fold at the same instant; He was present before the Apostles in body; every morsel of the bread eaten by the eleven disciples is supposed to have been the living person of Christ, and every sip of the wine which they drank is likewise supposed to have been Christ, body and soul, flesh and blood.

"It is inconceivable that human beings could invent such a chimera. No man and no spirit can multiply himself. Not even God can do so. No one, — not even God, — can be present in body in more places than one at the same time. No one can convert himself into another form and yet remain what he really is. Christ could not sit before His Apostles as a man while they were partaking of Him in the shape of bread and wine. Christ could not eat Himself, for inasmuch as He also partook of the bread of which He gave to His disciples, He was eating His own body, according to your view.

"I can find no words in your language adequate to brand this doctrine as the supreme exhibition of human delusion.

"Furthermore, you teach that the same transsubstantiation is effected daily by your priests and that when they pronounce the words: 'This is my body; this is my blood', every crumb of bread and every drop of wine consecrated by them are changed into the person of Christ. On this assumption, your priests presume to a power which not God Himself possesses, because not even He can bring about the inherently impossible.

"You may protest all you will that this is an unfathomable mystery; you may call it a mystery of the faith; the fact of the untruth of this doctrine remains. The word 'mystery' can be used to cover any human fallacy. Words are always available, even if they convey no sense.

"There is one thing in connection with this doctrine at which I never cease to wonder. You surely read the Bible; has it never occurred to you that in the entire New Testament there is not a shred of evidence to support your preposterous view? If, at the Lord's Supper, the bread and wine had been changed into the true Christ, the Apostles certainly would never have wearied of pointing to this incomprehensible miracle. It would have been recorded minutely in the Gospels, in addition to which the Apostles would have referred to this supper of leavetaking again and again in their Epistles to the early Christians. On the contrary, you cannot find one single reference to it. The Apostle John who reclined beside his Master during the supper and who was the first to receive a morsel of the consecrated bread, says nothing whatever in his Gospel of the distribution by Christ of the bread and wine. He relates that Jesus washed the disciples' feet. He relates His betrayal by Judas. Is it reasonable that he should have said nothing of the most mysterious and mightiest event in the life of Jesus? The Epistles make no mention of the Supper. In the Acts it is recorded only that the early Christians 'continued steadfastly in the apostles' teaching and fellowship, in the breaking of bread and the prayers'. Here therefore the observances of the Supper is described as 'breaking of bread', and not as the ceremony which you have made out of it today. The bread was broken as a symbol of the death of Christ and of the love which they bore to one another and to Him. It was bread that they broke and ate, but while so doing, their thoughts and their prayers were directed to Him Who had promised them: 'For where two or three are gathered together in my name, there am I in the midst of them'. The partaking of the bread and wine meant to them a sacred token of their spiritual fellowship with the Redeemer.

"The Apostle Paul who wrote numerous Epistles to the churches is the only one to refer to the Lord's Supper, as he does in his first letter to the Corinthians, but not even he would have mentioned it, had he not been compelled to do so by circumstances, having learned that the observance of the Supper by the Corinthian community was often marked by unseemly conduct.

"Among the early Christians the observance of the communion included partaking of a complete meal, as indeed had been true of Christ's supper in Jerusalem, for before He gave His disciples bread and wine in remembrance of Him, He had eaten of the paschal lamb and of the other dishes, and drunk wine together with them. So too the early Christians, when observing the communion, began with meats and other dishes, and partook of wine. Not until the end of the feast did they break bread, and drank from a common chalice in remembrance of Christ.

"They were, however, human, and had the same human failings that all men have, as unfortunately was made evident during the communion service in Corinth. This was held in private dwellings, and since the owners of these dwellings were in no position to supply the meal for the entire community — most of the early Christians belonging to the poor, — it was necessary for all who participated to bring with them their own food and drink for the meal that preceded the rite. Under the circumstances it sometimes happened that the very poor brought little or nothing at all, contenting themselves with partaking only of the communion-service proper after the conclusion of the feast. Too often they had to witness how the more affluent members of the community consumed plentiful repasts accompanied by copious drafts of wine, and how, upon occasion, they exceeded the bounds of discretion and became drunk. Conditions of this kind could not be tolerated, not alone because they gave offense to the poor who were obliged to observe them, but chiefly because they were entirely out of keeping with the solemnity of the occasion.

"When, therefore, Paul had heard of occurences of this sort in the Corinthian community, he stepped in and called the Corinthians sharply to task for their behavior, and in so doing he could scarcely avoid speaking to them of the true significance of the communion. He opens the subject by criticising their conduct at the Lord's table. 'When therefore you assemble yourselves together, it is not possible to eat the Lord's supper: for in your eating each one takes before others his own supper; and one is hungry, and another is drunken. What, have you not houses to eat and to drink in? or do you despise the congregation of God, and put them to shame that have not? What shall I say to you? shall I praise you? In this I praise you not'. *(1st Corinthians 11 : 20-22.)*

"He next proceeded to point out to them the significance of the rite, although in their case no lengthy explanations were necessary, since he had already taught them of the subject orally. Citing the words uttered by Christ at the supper in Jerusalem, he thus summarized their import: 'As often as ye eat this bread and drink the cup, ye proclaim the Lord's death till he come'. The Lord's Supper is therefore a partaking of bread and wine in token of the death of Christ, Who gave His life out of love for the fallen spirits, and those who during a rite observed in His memory treated the symbols of the Redeemer's body in so unworthy a manner as did some of the Corinthians, sinned not only against those symbols, but against Christ Himself, as he who misbehaves at a festival given in honor of his sovereign, commits an offense against the sovereign's person, and is punished accordingly. 'Wherefore whosoever shall eat the bread or drink the cup of the Lord in an unworthy manner, shall be guilty of the body and the blood of the Lord'. Paul now exhorts his hearers to search their souls before receiving the communion, in order to make sure that his thoughts are as the Savior would them be. 'But let a man prove himself, and so let him eat of the bread and drink of the cup. For he that eateth and drinketh, eateth and drinketh judgment unto himself, if he discern not the body'. But whosoever treats bread and wine, when administered as the tokens of the highest and holiest act of love in all creation, with indifference or contempt, whoever partakes of them while he is drunk or in some other equally objectionable state, draws upon himself the Divine ire, for even men will resent the slighting of a gift which they have made in memory of themselves. Lack of respect for the tokens of Christ's death and of His love manifests itself above all things in the communicant's frame of mind. At a rite held in commemoration of love, it is eminently unfitting that the hearts of the participants be filled with feelings of an opposite kind. The Lord's Supper is not a rite to be received when the heart is full of rancor, enmity, bitterness and other sentiments that offend against the love for one's neighbor. On this score also the Corinthians had sinned heavily, for as Paul says '. . . ye come together not for the better but for the worse. For first of all . . . I hear that divisions exist among you', indicating that they had sinned against the precept of neighborly love.

"Under these circumstances it is not to be wondered at that the Apostle stigmatized many of the Corinthian Christians as 'weak and sickly, and not a few sleep', by which he meant that they had gone to the length of becoming indifferent to God.

"As you see, nothing in Paul's Epistles indicates that he regarded bread and wine in any other light than as symbols of Christ's body and blood. Had the bread ceased to be bread, as you teach, and had it been changed into the body of Christ, Paul would have said so very clearly. How much more emphatically would this fiery disciple have spoken to the Corinthians, had he believed in the transsubstantiation of the bread!

"Already, in an earlier part of the same Epistle, Paul had mentioned the communion in connection with his discussion of idolatrous festivals. In that passage he compares these with the Christian observance of the communion-rite. The meaning of his words is as follows: By eating the flesh of beasts sacrificed to the idols, the Gentiles have communion with the demons. The flesh itself is nothing out of the ordinary; it is flesh, and remains such, like any other flesh. But the intention with which it is offered and eaten by the Gentiles is the factor which allows them to hold communion with the evil spirits. On the other hand, Christians have communion with Christ by receiving bread and wine, which do not change their nature by virtue of this rite, but remain what they were. It is only the intention with which they partake of the consecrated bread and wine that enables them to have communion with Him. Because of this, Christians are forbidden to take part in pagan sacrificial feasts, since thereby they would be in communion with the evil spirits. 'You cannot drink the cup of the Lord, and the cup of the demons; you cannot partake of the table of the Lord, and of the table of the demons'. *(1st Corinthians 10 : 21.)* The bread and the wine partaken of by the Christians are changed by virtue of the rite into the body of Christ as little as the flesh eaten by the Gentiles underwent any change whatever. In both cases it is true that communication is established with the spirit-world: in the case of the heathens this was a communication with the demons accompanied by the symbolical consumption of flesh and wine, while with the Christians it was a communication with Christ, symbolized by bread and wine. Furthermore, just as the heathens at their festivals came into communication not only with the particular demon in whose honor the feast was held, but with the entire world of evil spirits, which constitutes a single unit, so the Christians by receiving the bread and wine had communion not alone with the individual Spirit of Christ, but with all the spirits in God's kingdom whose ruler He is. Paul describes this great community by the term 'the Lord's body'. Christ is its head, and all created spirits of good, including all men who believe in God are its members. Whoever, therefore, is in communion with Christ, is in communion with the members of His spiritual body also. This communion is particularly symbolized at the Lord's Supper by single loaf; as this, prior to its distribution constituted a whole, so the many among whom it is distributed are held to constitute one unit in love. 'Seeing that we, who are many, are one bread, one body; for we all partake of the one bread'. *(1st Corinthians 10 : 17.)*

"The image, that all who belong to Christ form one spiritual body with Him is frequently employed by Paul in his Epistles. It is the same thing as that which you call the 'communion of the saints' in your creed.

"In support of your false doctrine of the transsubstantiation of bread and wine into the person of Christ, you quote the words allegedly used by Him: 'This *is* my body — this *is* my blood', emphasizing that in both cases He said 'is' and not 'signifies'. How do you know that in the language which He spoke He used a word corresponding to your word 'is'? You know nothing whatever of the Aramaic tongue spoken by Him and you no longer have the original Greek text of the New Testament. In reality, Christ at the Last Supper said nothing to indicate anything beyond a reference to the bread and the wine as symbolizing His impending death on behalf of the Redemption of the world.

"Let us assume, however, that He really said: 'This *is* my body — this *is* my blood'. Everyone familiar with the Bible knows that Christ prevailingly spoke allegorically, as He himself says: 'These things have I spoken unto you in parables: the hour comes, when I shall no more speak unto you in parables. . .' *(John 16 : 25.)* Do you recall when it was that He spoke these words? As you will find, it was on the occasion of the Last Supper, but a few hours before His death. As a man He spoke only in allegory. 'All these things spoke Jesus in parables unto the multitudes; and without a parable spoke he nothing unto them'. *(Matthew 13 : 34.)* Moreover, on the eve of His death He spoke not only of bread and wine as symbolical of His approaching end, but in another allegory he pictured His relation to the disciples: 'I am the vine, you are the branches'. *(John 15 : 5.)* If therefore you are not willing to accept the bread and the wine in a figurative sense, you cannot assign an allegorical meaning to His words of the vine and its branches, and are forced to admit that by speaking these words, Christ became a vine and His disciples became its branches. The mode of expression is the same in both cases, and one metamorphosis is no more difficult to conceive than the other, both being equally impossible.

"It is easy to understand why the Catholic Church should collect even the most far-fetched evidence contained in the Bible to support its preposterous doctrine. Thus it accepts other figurative expressions literally, as where Christ says of Himself that He is the bread that came down from heaven, and that His flesh is 'meat indeed' and His blood is 'drink indeed'. These sayings are to be taken in a spiritual sense, as Christ never wearies of repeating. It is the Spirit that gives life; the flesh profits nothing: the words that I have spoken unto you are spirit, and are life'. *(John 6 : 63.)* Speaking of Himself, He says: 'My meat is to do the will of him that sent me and to accomplish his work'. To the Samaritan woman at the well of Jacob He promises that the 'water' which He will give shall become a well of water springing up unto eternal life'. All of these sayings are allegories and can never be taken literally without involving the sheerest absurdities. Christ is not truly a vine nor are His disciples truly branches thereof. The bread and the wine at the Lord's table are not actually His body nor His blood. These expressions were meant in a figurative, spiritual, sense, and were so understood by the Apostles and by the Christians of the early centuries.

"The service which centers about the alleged transsubstantiation of bread and wine into the person of Christ is known to Catholics as the 'Mass'. It is also referred to as the re-enactment of the Crucifixion. There is no such thing as a re-enactment of the death of Christ, not even a bloodless re-enactment. Just how, do you imagine, Christ's death on the Cross would be re-enacted bloodlessly? You probably do not think at all, because the subject admits of no rational thinking.

"The Mass has come about by an amplification of the prayers offered at the Lord's Supper in early Christian times, but in the course of the centuries it has lost those features which made of it a communion rite and a rite commemorative of the Lord. Thus the present-day Mass retains nothing good except a series of prayers which can as well be said in private by anyone without the assistance of any priest. The faith placed by Catholics in the efficacy of paid-for Masses is unfortunately a great delusion.

"Restore to the people the communion-service of the Apostolic days, which was a sacred and beneficent rite! It should be observed frequently, the most appropriate occasion therefor being the eve or the day itself of your more important church-festivals. Other days also, which are of special significance to you, are appropriate times for observing this rite. You may do so without outside help, if you will, at home in your own family circle. No priests nor clericals of any other kind, no churches, are necessary. In every gathering of the faithful there will be someone qualified to conduct the communion-service in a becoming manner.

"Because of the importance of the subject I shall give you a brief outline of the ritual to be followed.

"The bread to be used had best be unleavened, or what you know as 'matzoth'. The wine, which may be either red or white, is contained in a chalice of glass or crystal. Both are placed upon a table covered with a white cloth, the vessel containing the wine being kept covered until it is used, in order to prevent any contamination of its contents. Similarly, the bread may be covered with a clean napkin. In addition, you may follow the custom of the early Christians by placing upon the table a simple cross, not a crucifix. Behind the cross are ranged seven candles, so placed that the center one is directly behind the cross, and close to the same.

"When you have met at the appointed hour, open the service with a song appropriate to the occasion. After this, prayer is offered by the person officiating as leader, in his words, followed by the recital of some Psalm suited to the hour. He may, if he likes, select such verses from a number of different Psalms as he likes, considers most fitting. Next in order is a selected reading from the Holy Writ, and if, furthermore, anyone present is qualified to deliver a short address, this also will be of value.

"Thereupon the congregation devotes several minutes to silent reflection, each member thinking of his sins and short-comings and contritely asking pardon of God. This is followed by the recital by the leader, or by the whole congregation in unison, of the 130th Psalm: 'Out of the depths have I cried unto thee, O God!'
At the conclusion of this psalm, the leader approaches the table and in words of his own choosing prays that the Lord may bless the bread and wine, in order that they may conduce to the welfare of all who partake thereof. He thereupon breaks morsels from the loaf and hands them, one by one, to each worshipper present, with the words: 'Take, eat; this is in token of the body of Christ,

our Redeemer, Who died upon the Cross in order that we might be saved!' These words are pronounced once only, and very slowly, during the distribution of the bread, which the worshippers eat as soon as they receive it, the last in order to eat being the officiating member himself. In the like manner he then passes the cup from member to member, saying: 'Drink ye all of it; this is in token of the blood of our Lord Jesus Christ, which was poured out for us unto the remission of our sins!' Again, the leader is the last to drink of the cup. He then offers a prayer of thanksgiving and the rite is closed with a song.

"If a deep-trance medium should be present, the spirit which speaks through him will take charge of the service and give the needful directions.

"It is in no sense out of place that the communion-service be followed by a social occasion which may include a supper and an evening spent in enjoyable conversation, for it is right that you should feel happy and manifest that feeling outwardly. It is right that you should enjoy not only the spiritual gifts of God, but also His temporal blessings joyously and cheerfully, without exceeding the bounds of propriety.

"d. The Catholic Church has a *Sacrament of Penance.* According to the precepts of the New Testament, 'penance' signifies a change of heart. John the Baptist preached repentance as a means to obtain forgiveness for sins, and of Christ it is related: 'From that time began Jesus to preach, and to say, Repent you; for the kingdom of heaven is at hand'. *(Matthew 4 : 17.)* The words: 'Repent ye', literally translated, read: 'Change your manner of thinking'. Repentance is therefore a spiritual change, by which the mind ceases to harbor evil thoughts and turns to God. Whoever lays aside a former evil habit and acquires a good one, gives evidence of a change of heart, and numbers among the penitent.

"The Catholics give a far wider scope to the sacrament of penance. They do not regard reformation in thought and conduct as sufficient, but their Church demands rather, as unconditional for such reformation and reconciliation with God, the confession of each individual grave sin before a Catholic priest, who alone, according to its teachings, has the power to act in God's place in granting pardon. For Catholics, there can be no pardon without priestly absolution, and in this way the Church binds its adherents fast to the priesthood and to the churchly organization. This is the spiritual club by which it exercises unrestricted domination over their souls.

" 'Who can forgive sins, save God alone?' In addressing this question to Christ, the scribes were in the right. No mortal, and no priest, can grant absolution; even Christ could not. It is true that God can commission a mortal as His instrument to tell a sinner that his sins are forgiven. An instruction of this kind was given by Him to the prophet, Nathan, whom God sent to David to say that He had pardoned him for the sins of adultery and murder. Similarly, Christ had been specially empowered by God to remit sin in the individual cases in which He told the sinners that they had been forgiven. He did not grant this pardon as coming from Himself nor at His own discretion, but announced it only to those whom God, through His spirit-messengers, had designated as being worthy of it. This is confirmed by Christ, in that He expressly tells His opponents that He has been given authority on earth to forgive sins, not an authority to cover all cases at His own pleasure, but special authority in each individual instance.

"The Catholic priest, however, asserts that he has been invested by his bishop with the power to grant or deny absolution according to his own human judgment. How can he tell whether God has pardoned the sins in one case and not in another? Or does he delude himself into thinking that God will pardon one sinner because he has been absolved by a priest, and deny pardon to another because a priest has refused to absolve him? Or do the Divine spirit-messengers direct the priest when to grant and when to deny absolution? Has the priest any other supernatural gifts to guide him in this decision? Can he read in the hearts of his confessants whether God has forgiven their sins? The Catholic priesthood must admit that it is not so gifted. How can they assure a fellow man that God has pardoned his sins, when they have not the slightest grounds for knowing whether they are telling him the truth? The priest can neither read the heart of his confessant, nor know the will of God, and if you reply that absolution is given only on condition that the confessant truly repents of his sin and strives earnestly to mend his ways, the futility of priestly absolution lies in the very fact that the priest is never in a position to know whether his confessant is sincere. He cannot, therefore, in any instance say: 'I absolve thee', but at the most he may say: 'May God absolve thee!' One need not be a priest in order to utter a wish of this kind, which is merely the expression of a desire that exerts no effect and may be spoken by anyone. However, the priest says, 'I absolve thee', and thereby pronounces a sentence of whose validity in the eyes of God he knows nothing.

What would be thought of a judge of your temporal courts who pronounced sentences without knowing whether they were legally valid? His proceeding would be considered farcical. This applies to the Catholic doctrine of the remission of sins through a priest, as your common sense will tell you. The truth of the matter is this: whoever sincerely repents of his sins and turns to God, will be forgiven by Him, regardless of whether or not he has received the forgiveness of a priest, and whoever does not repent, will not be forgiven by God, no matter how often he may have received priestly absolution. Your doctrine of the remission of sins by priests is therefore one of the great human fallacies which have crept into religion in the course of time.

"In support of its contention that its priests have the power of granting absolution, the Catholic Church invokes a spurious Biblical passage, to which I called your attention on the occasion of our first meeting. This reads: 'Whose soever sins you forgive, they are forgiven unto them; whose soever sins you retain, they are retained. *(John 20 : 23.)* As you already know, a slight alteration of the Greek text has been made at this place, thereby completely changing the sense of the passage. Instead of 'unto them' the original text read 'unto you' whence the passage would read: 'Whose soever sins you forgive, they are forgiven unto you. Whose soever sins you retain (or do not forgive), they shall be retained unto you'. In these words Christ voices the same precept that is contained in the words of the Lord's prayer: 'Forgive us our trespasses, as we forgive those who trespass against us', and in the words that He uttered immediately thereafter: 'For if you forgive men their trespasses, your heavenly Father will also forgive you. But if you forgive not men their trespasses, neither will your Father forgive your trespasses'. *(Matthew 6 : 14.)*

"Inasmuch as the faculty of remitting sins, such as is claimed by the Catholic Church, does not and cannot exist, it was never either taught nor exercised in the early days of Christianity. Hence the Christians of those times were never required to confess their sins to a priest, but were urged, in accordance with the precepts of Christ, to confess their sins to *one another,* namely those sins which one of them had committed against his fellow-Christian. They were expected to acknowledge those wrongs which they had committed against their neighbors to the neighbors themselves and thereby effect a reconciliation, for this, after all, is the only and the quickest way of making atonement. If a person who has offended you comes to you and admits that he was in the wrong, you will gladly make up with him. It is this that Christ means when He says: 'If therefore thou art offering thy gift at the altar, and there remembered that thy brother hath aught against thee, leave there thy gift before the altar, and go thy way, first be reconciled to thy brother, and then come and offer thy gift'. *(Matthew 5 : 23, 24.)*

"If confession before a priest and absolution by him were necessary for the remission of sins, Christ would not have neglected to point this fact out to the Apostles, inasmuch as it would have constituted the most important part of the Gospel, since without forgiveness no one can enter the kingdom of Heaven. Nevertheless, neither Christ nor the Apostles make any mention of confession before a priest, nor of absolution by the same.

"Confession and absolution by a priest are human institutions which do not make the road to God any easier for the believer, but render it more difficult for him by lulling him into a false sense of security. He confesses, receives absolution, and goes his way, thinking that he has made his peace with God, and thereby suffers a great deception. Every error incurred on the road to salvation is like the wrong path taken by the wanderer, leading him away from, rather than toward his goal.

"No little importance is attached by your one-time religion to penitential exercises. This creed prescribes abstinence from certain kinds of food on certain days, considers physical castigation in the light of a high degree of excellence, recommends pilgrimages, and demands celibacy of its priests and monks. None of these things have any connection with the true idea of repentance and inner perfection. Christ never fasted voluntarily and never mortified the flesh. When He fasted in the wilderness it was because of necessity, since the desert offered no nourishment. Consequently you will not find a word in the teachings of Christ or in the Epistles of the disciples enjoining abstinence from given kinds of food, or physical castigation. On the contrary, matters of this kind are described as being of no value; thus Paul writes to the Corinthians: 'The food which we eat in no way affects us in the eyes of God'. *(1st Corinthians 8 : 8),* and to the Colossians: 'If, then, being members of Christ, you have freed yourselves wholly from the spirit powers that rule the world, why do you still submit to its ordinances, as though you were worldly? Among these ordinances I might mention: 'Do not touch this, do not eat that, — do not handle this'. According to the laws and doctrines of men, whoever violates these ordinances shall perish. It is true, that all such ordinances are reputed as wise; that they acquire the standing of religious precepts and are regarded as a sign of humility and as serving to subdue the flesh, but they have no real value whatever, and serve only to make men self-sufficient'. *(Colossians 2 : 20-23.)*

"All of the ordinances imposed upon men by the various Christian denominations originated not with Christ, but, as Paul writes to Timothy, with those who have fallen away from the faith, 'God's spirit declares expressly that in times to come many will fall away from the faith, and, turning to the spirits of deceit, will spread doctrines inspired by demons. They will be led into this by lying preachers who stamp their own consciences with the brand of guilt. These men forbid marriage and exact abstinence from certain foods which God has created to be eaten with thankfulness by those who believe and by all who have come to a full knowledge of the truth. For all things created by God are good and nothing is to be reckoned among the things forbidden, if you can partake thereof with a prayer of thanks to God, seeing that it has been sanctified by the world by which God created it, and by your prayer'. *(1st Timothy 4 : 1-5.)*

"The Catholic Church is one of those which lays great stress upon abstinence from food on specified days, for which a single meal is prescribed by it. It forbids its clergy to marry and regards the monastic state as the most perfect. That church also has 'given heed to doctrines of demons', for these precepts are purely human ordinances, which according to the words of the Apostle, may 'have a show of wisdom', but are not of any value for the salvation of men, and consequently, no church has the right to force such ordinances upon its followers and to brand any infraction thereof as a grave sin.

"It is true that your Church maintains, as regards its ordinance of celibacy, that there is no compulsion in the matter, since no one is obliged to enter the priesthood or any of the orders. True enough, nobody is forced to become a priest, a monk, or a nun, but if anyone believes that he has been called to proclaim the Gospel in the capacity of a priest, that Church does compel him to vow celibacy, giving him the choice only between abandoning his chosen calling, or taking the vow to live a life ordained not by God but by ecclesiastical precept. He is, therefore, subjected to the greatest moral stress which can be exerted upon man, for although the church openly compels no one to join a religious order and in consequence, to remain unmarried, it nevertheless exercises psychic pressure of the most powerful kind by picturing a monastic existence as the acme of perfection. Now it so happens that it is precisely the best who regard it as their duty to attain to this ideal, and since this has been falsely held up to them as a celibate life as the member of some order, they are ready to make this sacrifice, impelled as they are by an irresistable desire to become perfect.

"Let it not be said that God gives strength to those who feel called to join the priesthood or a religious order to lead a life of unblemished chastity. That is an utter delusion. God gives strength only for the fulfillment of His own will, not for the accomplishment of that which men impose upon themselves or on their fellows out of an outward show of voluntarily assumed saintliness, as they call it, and in violation of His laws. Goodness and perfection lie only in doing that which is in keeping with the will of God and the performance of which is at all times wholly voluntary. Nothing, however, can be good or perfect if done under compulsion, not even if the first step be voluntarily taken and subsequently involves lifelong compulsion. Not even God exercises compulsion upon any man to force him to do His will. How then can a church deprive man of his right of self-determination, a right upon which God Himself never encroaches? Compulsion and enslavement are the measures by which Evil governs; the rule of Goodness is based on liberty. Evil, and nothing else, has introduced oppression into religion. The mania for unrestricted power over others is responsible for the introduction into the Catholic Church of the suppression of personal liberty in the guise of achieving saintliness. The celibacy of the clergy as well as the monastic life with its vows of poverty, chastity, and implicit obedience to spiritual authority are the most powerful weapons of the Catholic religion for strengthening its internal organization. Neither Christ nor the Apostles have any knowledge of a priesthood such as the Catholic; they know nothing of any religious orders. They never taught nor founded anything of that nature. They did not proclaim that ideal perfection lay in taking vows of poverty and of chastity in the form of celibacy, and least of all, in blind obedience to ecclesiastical superiors.

"They know of no *voluntary poverty* as the Catholic Church defines the term. They founded no monastic orders, nor did they teach that such should be founded for men to enter, and on entering, endow them with their worldly goods. Can the members of monastic orders truthfully be called poor? Are they not rather relieved for the rest of their days of all worry on the score of support? Is not the table set for them every day? Is that what you call poverty? If all men were as well off, there would be no poverty in the world. And if ideal perfection is to be found in poverty, how is it that so many monasteries are rich in worldly possessions? If poverty is the ideal condition for the individual, it must also be the ideal condition for the community. Again, why do not your clergy who preach voluntary poverty as the highest form of saintliness, practice it themselves? He who preaches an ideal should surely be the first to practice it himself. Or do you perhaps call your clergy poor? Is the Pope poor? Are the bishops? Are the priests? There would be no poor people on earth if every man were blessed with worldly goods possessed by those who preach poverty as a virtue.

"In order to prove that voluntary poverty is necessary to perfection, you invoke Christ's speech to the rich youth, but your interpretation of His words is quite incorrect. When Christ said: 'One thing thou lackest yet: sell all that thou hast, and distribute unto the poor, and thou shalt have treasure in heaven: and come, follow me', this advice was tendered to that particular youth whose heart was set upon his wealth, which had become a snare unto him and a hindrance on the road Godward. When, on receiving this advice, the youth turned away, the Lord said to His disciples: 'How hardly shall they that have riches enter into the kingdom of God'! Not all, however, who are blessed with worldly goods are rich in the sense in which Christ used the word, but only those whose hearts are set upon Mammon and who make a god of him. Abraham, Isaac, Job, and David were wealthy in the worldly sense, without belonging to that class of the rich to which Christ referred, for their wealth did not stand in their way on their road to God. Not men like them would He have counselled to sell all they had, in order to lay up treasures in heaven. It was a different matter in the case of the rich youth whose love of riches was such that it would not let him follow the call of God. Rather than renounce these, he renounced the kingdom of heaven.

"All men encounter obstacles when they attempt to come nearer to God, the nature of these obstacles varying with the individual. It is the task of everyone to remove the obstacle peculiar to himself, as is indicated in the words of Christ: 'If thy eye causeth thee to stumble, pluck it out, and cast it from thee'. If there is anything in your life that hinders you from fulfilling the will of God, put it away, though it be as dear to you as your eye. In the case of the rich youth, that hindrance was his wealth, which he was invited to put away by selling all he had and giving the proceeds to the poor; if, however, wealth does not constitute a hindrance to progress Godward, its owner has no occasion for parting from it. Furthermore, if it were incumbent upon all to sell their property in order to attain perfection, it would be wrong for anyone to acquire property, for if the retention of wealth is an offense against righteousness, so, surely, would be its acquisition, and in that case the churches and monasteries would certainly be committing a wrong by holding and acquiring property.

"Christ Himself, before His appearance in public, was not abjectly poor. He owned several houses which He had acquired by dint of hard work and which He sold when He began to preach, giving the proceeds to those of His friends with whom He lodged while on His travels. Therefore, although He no longer owned property after He had entered upon His career as a teacher, He had no need to beg of anyone.

"Another of the ideals of saintliness according to the views of your former belief is that of *absolute chastity* in the form of celibacy. Absolute chastity is something that everyone should and can observe, but it has no connection with celibacy for there is nothing unchaste in matrimony. Married people can be perfectly chaste, and the unmarried ones quite the reverse, even if they do belong to the clergy.

"True chastity consists in exercising moderation in matters pertaining to the natural laws of sexual life. Just as moderation in eating and drinking does not lie in the forcible suppression of hunger and thirst, but in refraining from consuming food and drink to excess, so in the case of sex-life. The sexual impulse has been implanted in all created beings by the Maker, as one of Nature's laws, and since whatever He has created is good, it should not be forcibly suppressed by men, but should be used by them within the limits set by the Divine will.

"The law of procreation applies to all men, and the founding of families is a sacred duty which no one may shirk with impunity. Procreation on earth is the way by which the fallen spirits must progress through the stages of Nature, in order that they may reach perfection. It is a manifestation of God's wisdom, that those of the fallen spirits which have progressed to a given terrestrial stage may, by way of procreation, assist their fellows to rise from the lower to the higher orders of Nature. If several brothers are precipitated into the same pit, the first one to succeed in climbing out of it will lend the others a hand, in order that they too may escape. That is a duty which brothers owe one another.

"It is from this viewpoint of God's wisdom and mercy that you should consider the law of sex-life. God has made the sexual instinct as strong as it is, because procreation is a part of His plan of salvation, and in order that His creatures may find it less easy to shirk their duty of collaborating with Him in carrying out that plan.

"Manifestly, therefore, the question involves a duty from the performance of which only the weightiest of reasons can absolve a man, and hence the vow of celibacy is a grave offense against the will of God. Neither the priests nor the members of the monastic orders of the Catholic Church have any adequate grounds in the eyes of God for their attitude toward marriage.

"I know that celibacy has been defended on grounds derived from the seventh chapter of the first Epistle to the Corinthians, in which Paul alleges several reasons, because of which the single state is to be preferred, recommending that only those should marry for whom celibacy has perils.

"This attitude of the Apostle was a mistaken one, neither had he received any authority from Christ to preach such a doctrine. Of this Paul himself was well aware, as you will see if you will read that chapter carefully, for if you do, you will notice something that occurs nowhere else in any of his Epistles, namely, Paul's repeated insistence upon the fact that he is voicing his personal views only as regards celibacy, and that in this respect he is speaking under no mandate from the Lord. Hence the constant reiteration of the words: 'I say'. 'But *I say* to the unmarried and to widows. . .' 'But unto the married I give charge, yea, not I, but the Lord. . .' 'But to the rest say I, not the Lord. . .' 'Now concerning virgins I have no commandment of the Lord: but I give my judgment. . .' At the end of the chapter he again says: 'But she is happier if she abide as she is, after my judgment. . .' His judgment was mistaken, even if he closed his last sentence with the remark: 'and I think that I also have a spirit of God'.

"Paul himself was not married, a state which he justified by the fact that his calling required him to make long and frequent journeys. Had he had a family, these would have been impossible, for he could neither have taken his wife and children with him nor have abandoned them for months and years at a time. Paul's own state of celibacy made him narrow-minded and fanatical upon this subject. All men have their faults, a fact for which allowance must be made even in the case of the Apostles.

"Paul was subsequently enlightened by Christ as to his misconception on the score of celibacy, and was directed to retract his views in a letter addressed to all of his communities. This is the letter of which I spoke to you on the evening of our first meeting and in which a number of other earlier mistakes are corrected. On that occasion I told you that this letter had afterwards been destroyed because a number of the explanations and amendments which it contained did not accord with the views of the Church of the later age.

"How radically Paul changed his views concerning celibacy, in consequence of the enlightenment he received from his Master, may be gathered from his writings to Timothy and to Titus. He who had written to the Corinthians that he wished all men were even as he himself, now no longer tolerates the appointment of the unmarried to any ecclesiastical office in the community. Judging from his Epistle to the Corinthians it might have been expected that he would have preferred these for the places in question, but the exact opposite is the case. 'The bishop therefore *must be* . . . the husband of one wife, temperate, sober-minded, orderly . . . one that ruleth well his own house, having his children in subjection with all gravity; but if a man know not how to rule his own house, how shall he take care of the church of God?' 'Let deacons be husbands of one wife, ruling their children and their houses well'. *(1st Timothy 3 : 2, 13.)* A similar injunction is addressed to Titus: 'That thou shouldest set in order the things that are wanting, and appoint elders in every city as I give thee charge; if any man is blameless, the husband of one wife, having children that believe. . .' *(Titus 1 : 6.)* Whereas he writes to the Corinthians that a widow is happier to abide as she is, he writes to Timothy: 'I desire therefore that the younger widows marry, bear children, rule the household. . .' *(1st Timothy 5 : 14.)*

"When Paul stresses the point that bishops and deacons must be 'husbands of one wife' he is not referring to men who have contracted a second marriage, for if he recommends that widows remarry, as he does in his letter to Titus, then surely he concedes the same right to widowers. The term 'husbands of one wife' is used because several men who became converted from paganism to Christianity had concubines in addition to their wedded wives, a fact which was generally known, and because of the scandal to which it gave rise, Paul would not tolerate their appointment to positions of responsibility in the religious communities. For such offices he desired only men in good repute among both Christians and non-Christians, as he writes to Timothy: 'Moreover he must have good testimony from them that are without, lest he fall into reproach and the snare of the devil'. *(1st Timothy 3 : 7.)*

"For a thousand years, matrimony, which Paul enjoined upon the elders, bishops and deacons was permitted to Catholic priests also, and if the Papacy forced celibacy upon the clergy eventually, its motives for so doing were not based on any lofty religious grounds, for such could hardly have existed, since otherwise they would have led to the enactment of the rule of celibacy in the first days of the Christian Church. The determining factor in the matter was a purely worldly one, namely, a desire to increase the powers of the Pope, for a clergyman who is bound by no family ties is a far more pliable tool of his ecclesiastical organization than is a priest who enjoys the moral and material support of a wife and children. It might be added that the celibate priest bequeathed his property to the Church.

"The dangers of celibacy which caused a man like Saint Paul to discriminate against unmarried collaborators as servants of the church are the same in all ages. They were no greater then than they are today. The alleged gain in purity of morals and devotion to the cause of God in the case of a celibate clergy is a mere pretext which has ever proved fallacious.

"What has been said concerning the vows of absolute poverty and perfect chastity at all times applies to the same extent to the vow of *unquestioning obedience to human superiors.* This also is contrary to the will of God, being merely an invention of man's lust for power.

"To every spirit at the moment of its creation, God gave as His greatest gift that of freedom of will. The liberty accorded to men to govern their actions by their own personal decision is something which God does not restrict in the case of anyone, nor is it His will that it should be restricted by man, since all must answer throughout life for all acts committed by them. It is a responsibility which no one can evade. No one can justify himself before God by alleging that he subordinated his will to that of another. As soon as a person has reached the age of discretion, he may never subordinate his will blindly to that of a fellow-man, whether that fellow-man be his ecclesiastic or a temporal authority. Blind obedience is due to God only. 'To obey is better than sacrifice', refers to obedience to God, never to obedience to men, in spite of the fact that people in authority, and in particular, ecclesiastics, are prone to quote this passage from the Bible in order to secure the blind obedience of their subordinates. The doctrine has also been set up that blind obedience to an ecclesiastic superior relieves the person that renders it of all responsibility as to the action involved, except insofar as he may not carry his obedience to the extent of committing a sin. This is a sheer fallacy, for man is personally responsible not only for such wrongs as he may commit, but equally so for any good acts which he fails to perform. In fact, the sins of omission may often be more serious than those of commission. According to your doctrine, if an ecclesiastical superior orders a subordinate to commit theft, that order must not be obeyed; if, on the other hand the superior forbids his subordinate, for example, to aid a fellowman when it is in the subordinate's power to do so, the latter must refrain from giving help, despite the fact that in the eyes of God the refusal to extend assistance might be a far greater sin than theft. In such a case the subordinate could not justify himself before God by contending that his duty toward his superior prevented him from doing a good act which he would have performed had he been free to follow the dictates of his own conscience. On the contrary, it is his duty to obey those dictates under all circumstances; a man's own conscience can never be replaced by that of another. To every man God has allotted a given task, which he must fulfill, without allowing himself to be diverted by human orders or manmade ordinances. It follows that no man should subordinate his own will to that of another by virtue of a vow of obedience. This vow which is rendered by your priests and monastics is therefore in opposition to the Divine will.

"In the case of temporal authorities also, obedience is due them only to the extent that their laws do not conflict with those of God.

"You cite the words of the Apostle Paul found in the opening lines of the 13th Chapter of the Epistle to the Romans, as a basis for your doctrine that man owes obedience to his human superiors, but you have completely misunderstood the sense of these words and have translated them quite incorrectly. Paul is not speaking here of temporal authorities but of the spiritual ones which God assigns to every man. To each of you God has allotted His spirits for your guidance in greater or smaller numbers, according to the individual and depending upon the scope of the task Divinely set. These spirits are sent not only to protect, admonish, warn, and direct you and to incite you to do good, but they also have the right to punish you. They bear God's sword of vengeance, for the punishments which He inflicts are executed by His spirits, as you know from numerous passages of the Bible.

"I shall now give you the correct rendering of the words of Paul:

'Let every soul be in subjection to the spirit-powers under whose guidance it is: for there are no spirit-powers but of God and the spirit powers that are ordained of God. Therefore he that resisteth these powers withstandeth the ordinance of God: and they that withstand shall receive to themselves judgment. For these powers are not a terror to the good work, but to the evil. And wouldst thou have no fear of the power? do that which is good, and thou shalt have praise from the same: for it is a minister of God to thee for good. But if thou do that which is evil, be afraid; for it beareth not the sword in vain: for it is a minister of God, an avenger of wrath for him that doeth evil. Wherefore ye must needs be in subjection, not only because of the wrath, but for your conscience's sake. For this cause ye make sacrifice also; for they are ministers of God's service, attending continually upon this very thing. Render to all their dues: sacrifice to whom sacrifice is due; custom to whom custom; fear to whom fear; honor to whom honor. Owe to no man anything, save to love one another: for he that loveth his neighbor hath fulfilled the law'.

"How can you interpret these words as referring to your temporal rulers? Do you seriously believe that every temporal authority is appointed by God? Were by any chance the countless kings and princes of history, who in many cases were instruments of evil, rulers 'by the grace of God', or were they not rather rulers by the 'grace of the Devil?' Do the words from the passage I have quoted: 'for they are ministers of God to thee for good', apply to those rulers also who committed the greatest acts of cruelty, injustice and oppression against their wretched subjects? It is you mortals who put your temporal and spiritual rulers into power by virtue of manmade ordinances — it is not God who does so. No Divine spirit functions either at your coronations nor at the election of your Popes and bishops.

"When in the text in question you speak of 'tribute' and 'custom' and arrive at the conclusion that the passage refers to the temporal rulers to whom these are due, you forget that there is a spiritual tribute which you owe to God. This tribute is the fruit of your spirit. Just as the annual tribute paid by a tree consists of the fruit it bears, so you too are called upon to render as tribute to God the fruit which the spirits Divinely assigned to you are constantly endeavoring to bring to maturity.

"As you may see, the Catholic ideals of saintliness: voluntary poverty of the members of the orders, chastity in the form of celibacy and blind obedience to ecclesiastical superiors are in reality great fallacies, entirely unknown to Christianity in its early days.

"In connection with the doctrine of your previous creed concerning penance and the remission of sins, I shall mention one strange doctrine held by that church, namely that of *indulgence.* This is a corollary of the doctrine of the remission of sins, for if it lies within the power of a church to forgive offenses, why should it not also have the power to remit the punishment therefor? By virtue of this doctrine the church therefore lays claim to a pardoning power, but inasmuch as only God can pardon sins, so only God can remit the punishment of the same. Strangest of all is the reason advanced by the Catholic Church in support of this particular claim, namely that it rests upon the application of the merits of Christ and of His saints to the contrite soul through the Church. Upon this fund of merits the Church draws in the shape of an indulgence to the extent required to compensate for the lack of merits on the part of the sinner, in order that his punishment may be remitted wholly or in part, according to whether the indulgence is plenary or otherwise.

"On various grounds this doctrine is contrary to all reason.

"In the first place, no creature of God's, whether man or spirit, can render to Him more than is due Him. In the eyes of a God of whom it has been said: 'Yea, the heavens are not clean in his sight', even the most perfect of spirits is but a servant who is doing no more than his duty, even when exerting himself to the utmost. *God recognizes no surplus of merit.* Not even Christ had performed more than in duty bound, for had He done less than He did, He would not have accomplished His exalted mission; He would have succumbed to Hell, and have fallen from God. No one can do more than fulfill the will of God, and even if he does this, he is doing no more than his duty. He has no merits to spare for others who may fail to do theirs. Everyone must work out his own salvation, another reason because of which the merits of one may not be applied on behalf of another. A thing that is inadmissable in your courts of justice on earth, is equally inadmissable in the court of God. Precisely as your judges would never think of tempering the severity of the punishment of a lawbreaker on the ground that other citizens have observed the law, so no remission of punishment can be made to a sinner by virtue of the merits of the righteous. If it could, wherein would God's justice lie?

"Again, just how do you picture to yourselves this fund of the surplus merits of others? Do you imagine by chance that spiritual life in God can be stored in a vault like the worldly treasures of your churches, to be drawn upon as needed? How irrational you mortals can be at times! And how unutterably absurd are the formalities observed by your former church in the granting of indulgence! Can you, as reasoning beings, believe it possible that the remission of punishment is contingent upon the observance of external trivialities? Do you think that your punishment will be remitted if you recite your prayers upon a consecrated rosary, but not, if you fail to take the rosary in hand? Do you think that you will receive plenary remission by virtue of reciting a certain prayer upon a certain day in a certain church, but not if you recite the same or even a better prayer in the privacy of your own room? Will all punishment for your sins be remitted at the hour of your death, merely because you are holding a crucifix in your hand or wearing a scapular, associated by your church with so-called plenary indulgence? Do you honestly believe that the crucifix or the scapular can save you, if without them you would have incurred God's chastisement? Or that there is any connection between remission of punishment as determined and regulated by the church, and certain prayers, pilgrimages to shrines, and similar rites? Is it not rather blasphemy against a great and holy God to regard His manifestations of love and mercy as being contingent upon such absurdities? No human being, not even a pope or a bishop, can grant remission of punishment. God alone can reward or punish according to merit.

"God pardons and remits punishment according to the measure

of the sinner's contrition and works of love. Whoever turns to God in repentance will be pardoned by Him for his sins, and if in addition, he strives to perform labors of love by forgiving the faults of his fellow men and by helping them to the extent of his ability, the punishment which he may have incurred will be remitted correspondingly, as Christ says of Mary Magdalene: 'Her sins, which are many, are forgiven; for she loved much: but to whom little is forgiven, the same loveth little'. Naturally, the reference here is not to sexual love, but to love of God and one's neighbors. To him who gives evidence of abundant love for his fellow men, much of the punishment which he has incurred by his sins will be abated. In one scale are placed the penalties incurred through sin, in the other the sinner's works of love, and to the extent that the penalties outweigh the good deeds, to that extent will he be punished. Thus he to whom little is forgiven, has little to show in the way of good deeds.

"Mary Magdalene had sinned greatly, but she had always shown herself to be ready to help the suffering and those who were persecuted unjustly. On that account much was forgiven her after she had abandoned her life of sin.

"It is true that Christ speaks of one sin which will not be forgiven either in this world or in that which is to come. The word 'forgive' is used in this, as in so many other places in the Bible, in the sense of 'remit'. In the case of the sin which He had in mind, there is no remission; it must be expiated in full, 'paid for to the last farthing'. This is the sin referred to in the words: 'Every sin and blasphemy shall be forgiven unto men; but the blasphemy against the Spirit shall not be forgiven. And whosoever shall speak a word against the Son of man, it shall be forgiven him; but whosoever shall speak against the Holy Spirit, it shall not be forgiven him, neither in this world, nor in that which is to come'. *(Matthew 12 : 31, 32.)* Whoever shall have been made aware of the workings of the Spirit of God and whose soul shall have been enlightened by the truth imparted to him by the Divine spirits under God's guidance, and who for worldly considerations shall nevertheless reject the truth, shall incur a penalty for which there is no commutation. The ground for the refusal to extend mercy in this case lies in the nature of the sin, for if the most convincing proofs of the truth which the Divine spirits can bring fail to induce a man to accept it, even though in his heart he recognizes it as such, what more can be done to force his acceptance? One thing only remains: he must be brought to terms by means of complete expiation; he must suffer hunger and want, like the prodigal son. Only then will he be in a fit frame of mind to be offered the truth anew.

"This was the sin which was committed by the Jewish priesthood, the Pharisees and the scribes. Daily they had listened to the gospel preached by Christ and had seen with their own eyes its confirmation by the workings of the Divine spirits, through which He healed the sick and raised the dead, and performed other miracles. Surely more convincing proofs could not have been offered, but in spite of them, His enemies would not accept the truth. On the contrary, they blasphemed against the Divine spirits working in Christ by referring to them as 'devils'. In the same way you would sin against the Spirit if, in the face of the overwhelming proofs given to you by the good spirit-world you were to reject the truths that have been presented to you, out of fear of your fellow men or from any other reason.

"In the case of all other sins God shows far greater mercy than men deserve, provided they give evidence of good intentions, and strive to turn unto Him. All men and all sinful spirits have need of His mercy, for there is none who is without sin and enters spotless from this life into the Hereafter. There are no 'saints' in the sense taught by your former Church.

"By 'saint' the Catholic Church understands something far different from the meaning attached to the term by the early Christians. The Apostles make frequent use of the word in their Epistles, applying it to all who accept Christ's gospel as the Divine truth and who endeavor to live accordingly. Hence they address the members of the Christian communities as 'saints'. In so doing they are not implying that the early Christians were free from sin; on the contrary, they censure these in every epistle for their sins and their human infirmities. They knew that all men sin. 'If we say that we have no sin, we deceive ourselves, and the truth is not in us', writes John.

"Your Church takes a different view of the matter, maintaining that those whom it venerates as 'saints' were either entirely free from sin throughout life, like the Mother of Jesus, or that they committed no further sins after the day of their conversion. It preaches that these 'saints' went directly into the presence of God after their death, and that God had confirmed their standing as saints by means of miracles. It furthermore presumes to pronounce infallibly whether or not a given person is to be venerated as a 'saint'.

"Saintliness lies in a person's thought and disposition, and since no man, even though he be a pope, can infallibly read and judge another's disposition, no further proof is needed of the fallaciousness of canonization by human agencies. God alone is the judge; there is no other. Only God knows the heart of man; it is not for men to say whether a fellow man has merited God's love or incurred His hatred. It is a piece of monstrous human presumption to claim the ability to decide infallibly the standing of this man or that in the eyes of God, for aside from true saintliness there is such a thing as sanctimoniousness, and often the two cannot be told apart.

"As for the alleged miracles which God is said to have performed through the saints, many of these can be relegated to the realm of fable out of hand. Other things in the lives of these saints which may appear miraculous to you rested on various mediumistic gifts, by which they stood in communication with the spirit-world, but whether it was the good or the evil spirits that manifested themselves is something which you have no means of knowing at this late day. The Egyptian sorcerers of the time of Moses, and the magician Simon of Samaria whom his contemporaries called 'the great power of God', performed more miracles than any saint in the Catholic calendar. Nevertheless, they worked under the spell of Evil, disguised though it was under a semblance of good.

"God is not interested in revealing to you by means of miracles whether or not a person is a saint, for He desires no veneration of saints or of their relics, no pilgrimages to the tombs of saints or to any other shrines. All these things are nothing but glorified idolatry. Why did the Devil dispute about the body of Moses? Because he wanted to deliver it to the people of Israel as an object of veneration of the same sort which you pay to the remains of your 'saints'. Again, why did Michael contend with Satan for the body of Moses? For the same reason for which it is wrong that you should continue to venerate saints and their relics and to hold pilgrimages, namely because the people of Israel would have diverted a large part of their worship from God to the body of Moses, and would have made this the object of a cult similar to that which you render today to the remains of your saints. You may say that you are worshipping God through the saints, but that is a mere pretext. In reality, a great part of the faith that should be placed only in God, is placed by the Catholics in the saints and in their images, statues and relics. If this is right, then God could have allowed the Israelites to have the body of Moses, and have accepted the veneration paid to it as addressed to Himself.

"Nothing was known in the early days of the Christian era of the veneration of the saints or of the Virgin, to which, as you know yourself, more attention is given by your Church than to the veneration of God. The "Ave Maria" is recited far more often than the Lord's Prayer. Think of your Rosary, which is repeated in prayer on every possible occasion.

"Christ and His Apostles, as well as the early Christians worshipped God only; they recognized no worship of any of His spirits, despite the fact that even in their time there were mortals who died the death worthy of any saint, according to all human standards. Among these were John the Baptist whom Christ called the greatest of all born of women: Stephen, who died a martyr's death, and the Apostle James to mention only a few of those whose death took place in Biblical times. Nevertheless, it never occurred to the Apostles even to mention these men as saints, much less to make them the objects of devotional veneration as is the case today. Nor is Mary ever mentioned by them. The whole practice of the veneration of the saints is of human origin, and of a much later date. The Apostle Paul censures those who worship angels, meaning by the word all spirits residing with God, or what you designate as 'saints'.

"No holy spirit created by God possesses anything whatsoever in its own right, nor can it, of its own accord, surrender anything thereof to men. Hence let all glory be to God alone! This also is the reason why God's spirits, when they manifest themselves, invariably decline your thanks, for whenever you tried to thank them they would reply: 'Give thanks to God!'

e. The Catholic Church has a sacrament which you call the *'extreme unction'*. The early Christians also had the practice of anointing the sick with oil, but its significance was quite different from that now attached by you to the 'extreme unction'. You anoint only in cases in which life is in imminent peril, and do so, primarily, to secure the forgiveness of the sufferer's sins, and incidentally, an alleviation of his sickness. Among the early Christians, however the anointment of the sick was practised as a physical remedy the value of which depended upon the patient's eradication of sin from his heart.

"In the Epistle of the disciple James you read: 'If any man of you is sick, let him send for the elders of the congregation and let them pray over him, anointing him with oil in the name of the Lord.

Their prayers, offered in faith, will bring aid to the sick man, and the Lord will raise him. If he has committed sins, they will be forgiven. Confess the wrongs that you have done to each other and pray for one another, that you may be cured of your diseases. A righteous man's insistent prayer is of great avail'. *(James 5: 14-16.)*

"The 'elders' as they were called, of the Christian communities were men who stood high in God's favor and were endowed with the power of healing, their visits to the sick being among the most important features of their work. By the unction which they administered, to the accompaniment of prayer, they transmitted their power to heal to the patient. By means of prayer, man comes into closer communion with God, Who is the source of all healing, and the closer that communion, the greater the power derived from that source by the supplicant.

"From the cures effected by Christ you know that certain sicknesses are punishments for sins, particularly for sins against the love of one's fellow man. Thus Christ repeatedly warns those whom He had cured: 'Sin no more, lest a worse thing befall thee!' Hence it was necessary to remove first of all the sin, which was the cause of the disease, and this was done by the confession on the part of the patient of the faults which he had committed against his neighbors. He would therefore cause any man whom he had wronged to come to the sick-bed, where a reconciliation would take place. It is for this reason that the Apostle James admonishes you: 'Confess therefore your sins to one another, that ye may be healed'. His hearers were not directed to confess their sins to any man indiscriminately, nor to a priest, but to those against whom they had sinned. After the reconciliation had taken place God forgave the sin and the patient's sickness left him by virtue of the elder's healing power, transmitted to the patient, as has been said, by anointment and prayer.

"The words of the Apostle describe the noblest form of healing offered to men. It was a cure for both body and soul.

"Today, what has become of this anointment and healing of the sick? According to your doctrine, the oil used must be consecrated by a bishop and may be applied only by a priest ordained by the same, who must recite a prescribed prayer while administering the unction. This, you believe, will bring about forgiveness of the sick man's sins, going so far as to administer the extreme unction to a person who has lost consciousness, in the belief that even though he be in that condition, the unction will effect forgiveness. Common sense should tell you that the anointing of an unconscious person can in no way affect the state of his soul. Among the early Christians also it was not the anointing that brought about the forgiveness of sin, but forgiveness preceeded the administration of the unction and thus paved the way to healing, allowing the oil to exert its curative properties upon the patient, Inasmuch as in the unction as practised today all of the prerequisite conditions which existed in the early Christian communities are generally lacking, the so-called 'extreme unction' is a purely external ceremony, of no inward effect whatever.

f. Early Christendom knew nothing of the *ordination of priests*. The word 'priest' which is derived from the Greek word 'presbyter' used by the early church, signifies the 'oldest'. As so used, however, it did not refer to age in years, but to maturity in the cause of God, in the case of the persons selected, to whom were applicable the words from the Wisdom of Solomon: 'For honorable age is not that which standeth in length of time, nor that which is measured by number of years. But wisdom is the gray hair unto men, and an unspotted life is old age'. *(Wisdom 4: 8, 9.)* Hence the presbyters of the early Christian church were not selected for their office by men, since these are unable to judge of a fellow man's merits, but were appointed at the religious gatherings of the communities by the manifestant Divine spirits, as those chosen by God for His purposes. They were then solemnly recognized by the members of their communities as invested with their office by virtue of God's wish, by the laying on of hands.

"Wherein did their duties consist? Did they possess higher spiritual gifts than did the other Christians? Did they possess spiritual powers which they exercised over their fellow-Christians, making the latter dependent upon them in their relations toward God and for the attainment of salvation? By no means! There was no priesthood, such as you have today. In those times there were no priests, endowed with special spiritual powers which they alone could exercise. There were no priests to administer the so-called sacraments, to forgive sins, or to dispense other forms of spiritual grace. There were no bishops by whom others were ordained as priests and invested with spiritual powers. The office of an 'elder' or 'presbyter' involved duties of quite another nature.

"Wherever men unite and assemble for a given purpose there must be a leader to maintain order and to see to it that all formalities shall be carried out as required to achieve the end in view. This was true also of the early Christians. They met for the purpose of worshipping God, of holding the communion-service, and of mutual fortification in the faith, and edification. Someone was needed to find quarters for these meetings, to prepare these quarters, to fix the hours, lead the service, and to see to it that all things should be done in order and harmony, for God is a God of order throughout all Creation. Just as He has appointed leaders and guides for the spirit-world to supervise the execution of His ordinances, so it is His will that there should be leaders and guides in religious communities on earth, who shall arrange all things in such a manner that all the members may derive the greatest possible benefit.

"This was the duty of the presbyters. First of all they attended to the practical details, determining the house at which the meetings were to be held, seeing to it that the premises were suitably arranged and provided with whatever might be needed, fixing the time of the meeting and, in general, looking after all requirements.

"However, they had even more important duties to perform in regard to the spiritual life of the community. During Divine worship many directions were given by the manifestant spirits conducive to the spiritual progress of the community, and it was the presbyter's task to see to it that these directions and orders were obeyed promptly and conscientiously.

"Inasmuch as true religion is one of service to one's neighbor, the early Christians laid great stress upon the assistance given to the truly needy of the community, and it was the presbyter whose task it was to keep in constant touch with the families of his congregation and who consulted with them about all their troubles of body and soul. He was everyone's best friend and everyone had unlimited confidence in him because he had been named by the Divine spirit-messengers as the one who was to share their sorrows and joys and to whom they could confide everything. In consequence of his selection by the spirit-world he also possessed the Divine gift of always giving them the best of everything in the way of help and advice. He found out who needed help, visited the sick and the lonely, the widows and orphans, and looked to it that they received help from the other Christian families.

"It was the custom of the early Christians to bring to the meetings numerous gifts of the most varied nature and to entrust them to the elder in order that he might distribute them among the needy.

"Since he also possessed the power of healing and was of great help to the sick, it naturally followed that he won the love and affection of his fellow Christians on purely human grounds by virtue of his activities. Moreover, because of their perfect confidence in him, the members of the community confided to him all their mental troubles, frequently also confessing to him their sins and asking him for counsel. He on his part would advise, console and encourage them, pray with them, and be in every way a spiritual guide and a faithful shepherd.

"The early Christian congregations were composed of groups of neighbors, being formed of a given number of families living within a certain radius. They could not be very large, since otherwise the limited accommodations of a private house would not have held them, and for this reason the number of congregations in a large town or a populous district was often very considerable, each congregation having a presbyter of its own. Now it often happened that one congregation was composed prevailingly of families in fairly easy circumstances while another might consist almost entirely of the needy, and since the well-to-do families were eager to do as much good as possible with their wealth without having the opportunity therefor in their own circle, the following situation eventually arose: it was found necessary to establish an interrelation between the separate communities in the sense that someone was selected to keep in touch with all the presbyters of the district. It was that person's task to ascertain the number of those in need of help and the means available for supplying it. In this way a system of giving and reciprocating help could be inaugurated, for the presbyters kept an accurate record both of the number of the poor and of the means available for their relief in their respective communities.

"The person who took charge of the exchange and distribution of supplies and relief for the congregation of an entire district, was called the 'episcopos' the word from which your modern word 'bishop' is derived, and which signifies a supervisor. He had no dealings whatever with the members of the individual congregations, his duty being to meet the presbyters of his district, discuss with them the co-operation in the field of lending assistance to the Christians and to organize the same, and to forward supplies to the various presbyters for final distribution. That during the conferences between the presbyters and the episcopos or bishop, questions relating to the welfare of the soul should have been discussed, was but natural.

"Like the presbyters, the bishop was not elected by men, but was appointed by virtue of a manifestation from the spirits of God. As was natural, his influence upon the life of the Christian communities was very great, but it was an influence which rested upon his worth of character and his examplary conduct. For this reason his opinion was sought on all matters of importance. In all questions affecting all of the Christian congregations of a given district, the spirit-world referred the presbyters to their respective bishop who was instructed as to his course of action by a spirit sent by God.

"However, you mortals are prone to abuse any influence which you may acquire over your fellow men, and the early Christian communities were no exception to this rule. In the course of time, God's spirits were banished from the Christian religion, and thereafter, presbyters and bishops were no longer appointed by the spirit-world, but by men of influence. Lust of power and other human vices made their appearance, for where God's spirits are absent, other spirits, concerned not with man's salvation but with his perdition, are at work. Goodness governs through liberty, evil through compulsion. The original Church in which God's spirits bore the scepter was a church of liberty for God's children. The later Church which banished the Divine spirits became, under the influence of the Powers of Evil, a church of spiritual slavery in which the leaders arrogated to themselves an authority which clashed with the will of God, and by virtue of this authority, barred the direct path to God to the faithful. This is the situation in the Catholic Church today. Its adherents are tied fast to the skirts of the priesthood, for without the intercession of that priesthood, there can be, according to the doctrine of that church, no forgiveness for sins, no presence of the Spirit of God, no communion, no anointment of the sick, and no valid marriage. The last-mentioned has also been classed by your Church as a sacrament, concerning which, however, I need not speak further after what I have already told you about the subject.

"If Christ were to come back to earth today, He would again be forced to exclaim: 'I have compassion on the multitude!' If the Christian churches of today are to become once more the bearers of the true gospel of Christ, they must return to the form of service observed by the early Christian church. That a return to the Christianity as preached by Christ will be inaugurated by the leaders of the churches of this age, is not to be hoped; it is the people among whom the movement must originate. The people, who have been burdened with so many manmade rules in the name of religion must learn anew to seek their God and to serve Him as did the early Christians under the guidance of the Divine spirits, for the words which the primitive Christian Church took as its axiom:

" 'Wherever God's spirits are, there, also, is the truth!' hold good to the present day."

Conclusion

WE are all prone to oppose any innovation that conflicts with our traditional views. This is a part of man's nature. Custom is the strongest of all forces in the life of the individual as in that of a nation. For this reason man clings so closely to habits and usages handed down to him by his parents and observed by him from childhood up.

This is particularly true of anything related to the religion of our forbears. Whatever a child's parents hold up to it as sacred and divine, whatever they practised as a religious duty and inculcated to the child as such, is difficult to eradicate completely, and even though most of us in after life do not guide our conduct in entire accordance with our early teachings, we continue to regard them as something to be held in veneration, as something of which we should stand in awe and which we are not ready to discard, outwardly at least. We still feel that our own funeral should be conducted as were those of our forefathers even if we have led lives not consistent with their faith, holding that we owe so much at least to family and religious tradition. We are all so strongly tinged with the colors of religious opinions and ways of the parental home and of our co-religionists, that something of the hue remains, no matter how often we may have bathed in the waters of an irreligious daily life.

This power of custom is the greatest enemy of truth in all fields and particularly in that of religion, not only discouraging men from seeking the truth by their own efforts, but driving them instinctively to reject without further investigation anything that may conflict with their previous ideas. For this there is only one remedy: *a personal witnessing of the truth.*

My own experience with respect to the truths related in this book was not very different.

My religion had taught me that there is a God and a spirit-world, and of so much I was convinced, but the fact that communication perceptible to the human senses could be established with that spirit-world conflicted with the doctrine of my church, and I regarded any such idea as mere folly. Consequently when I was called upon one day to investigate matters which were allegedly connected with spirit-messages I was inwardly convinced that I would be able to expose the whole affair with ease as a fraud. True, I realized that any such investigation could be conclusive only if conducted on the same scientific principles as those which must be applied in all fields if the truth is to be discovered, namely, in the light of the laws of cause and effect which are valid in all things and admit of no exception. An effect without a corresponding cause is unthinkable in any field. Thus, wherever thoughts are uttered clearly and distinctly, there must be a bearer of these thoughts, a thinking "ego". Again, if a human being utters thoughts which are and always have been unfamiliar to him, if he speaks and writes in foreign languages whose very sound he has never before heard, then it cannot be that person's own "ego" which is the cause of the effect produced. This is all the more true if the speaking and writing are done during a state of utter unconsciousness, it being contrary to all reason to believe that a person in that condition can speak rationally for hours on the most difficult subjects and answer and discuss all questions and side issues in an intelligent manner. Still less would an unconscious person be able to speak and to write in a language which he had never heard or studied. In a case of this kind we cannot accept the "ego" of the person in question as the bearer of such messages and are driven to assume the presence of some other thinking entity which employs that person's body as an instrument for speech and writing. This conclusion is unescapable, even if we apply the principles of the exact sciences.

If, furthermore, these thinking entities, invisible to our eyes, assure us again and again that they are discarnate spirits, and if they give us a circumstantial account of the laws which enable them to communicate with mankind, we have the means of testing the truth of their statements. We need only to fulfill the conditions which, according to the spirit-world, are required for communicating with us. If now it develops that, subject to the observance of the said conditions, communication with the spirits actually does occur, and, what is more, everywhere and in every case, then spirit-communication is as undeniable as is the fact that by the observance of certain laws we can receive radio-messages from points at a far distance from us. The validity of the laws is the same in both instances. The laws governing transmission by radio were not created today; they are as old as the universe, but they have been discovered only recently. So too the laws governing communication between the spirit-world and mankind have always existed and are not even a recent discovery but have been known to men of every country and of every age, and were used by them for communicating with the Beyond.

In the case of my own experiences in this field as in that of a thousand others, among whom were numerous scientific investigators, illusion, hallucination and similar deceptions of the senses did not enter into the problem in any way. The occurrences witnessed were of a purely objective kind. For my own part I was in the full possession of my senses while observing and testing the things I witnessed. I have no mediumistic gifts, being neither clairvoyant, clairaudient, nor sensitive on any other score. Personally, I have never experienced a state of trance. Blessed as I am with good health and steady nerves, I made my observations at the age of fifty, and after twenty-five years of service as a Catholic priest had familiarized me with the ups and downs of human existence. I had seen innumerable cases of symptoms of hysteria, extreme nervousness, insanity, epilepsy, and similar mental conditions in the daily discharge of my clerical duties, but what I saw in connection with spirit-communication as related in this book, was something utterly different, something that bore not even the remotest resemblance to the symptoms of psychic abnormality mentioned above.

The reflection that I had everything at stake was in itself enough to compel me to conduct my observations with the utmost seriousness and conscientiousness. As a clergyman I held a position which relieved me from all worldly care for the rest of my life, and it requires no proof to show that no one will surrender such a position to face the world without means of support except for reasons of the weightiest kind. But surrender it I must, if the things that I had learned through what I took to be communication with the spirit-world should prove to be true, for these were in conflict with the doctrines which I, as a Catholic priest, was called upon to preach to my co-religionists, and to uphold, as a part of my other duties as the guardian of their souls. If the messages brought to me by the spirit-world were based upon the truth, I would have to relinquish my position as a Catholic divine.

There is one more word which I wish to say to the reader of this book, in answer to the question whether it is *imperative* that everyone should strive to enter into communication with God's spirit-world in the manner herein described. It is not. Whoever believes in God and relies upon Him, whoever obeys God's will according to the best of his knowledge, will arrive at God. This end can be achieved without a palpable communication with His spirit-world. But whoever harbors any doubt as to God's existence, whoever wishes to be assured whether or not the doctrines of his religion are true, whoever seeks enlightenment upon the great questions involving the Here and the Hereafter can learn the truth in one way only: by communicating with the world of good spirits.

To arrive at a firm conviction with regard to his relation to God and to the Hereafter is the duty of every man, according to the words of the Apostle Paul: 'You may have your own convictions in certain matters; well then, keep them to yourself and let them be known to God alone. Happy is the man whose conscience does not reproach him, but he who eats of a food despite the voice of his conscience has brought his punishment upon himself. He did not feel assured that he might eat of that food, and any act committed without a firm conviction of its lawfulness, is a sin'. *(Romans 14 : 22, 23.)*

For the sincere truth-seeker, truth is the treasure of which Christ says in a parable: 'The kingdom of heaven is like a treasure buried in a field, which someone found and buried it again, and rejoicing in his find, went home and sold everything that he had, and bought that field'. *(Matthew 13 : 44.)*

Another work by **JOHANNES GREBER**
Theologian and Biblical Scholar

THE NEW TESTAMENT

A new translation from ancient Greek manuscripts into German and English

The Bible and the New Testament have probably been translated into more languages than any other book in the world. In its quest for the meaning of life, mankind at all times has sought the answer to this burning question in the Holy Scriptures.

However, throughout the ages, errors have crept in through carelessness, ignorance or political expediency. Specific references have been made to some of the falsifications in "Communication with the Spirit World of God." These errors are by no means confined to minor points. Indeed, they touch upon the very foundation of Christian belief today.

Through personal revelations received from the spirit world of God, Pastor Johannes Greber realized it was his mission to bring the Truth to mankind. For, in the words of Jesus Christ: "The Truth will make you free." (John 3:32)

Therefore, he began the painstaking work of collecting the oldest manuscripts in ancient Greek in order to translate a New Testament closer to the original text. This task was not simple. Many contradictions arose between the ancient texts and the existing versions. Only through constant prayer and guidance from the holy spirit world was he able to clarify these discrepancies and eliminate the erroneous material.

What remains is an inspired translation, written in a text so clear and simple that a child can understand. It is a work free of dogma or doctrinal prejudices and beliefs, revealing to the reader a truer understanding of God's magnificent plan of salvation for mankind, the real part played by Jesus Christ in that plan and the role of the holy spirit world. Its truths are relevant to the past, present and future destiny of mankind upon earth.

CPSIA information can be obtained
at www.ICGtesting.com
Printed in the USA
BVHW071951270620
582383BV00001B/18

9 780974 807300